The Crisis of Global Moder.

M000167308

In this major new study, Prasenjit Duara expands his influential theo-retical framework to present circulatory, transnational histories as an alternative to nationalist history. Duara argues that the present day is defined by the intersection of three global changes: the rise of non-Western powers, the crisis of environmental sustainability and the loss of authoritative sources of what he terms 'transcendence' – the ideals, principles and ethics once found in religions or political ideologies. The physical salvation of the world is becoming – and must become – the transcendent goal of our times, but this goal must transcend national sovereignty if it is to succeed. Duara suggests that a viable foundation for sustainability might be found in the traditions of Asia, which offer different ways of understanding the relationship between the personal, ecological and universal. These traditions must be understood through the ways they have circulated and converged with contemporary developments.

PRASENJIT DUARA is Raffles Professor of Humanities, National University of Singapore, and Professor Emeritus of the University of Chicago.

ASIAN CONNECTIONS

Series editors
Sunil Amrith, Birkbeck College, University of London
Tim Harper, University of Cambridge
Engseng Ho, Duke University

Asian Connections is a major series of ambitious works that look beyond the traditional templates of area, regional or national studies to consider the trans-regional phenomena which have connected and influenced various parts of Asia through time. The series will focus on empirically grounded work exploring circulations, connections, convergences and comparisons within and beyond Asia. Themes of particular interest include transport and communication, mercantile networks and trade, migration, religious connections, urban history, environmental history, oceanic history, the spread of language and ideas, and political alliances. The series aims to build new ways of understanding fundamental concepts, such as modernity, pluralism or capitalism, from the experience of Asian societies. It is hoped that this conceptual framework will facilitate connections across fields of knowledge and bridge historical perspectives with contemporary concerns.

The Crisis of Global Modernity

Asian Traditions and a Sustainable Future

Prasenjit Duara

National University of Singapore

CAMBRIDGE
UNIVERSITY PRESS

University Printing House, Cambridge CB2 8BS, United Kingdom

One Liberty Plaza, 20th Floor, New York, NY 10006, USA

477 Williamstown Road, Port Melbourne, VIC 3207, Australia

4843/24, 2nd Floor, Ansari Road, Daryaganj, Delhi - 110002, India

79 Anson Road, #06-04/06, Singapore 079906

Cambridge University Press is part of the University of Cambridge.

It furthers the University's mission by disseminating knowledge in the pursuit of education, learning and research at the highest international levels of excellence.

www.cambridge.org
Information on this title: www.cambridge.org/9781107442856

© Prasenjit Duara 2015

First published 2015
Reprinted 2015

A catalogue record for this publication is available from the British Library

ISBN 978-1-107-44285-6 Paperback

"I wonder from where these notes come."
– Kishori Amonkar

Gaan Saraswati,
Chanteuse extraordinaire

Sounding the transcendent
    across imagination's frontiers

Contents

Figures and maps

Preface and Acknowledgements

For the roughly ten years I have been researching, thinking about and writing this book, I was sure I wanted to call it "Transcendence in a Secular World" accompanied by a subtitle that included Asian traditions and sustainability. My editors at Cambridge University Press wisely counseled me to change the title to "The Crisis of Global Modernity." Since the latter better captures the imperative of the work, I quickly saw the wisdom of their advice. However, in my personal journey, it remains a book that seeks to understand the wellsprings of human commitment to a larger good beyond or 'after' religion and across various historical circumstances. The existence of the so-called altruism gene is a neutral matter because epigenetic conditions may allow it to be expressed in many ways or not at all. Thus, if the book is first of all about the crisis of sustainability, it is also about the crisis of transcendence and the search for sources and resources of self and communal regeneration in historical cultures.

A book composed in the later stage of one's career cannot but also represent a stock-taking of one's previous writings, recognizing how ideas and materials that once seemed to belong to a different realm fit into this. As such it draws on several of my earlier works and also more recently published essays. In each case, however, the original essay or material is transformed in this study. The database has been empirically expanded and the arguments intellectually developed to contribute to the overall theses of this book.

The work was principally written during the last six years at the National University of Singapore (NUS). I want to acknowledge the generosity and kindness of the senior administrators at NUS, especially President Tan Chorh Chuan and Deputy President Barry Halliwell for giving me the freedom and wherewithal to conduct this work. I keenly hope that the wise administrators in Singapore will continue their commitment to the humanities and social sciences.

One of the most fruitful endeavors that we initiated was the network of reading groups in the Humanities and Social Sciences at NUS. The groups in which I participated metamorphosed over time as our explorations deepened. But without my participation in the overlapping religion and historical sociology reading groups, this book would have been much poorer. I know many of the participants have also been producing their own work, and I fully expect that they too will be highly influenced by our energetic discussions over the years.

I cannot mention every name among the many dozens of people who participated in all the discussions I have had over the years, but I must thank those who have repeatedly and closely read my work in the context of our discussions and have helped me immensely. I single out with special gratitude Arun Bala, Viren Murthy and Rada Ivekovic, my generous philosophical interlocutors, for rescuing the analysis from being more naive than it is. Michael Feener, Ken Dean and Tansen Sen were critical fellow travelers through the entire process of conceptualizing and writing the book. Armando Salvatore, Robert Bianchi, Richard Bensel, Mayfair Yang, Amitav Ghosh, Andrea Acri, Pheng Cheah, Liang Yongjia, Roger Ames, Nazry Bahrawi, Manjusha Nair, David Strand, Anne Blackburn, Janet Hoskins, Purnima Mankekar, Zhong Yijiang, Han Suk-jung, Bob Gibbs, Wendy Larson, Misha Petrovich, Daniel Goh, Kurtulus Gemici, Michael Hathaway, Rick Weiss, Michael Radich, Sekhar Bandopadhyay, Wang Xiaoming, Bill Callahan, Srirupa Roy, Ward Keeler, Lee Haiyan, Tim Winter, Kirin Narayan and the late S. N. Eisenstadt all gave generously of their time and goodwill. Mohammad Faisal, Huang Yanjie and Arnab Roychaudhury served doubly as research assistants and intellectual discussants. I owe special gratitude to Tay Wei-leong for his fine research assistance in all periods of Chinese history. Brenda Lim and Kristy Won handled the logistics and protected my time with the famed Singapore efficiency and care.

I thank Lucy Rhymer for placing her faith or, rather, hope in me when others thought this was a hopelessly ambitious work and for stepping far beyond her role as acquisition editor to help me draw my wandering gaze back to the reader. The five readers of the manuscript for Cambridge University Press also gave invaluable comments to improve the book. Finally, to Juliette and Nisha, my eternal love.

Introduction

In this work of historical sociology, I explore various Asian social and cultural responses – actual and potential – to the unsustainable nature of global modernity as we have known it. While the period of this study covers the last hundred years or so, I range back in time to better understand these responses in our present moment that is characterized by three global changes: (1) the rise of non-Western powers; (2) the loss of authoritative sources of transcendence (e.g., Marxism or religion); and (3) the looming crisis of planetary sustainability.

I believe that these changes require us to revisit the paradigm of historical sociology deriving from the nineteenth century which essentially seeks to explain the rise of the West. This narrative was most sharply and exhaustively theorized by Max Weber (1864–1920), a scholar for whose work I have the greatest respect. Weber believed that it was only in the West that knowledge came to have "universal significance and validity." The overarching theme of Weber's historical sociology was to trace the long history of the rationalizing process which culminated in modern Western civilization. Rationalization, by which he meant world mastery by calculability and prediction, was made possible by the process of 'disenchantment' whereby religious and irrational knowledge came to be replaced by science and technological knowledge. Yet, this very process was itself germinated by certain forms of religious knowledge, ethics and disciplines – namely, Protestantism.[1]

There has also been a great deal of critical work directed at this literature since, perhaps, the writings of Oswald Spengler at the time of World War I, followed by the de-colonizing nationalist historians of the mid-twentieth century and, more recently, a school of economic historians who argue that Asia, particularly East Asia, was just as highly developed

---

[1] Max Weber, *The Protestant Ethic and the Spirit of Capitalism*, Trans. Talcott Parsons with introduction by Anthony Giddens (London: Routledge, 1992). See in particular the author's introduction, pp. xxviii–xlii.

1

as the West and witnessed proto-industrialization (or the 'industrious' revolution) right up to the early nineteenth century.

While not unsympathetic to these critics, I have a different goal. Rather than criticize Weber and his colleagues for their empirical lacunae and biases, I wish to stand the Weberian tradition on its head; that is, to trans-value or re-evaluate it by a different standard. I have no major quarrel with Weber in his assessment of Protestantism as *a* key to the emergence of the disciplines of the modern West, nor do I radically disagree with his thesis that neither the 'religion of China' nor the 'religion of India' had the capacity by themselves to bring about the modern revolution.[2] Rather I want to shift the paradigm to suggest that the cultural and subjective conditions needed for the modern revolution are no longer necessary. They have resulted in human *overreach* in the conquest by man of nature, and we are confronted today with the crisis of sustainability whereby a large proportion of living beings will not be able to survive the combined effects of climate change.

If so, might it not be time for us to revisit the alternative traditions from China and India, many strains of which have adapted to the unceasing circulations of modernity, to examine whether they allow a more viable cosmological foundation for sustainability? To be sure, the cultures of these societies have many strains that are abhorrent to modern sensibil-ities and other strains that have adapted all too well to the desires for human overreach, nationalism and profit maximization. But for many, the older cosmologies – or parts of them – are still relevant and are particularly important for the discipline of self-formation or self-cultivation and the methodologies of linking the self to locality, community, environment and the universal. These older modes of self-formation are important to my understanding of the responses to the crisis in Asia.

In his late writings, Michel Foucault examined classical Roman biog-raphies to probe how individual subjects came to be formed not only through relationships of power and knowledge (or power/knowledge) but also co-constituted themselves through intentional practices as ethical subjects.[3] The history of Asia is crowded with competing theories and practices of cultivating the ethical and disciplined self. For instance, the great sixteenth-century Confucian philosopher and statesman, Wang Yangming, developed a distinct philosophy of self-cultivation as a guide

---

[2] For a reinforcement and development of the Weberian argument, see Philip S. Gorski, *The Disciplinary Revolution: Calvinism and the Rise of the State in Early Modern Europe* (University of Chicago Press, 2003).

[3] Michel Foucault, *The History of Sexuality*, vol. III: *The Care of the Self*, Trans. Robert Hurley (New York: Vintage Books, 1988).

to a perfect moral life that departed significantly from earlier Chinese ideas and practices. For him the human mind already possesses the moral principle of Heaven, but it is obscured by selfish desires which can be overcome not by scholarly investigation of the prevailing Confucian paradigm of the 'principle of things', but through rectification of thought and moral action.[4] Wang's ideas and his school of self-cultivation became widely popular among many communities and groups across East Asia, including the Japanese samurai.

Two master concepts pervade the study: circulation and transcendence. Analytically central to my project, both are highly important but neglected phenomena and categories in the field of historical inquiry. What I call 'circulatory histories' is, to some extent, gaining acceptance and there is now an enormous quantity of historical data on transnational and trans-local flows. However, the conceptualization and larger implications of foregrounding circulatory histories over linear and bounded national or civilizational histories are yet to be elaborated, and my early chapters represent a preliminary effort in this direction. If circulatory history may be more acceptable to historians, the idea of transcendence is a definite turn-off for most social scientists. Yet, it is not difficult to show that many important and eventful changes in world history have in one way or another been tied to transcendent sources of imagination, inspiration, commitment and resolve, even though these qualities have hardly been sufficient in themselves as explanations unless they are grasped in relation to societal structures and environmental conditions.

Circulatory histories and transcendence

Given the importance of the concept of transcendence in my study, I will discuss it in greater depth in this introduction. In the first place, I distinguish the different meanings of transcendence in the social scientific literature and clarify my usage of it. Second, I briefly introduce my notion of dialogical transcendence, and, finally, I touch on the ways I think of the relations between circulatory histories and transcendence.

Academic theories of transcendence have been most developed by the tradition of historical sociology known as theory of Axial Age civilizations. I draw upon this school of thought but also take their ideas as a significant

---

[4] P. J. Ivanhoe, *Ethics in the Confucian Tradition: The Thought of Mengzi and Wang Yangming* (Indianapolis, IN: Hackett, 2002), pp. 96–8. See also the work of Judith Farquhar and Zhang Qicheng, *Ten Thousand Things: Nurturing Life in Contemporary Beijing* (New York: Zone Books, 2012), for the recent revival of everyday practices of nurturing forms of life that reach back to the Chinese classics.

point of departure for my own conception. Their ideas are derived from the insights of Karl Jaspers and were developed most famously by S. M. Eisenstadt, Benjamin Schwartz and Robert Bellah. The Axial Age refers to the sixth century BCE when revolutionary developments in society, philosophy and religion occurred across the Eurasian axis of China, India, the Middle East and Greece. Philosophers, prophets and what we would today call religious thinkers pursued the quest for human meaning and effected world-transforming changes by appealing to transcendent sources beyond the known world and magical explanations.[5]

There are several ways in which transcendence is understood even by Axial Age theorists. At a most basic level it refers to transcending the here and now of the world. This going beyond typically embeds a *critique* of existing conditions and posits a non-worldly power and vision to morally authorize an alternative to the existing arrangements and structure of power. In other words, transcendence is a source of non-worldly *moral authority* that can speak back to power. Moreover, this transcendence does not simply imply a temporal transcendence from the present but also its messengers or prophets often claim a *universal* applicability. Finally, *reflexivity*, rational knowledge and a synoptic view of the world are seen by many to be a product of the Axial Age. The philosopher Jurgen Habermas makes the most far-reaching claims for this breakthrough.

The Axial Age, captured by the First Commandment, is emancipation from the chain of kinship and arbitrariness from mythic powers. Axial Age religions broke open the chasm between deep and surface structure, between essence and appearance, which first conferred the freedom of reflection and power to distance oneself from the giddy multiplicity of immediacy. For these concepts of the absolute or the unconditioned inaugurate the distinction between logical and empirical relations, validity and genesis, truth and health, guilt and causality, law and violence, and so forth.[6]

Habermas may be rather rashly identifying the unconditioned with the absolute since transcendence as a concept does not necessarily involve the idea of God or gods. Axial Age philosophies such as Confucianism kept the realm of gods quite separate from worldly changes, although an

---

[5] Karl Jaspers, *The Origin and Goal of History* (New Haven, CT: Yale University Press, 1953); Shmuel Eisenstadt, Ed., *The Origins and Diversity of Axial Age Civilizations* (Albany, NY: State University of New York Press, 1986).

[6] Jurgen Habermas, *Time of Transitions*, Ed. and Trans. Ciaran Cronin and Max Pensky (Cambridge: Polity Press, 2006), p. 160. According to Bellah, "Without capacity for symbolic transcendence for seeing the realm of daily life in terms of a realm beyond it, without the capacity of 'beyonding' ... one would be trapped in a world of what has been called dreadful immanence," Robert N. Bellah, *Religion in Human Evolution: From the Paleolithic to the Axial Age* (Cambridge, MA: Harvard University Press, 2011), p. 9.

impersonal moral order of Heaven was certainly relevant to it. The Buddha was still more skeptical and denied any form of transcendent Being, even though the ultimate truth and morality could be achieved from closeness to the state of pure nothingness, or Nirvana. A certain measure or type of transcendence is often necessary as a foundation of ideals and values, but the radical transcendence of the Abrahamic religions of an absolute and omnipotent God – or what A. N. Whitehead called "an all-powerful imperial ruler or an unmoved mover" – is by no means the only expression of transcendence.[7]

The concept of transcendence that I deploy analytically in the book does not refer to an ontological status in itself and, although it is subjective, it is better thought of as occupying a meta-epistemic locus. In other words, it is not about how we know but about a *way* of knowing and as such is structured by worldly conditions. After long years of searching for an adequate conceptualization of this category, I ran into Georg Simmel's discussion of religion, which has been most helpful. Simmel views religion like art, as something that bridges the gap between the subjective and the objective. To be sure, I distinguish between transcendent and immanent expressions of religion, but my use of transcendence fits his description of religion as the objectification of human yearning – a metaphysical dimension of humans – by means of human interaction. Note that Simmel insists this dimension has little to do with whether or not the transcendent is out there, but, rather, it is an aspect of human subjectivity.[8]

Simmel asks whether this metaphysical yearning "once fulfilled by the idea of transcendence, and now ... paralyzed by the withdrawal of the content of faith and as if cut off from the path to its own life" can survive in a secular age. Can its lofty meaning be found in the depths of life itself?[9] I try to show that in a transfigured way, this yearning – or calling – can and needs to survive, although there are severe challenges. Indeed, Simmel suggests this survival is part of what it means to be human – at least for humans who are 'religiously musical', the phrase that Weber used to describe Simmel himself. Although I am not sure what Simmel means by the person of an 'erotic nature', his general meaning is abundantly clear; "[J]ust as an erotic person is always erotic in nature, so too is a religious person always religious, whether or not he believes in God."[10]

---

[7] Alfred North Whitehead, *Process and Reality: An Essay in Cosmology*, Ed. David Ray Griffin and Donald W. Sherburne (New York: Free Press, 1978), p. 275.

[8] Georg Simmel, *Essays on Religion*, Ed. Horst Jürgen Helle in collaboration with Ludwig Nieder (New Haven, CT: Yale University Press, 1997), ch. 1.

[9] *Ibid.*, p. 9.   [10] *Ibid.*, p. 5.

To sum up, by *transcendent* I mean *a way of human knowing* based upon an inscrutable yearning or calling with several attributes that coexist in varying degrees. It is a critique of existing conditions that draws on a non-worldly moral authority. This authority is frequently justified by a reflexive and holistic worldview involving rational, mystical and practical knowledge and behavior designed to affect and often change the self and the world. A reader of the manuscript of this book was puzzled as to why I considered Marxism (which is not a religion) to be transcendent and Shinto (a religion) not to be so. To the extent that Marxist and Shinto ideals or utopian goals can effectively appeal to a source of universal authority beyond the existing structure of power, these ideals remain transcendent. When this source of authority is appropriated by worldly powers and rendered inaccessible to others, it can no longer be said to be truly transcendent. The history of the world may, from one perspective, be seen as the recurrent capture and institutionalization of transcendent authority. Historically, however, it has reappeared as the source of renewal though sometimes accompanied by devastating violence when its agents are convinced of the absolute truth of the transcendent vision. The task of this work is to see if it still has the capacity for renewal in our time and whether it can do so without the violence of absolute conviction.

Historically, a less radical, 'dialogical transcendence' has pervaded most Asian societies. The ultimate truths and ethics of these traditions to which the *virtuosos* – who are not necessarily the elite – have special access through their knowledge and cultivation of the practices of the mind and body, are open to most people with the material, social and spiritual capacities to access these truths. Despite the harsh forms of discrimination levied against them, even the Untouchables in Indian society, like slaves in other societies, could develop and access forms of transcendence drawn from but also opposed to the wider cosmology that oppressed them. This kind of transcendence is *dialogical* insofar as it permits coexistence of different levels and expressions of truth. As such, it is to be distinguished from the Hegelian idea of the dialectic where one of the two terms negates and supersedes the other. This coexistence took place by debate and disputation, through mutual disregard, and more often by covert circulatory practices of absorption or unacknowledged 'borrowings' and hierarchical encompassment. Disciplinary practices of self-cultivation and self-formation that sought to link the self, and/or the community or locality to the transcendent ideals did not typically or historically eliminate other groups or immanent expressions of religion based on doctrine, although there were certainly historical cases in which it did occur.

The relationship between circulatory history and transcendent authority is a fundamental historical problem I probe in this work. As we have
noted, transcendent movements are also historically prone to become
congealed or institutionalized in orthodoxy or high Culture – such as
Christianity, Hinduism, state Marxism, modernization theory, etc. –
until challenged once again often from the *locus* of transcendence. In its
crystallization as worldly power, institutionalized transcendence serves to
discipline unruly and disruptive forces. Analytically, the relationship has
been a necessary one for societies to organize, order or control the un-
piloted flows and circulations of events and processes. But that ordering is
historically variable in different locations and times. The nature or kinds
of transcendence that I have distinguished above – most broadly between
radical and dialogical transcendence – can, under certain circumstances,
make an important difference to the kind of society that emerges.

The historical argument

The principal historical argument of this book is that the dynamic between
circulatory history and institutionalized transcendence becomes radically
transformed under the conditions of the capitalism and the nation-state
that it has itself fostered. I focus on the distinctive ways in which doctrine,
or *doxa*, intertwines with the material and ideological forces of change.
I synthesize the literature that suggests to me that competitive nationalism
in the early modern West developed in relation to the 'confessional nationalism' of the 'chosen people' during the religious wars of the Reformation
and Counter-Reformation of the sixteenth and seventeenth centuries.
Thus, the first phase of modernity is not the story of secular toleration
brought about by the commercial expansion, the Renaissance or even the
Enlightenment. Rather it is the sharpening of certain forms of radical
transcendence that contribute in particular to confessional nationalism,
disciplinary revolutions, and social and political mobilization. To be sure,
over time, the development of capitalism, industrialization and the force
of Enlightenment ideas transform confessional nationalisms into secular
expressions of nationalism in the disenchanted polity.

The early modern period is simultaneously the period when expanding
and accelerating circulations bring parts of the world closer to each other
through exchange of knowledge, technologies and ideas, and the period
when Western Europe is able to dominate or control the emergent global
networks of exchange. It is also the period when the circulatory/tran-
scendence dynamic in Western Europe departs significantly from much
of the rest of the Eurasian and especially the non-Abrahamic world – until
the rest of the world begins to adopt and adapt that relationship from the

late nineteenth century. The circulation of power-promising confession-alist ideas in the nineteenth century affected many Asian intellectuals and leaders who sought to convert their less radically transcendent and exclusivist traditions. This was the case among Hindu groups in India, Shinto sectarians in Japan, Buddhists in Sri Lanka and Southeast Asia, Taiping Christianity and the anti-Christian Boxers, and other popular groups in China. To be sure, each society adapted these ideas to their particular institutions and modes of regulating circulatory ideas. At the same time, many communities and groups continued to pursue modes of life and occupy ecologies that accommodated pluralities, albeit often hierarchically. Dialogical transcendence continued to shape self-formation in Asian societies even as they absorbed new ideas and ideals of the time.

The modern determination to conquer a disenchanted nature and subject the commons – natural resources such as water, air and forests necessary to all life – and, indeed, all beings – to resource mobilization has also advanced in these Asian societies, leading to an unsustainable and dystopian future. Although it is today mostly thought of as a secular ideology, nationalism and the nation-states have in many ways displaced or 'trafficked' the confessionalist forms and ideas of a chosen people that I discuss in the middle chapters of the book. While circulatory forces continue to make nations increasingly interdependent in the contempo-rary round of globalization, the ideology of national exclusivism continues to hamper efforts to counter global degradation and unsustainability. In this impasse, the environmental movement in parts of the developed world has fashioned important responses to the crisis which is already upon us. At the same time, communities in developing Asia have also begun to reach back into the values and practices of dialogical transcen-dence to salvage their worlds. Can the ensemble – or perhaps *gamelan* – of these forces attain a momentum that may be able to develop a vision of sustainability as a new transcendence?

In my oral presentation of some of these chapters, I occasionally encountered a fierce resistance to what is seen by some scholars as an essentialization of the differences between the Abrahamic and non-Abrahamic religions. Let me clarify my position at the outset. I believe that there are doctrinal differences between the monotheistic Religions of the Book that are characterized by a powerful dualism of the saved and the damned and an injunction to proselytize (in the later Abrahamic faiths), on the one hand, and, on the other, traditions of transcendence that coexist with polytheistic, pantheistic, panentheistic – where the divine interpenetrates the natural world but is also timeless – traditions through hierarchical modes of accommodation. The effects of these doctrinal differences should not be overblown because for much of human history there was considerable coexistence of both tendencies in all religions.

There were countertendencies towards radical transcendence and dualism in the non-Abrahamic traditions, albeit in a minor key, while, as we know, many versions of Sufism were accommodative and the very word *Catholicism* – presumably a Protestant nomination – came to mean undiscriminating acceptance or practical absorption of paganism. Of course, there were powerful episodes of confessional differentiation and intolerance as during the *jihads* and Crusades of the first half of the second millennium or the later religious wars in Europe.[11] It was when a mode of community-formation that I have called confessional nationalism became suitable for the competitive pursuit of global resources that doctrinal differences became salient. History is the circulatory and dynamic repository of live possibilities for future actions. When and how some currents become activated lies at the crux of the relationship between ideas and other historical forces.

The confessionalization of religion was not the only way in which religious circulations in the nineteenth century affected the world. The nineteenth- and early twentieth-century modes of secularization in several Western countries also generated the modern concept of 'spirituality' freed from institutional control by clergies – for example, among the Theosophists or Unitarian Universalists – that began a new dialogue with the syncretic or accommodationist religious traditions of Asia. In many ways, it is this hybrid product of circulation that represents the more transgressive and even challenging dimension of transcendence in contemporary Asia. Beginning with M. K. Gandhi's exemplary challenge to the Leviathan of modernity and the Gandhian environmental movement in India, the Buddhist environmental and activist forest monk movements in Thailand and Southeast Asia, and the Chinese Buddhist groups led by the nun Ciji, many religious, spiritual and inspired secular movements and non-governmental organizations (NGOs) have emerged in Asia to critique, oppose or alleviate the devastation being perpetrated on the planet by the combined assault of capitalism and nationalism.

I try to assess the role and – to a limited extent – the impact of these religious and secular civil-society movements upon contemporary Asian societies. The nature and rate of economic, population and urban growth in India and China in particular, which continue the model set out by the West two centuries ago, will almost certainly cause desolation on the

---

[11] For the importance of the ideology of the *Reconquista* in Andalusia as the crucible of the Crusades, see Roberto Marin-Guzman, "Crusade in al-Andalus: The Eleventh Century Formation of the *Reconquista* as an deology," *Islamic Studies*, *31*(3) (1992): 287–318.

planet. While both societies are making laudable environmental efforts, their impact on relieving the wreckage being produced by their current models is quite inadequate. A global effort with justifiable sacrifices on all sides is the urgent call of the day. At the same time, both societies will have to make special efforts. They can still look to their local and indigenous traditions, which, when re-energized by circulatory ideas and practices of our time, can and have begun to address the problems more dramatically. Of course, finding the cultural and intellectual resources in the tradition scarcely means that people or communities pursue the ideal practices in reality. As Mark Elvin has pointed out, late imperial China witnessed almost the entire spectrum of attitudes towards nature from undertaking large-scale engineering schemes on land and water to reverential approaches to an anthropocosmic order where cosmic energy flows (*qi*) unified humans, nature and Heaven.[12]

The goal of this work is to identify traditions in Asia that have been consonant with global imperatives in the Anthropocene – when humans have begun to significantly affect nature and the environment – not only by revealing different attitudes and ideals regarding nature (and other subjugated entities) but also by showing us different methods and techniques of self-formation that can link the personal to the social, natural and the universal to counter the consumerism and nationalism of our times. As in earlier times, these modes and 'techniques of the self' will inspire only a minority, but, through their leadership, this minority can develop the capacity to mobilize around policymaking and questions of state sovereignty in the way that the Green parties have sought to do in Europe and elsewhere.

This work is also a quest for answers to a personal question, which, it turns out, is close to Simmel's question. What causes certain people – often at different stages in their lives – to undertake altruistic, if not saintly, activity, whether through philanthropy, social work, NGO activism or political resolve? The 'altruism gene' is not relevant to my question because it has long been established that the epigenetic cultural conditions may allow it to be expressed in many ways or not at all. Religious transcendence, which motivates people in a great variety of ways, many of which are unsuited to our contemporary concerns, has, historically, been an obvious source of such commitment and empathy. It is affiliated with a host of related concepts: resolve, sacrifice, suffering, compassion, faith, love and selflessness. In the absence of a religious culture with the ability to sustain such commitment when the world is in urgent need of *physical*

---

[12] Mark Elvin, *The Retreat of the Elephants: An Environmental History of China* (New Haven, CT: Yale University Press, 2004).

salvation, it is, I believe, of utmost importance to investigate the historical and cultural sources for such commitment.

Chapter descriptions

This work has, roughly speaking, three categories of investigation, which are not neatly divisible into different chapters or chapter groups, although each chapter tends to emphasize one or the other. The first two are historical: first, to identify the historical forces and developments that have led to the path of unsustainability, entailing a broader history than is to be found in the narrative of modernization or a reductionist critique of capitalism; and, second, to identify alternative sources, methods, ideas and movements in history and the contemporary world, as seen from a longer historical perspective, that could be of help in restoring a more sustainable world. The third category is methodological and conceptual. My goal as a scholar is to replace the still dominant 'national-modernization' model with the paradigm of 'sustainable modernity' for the humanistic disciplines. The concepts of circulatory history, the 'logics' of history, dialogical transcendence, and the pre-reflexive traffic of ideas and practices into different institutional spheres, and the notion of a 'network region', among others, represent a preliminary effort to move into that other paradigm. Chapters 2, 3 and 4 represent the more methodologically oriented chapters, although they also contribute to the historical understanding.

The first chapter, "Sustainability and the Crisis of Transcendence," lays out the nature of the global crisis, the quest for and problems with universalist visions, and emergent efforts in Asian societies to address these issues. The rise of Asia, and China in particular, has been accompanied by the need to project a new, more just vision of the world that is not simply a new hegemony. Many Chinese intellectuals have sought to find inspiration in their historical and transcendent universalisms such as 'all under Heaven' (*tianxia*). The chapter presents an effort to think through the conceptual and political framework for understanding transcendence in post-Western modernity.

Historically, universalisms have been the source of ideals, principles and ethics. Modern universalisms – developed from Kant to Marx – are apparently in retreat, yielding to nationalism and consumerism. Yet, the physical salvation of the world is of greatest urgency and is becoming, in some quarters, the transcendent goal of our times. It will, however, need to transcend *exclusive* national sovereignty for its realization. The role of transnational civil society and NGOs, as much as quasi-governmental and transnational agencies, is crucial for this realization. Older approaches of dialogical transcendence may furnish us with useful methodologies of linking the personal, the community, the environment and the world.

Chapter 2, "Circulatory and Competitive Histories," develops and illustrates the concept of circulatory histories as the basis of the critique of sovereignty in the 'national modernization' narrative. To be sure, narratives of the past are perhaps necessary in all collectivities that seek to constitute themselves as such. Before the modern nation-state, however, these narratives not only embedded differences and contestations but also bore a relationship to universal or cosmological time. The emergence of the modern disenchanted polity converged with the rise of competitive states which viewed nature and humans as resources and bio-power susceptible to mobilization. The reified idea of linear histories of the state, nation and civilization was crucial for this mobilization, but, ironically, it became regnant at a time when the world was globalizing more actively than ever and when these very histories were being shaped by circulating global forces.

While the historical enterprise of collective formation remains important for local or national community building, narratives also embed structures of power. Scholars have analyzed these structures of power within a society, but my goal is to view the ideological structures that occlude the role of cosmopolitan circulations which have enabled and co-produced this society. A good case can be made that the most significant Eurasian historical developments were circulatory and shared over several thousand years. Empirically, I explore the exchanges of knowledge, technology and ideals in the *early modern era* which is 'good to think' because particularist perspectives of the past of that time were not usually in contradiction with either local or universal ends; state territoriality and culture were not conflated. How might the concept of national sovereignty be influenced if foundational histories were not linear, exclusive accounts of nations, civilizations or other bounded subjects but rather dispersed, cross-referenced, circulatory and shared histories?

Chapter 3, "The Historical Logics of Global Modernity," continues the methodological discussion of the concepts required to re-valuate historical sociology. If the world has been interlinked for well over a thousand years, it has been more intensively linked by capitalism for several hundred years. Modernization theory has had a normative, Eurocentric bias, neglecting the manifold role of capital in the peripheries which have also been an integral part of capitalist modernity. I propose an alternative, more inclusive and *longue durée* understanding by invoking the logics of global modernity which can account for the newer and unpredicted aspects of modern society, particularly as seen from China and Asia generally.

Complexity theory and 'big history', particularly notions of pulsating global networks of exchange, allow us to grasp changes through three logics: of capital, of political systems, and of culture, by which I refer to the formation of subjectivity and social actions. 'Logics' seek to grasp patterns of change within and at the limits of capitalist modernity. Politics and culture have often been reactive to the logic of capital in the last two centuries, but they have demonstrated considerable autonomy, as revealed by the history of socialism.

While the dominant logic of capital may be de-territorializing, seeking markets and resources beyond all kinds of boundaries, it is inherently characterized by cores and peripheries. The current era has not merely reterritorialized cores and peripheries away from groups of nations to those within and across nations but has also respatialized this division beyond geography (e.g., cyber-divisions and groupings). Politically, the system of nation-states is characterized by the tension of 'misrecognition' in the constitution of the nation versus the world in order to achieve sovereignty in a competitive and anarchic world. The logic of culture moves between the unmarked, circulatory culture of global networks versus the 'high Culture' of (often) institutionalized transcendence and intentional transformation. How do movements founded on transcendence seek to control, shape and authorize circulatory forms even as they themselves may be shaped by circulations?

The logics disaggregate the preclusive bundling of institutions within particular territorial boundaries. Modern history emerges from the impact of events on the logics; to illustrate, I will explore the end of the Cold War from this perspective in Asia, arguing that certain transcendent movements (the Islamic revolution in Iran and Maoism, like Solidarity in Poland) were as important to the unraveling of the Cold War as any other development in the West. The transition from the Cold War configuration of capital, politics and culture has tended to subordinate the relative autonomy of the nation-state to the interests of capital at various scales of global society. While this collusion is disastrous for the regulation of capital, the new opportunities opened up by forms of private–public partnerships, social media and, in particular, the efflorescence of civil-society networks present us with possibly novel modes of balancing the logics. However, the autonomy of culture is essential for a just balance, a balance capable of articulating new goals and programs for global sustainability.

The next three chapters explore the historical logic of 'high Culture' versus circulatory culture in Asian modernity, expressed especially in the relationship between transcendent authority and circulatory history. They will deal with the sources and forms of transcendence and how the constitutional division between religion and secularism has come to be understood and practiced. By exploring the various ways in which circulatory notions reflecting Protestantization, secularization, spiritualization and nationalization have affected transcendent traditions in Asia, the chapters will show the ways in which they have adapted to and/or transformed global modernity in the realms of self and collective formation.

In Chapter 4, entitled "Dialogical and Radical Transcendence," I distinguish two traditions of transcendence in Eurasia: radical transcendence mostly associated with an absolute notion of the creator God and the more dialogical religious traditions, where transcendence is interwoven with immanent, polytheistic, pantheistic and plural religious practices. This way of distinguishing the two traditions allows us to see dialogical trends and sects within the Abrahamic traditions as well as radical tendencies in non-Abrahamic ideas of transcendence. The chapter describes at some length the various different traditions of dialogical transcendence in Asia and focuses on historical and institutional contexts in which these traditions have circulated, survived and flourished in Asia, particularly in the Sinosphere and the Indosphere. How did religious elites, intellectuals, sects and communities in these societies, accommodate, incorporate or hierarchically order the pluralities and circulatory phenomena? It also explores the various practices and techniques of self and bodily cultivation and attends to philosophical and doctrinal features that under certain circumstances could dispose them in the direction of sustainability.

Additionally, the chapter juxtaposes the philosophical presuppositions of the various traditions of dialogical transcendence with ideas of 'emergence' in 'complexity theory' and 'process philosophy'. The effort is to show how the two otherwise very heterogeneous bodies of ideas share certain non-dualistic assumptions about the subject and object. As alternatives to the radical dualisms of religion and science historically available in the world that have been marginalized in recent centuries, these philosophies can collaborate to create a more integrated vision of the world and nature that does not make the world an object solely of human desires and control. Although it can hardly be a sufficient condition for sustainability, this philosophical value will be necessary for it.

Chapter 5 is entitled "Dialogical Transcendence and Secular Nationalism in the Sinosphere." Secularism and nationalisms, circulating largely through imperialist channels, began to take recognizable shape in most Asian societies from the late nineteenth century, although their institutionalization often had to wait until well into the middle of the twentieth century. In this chapter, I explore this process in East Asia, where institutionalization took place somewhat earlier largely because of the existence of semiautonomous rather than fully colonized states. In order to track the impact of these changes, I will explore the relationship between state and religions in late imperial China, focusing especially on the Qing period (1644–1911). What were the methods of dialogical transcendence whereby segments and groups in popular religion accommodated diversity? What were the techniques of self-formation linking the self/body to the local and to universal ideals in late imperial China?

I argue that the Chinese case has largely escaped the conflicts among confessional communities through much of its history. It also largely escaped the late nineteenth- and early twentieth-century penetration of faith-based models of nationalism that appeared in Japan and India. But if the Chinese case escaped both these developments, it suppressed and continues to deal with another type of problem: a vertical division –state and elites versus popular religiosities – rather than a lateral competition in the realm of transcendence and faith in the modern transition. In significant part because our notions of religion in Asia derive from the radical categories of the Abrahamic faiths, we see why the idea of secularization seems to do so little for our understanding of modern China even though the question of religion is an explosive one. A comparative excursus tracking the fate of confessionalized religion in modern Japan concludes Chapter 4.

In Chapter 6, "The Traffic Between Secularism and Transcendence," I examine the many religious traditions in Asia that sought to adapt to the new models of religion emanating from the powerful West in the nineteenth century. They responded in two ways – sometimes combining both. The first was the confessionalization of religion built around the self–other distinction, which was sensed as critical to the survival and advancement of nations in the new world. The second was the development of the modern realm of spirituality as a source of the self- and collective formation that often accompanied the demarcation of the secular from the religious spheres.

I try to gain a better understanding of the process of secularization in Asia by developing the idea of 'traffic' between religious and secular spheres. Traffic belongs to the family of circulation within a society and refers to the redistribution of qualities and attributes associated with religion in earlier periods (or elsewhere) in the process of creating the secular. Conversely, it also refers to the transference of modern elements often thought of as belonging to the political realm – such as citizenship – to the newly constituted religions. We recognize Max Weber's concept of the penetration of the Protestant ethic into capitalist practice and Carl Schmitt's concept of confessional principles shaping the nation as prime instances of traffic.

I discuss the recent debates about secularism and analyze several episodes, practices and figures in modern Asian history to illustrate how the transcendent and other religious ideas often do not disappear but, rather, migrate into different spaces and institutions with sometimes remarkably generative and, equally, constraining, effects. I explore the range of traffic in modern Asia, referencing ritual, faith, duty, interiority, charisma, spirit, cultivation practices and techniques, as well as the political theology of citizenship, revolution and state, and much else, traveling between the sphere of religious practices to the institutions of the 'secular'. This chapter deals in some depth with the Indian materials primarily because both secularism and transcendence are sharply developed in India, which remains an important space for experimenting with their relationships. The significance of the idea of traffic arises from its ability to grasp how transcendence can be reimagined in the contemporary world, whether through forms of nationalism, spirituality or cultural autonomy.

Chapter 7 is entitled "Regions of Circulation and Networks of Sustainability in Asia." Regionalism has accompanied globalization in the contemporary world. Note the appearance or strengthening of the (idea of) the European Union (EU), the North American Free Trade Agreement (NAFTA), the Southern Common Market (MERCOSUR), Asia-Pacific Economic Cooperation (APEC), and the Association of Southeast Asian Nations (ASEAN) (+3; +6 – i.e., the East Asian Summit). Much of the literature views this regionalism in terms of global economic and strategic competition. While this aspect is undeniable, I view it in terms of the circulatory forces and networks that have created and often recreated interdependence among these societies. Even more, the imperative to collectively manage the regional and ultimately global commons – those resources of the world that are critical to life and over which no private body or nation can have exclusive ownership – is a more compelling reason to attend to these transnational efforts. Today regionalism can become an emergent, albeit unstable, space for mediating between the global sources of *national* wealth and the global sources of national *problems*.

What we call Asia has never been much more than a networked region. This has been facilitated or hampered by vast empires, including modern colonial ones. These networks have, however, been profoundly influential, enabling historical circulations that led to the exchange of goods, knowledge, technologies and, not least, religions that transformed entire civilizations. I discuss the role and conditions under which some of the networks functioned and developed in maritime Asia; I go on to assess the significance of the current resurgence of activities around ASEAN among the major economies and societies of Asia – chiefly, China, Japan and India. These activities have created important interdependencies in the economic realm and renewed exchanges and flows in the social and cultural realms. But they have also brought to the surface many problems which can only be addressed by the practical modification of existing models of national sovereignty.

For instance, transborder regimes today are critical to manage regional commons such as cross-border river waters and interconnected environmental, epidemiological, security and labor-migration problems. Alternative ideals that transcend national exclusiveness and create the foundations of shared sovereignty have become necessary in facing the crisis of planetary sustainability. I examine several social movements committed to environmental sustainability in the region that have succeeded in networking with global and regional partners to push ahead their agenda in the face of enormous challenges.

The Reprise and Epilogue summarizes the principal arguments and their connections in the book. It also suggests some ways of thinking about a few of the fundamental problems that remain unresolved in the work. These include the embryonic idea of treating the commons as a new area of inviolability, sacredness and transcendence. I also signal the growing importance and role of a highly networked civil society and its allies joining different scales of activity and joining ideas from diverse realms regarding, for instance, sacred groves and scientific accountability. These groups are struggling to emerge as watchdogs and custodians of sustainability.

1 Sustainability and the crisis of transcendence

Three developments in the present century frame my study: the rise of Asia – in particular, China; the crisis of planetary sustainability; and the decline of transcendent and universalist ideals. To what extent are Chinese and Indian intellectuals and activists beginning to address these issues? I will first consider some Chinese approaches and subsequently also turn to Indian responses. The rise of China has been accompanied by a palpable need to understand the significance of this ascendance and project a vision of the world – a universalism – that does not reproduce the injustices of the earlier orders, whether under the empires or modern imperialism.

The Asian tsunami of 2004 and the Sichuan earthquake in 2008 triggered a moral awakening in China which led to an intense debate about 'universal values' (*pushi jiazhi*) as a goal of the Chinese people. Supporters, both within and outside the Communist Party, upheld the idea of a universal human bond transcending nation and ideology, whereas opponents decried universal values (which include democratic values, human rights and philanthropy) as eyewash to advance Western capitalism.[1] Chinese intellectuals and others have turned to resources within the Chinese tradition of universalism and transcendence. Given, as I will argue later in the book, that all nations originate in and remain deeply embedded in global norms and institutions, this is a welcome recognition of the necessity of aligning the global and circulatory conditions of national welfare. But approaches to sustainability, which we will consider here, have yet to be integrated with these espousals.

Why universalism? In my understanding, a cosmopolitan world is now more necessary than ever before in history because the nation and the world are grossly mismatched. If the 'nation form' itself is a global design for competitiveness and nations have from the start been competitive engines to acquire global resources, globalization today has reached a

---

[1] Jianmin Qi, "The Debate Over 'Universal Values' in China," *Journal of Contemporary China*, 20(72) (2011): 881–90 (http://dx.doi.org/10.1080/10670564.2011.604506).

point where no nation in the world is solely responsible for its wealth or poverty. Most alarmingly, the turn to neo-liberal globalization over the last several decades has devastated the planetary environment. The debate among ecological scientists today is whether the Anthropocene – the era when human activity has become the dominant influence on the global ecosystem – has already advanced to irreversibility, or whether humans can still do something about it. A lively debate in *The New York Times* in 2012 nourished my hope that it may still not be too late, though undertaking major changes in our economic, political and social systems will be necessary.[2] The incongruity of the source of our problems, which are global – but where cause and effect are not directly visible – and the institutions of justice, which are, by and large, limited to the sovereign nation, requires that the sacred notion of the singular sovereign has to be restructured or give way to be shared with regional and global entities. Global sustainability requires a cosmopolitanism that is able to transcend the nation.

Thus, in my view, the Chinese conceptions of the new world order will need to respond to this fundamental mismatch and develop a cosmopolitan ideal whether from historical traditions, from new conceptions of universalism, or from some emergent combination thereof. The Chinese ideal of *tianxia* was perhaps the last archaic universalism to have survived institutionally until the end of the nineteenth century. *Tianxia* may be seen as the imperial ideology based on *Tian*, or Heaven, the pre-eminent locus of transcendence in Chinese culture – one that has authorized not only powerholders such as the emperor and his bureaucracy but also those who would challenge the imperial claim to its mandate.

Archaic universalisms tend to assume an unprovable, Archimedean position located outside the world. Thus, from the perspective of situated knowledge, they must reflect a particular origin and utility. Particular origins, however, cannot disprove the possibility of universal scope and acceptability, so their value remains. But so does the problem of historicizing their human and teleological values. Modern universalisms seek to justify their vision as non-particularistic as well as non-transcendent. Let us start by assessing whether this ambition can be sustained and if so whether their effectiveness can be retained.

---

[2] See Roger Bradbury, "A World Without Coral Reefs," *New York Times,* July 13, 2012 (www. nytimes.com/2012/07/14/opinion/a-world-without-coral-reefs.html?src=recg&_r=0), and the response by Andrew C. Revkin, "Reefs in the Anthropocene – Zombie Ecology?," *New York Times,* July 14, 2012 (http://dotearth.blogs.nytimes.com/2012/07/14/reefs-in-the-anthropocene-zombie-ecology/?ref=opinion).

Modern universalism

I offer a working definition of cosmopolitanism. It is the idea that all humans belong non-exclusively to a single community. Thus, while this sense of belonging may be shared with other communities of identity, such as the locality, nation or religion, the cosmopolitan community must be able to share sovereignty with any of these other communities of affinity. In other words, the institutions or representatives of the cosmopolitan community must be able to make sovereign decisions in some (mutually agreed upon) areas of political society.

Modern efforts to locate universalisms in secular ethical tenets –such as Kantian moral universalism, communism or modernization theory – are in apparent retreat, precisely at a time when nationalism has succumbed to capitalist forms of universal commodification. Modern universalisms have not been able to link the goals they advocate successfully with the affective and symbolic force of the lived experience. Whether or not this has to do with the destabilizing effects of accelerating time or to alternative ideologies like nationalism is a historical question that I have explored elsewhere. It is in this context that we will later try to grasp how older universalisms sustained their ideals, even if the reality fell far short of the rhetoric.

Let me first turn to the reasoned cosmopolitanism or universalism of Immanuel Kant (1724–1804).[3] Kant's universalism is based on his moral concept of the categorical imperative, which holds that one "must act through the maxims which one can at the same time will that they be universal laws." A leading interpreter of Kant's moral philosophy, Onora O'Neill, has sought to demonstrate that the moral imperative furnishes the most elemental vindication for reason and human life (as social life). Reason is calculative and instrumental, but its fundamental character does not reside in these algorithmic functions. It lies rather in the moral authority that regulates and permits reason to realize its designs. It is only through its moral authority that reason can overcome the disagreements

---

[3] Contemporary theorists have sought to distinguish cosmopolitanism from universalism because the latter is believed to presuppose a religious, particularly Christian, conception of common belonging of all as creations of God. Cosmopolitanism is regarded as less impositional (or universal from a particular perspective) because it is based on *practices* of common living and belonging in the world. Yet, cosmopolitanism is also founded on a certain conception of universalism that denies other expressions of universalism. In a way, Kant's tendency not to differentiate the two sharply reflects the reality of their interpenetration. See Daniel Chernilo, "Cosmopolitanism and the Question of Universalism," in G. Delanty, Ed., *Handbook of Cosmopolitan Studies* (New York: Routledge, 2012), 47–59. See also Carolina Moulin Aguiar, "Cosmopolitanism," in *Globalization and Autonomy*, CAPES Foundation (http://globalautonomy.ca/global1/servlet/Glossarypdf?id=CO.0074).

among members of society or manage the paucity of resources. Moreover, reason cannot appeal to an external authority – outside debate – such as a dictator because then reason's power and abilities will break down.[4]

In this context, O'Neill emphasizes that the categorical imperative does not posit any substantive goals. Its regulatory function is negative. It only prevents any person or group from claiming a special privilege or harming the interests of others. Thus, it undertakes the standpoint of everyone else – a universal point of view. Significantly, O'Neill seeks to demonstrate that this is not a transcendent position. She says, "The universal is not Archimedean. Rather the thinker constructs it by shifting his ground to the standpoint of others."[5] To be sure, she recognizes that this is Kant's greatest difficulty because it can produce inconsistency (and irrationality). But she nonetheless remains persuaded that Kant's categorical imperative does not deify reason; reason has to respond to the demands of justice in this world. The categorical imperative is thus quintessentially an Enlightenment product: it represents neither a particular point of view, nor is it transcendent.

Other interpreters of Kant see the categorical imperative in a distinctly religious light. Stephen Palmquist, a contemporary expert on Kant based in Hong Kong, begins with the proposition that Kant regards Jesus Christ as the first person to view the coming kingdom of God as a radically *moral* kingdom. The kingdom of God in religion is closely related to the 'realm of ends' – where humans work together through their mutual obedience to the moral law. That the world's political and religious kingdoms will become the universal kingdom of God is the kernel of rational truth. According to Palmquist, when the goal comes into full view, "the idea of immortality will no longer refer merely to a hope for everlasting life in another world – but to the realization of another way of life in the present world where the moral law is fully regulative in the heart of every human person."[6]

With my restricted reading of Kant, I can only make a limited intervention in this debate. I am interested in seeing to what extent Kant required or utilized such concepts as faith and transcendence to construct the modern universal. Interestingly, we may see this in his conception of history, particularly in the essay "Idea for a Universal History from a Cosmopolitan Point of View." Whereas transcendent religions equate

---

[4] Onora O'Neill, *Constructions of Reason: Explorations of Kant's Practical Philosophy* (Cambridge University Press, 1989), pp. 13–23.

[5] *Ibid.*, p. 26.

[6] Stephen Palmquist, "'The Kingdom of God Is at Hand!' (Did Kant Really Say That?)," *History of Philosophy Quarterly*, *11*(4) (1994): 421–7, at p. 434.

the universal with God, Kant's starting point of inquiry into the history of humans is not God. Rather, it is, as he says, "this idiotic course of things human" from which the philosophical historian must seek the natural laws and end of history. He avers that history "is like the unstable weather, which we likewise cannot determine in advance, but which in large, maintains the growth of plants, the flow of rivers, and other natural events in an unbroken, uniform course."[7]

The "unsocial sociability of men" is the antagonism that produces creativity and culture but simultaneously threatens the fabric of society, which humans are also bound to enter. The philosopher recognizes that the history of mankind is the realization of nature's secret plan to bring forth a perfectly constituted state as the only condition in which the capacities of mankind can be fully developed, and, further still, a cosmopolitan condition to secure the safety of each state and the *civic union of the human race*. Thus, "such a justification of Nature – or better, of Providence – is no unimportant reason for choosing a standpoint toward world history."[8]

In other words, while God does not play a directly causal role in the world, the idea of history posits that its moral 'end' can be achieved if we *act in the faith* that it can be realized and in an exemplary way. This seems to be a transcendent position that acknowledges the temporal and human condition of the world but locates the equivalent of the kingdom of God in what we might call a 'utopian' end in this world. This is, of course, a position that would later be developed by Hegel and Marx. Moreover, Kant locates nature or Providence as a placeholder for God that requires considerable faith and sacrifice. Kant says that nature has willed that man should aim at producing everything that goes beyond animal existence, and "that he should partake of no other happiness or perfection than that which he himself, independently of instinct, has created by his own reason." Nature aims more at man's "rational self-esteem than at his well-being."[9]

I want to identify a syndrome here associated with modern universalism. The role of God or the transcendent is not causal, but there are nonetheless larger moral forces working through history. These forces promise deliverance at the *end of history*, not by a transcendent salvation of individual beings but through a deferred utopian salvation of humanity. However, this will not happen unless we will and act in the faith that this

---

[7] Immanuel Kant, "Idea for a Universal History from a Cosmopolitan Point of View," in Kant, *On History*, Ed. (with introduction) Lewis White Beck (Indianapolis, IN: Library of Liberal Arts, 1963), p. 11.

[8] *Ibid.* (emphasis added), p. 25.   [9] *Ibid.*, p.14.

can be realized. Its realization requires great sacrifice of our animal nature. Note the similarities and differences in this syndrome with historical conceptions of transcendence.

The principal difference with archaic thought is that transcendence now no longer trumps history. Rather, transcendence in modern universalism is located at the end of history as a utopian moment that can be realized by willing and acting through history. A second point of comparison lies in the combination of reason and the sacred. There were few ethical philosophies of the premodern age where the reasoned discussion of the good was not also bounded by the inviolable symbolism of the sacred, whereas most modern universalisms tend to deny the sacred. Historical sociology also reveals that the sacred bindings of the truth, *telos* or *Dao* can be more or less tight. In this regard, the limited causative or injunctive agency of dialogical transcendence, such as the Confucian ideal of Heaven, or *Tian* (beyond correlative cosmology of the early period), or the Buddhist Nirvana, makes them more interesting cases for the modern period.

The relocation of the transcendent to the end of history is not, strictly speaking, parallel to the arrival of 'the kingdom of Heaven on Earth' because humans alone can will this moment into existence. But the radical dualism underlying the relation of God to humans appears to remain, and the absolute power of God has now migrated to the relation between the scientific human and the rest. However, the philosopher Jurgen Habermas reminds us that the tensions between the sacred and reason in Axial Age thought basically remain with us today, as, for instance, in the human-rights movement, albeit its expression has changed.[10] As my discussion of Kant and the modern universalism of Marxism and modernization theory reveals, reasoned analysis also requires a sacralization of the *telos* – here the utopian goal at the end of history. Faith and sacrifice remain necessary for human salvation. At the same time, the radical transcendence of the scientific human tends to blind us precisely to the elements of faith and sacrality that are often involved in the efforts to achieve the goals of human design. By associating faith, the sacred and the affiliated ideal of hope with

---

[10] Jurgen Habermas, *Time of Transitions*, Ed. and Trans. Ciaran Cronin and Max Pensky (Cambridge: Polity Press, 2006); see in particular chs. 5 and 12. It is my misfortune that I came across a fine book on the human-rights movement by Samuel Moyn – *The Last Utopia: Human Rights in History* (Cambridge, MA: Harvard University Press, 2010) – just as this book was going into press, so I cannot engage it more directly. My intellectual concerns converge with his on several points, regarding, for instance, the transfiguration of Christian ideas in the human-rights agenda and movement (pp. 74–6); the view of human rights as a moral transcendence of politics based on an authority beyond national sovereignty (pp. 221–3); and the incrementalism of the human-rights agenda (to save one individual at a time). These points speak to the themes of dialogical transcendence and the traffic of ideas from the religious to the secular that I develop in later chapters.

the opposite of all that is scientific and true, we have enfeebled the emotional investment of the transcendent or utopian *telos* and rendered modern universalism a weak force compared to its predecessors.

Tianxia and Tian

In contemporary China, one of the most noted advocates of *tianxia* for a new global order is the philosopher Zhao Tingyang. Zhao advocates a global philosophy "through the world" rather than "of the world," which is a perspective that would necessarily represent only the views of a certain part of the world. In a recent essay, Zhao gives us some insights about how the *tianxia* worldview emerged in the transition from the Shang to the Zhou dynasty at the beginning of the first millennium BCE. A limited power that succeeded a much larger empire, the Zhou dynasty devised a worldview to control the larger entity by making global politics a priority over the local. As such, it was a strategic act that eventuated in a long-lasting peace governed by a global worldview harmonizing differences in the world.[11]

In Zhao's view, the contemporary extension of the *tianxia* model would involve a 'world institution' controlling a larger territory and military force than that controlled by the autonomous substates. These substates will be independent in most respects, except in their legitimacy and obligations, for which they will depend on the recognition of the world institution. Rather than being based on force and self-interest, the cultural empire would use ritual as a means to limit the self and its interests. *Tianxia* is a hierarchical worldview which prioritizes order over freedom, elite governance over democracy and the superior political institution over the lower level.[12]

The China scholar William Callahan, who has launched a critique of Zhao's conception, suggests that his conception of *tianxia* as a top-down project of bringing order to a chaotic or potentially chaotic world cannot be derived from the thinkers Zhao uses such as Laozi and Zhuangzi. In their conception of utopia, *luan* represents a form of 'de-centered multi-ordering,' and not the kind of chaos which requires ordering from above.[13] Additionally, Wang Mingming tells us that the cosmology of

---

[11] Zhao Tingyang, "A Political World Philosophy in Terms of All-Under-Heaven (Tian-xia)," *Diogenes*, 56(5) (2009): 5–18, at pp. 6–8. See also his "Rethinking Empire from a Chinese Concept 'All-Under-Heaven' (Tian-xia)," *Social Identities: Journal for the Study of Race, Nation and Culture*, 12(1) (2006): 29–41.

[12] *Ibid.*, pp. 11–18.

[13] William A. Callahan, "Chinese Visions of World Order: Post-Hegemonic or a New Hegemony?," *International Studies Review*, 10 (2008): 749–61. For the critique, see pp. 753–6.

tianxia cannot be grasped in a singular fashion. Rather, it has to be understood in its two different varieties datable to the periods before and after the Qin unification of 221 BCE.

In the classical pre-Qin period, *tianxia* represented a religious cosmology in which there was no strict demarcation of the human, natural and divine order. There was no outside to this system which encompassed the different kingdoms, or *guo*. *Tianxia* was organized according to a hierarchical theory of concentric circles around a cosmic-moral core of closeness to a transcendent Heaven. Instead of a self–other relationship, a reciprocity of ritualized relationships existed within this concentric world. Wang Mingming describes the means by which the ritual society was created in the Zhou period by the *shi* class in order to build the ideal of *tianxia*, or the Great Unity (*datong*). Not only did the rituals prescribe proper conduct and obligations for different classes of people but also the emperor himself as the Son of Heaven was subordinated to Heaven in the name of *tianxia*. In this ritual order, the "other" was not strictly separated from the self but existed in a reciprocal relationship with it.[14]

Wang argues that, after the imperial unification, *tianxia* cosmology became subordinated to the imperial state (*guo*) and the earlier distinction between the Zhou imperial state and the realm of *tianxia* began to disappear. Imperial *tianxia* was also creatively deployed to create a Sino-centric order of hierarchy in the empire and superiority in dealing with foreign tributaries and vassals. Access to the transcendent power of Heaven became increasingly monopolized by the imperial center, especially through its elaborate and synchronized system of official sacrifices and rituals in authorized ceremonial centers through the world. The concept of Heaven and all under Heaven now became manifested in the idealized perfect union between Heaven and Earth and the core role of the Son of Heaven in it.[15]

While Zhao acknowledges that the post-Qin ideal of *tianxia* is transformed, his conception continues to offer a top-down method of political ordering as the essence of the *tianxia* system. I submit that I have trouble with this model. Do we not presuppose a highly idealized conception of humanity and a literalist reading of rhetoric if we think that ritual-familial order alone will restrain the politically superior to act benevolently? If it did work well in the Zhou period, we will need to consider a multiplicity of factors including kinship ties, a differentiated control of resources and a complex balance of power. With regard to the contemporary utilization of

---

[14] Wang Mingming, "'All Under Heaven' (Tianxia): Cosmological Perspectives and Political Ontologies in Pre-Modern China," *Hau: Journal of Ethnographic Theory*, 2(1) (2012): 337–83, at pp. 343–7.

[15] *Ibid.*, pp. 351–4.

tianxia, it seems rather odd to be applying an ancient system quite so mechanically to an entirely changed world. Moreover, since the political system is not based upon democratically elected leaders, we do not know who will represent world government and its vast resources. While Zhao's effort to create a blueprint for an alternative to the Westphalian/Vatellian/ UN order is laudable, it seems quite impracticable for the foreseeable future.

A feature of the *tianxia* order in this discussion that is worth dwelling upon is the method by which this order is secured. In his top-down system, Zhao believes that political leadership must emanate from the highest level – the *tianxia* political institution – which must then be "transposed" to the lower levels (how the top controls the bottom is not clear), and not vice versa. This is a thus a descending order from "all under Heaven" to nation-states to families. At the same time as political order or control descends, an ethical order ascends from families to states to *tianxia*. Thus, this results in a relationship of mutual justification but would presumably also act as the system of mutual checks.[16]

The extent to which the ethical order was able to check political power, needless to say, is a highly contested issue. My own view is that ethical remonstrance in late imperial society did not achieve a great deal *politically* within the court. Nonetheless, the ethical life was undoubtedly a deeply meaningful and important ideal in Chinese society, and not merely for potential sage kings. The ritual system of imperial *tianxia* played a significant role not only in sustaining rituals in Chinese society but also in the ethical ideals embodied in *Tian* – if not *tianxia* – which served as the transcendent framework of reference in the imperial Chinese world.

Tian remained very powerful in projects of self-formation and self-cultivation from such Confucian ideals of righteous service, remonstrance and renunciation to syncretic ideals of spiritual and bodily empowerment and ethical duty. It is in these modes and methods of self-cultivation and their extension to wider levels of community and universe that we might find the historical sources of a new universalism. There were at least two modes whereby the committed Confucian sought to remain true to the sagely ideal when government service had become too corrupt to realize it in society. The first was the tradition of Confucian eremitism or renunciation whereby the true Confucian sage not only rejected the office and the imperial examinations through which the prestigious bureaucracy was selected but also refused to meet with the emperor. Liang Yongjia has argued that these renunciatory or *yin* (hidden) scholars were believed, ironically enough, to have been sought out by the emperor to grant

---

[16] Zhao Tingyang, "Rethinking Empire from a Chinese Concept," p. 33.

legitimacy to his power – usually in vain – precisely because their renunciation embodied the fullness of moral authority. This was a topos to be found in the literature about the late Ming period when corruption was rampant across society, most centrally in Wu Jingzi's (1701–1754) *Rulin Waishi* (*The Forest of Scholars*).[17]

The second mode was less other-worldly but equally committed to the pursuit of the ethical ideal by avoiding government office and turning one's attention to service of the locality as teachers or promoters of local morality and to other local duties. The neo-Confucian ideal of society was the creation of a voluntary moral community led by cultivated persons who approached the ideal of the sage or gentleman (*junzi*).[18] The popularity of this kind of local service is evidenced by the numerous shrines to notable Confucians that were created in late imperial local society. Indeed, many of these local Confucians were adherents of Wang Yangming or the Taizhou school of Neo-Confucianism which also played an important part in the popular syncretic movements (*sanjiao heyi*) that became a dominant form of religiosity in Republican China. While not intrinsically oppositional or political, the syncretic movement was deeply redemptive and appealed to a notion of transcendence that combined the Buddhist and neo-Confucian doctrines of the mind.

It seems to me, at least as an initial step, that we should be thinking about such modes of commitment through transcendence when we consider the possibilities of a universalism that may emanate from Chinese historical culture. Admittedly, this does not get at how a world political order may be generated, but it may be more useful to understand the methodology of how a commitment to such an order may be generated. One may well ask why we need to turn to archaic forms when there have been other modern modes of generating commitments.

Of course, revolutionary self-formation had a powerful impact in twentieth-century China. Through rituals of revolutionary rebirth such as *fanshen* (to turn over the body), 'speak bitterness' sessions and other campaigns, the Communist Party set the stage for powerful, semi-scripted performances expressing many real grievances of ordinary people – even when the targets or 'enemies of the people' were not necessarily responsible for many of these grievances. David Apter and Tony Saich have explored some of these practices in Yan'an – most prominently what they call

---

[17] Liang Yongjia, "Shehui Yishi zhong de Yin" ("Renunciation as Ideology"), *Shehuixue Yanjiu* (*Sociological Studies*), 23(5) (2008): 43–56. See also Ronald G. Dimberg, *The Sage and Society: The Life and Thought of Ho Hsin-yin*. Monographs of the Society for Asian and Comparative Philosophy, no. 1 (Honolulu, HI: University of Hawaii Press, 1974).

[18] Youngmin Kim, "Political Unity in Neo-Confucianism: The Debate Between Wang Yangming and Zhan Ruoshui," *Philosophy East and West*, 62(2) (2012): 246–63.

'exegetical bonding' with the Maoist nationalist-communist scriptures – and have also revealed the limits and counterproductive consequences upon its extreme politicization, particularly in the People's Republic of China (PRC). Over time, the new revolutionary identities thus formed often became too closely controlled, mobilized and manipulated for larger political or statist ends to be able to sustain the commitment to the larger or universal goal that communism had originally intended.[19]

Indeed, the Great Leap Forward, which was launched in China in 1958–9, exemplifies both the utopian vision and the controlled mobilization of identity (which also applies to the Cultural Revolution) that can accompany modern universalisms. During the Great Leap Forward, the confidence and energy that issued from the possible realization of a communist society, by drawing upon the rational procedures of (an alleged) Marxism and the creation and mobilization of a highly committed citizenry, represented, ultimately, a leap into faith. Faith, as we have discussed above, is the essential ingredient between the boundaries of knowledge and the realization of the *telos*.

Nationalism is probably the most successful of modern techniques of creating commitment and resolve. But we will see how it too depends on the old religious values of sacrifice and suffering. Indeed, nationalisms also posit a transcendent point of reference that exceeds locality, family and other particularisms for the sake of the 'imagined community'. But the nation is a severely limited expression of transcendence precisely because it is based on a tribal self–other distinction. It is exactly what we need to transcend. Moreover, even for this limited form of transcendence, the nation has mobilized a panoply of sacred imagery through which it channels the loyalty and commitment of compatriots.

The problem with nationalism lies not only in that it limits transcendence and sympathy to the national community but also in that it subordinates or devalues the links between individuals and other expressions of community at scales below and above the nation.[20] A program of shared sovereignty – a new universalism – can gain meaning only if it develops from the ground up, only if it can relate everyday experiences of the good to the universal. The local and the transcendent can be mutually vindicating. I want to see how the environmental program and movement in China may be able to incorporate such a long-term salvationist agenda

---

[19] See Ann Anagnost, *National Past-Times: Narrative, Representation, and Power in Modern China* (Durham, NC: Duke University Press, 1997); David E. Apter and Tony Saich, *Revolutionary Discourse in Mao's Republic* (Cambridge, MA: Harvard University Press, 1994).

[20] Approaches that unconsciously adopt the nation-state's claims in history or in contemporary space adopt what has been dubbed methodological nationalism

of sustainability by touching upon the discourses and practices that are shaping it.

Approaches to sustainability

The greatest obstacles facing the elevation of sustainability to a transcendent level are the untrammeled power of capitalist consumption and the imperative felt by national populaces and their leaders to avoid sacrificing national interests at all – or perhaps, almost all, costs. We will see how the post-Cold War realignment of state and capital has been particularly conducive to these developments. The process of overcoming such resistance is, of course, multipronged, but it will require bodies of committed activists in civil society and the state attuned to the urgency of planetary sustainability. Moreover, the methods used by such bodies are and will have to be both rational and symbolic. As we know, environmental organizations across the world from the radical Earth First! to the UN's scientific Intergovernmental Panel on Climate Change (IPCC) have been increasingly active. Intellectually and academically, the ground has been laid globally by the spread of the general field known as 'environmental ethics' over the last thirty years. Movements following E. F. Schumacher's book, *Small Is Beautiful*, such as deep ecology, Buddhist economics, dark green religion, animal ethics, ecofeminism and, not least, Green political ideology, have already established the possibility of elevating nature and natural sustainability to a transcendent ideal.

Deep ecology is a philosophical and social movement that seeks to de-privilege humans as the center of the planet because this has led to untold destruction and mass extinction. The movement advocates a holistic philosophy that takes non-human life as an intrinsic value and seeks a better quality of life grounded by values rather than goods. This holism is particularly sympathetic to Asian and pantheistic wisdom traditions such as Daoism, Buddhism and Native American religions. Advocates of deep ecology also seek to affect policies and undertake activities that will achieve their goals. Roger Gottlieb, a deep ecology philosopher, has underscored the mystical and transcendent basis of "earth and all its life as an ultimate truth" in the movement against the collective violence towards the environment that is destroying the support systems of human life.[21]

He speaks of a "passionate, spiritually oriented, mystical communion with the earth and its many beings, recognition of kinship with those

---

[21] Roger S. Gottlieb, "The Transcendence of Justice and the Justice of Transcendence: Mysticism, Deep Ecology, and Political Life," *Journal of the American Academy of Religion*, 67(1) (1999): 149–66, at p. 155.

beings that no more requires philosophical justification than does the connection we feel with our parents, pets, or lovers. As such, deep ecology is a spiritual philosophy; and the deepest experiences that animate its adherents are profoundly mystical." At the same time, Gottlieb wants to balance this mystical core with a less escapist and a more contemporary and rational view of social justice. He concludes thus, "And so, paradoxically, the wisdom of a mystical Deep Ecology can augment the powers and promises of the secular drive for just social transformation."[22]

Several philosophers who identify with the ideas of A. N. Whitehead (to be discussed in Chapter 4) have sought to ally themselves with deep ecologists since they have much in common, particularly with regard to the interconnectedness of the universe. Their differences emerge from the relative valuation of humans in relation to the intrinsic value of other creatures and nature. Whiteheadians recognize the importance of 'vital' human needs as an aspect of the human propensity for gradations of value.[23] This question is, as we will see below, fundamental to much environmental debate between advocates of environmental preservation and sustainable development.

According to the great historian of Chinese science, Joseph Needham, nature, in Chinese organismic cosmology, represented perhaps the greatest of all living organisms, and its governing principles had to be well understood so that human life could live in harmony with it.[24] The process of self-formation was inseparable from nature. The indivisibility of nature between inner self and outer nature in a neo-Confucianism highly influenced by Daoism and Buddhism is the condition for the quest of the true nature within that represents the elusive heavenly principles (*tianli*).[25] From the Daoists to the neo-Confucians (*xinxue*) right up to the adherents of the syncretic Morality Society, the practices of self-cultivation have represented a turning back towards one's original nature that was simultaneously a move towards the quiet and pure "nature of Heaven-and-Earth." It was through this process that practitioners were able to fully develop their

---

[22] *Ibid.*, p. 165.

[23] John B. Cobb, Jr., "Deep Ecology and Process Thought," *Process Studies*, *30*(1) (2001): 112–31 (www.religion-online.org/showarticle.asp?title=3025). See also S. Armstrong-Buck, "Whitehead's Metaphysical System as a Foundation for Environmental Ethics," *Environmental Ethics*, *8* (1986): 241–59.

[24] Joseph Needham, *Science and Civilization in China* (Cambridge University Press, 1956), vol. II, pp. 242–4, 281. Needham also finds parallels with Indian thought of the 'organism of the universe' (p. 281, note c) and with the ideas of Whitehead (p. 454); see also vol. III (1959), pp. 152–3; 163–5, 196.

[25] Zhu Renqiu, "The Formation, Development and Evolution of Neo-Confucianism, with a focus on the Doctrine of 'Stilling the Nature' in the Song Period," *Frontiers of Philosophy in China*, *4*(3) 2009: 322–42, 335.

original nature while realizing the metaphysical character of the Dao, the true nature or essence of the universe.[26]

Similarly, Purushottama Bilimoria and others have shown that in Vedic religion the highest good was identified with the total harmony of the cosmic or natural order. Indeed, the social and moral order was seen as a correlate of the natural order, and both reflected the unity of an inner order. Classical Hinduism and the parallel traditions of Buddhism and Jainism developed the moral concept of *dharma* as an abstract, author-itative and autonomous idea (in the Axial Age mode), but it served to preserve the organic unity of 'beinghood'. One of the cardinal values in *dharma* is non-injury to all beings, or *ahimsa*, a universalization from one's experience of pain to others. *Ahimsa* was also a virtue that was central to Buddhism, and particularly to Jainism. As is well known, in the modern era, it also influenced Mahatma Gandhi, who sought to turn it into a dynamic force of passive resistance.[27]

The presence of norms and ethics regarding care of nature may be necessary but hardly sufficient to guarantee its careful husbanding in practice. Mark Elvin has cautioned that late imperial China witnessed almost the entire spectrum of practices towards nature, from reverential approaches to an anthropocosmic order unified by *qi* cosmic flows to large-scale engineering schemes on land and water. By the late imperial period, the toll taken by massive hydraulic projects, deforestation and intensive agriculture put more pressure, certainly in parts of China, than in many other parts of the premodern world.[28] At the same time, as Robert Weller argues, premodern views in China did not sanction the complete subjugation of nature by humans.[29] Needham points to the importance of ideas of *wuwei* and *fengshui* as constraining ideals, and cites the example of the Han dynasty hydraulic engineer Chia Jang (Jia Rang), who practiced 'Taoist hydraulics' and believed the river should be "given plenty of room to take whatever course it

[26] Xiang Shiling, "A Study on the Theory of 'Returning to the Original' and 'Recovering Nature' in Chinese Philosophy," *Frontiers of Philosophy in China*, 3(4) 2008: 502–19; *passim.*

[27] Purushottama Bilimoria, "Environmental Ethics of Indian Religious Traditions," paper presented at a symposium on Religion and Ecology at the American Academy of Religion Annual Conference, San Francisco, November 1997 (http://home.cogeco.ca/~drheault/ ee_readings/East/Suggested/Bilimoria.pdf).

[28] Mark Elvin, *The Retreat of the Elephants: An Environmental History of China* (New Haven, CT: Yale University Press, 2004). See also the debates surveyed in Bron Taylor, "Environmental Ethics," in Bron Taylor, Ed., *Encyclopedia of Religion and Nature* (London and New York: Continuum, 2005), pp. 597–608.

[29] Robert Weller, *Discovering Nature: Globalization and Environmental Culture in China and Taiwan* (Cambridge University Press, 2006).

needed."[30] The doyen of Indian environmental history, Ramachandra Guha, observes that since the strongest forces of environmental destruction lie not in premodern societies nor in religions – whatever they may say or do – it follows that the relationship between religion and environmentalism will be tested only after industrialization has proceeded. The lesson to be learnt from these cautionary statements is that moral norms by themselves will have limited effects without a program of action that mobilizes these dispositions.[31]

In the large societies of contemporary China and India, the continued patterns of present use and consumption of environmental resources will have incalculable consequences upon the world's environment. In 2012, global carbon emissions per capita worldwide were 4.6 tonnes, and while the United States continues to emit 18 tonnes per person, China has exceeded the world average by an emission rate of 6.3 tonnes per person. The country as a whole already emits more carbon dioxide than the United States and Canada put together. India is ranked third in total emissions, but its per capita carbon footprint still remains small at 1.4 tonnes.[32] Geoengineering schemes to counter global warming involve known and unknown costs and side effects which would probably worsen the problem – at least in some parts of the world.[33] In the foreseeable future, there are no quick fixes beyond developing global agreements on curbing emissions and changing lifestyles and values. While present governments are making important efforts, their policies will have effects only if there is a sea change in the attitudes, lifestyles and aspirations of populations and their organizations. In turn, committed social organizations can both feed this change and steer policy towards more sustainable options, as we have seen through such organizations as Greenpeace and the Green parties in Europe and New Zealand.

[30] Joseph Needham, *Science and Civilization in China* (Cambridge University Press, 1971), vol. IV, part 3, pp. 234–5.

[31] Ramachandra Guha, *How Much Should a Person Consume? Environmentalism in India and the US* (Berkeley and Los Angeles, CA: University of California Press, 2006), pp. 5–8. The idea that Christianity is responsible for this attitude towards the conquest of nature was developed in an essay by Lynn White in 1967. Subsequently, advocates of non-Christian traditions began to suggest that the non-Christian traditions sought to protect and cherish nature. Guha suggests that this earlier history may simply not be relevant. See also J. Baird Callicott, *Earth's Insights: A Survey of Ecological Ethics from the Mediterranean Basin to the Australian Outback* (Berkeley and Los Angeles, CA: University of California Press, 1994), pp. 53–69.

[32] "World Carbon Emissions: The League Table of Every Country," *The Guardian*, June 21, 2012 (www.guardian.co.uk/environment/datablog/2012/jun/21/world-carbon-emissions-league-table-country).

[33] Clive Hamilton, "Geoengineering: Our Last Hope, or a False Promise?," *New York Times*, May 26, 2013.

In modern Asia, the mainstream obsession with pursuing the goal of controlling and manipulating nature has not provided us with too many helpful examples of efforts to realize alternative goals. Nonetheless, in India and China there were efforts at rural revival and sustainable development, including, most famously, Mahatma Gandhi's projects to revive simple rural industries like spinning and weaving and reduce consumer needs. Gandhi's legacy in the environmental movement in India today is immeasurable. Less known are Rabindranath Tagore's efforts to invoke what we today call sustainability – but which was called pantheistic philosophy in the 1920s – as a transcendent ideal for the world. In his critique of nationalism and instrumental modernity, Tagore sought to realize an alternative cosmopolitanism drawn from Asian traditions and embodied in Visva-Bharati (India of the World) University at Santiniketan. In the realm of Indian history, he was drawn to alternative popular traditions identified with medieval Bhakti seers and sages such as Kabir, Nanak and Dadu, who broke through barriers of social and religious exclusiveness and brought together communities based on spiritual reform.[34]

What was unique and worthy of further inquiry in Tagore's effort was his approach to linking locality and local identity with the transcendent goal. It was a form of rooted cosmopolitanism that was expressed in the spirit of Santiniketan. While education had to be undertaken in a universal framework of understanding, the local represented the means of this understanding. The educational projects in Santiniketan celebrated different world traditions, but students also engaged with their environment and traditions. Tagore invented secular festivals for the celebration of the different seasons in the region and brought together the urban and the rural during harvest festivals. He started cooperative movements among the tribal peoples and the rural folk, seeking to educate them in health, agriculture, savings and other modern ways of survival, while encouraging the maximum preservation of their own local culture.[35]

We can find similar efforts in the grass-roots movements that were begun in Republican China by Liang Shuming and Tao Xingzhi, the mass-education movement of Jimmy Yan, the folklore movement of Zhou Zuoren and Gu Jiegang, the industrial cooperative movement that was simulataneous with the Yan'an cooperatives of the late 1930s and 1940s, and the early work of Fei Xiaotong, among others. Of course, these

---

[34] See Uma Das Gupta, Ed., *Tagore: Selected Writings on Education and Nationalism* (Delhi: Oxford University Press, 2009), p. 172. For more extensive discussion of Tagore, see Chapter 7 in this book.
[35] Nabaneeta Dev Sen, "Crisis in Civilization, and a Poet's Alternatives: Education as One Alternative Weapon," paper presented at Tagore's Philosophy of Education: a conference dedicated to the memory of Amita Sen, Kolkata, India, March 29–30, 2006.

various movements spanned an entire range of activities designed to 'recon-struct' Chinese villages, from Liang Shuming's Confucian approaches to restoring the ecology of the ethical community to the industrial cooperative movement, whose leaders sought to bring modern industry on the basis of cooperative ownership to the countryside.

Most of these reformers were motivated not only by their concern about poverty and economic decline in China's villages but also by the 'erosion' of talent and values in the village following the impact of the industrial city. Liang Shuming, who may have been the most successful of these reform-ers until the Japanese occupation of 1937, distinguished the goals of Chinese paths of reform from the Western ideal of the conquest of nature. The Chinese path was different also from the Indian path, which, in his view, regarded the contradiction between humans and nature to be illu-sory. Liang, who occasionally also called himself a Buddhist, believed that the Indian path which sought human happiness in spiritual enlightenment was a worthy goal, but only after the needs of human material and social life were addressed. The Chinese represented the middle option, which was the way of living harmoniously with members of family and society and balancing human relations with nature.[36]

Of course, rural reconstruction was not necessarily based on ideas of sustainability in the contemporary sense. Indeed, with the establishment of the PRC, even pioneer reformers, such as the doyen of Chinese rural studies, Fei Xiaotong, who had sounded the clarion call for rural recovery early in his studies in the 1930s of the intimate relations of the Chinese peasant and the soil (*xiangtu Zhongguo*), became intoxicated by the dom-inant approach of subjugating nature. Fei championed rural industrializa-tion and neglected or ignored its environmental effects until very late in his life. Zhang Yulin has shown that of the 747 articles carried by the flagship journal *Observations of Chinese Villages* between 1994 and 2007, only 11 dealt with environmental issues. Zhang believes it is the drive to increase rural production at all costs and the nexus of interests pushing commercial technologies of intensive agriculture that are responsible for much of the degradation of the environment and of rural self-governing and cooperative institutions. This drive also influenced the academic neglect of these issues.[37]

---

[36] An Yanming, "Liang Shuming: Eastern and Western Cultures and Confucianism," in Chun-Ying Cheng and Nicholas Bunnin, Eds., *Contemporary Chinese Philosophy* (Oxford: Blackwell Publishers, 2002), pp. 147–63.

[37] Zhang Yulin, "'Tiandi yibian' yu Zhongguo nongcun yanjiu" ("'Upheaval on Heaven and Earth' and Research on Chinese Villages"), *Zhongguo yanjiu*, Spring (2009): 1–17. For his earlier views, see Fei Xiaotong, "Xiangtu bense," in *Xiangtu Zhongguo* (Shanghai: Guanchashe, 1947), pp. 1–7.

Nonetheless, the early twentieth-century traditions of rural reconstruction, especially the ideas of Liang Shuming, have had a major impact on the contemporary rural-reconstruction movement in China. Since the 1990s, in the new rural reconstruction movement (*xin xiangcun jianshe yundong*), leading figures like Wen Tiejun, Cao Jingqing, Li Yuanxing and Li Changping have linked this movement to the early twentieth-century tradition. They have been active in developing cooperative, protective and integrated movements that do not focus only on economic or technical solutions for problems in rural society. Just as Liang Shuming pointed out earlier, Li Yuanxing declared that urban-based industrialization is unsustainable and destructive both economically and socially. Land as a subsistence need and rural cooperatives as a protective strategy should not to be trumped by efficiency considerations, and both tasks require strong initial government support. Note, moreover, that these new rural reconstruction activists do not necessarily stake out an antistate position. Indeed, some of them proactively insert their agenda into the government's policies for ameliorating rural conditions, and they have, arguably, shaped government discourse of rural problems. Moreover, while these leaders see themselves as inheritors of a century-long quest to revive the values of human relations and relations with nature that were hallmarks of Chinese culture, they have also clearly affiliated their movement to the wider global problems of sustainability.[38]

Despite progress in research on the rural-reconstruction movements, we are still missing some important questions related to their connective methodology. How was the self to articulate with the local, national and the global? How was the self to manage the inevitable tensions in the pull of these scales, but especially the tensions between the local and transcendent on the one hand and the national on the other? What were the ways in which different civilizational traditions expected to interact to form the alternative global one?

The environmental movement in contemporary China

We turn now more specifically to environmental issues in China today. While the daily news is filled with small and large environmental disasters, China has also witnessed some remarkable developments in the environmental sphere. Among all developing countries, the Chinese government's efforts in environmental education are probably the greatest. In 2007, President Hu Jintao coined the idea of ecological civilization

[38] Alexander Day, "The End of the Peasant? New Rural Reconstruction in China," *Boundary 2*, 35(2) (2008): 49–73, at pp. 55–62.

through which he sought to replace economic construction as the core of development with sustainable development that must incorporate a balanced relationship between humans and nature. The central government in China has been steadily developing the institutional and financial infrastructure of environmental protection. In 2005, China raised its expenditure for environmental protection in the national budget to 1.4 percent of GDP and in 2008, the State Environmental Protection Agency was given full ministerial status and established local environmental protection branches all over the country.[39]

Top-down state mandated agendas, however, are unlikely to fulfill the task of environmental protection despite the commitment of the central government, in part because the state itself sends mixed messages and is constituted by different agencies and levels of government with varying if not contradictory attitudes towards the environment. Principally, environmental protection has to compete with high production goals and targets, particularly at the local levels of government, which depend upon revenues from industrial and real-estate development. It is in this context – of the environmental crisis accompanying breakneck economic growth and industrialization, including the widespread development of rural industry in the 1980s and 1990s – that Chinese society has responded with perhaps the most vibrant social movement the PRC has seen in many decades.

Over the last twenty years, environmental NGOs (ENGOs), as well as informal groups and movements, have mushroomed across the country. Indeed, Guobin Yang and Craig Calhoun have dubbed this activism the 'Green public sphere' in China.[40] According to the government-affiliated NGO (GONGO) All-China Environmental Federation, in 2008, there were 2,768 ENGOs (employing 224,000), which rose to almost 8,000 in 2013. There are many thousands of others which are not formally registered as ENGOs. Their role has been enhanced by recognition at higher levels of government for the environmental services they can render such as enhancing environmental consciousness among the public and mobilizing for projects like reforestation. More importantly, they are able to serve as watchdogs to expose the violation or non-implementation of environmental laws. Of course, as civic organizations in the PRC, they occupy a vulnerable status and most organizations are careful not to

---

[39] Bryan Tilt, *The Struggle for Sustainability in Rural Society: Environmental Values and Civil Society* (New York: Columbia University Press, 2009), pp. 109–10.

[40] Yang Guobin and Graig Calhoun, "Media, Civil Society and the Rise of a Green Public Sphere in China," *China Information*, 21 (2007): 211–34.

oppose state policies, but serve rather in a vital 'supplementary' role as pressure groups, guardians and enablers for the victimized.[41]

Nonetheless, ENGOs, perhaps unexpectedly, have been successful in influencing state policies over the last decade – until very recently. A land-mark event for Chinese environmental history was the halting – or shelving – of the massive Nu river dam project in 2004, as discussed in Chapter 7 (see Maps 7.1a and 7.1b). The event was important for various reasons, including the collective action taken not only by the Chinese groups but also by international NGOs and groups and governments in Southeast Asian countries that would have been affected by the enormous environmental impact on their societies.[42] The Chinese groups also ignited the media campaign – including both the old and new media – that launched the vigorous 'Green public sphere' and 'Greenspeak', which are remarkably consistent with the global Green discourse of climate change, sustainable consumption, biodiversity, desertification, etc. Although activists in rural and urban society utilize Web platforms for groups to self-organize and twitter for flash mobilization, the ENGOs operate largely within the scope of state policies, and this explains their ability to survive and even flourish.

The profile of activists and the activities of the ENGOs suggest an orientation that transcends consumerist and materialist approaches to life, at least among the youth for the time being. Bao Maohong notes that 80 percent of the staff of the registered ENGOs are under 30 years old, and although over half of them have college degrees, they are moti-vated by their mission rather than their rather paltry, if any, salaries. Greenspeak tends to promote a new moral-spiritual/religious vision and practices, and promotes volunteerism and civil participation in opposition to materialist and consumerist practices. The All-China Environmental Federation notes that 70 percent of the public surveyed by it recognized and supported the activities of the ENGOs.[43]

China has also made considerable investment in environmental educa-tion. Together with many developed countries, China, in 2003, mandated environmental education in the public schools of the nation. It has encouraged many local governments and groups to produce texts and programs for schoolchildren. Yet, there are significant obstacles to the development of environmental education as a transformative force in society. The courses tend to be formalistic and the seriousness of the enterprise may be undermined by the non-inclusion of environmental

---

[41] Bao Maohong, "Environmental NGOs in Transforming China," *Nature and Culture*, 4(1) (2009): 1–16; "China's ENGOs Increase by Almost 8,000," *People's Daily* (English Edition), March 5, 2013.

[42] *Ibid.*, pp. 8–10.   [43] *Ibid.*, pp. 3–8.

education in the core official examinations. More generally, children as much as adults are increasingly alienated from the natural environment in their everyday activities. They cannot yet see how conserving the environment can contribute to their future careers. There is no engagement with self-transformation.[44]

Nonetheless, there are some interesting experiments in environmental education among grass-roots environmental NGOs, especially in Yunnan, a province rich in biodiversity, which is called the "cradle of NGOs." Robert Efird's study of NGOs working in the Naxi region of Lijiang – particularly Lashihai – shows how some of these small, shoestring budget NGOs committed to environmental education have sought, not merely to tailor environmental learning to local circumstances but also to engage children in a practical, hands-on education about the environment.[45]

Historically, the Naxi Dongba religion revered nature. Water and forests were sacralized, and this permitted the people to manage these communal resources sustainably. Village regulations were set in stone steles and backed by threats of divine and communal punishment for activities such as unnecessary deforestation and overharvesting wild game. Some of these NGOs have clearly learnt the lesson of the importance of cultivating identification with this local and historically meaningful environment. For instance, the Yunnan Eco-Network (YEN) and its director, Chen Yongsong, work with school-age youth to protect their local environment by having them visit forests, learn about and weed out invasive plants, clear trash, create school gardens, etc.[46]

Efird emphasizes not only how environmental stewardship and sustainable behavior have to be learnt practically but also how education must *cultivate the motivation to engage in sustainable behavior.* The literature on this kind of motivation emphasizes personal understanding of nature – the process of self-formation – rooted in experiences of the non-human world. They have turned to education about the locality – and not the environment in the abstract – through materials (*xiangtu jiaocai*) based on specific cultural and ecological characteristics of a place or region in order to foster a sense of roots and a "spiritual home" (or *Heimat*) for the youth. The

---

[44] Caterina Wasmer, "Towards Sustainability: Environmental Education in China – Can a German Strategy Adapt to Chinese Schools?," Ed. Werner Pascha and Markus Taube. Duisburg Working Papers on East Asian Economic Studies (D-47048), Duisburg, Germany, pp. 20–4. A project of the Asia-Pacific Economic Research Institute (FIP), (www.econstor.eu/obitstream/10419/23138/1/AP73.pdf). See also Rob Efird: "Learning by Heart: An Anthropological Perspective on Environmental Learning in Lijiang," in Helen Kopnina and Eleanor Shoreman-Oiumet, Eds., *Environmental Anthropology Today* (New York: Routledge, 2011), pp. 254–66, at pp. 254, 259.
[45] Efird, "Learning by Heart."   [46] *Ibid.*, pp. 261–3.

local or *xiangtu* as the basis for larger commitments harks back at least to the rural reconstructionists of the previous century.[47]

The urgency to change environmental behavior has encouraged other interesting research in the reception of environmental ideas. In an ethnographic study of modern environmental ideas and movements in both the PRC and Taiwan, Robert Weller explores how awareness of the environment is often a product of the intertwining of government, civil society (NGOs) and local efforts that integrates past cosmological ideas and practices with contemporary concerns. But these activities also reflect divisions among these groups. Thus, nature tourism in both societies is sustained by local and traditional conceptions of the *qi* in stones and mountains, which become sources of art, reverence and worship. Forms of local religion including village deities, lineages and temple associations have often become the basis of mobilizing the local community and authorizing their opposition to the construction, say, of a polluting factory. At the same time, these communities also remain obstinately local, refusing to share the wider perspective of the elite NGOs on biodiversity, endangered species, etc., although they may cooperate with them on strategic issues.[48] This is an issue identified by many of the ethnographies of local environmental movements in China and Asia, generally. As Jun Jing observes, "These protests are not meant to save an endangered environment for its own sake, independently of its relevance to the people. Rather, they are aimed at seeking social justice to protect the ecological basis of human existence."[49]

We will return to this recurring problem of the tensions between the local and the universal, which is not unconnected to the problem of the sacred and the rational. Weller suggests that in both the PRC and Taiwan, the problem lies not only in the entrenched nature of local concerns and interests, but also in the global-speak – or Greenspeak – of NGOs concerned with biodiversity, nuclear threats and other seemingly distant and abstract issues. They may also be influenced by the global concerns of donor agencies.[50] Although the fit is not exact, we can think of these

---

[47] Rob Efird, "Learning the Land Beneath Our Feet: The Place of NGO-Led Environmental Education in Yunnan Province," *Journal of Contemporary China*, 21(76) (2012): 569–83, at pp. 577–82.

[48] Weller, *Discovering Nature*, pp. 80–97, 115–33.

[49] Jun Jing, "Environmental Protests in Rural China," in Elizabeth Perry and Mark Selden, Eds., *Chinese Society: Change, Conflict and Resistance* (New York: Taylor and Francis, 2010), p. 159; Tilt, *The Struggle for Sustainability in Rural Society*, p. 106; Ralph Litzinger, "In Search of the Grassroots: Hydroelectric Politics in Northwest Yunnan," in Elizabeth Perry and Merle Goldman, Eds., *Grassroots Political Reform in Contemporary China* (Cambridge, MA: Harvard University Press, 2007), pp. 282–99.

[50] Weller, *Discovering Nature*, pp. 132–4.

educated elites as representatives of universal ideals and abstract truth who are often frustrated by the limited horizons of local communities. Yet, they might reflect on older religious traditions which developed *frameworks* for engaging or assimilating these local truths, thus leading to new forms of dialogical transcendence. Let us turn to this local–universal tension from a somewhat different but closely related angle to put it in a wider perspective.

Conservation, sustainability and religion

In the 1980s, Ramachandra Guha identified two types of environmental movements that had begun to emerge across the world. The distinction was between what may be called the post-materialist or post-industrial environmentalism of the affluent world and the livelihood environmentalism of the developing world. This was also reflected to some extent within Asia where the effects of high-speed growth in much of East and Southeast Asia upon the natural conditions of livelihood and environmental degradation led to the emergence of environmental movements in the 1980s. By this time, a division had already begun to appear between developed or affluent Asia (Japan, Hong Kong, South Korea, Singapore and Taiwan) and developing Asia (the rest). Of course, since there were many developing world issues in several of the affluent countries, the division was by no means distinct.

As Guha elaborates it, the first group of countries was typically associated with an American ideal of wilderness protection, some lifestyle changes and even sacralization of wilderness as by Earth First! and other deep ecologists. In the second type, the developing countries, the impact of industrialization and urbanization was found to be felt most acutely by marginal populations, particularly peasants, forest and fishing communities and those displaced by large construction projects. For these populations, conserving the environment meant conserving the sources of their livelihood, and the environmental movement in much of Asia has been significantly shaped by their perspective. To be sure, the distinction also began to emerge within developing Asia between middle-class urban dwellers and marginalized sectors, but the livelihood environmentalist movement was becoming increasingly articulate and influential in countries like India.

Guha, who first visited the United States in the 1980s, has reflected on his experiences with the chauvinistic attitudes of deep ecologists like Roderick Nash, author of *Wilderness and the American Mind*. His response to Nash, who hoped that "the less developed nations may eventually evolve economically and intellectually to the point where nature preservation is more than a business," was the following:

This angered and irritated me, for I had spent five years studying what I thought to be rather evolved environmentalism in India. Where American environmentalists were hypocritical, driving thousands of miles in a polluting automobile to enjoy "unspoilt wilderness," men like Chandi Prasad Bhatt integrated their lives with their work. Deep ecology tended to ignore inequalities within human society, while the Gandhian Greens I knew worked among and for the poor.[51]

Although Guha later came to regard his own version of environmentalism to be similarly chauvinistic, his work triggered major debates in environmental studies, which remain with us today. Research on environmental movements in developing Asia confirmed that movements by people and communities whose livelihood was directly affected also associated ecological issues with issues of decentralized and democratic decision-making, whether in authoritarian or liberal regimes. This has been the case in Taiwan, Hong Kong, the Philippines, Indonesia and other places. In other words, environmental movements have become intertwined with the struggles for development and justice and are in the process transforming older notions of social conflict based on class struggle or the single-issue movements found in many affluent and urban societies.[52]

Indeed, it is arguable that the fight for a livable environment has transvalued our understanding of 'progressive struggles'. While they certainly hope to better their lives materially, these affected communities also seek to protect the natural resources provided by their local ecological systems that are threatened by logging, mining, trawler fishing, building, poisoning and flooding. In this context, it makes eminent sense for them to turn to their religious and cultural resources both to articulate their ideals and authorize their resistance, as well as to utilize local institutional resources for their struggles. Local religions have, in many cases, mutated into forms sanctioning the conservation and protection of these natural resources.[53] They have recovered their transcendent role, not necessarily by evoking a universalist view, but in invoking a moral authority that is higher than the worldly powers and their ideal of progress.

Yok and So have noted the important role that religious ideas, values, institutions and networks have played in the environmental movements in Asia. Folk religion, the Catholic Church (especially in the Philippines),

---

[51] Guha, *How Much Should a Person Consume?*, p. 27; see also Ramachandra Guha, "Toward a Cross-Cultural Environmental Ethic," *Alternatives: Global, Local, Political*, 15(4) (1990): 431–47.

[52] Yok-shiu F. Lee and Alvin Y. So, Eds., *Asia's Environmental Movements: Comparative Perspectives* (New York and London: M. E. Sharpe, 1999), pp. 10–12.

[53] Bron Taylor, "Popular Ecological Resistance and Radical Environmentalism," in *Ecological Resistance Movements: The Global Emergence of Radical and Popular Environmentalism*, Ed. Bron Taylor (Albany, NY: State University of New York Press, 1995), pp. 334–53.

Figure 1.1 Children sacralizing the landscape in the Cardamom Forest, Cambodia (Source: © Luke Duggleby Photography).

Buddhism, Daoism, familism, lineages, *fengshui*, indigenous traditions, symbols and rituals (the Catholic Mass, parades, funerals, martial arts performances that can turn into real resistance) have played a significant role in framing, empowering and enhancing the solidarity of local environmental movements since the 1980s. Thus, for instance, in 1987, the Catholic Mass was performed to launch the barricade of logging operations planned for San Fernando, Bukidnon province (Philippines), where the people linked arms while singing the praises of God.[54] In Sri Lanka, Buddhist monks have evolved a philosophy of development geared to meeting local needs through appropriate technology, and Cambodia and Thailand's forest monks have led a grass-roots movement of sacralizing trees by wrapping them in saffron robes and performing rites in order to save the remaining forests (see Figures 1.1 and 1.2).[55] In Hong Kong and Taiwan, Buddhism and Daoism are frequently mobilized to promote environmental protests. Buddhist lifestyles emphasizing vegetarianism, recycling and reduced consumption are increasingly adopted by the middle classes in both societies, especially as Buddhism has

[54] Lee and So, *Asia's Environmental Movements*, pp. 212–23, 289–303.
[55] Callicott, *Earth's Insights*, pp. 230–3.

Figure 1.2 Monk sacralizing the landscape in the Cardamom Forest, Cambodia (Source: © Luke Duggleby Photography).

begun to reflower among the Chinese communities in Taiwan and mainland Southeast Asia.[56]

In the PRC, the linking of religion with environmentalism is one way in which religions have actually found a new voice in society. The work of anthropologists, such as Adam Chau and others in north China, suggests that simply having a temple produces considerable volunteerism, models of organizational extension into the secular realm and leadership opportunities. Chau shows that in the villages he has studied in Shaanbei, the leadership – which was the temple leadership – undertook a slew of community initiatives, the most prominent of which was a large-scale reforestation project that drew the attention of international NGOs. The activism and good works of the village leadership secured the protection of the community from entrepreneurial local officials. Weller, Jun Jing, Ralph Litzinger and others cite several cases where religious groups have turned to ecological issues.[57]

---

[56] Lee and So, *Asia's Environmental Movements*, pp. 224–30.
[57] Adam Yuet Chau, *Miraculous Response: Doing Popular Religion in Contemporary China* (Stanford University Press, 2006), pp. 176–8; Jun Jing, "Environmental Protests"; Weller, *Discovering Nature*; Litzinger, "In Search of the Grassroots."

On a larger scale, it is no surprise that several agencies representing the world's historical religions have been eager to adopt ecological restoration and conservation as their goals. It is a *natural* extension of their mission for universal salvation. In this regard, their methods are possibly better equipped to foster personal and collective commitment than are secularist projects because they have tested methodologies for linking the personal and local to the universal. One of the most remarkable developments in the ecological and religious encounter in China has been the alliance between the Alliance of Religions and Conservation (ARC), a UK-based secular organization committed to assisting religions develop environmental programs, and the Chinese Daoist Association (CDA) (*Zhongguo daojiao xiehui*). Since the mid 1990s, the CDA has refashioned itself as a religious association committed to conserving the natural environment and promoting an environmental ethics, goals that are compatible with historical Daoism's sacralization of nature. The CDA has transformed itself from a loose and relatively passive agency dominated by the state to a more active organizational structure that steers temple activities while distancing itself from the older, allegedly 'superstitious' practices associated with the religion.

Jennifer Lemche has studied this process that she calls the "greening of Daoism," in which Laozi has morphed into the God of Ecological Protection (*Shengtai baohu shen* (生态保护神)). The transformation of the CDA has been made possible by its alignment with the environmental and religious goals of the PRC government but perhaps even more through the close collaboration with the ARC on developing its agenda for ecological practices and educational programs. The agenda seeks to create sustainable temples through various means from environment-friendly rules for tourists and pilgrims to water management, energy conservation, recycling and environmental audits at all temple sites. The CDA and ARC have held up two exemplars, the Maoshan and Tiejia Ecology Temples. To be sure, such agenda-driven projects are unlikely to rapidly transform beliefs and attitudes, and Lemche suggests a mixed record so far. Nonetheless, what is notable is that a national agency with local roots has, in close collaboration with a global NGO, taken the lead in changing environmental consciousness in China.[58]

---

[58] Jennifer Lemche, "The Greening of Chinese Daoism: Modernity, Bureaucracy and Ecology in Contemporary Chinese Religion." Master's degree thesis submitted to the Department of Religious Studies, Queen's University, Canada, June 2010.

Sustainability in contemporary India

The modern environmental movement in India is perhaps the most robust and diverse outside the West and was launched a decade or more before similar movements in Asia.[59] Although the foundations of it were laid by the earlier Gandhian movement and British pioneers such as the urban planner, Patrick Geddes, the now renowned Chipko (tree-embrace) movement in the Himalayan villages of 1973 is identified as the start of the popular movement. The Chipko was an indigenous peasant movement and revealed a strong role played by local women. Gaura Devi, an older peasant woman who faced down the loggers and armed guards, has subsequently been called the Rosa Parks of the Indian environmental movement. Chipko was a local movement of livelihood protection that had earlier antecedents, but its association with non-violent Gandhian techniques and with the sacred geography of the Himalayas and the Ganges endowed it with a wider symbolic significance. The movement succeeded in forcing a 15-year ban in commercial green felling in Uttar Pradesh and several other parts of India.[60]

The intertwining of local livelihood concerns with spiritual if not religious meanings would be repeated in many expressions of environmental protest across India. Two of the most dramatic and influential of such movements were related to displacement and environmental destruction caused by the construction of big dams in India: the antidam movements in Tehri Garwhal (also in the Himalayan Ganges region) in the 1980s and against the Narmada river dam (Sardar Sarovar Dam) in Gujarat during the 1990s. As a result of the protest movements which were allied with other large dam protests of the time across the world, not only has the Indian state largely stopped the construction of large dams but also the World Bank and other transnational agencies have reversed the trend of funding large dam projects (examined in Chapter 7).[61]

In these movements, local Gandhian activists like Sunderlal Bahuguna and Chandi Prasad Bhatt made common cause with national and global environmental activists and intellectuals such as Medha Patkar, Vandana

---

[59] Arne Kalland and Gerard Persoon, Eds., *Environmental Movements in Asia* (Richmond, Surrey: Curzon Press, 1998), p. 16.

[60] Vandana Shiva and J. Bandyopadhyay, "The Evolution, Structure, and Impact of the Chipko Movement," *Mountain Research and Development*, 6(2) (1986): 133–42, at p. 140.

[61] Sanjeev Khagram, *Dam and Development: Transnational Struggle for Water and Power* (Ithaca, NY and London: Cornell University Press, 2004), pp. 51–5. See also Sanjay Sangvai, *The River and Life: People's Struggle in the Narmada Valley* (Mumbai: Earthcare Books, 2000); Patrick McCully, "The Use of a Trilateral Network: An Activist's Perspective on the Formation of the World Commission on Dams," *American University International Law Review*, 16(6) (2001): 1453–75.

Shiva and, later, the writer, Arundhati Roy, all of whom happen to be women. Patkar and Shiva also framed their resistance as a non-violent, non-cooperation Gandhian movement of *satyagraha* committed to "sustainable ecological stability and politics of distribution of ecological cost."[62] The Gandhian movement in Garwhal was mobilized around the abuse and degradation of forests together with the problems of women (including antiliquor protests) and the protection of livelihood and culture.

The intellectual leadership of the Gandhian environmental movement more broadly and the Narmada Bachao Andolan (NBA) group, in particular, has developed a strong critique of the role of the state and the 'modern Western' scientific project, which, to be sure, has been controversial in India. Science in the service of large-scale capitalist and bureaucratic projects which appropriate natural 'commons' is seen as violent, and against people, livelihood and cultures. The Gandhians advocate replicable, small-scale, decentralized, democratic and ecologically sustainable activities. In place of the dams, the NBA calls for energy and water conservation based on improving dry farming technology, watershed development, small dams, lift schemes for irrigation and drinking water, and improved efficiency and utilization of existing dams.[63]

The Gandhian environmental movement professes to be not at all antiscience; rather, its advocates oppose the practice of science that dismisses ultimate values and cultural goals. They reject the idea that the plurality of life ways and knowledge systems must give way to the merciless machinery of progress.[64] To be sure, there are differences among these activists on how much modern technology they are prepared to accept. For instance, there is a tension between the two originally local activists, Bahuguna and Bhatt. Bahuguna, now a major figure in the deep-ecology movement, believes that economic growth takes place at the expense of ecological sustainability and the satisfaction of basic human needs. Bhatt refuses to see modern technology and nature as a zero-sum game; appropriate technology can be developed to increase the productivity of labor without destroying or increasing natural inputs.[65]

---

[62] Shiva and Bandyopadhyay, "The Evolution, Structure, and Impact of the Chipko Movement," p. 133.

[63] Robert Jensen, "Damn the Dams: An Interview with Medha Patkar," posted on *Alternet*, February 26, 2004 (http://uts.cc.utexas.edu/~rjensen/freelance/patkar.htm).

[64] S. Ravi Rajan, "Science, State and Violence: An Indian Critique Reconsidered," *Science as Culture*, 14(3) (2005): 10–12.

[65] Baird Callicott has suggested that the two attitudes towards sustainability also reflect gender perspectives. While males in rural areas welcome local industries such as sawing or making turpentine, females depend on the forest – for fodder, water, and firewood – where they toil daily for livelihood needs. Chipko thus endorses Bahuguna's 'deep ecology' whereas men are more likely to endorse Bhatt. Callicott, *Earth's Insights*, pp. 224–7.

From the perspective of contemporary politics, however, we have recently been alerted to a more potent danger that appears to be emerging in the environmental movement in India, a danger that anticipates the themes I will develop in the course of this work. The Gandhian approach to historical and spiritual sources of transcendence in order to develop an alternative path appears to have been penetrated by advocates of the ideology of Hindu nationalism. Mukul Sharma's book, *Green and Saffron*, provocatively argues that the highly developed religious symbology of the Green movement in India, including that of the Gandhians, has become in many cases the 'Trojan horse' for political Hinduism (Hindutva) or confessional nationalism, as discussed in Chapter 6.

While he continues to see the Indian environmental scene as dynamic and diverse, Sharma notes several points of convergence between environmental organizations and a small number of highly organized groups of Hindu nationalists. These points include the evocation of sacred spaces and sites being violated, a knowledge format that associates ecology with the social body, and a common distaste for Westernization and globalization. While the environmental groups may be deeply committed to ecological goals and religious ideals, Hindu symbolism also gives them a wide platform to address the ocean of communities who continue to find such meaning in the land and waterscape. Hindu nationalists meanwhile insert strong nationalistic meanings into these very symbols directed against minorities and unfriendly neighboring countries. Their rhetoric connects the pollution of the land and waters with the pollution of the Hindu nation by the presence of 'aliens', particularly Muslims.[66]

Sharma explores three episodes or cases which in his view reflect either the infiltration by Hindu activists or the inclination of Gandhians themselves to appeal to nationalist or undemocratic social norms. The anti-Tehri dam movement, he believes, has been appropriated by the rhetoric of Hindutva, and its leader Bahuguna has apparently made a derogatory comment about the Muslim ruler, Aurangzeb (1618–1707). The second episode concerns the Vrindavan Conservation Project, a major campaign to revive the Vrindavan region, which is believed by Hindus to be the birthplace of the god Krishna, and its onetime forests, the sacred groves of his divine play (*leela*). This project has been launched by World Wildlife Fund (WWF)-India and has brought together major Hindu religious and temple authorities as well as the ARC, which we encountered in the

---

[66] Mukul Sharma, *Green and Saffron: Hindu Nationalism and Indian Environmental Politics* (Ranikhet, India: Permanent Black, 2012).

discussion of Green Daoism. The project sponsors plantings, nature clubs, citizens' action, a river watch and protection of sacred groves, together with improvement of civic facilities and environmental awareness education. But the Dalits, who continue to do the sanitation work, and resident Muslims interviewed by Sharma feel quite alienated from the place and its strong Hindutva narrative of history.[67]

Sharma's best-known case is his third instance – the 'exposé' of the model ecological village in western India, Ralegan Siddhi, created by the retired Indian army soldier and Gandhian, Anna Hazare. While Hazare has been well known and celebrated by the government and even by left-wing environmentalists, who have called him the "warrior of Indian environmentalism," his fame grew exponentially in the summer of 2011 when he arose as the leader of the massive, non-violent, anticorruption movement that spread like wildfire through the streets of New Delhi and other cities in India. Sharma, who was initially very impressed by Hazare's achievements in the village, which had gone from drought-ridden misery to a verdant, conservationist and self-sustaining community, became troubled by the means used by Hazare.

According to Sharma, "conservation and sustainable use of natural resources of the area are enmeshed in the creation and consolidation of a singular moral authority."[68] Hazare's Gandhian spiritualism is highly disciplinary, even militaristic, and undemocratic. The model works because of Hazare's personal moral authority, and village elections have not been held for many years. Vegetarianism and strict prohibition of alcohol consumption has been imposed on the villagers through social pressure of the majority – particularly upon the Dalits. While, as a Gandhian, he is committed and even passionate about equal rights for Dalits, he believes in a traditional Hindu order of castes that must perform their occupational duties righteously. Hazare's religio-moral "environ-mentalism is concerned not with democracy and social justice but with a system of reciprocal rights and duties and moral obligations of the village community."[69]

Sharma also surveys environmental conservatism in Europe to reveal what we might call a kind of 'Heimat complex' that associates deep affect for the 'native place' (xiangtu in Chinese) and its natural environment with the special quality – and prerogative – of the people who are allegedly 'of the soil'. Nazi ecological ideas, of course, represented one of the earliest expressions of modern environmentalism, and scientists like Ernst Haeckel, who influenced the Nazis, argued that ecology was a total science

---

[67] *Ibid.*, pp. 178–80.   [68] *Ibid.*, p. 78.   [69] *Ibid.*, p. 260.

that could explain the natural and social world and also change the latter. Richard Walter Darré introduced the idea of 'blood and soil' environmentalism into Nazi ideology and practice.[70] Incidentally, Nazi environmentalism also had a significant influence on the Japanese militarists in Manchuria and other colonies. While Sharma acknowledges that the overwhelming majority of contemporary Green movements and political parties are antiracist and in favor of global justice, he goes on to discuss contemporary right-wing environmental chauvinism in Europe, which often justifies racist, anti-immigrant and nationalist agendas by invoking protection of the environment. As a counterpoint, Joachim Radkau, among the leading historians of the environment in Europe, sees in early *Heimat* ideology a forward-looking, constructive love for one's land which restrained unchecked urbanization; its relative absence in the movement today is a weakness in his view. He challenges us to see the ecological insight of an otherwise brutal regime as "a thorn in the side of historical reflection."[71]

Sharma's book serves as an important warning by a radical, secular environmentalist of the dangers of sacralizing nature and the environment. It alerts us to the various interrelated problems that emerge in the effort to mobilize people to greater awareness, action and, indeed, self-transformation in relation to their natural environment and its abuse. We have seen earlier the problem of localization and the deployment of religious resources to empower the local community in relation to outside forces, especially in the examples from Weller's study of the PRC and Taiwan. In a way, although the process is complicated by Gandhianism in the Indian context, it also reflects religiosity as a limited and limiting project, whether to the Hindu nation or the traditional community. These religions may have found it difficult to resist the kind of confessionalization that seeks to transform its adherents into communities of identity, particularly in a world where global prestige belongs to strong nations. Even more, in a scientific world, they lack confidence in the transcendence of their ideals.

I do, however, take some comfort in the democratic diversity and prominence of Gandhian environmentalism in India. It has the potential to become a locally bred expression of dialogical transcendence in our times. In a recent study of the effects of globalization in India, *Churning the Earth*, Shrivastav and Kothari have produced a most disturbing critique of the environmental plunder and gross injustice being perpetrated by the

---

[70] *Ibid.*, pp. 195–201. See also Joachim Radkau, *Nature and Power: A Global History of the Environment* (Cambridge University Press, 2008), pp. 260–3.
[71] Radkau, *Nature and Power*, pp. 230–6.

urban, national and transnational, corporate and political elites on the rest of society and the land. Although the bulk of the book dissects the problem, they also devote two chapters to the buds and shoots of what they call radical ecological democracy. They see many tens of thousands of civic organizations and networks – communities, cooperatives, self-help groups, NGOs, occasional government agencies and others, "many wildly successful, others struggling, but all pointing to the immense possibility of a world that is more ecologically sustainable and socially equitable than what globalized growth has given us."[72]

In 1993, on the forty-second anniversary of Gandhi's martyrdom, Medha Patkar resolved to drown herself in the filling reservoir of the Narmada dam for the sake of "our ultimate goal of [a] socially just and ecologically sustainable model of development." The Indian government prevented the martyrdom by agreeing to a set of compensation measures for the displaced. Guha has compared her attempt at martyrdom with that of Mark Dubois, who chained himself to a boulder to sacrifice his life to protest the damming of the Stanislaus River in California in 1979; Dubois was saved by a helicopter search team. While both acts of intended self-sacrifice derived from commitment to a transcendent ideal, Dubois sought to rescue the wilderness; Patkar, to save livelihoods and sustainable ways of life.[73]

Conclusion

Whether in the developing or developed world, planetary sustainability requires grass-roots activists and leaders who comprehend the necessity of transcending the limits of interests and place while pursuing ways to respond to local problems. Some transnational NGOs such as Conservation International – to be discussed further in Chapter 7 – already work with corporations to develop economic models to compensate local interests for the loss of a community's livelihood resources and restore local biodiversity. While such activity is particularly worthwhile because it shows how a transnational body is able to respond to local needs, the need of the hour is to develop a new type of transcendent framework capable of motivating persons and groups to work for themselves, their communities and the planet. Advocates of global sustainability not only need strong institutional and scaling capacities, but they

[72] Aseem Shrivastava and and Ashish Kothari, *Churning the Earth: The Making of Global India* (New Delhi: Penguin/Viking, 2012), p. 255.
[73] Cited in Guha, *How Much Should a Person Consume?*, pp. 66–7.

also require the moral force of popular support to compel governments to share sovereign power in the near future.

An environmentalist such as Vandana Shiva directs her critique and ire less at national governments than at the idea of the global itself. She suggests that global Greenspeak about biodiversity, ozone depletion, etc., has erased the local from environmental concerns by suggesting that the solution can only be global. The Biodiversity Convention, the Agreement on Trade-Related Intellectual Property Rights (TRIPS) and the World Trade Organization (WTO) have become forums to negotiate the ownership of living resources. Global Greenspeak has become a signifier that hides the predatory interests of particular multinational corporations who plan the "final colonization of life itself" by seeking to patent plant genes and germ plasms.[74] But, surely, since national governments are often reluctant to defy powerful multinationals, these movements – such as the Seed Satyagraha of Karnataka – will still have to rely on the alliance of locally empowered movements with other global forces to press national governments to action.

To give one example of the kind of difficulties presented by nationalism, take the proposal of Mutsuyoshi Nishimura, member of the UN Secretary-General's High-Level Advisory Group on Climate Change Financing (AGF), that world governments should collectively own the capped "carbon budget" of 660 billion tonnes of carbon dioxide in total emissions between 2010 and 2050, the maximum that scientific research tells us may be emitted into the atmosphere to limit the rise in global temperature to $2\,°C$. Whereas the existing model is based on a government's voluntary determination to reduce national emissions, Nishimura's model requires polluters – no matter where – to pay for global commons. Carbon credits can be auctioned off on a polluter-pays principle. Autonomous global agencies can work out special provisions for developing countries. Capping carbon by a global budget rather than by a patchwork of national pledges can dramatically reduce emissions.

Yet, despite enormous support from environmental organizations, whenever this or this type of proposal is put on the table in climate change summits, it always faces 'national mitigation obligations' (i.e., my 'fair' share) from both developed and developing countries. China demands that the United States and other advanced countries take the lead because of their historical responsibility, whereas the United States insists that China and India must participate together with it from the start. Nishimura believes that a nation-state-based analysis not only limits our

---

[74] Vandana Shiva, "Conflicts of Global Ecology: Environmental Activism in a Period of Global Reach," *Alternatives*, *19* (1994): 195–207.

vision but also highlights our hypocrisy by limiting our complicity and responsibility in what is no longer a national issue. We live, he says, "in a world of global interdependency and of global subcontracting networks. It is global production in which we use China as an industrial platform." Climate change is "an issue for you and for all of us as nature does not make [a] distinction whether it comes from the US, China and Japan."[75]

There is no mystery to the task ahead of us. The machineries of national governments need to be persuaded to devote as much time and importance to planetary sustainability in their educational and pedagogic projects as they do to national studies and national identity-building. The next chapter probes the foundations of national identity and pedagogy in the ways in which history has been written in the modern period. Linear, tunneled histories have supplied a vital justification for the sovereignty claims of the nation. Yet, an emergent field of circulatory histories reveals that histories are shared, and there are many other modes of affiliation with peoples, the commons and the natural world that may serve our goals much better today.

[75] "Climate Change and Asia," presentation of Mr. Mutsuyoshi Nishimura, Special Advisor to the Cabinet of the Government of Japan and Senior Fellow at JIIA, IISS-JIIA Conference June 2–4, 2008, Hotel Okura, Tokyo, Japan: Second Session – Asian Environmental Nightmares, "Climate Change and Asia" (www.iiss.org/conferences/global-strategic-challenges-as-played-out-in-asia/asias-strategic-challenges-in-search-of-a-common-agenda/conference-papers/second-session-asian-environmental-night mares/climate-change-and-asia-mutsuyoshi-nishimura).

2 Circulatory and competitive histories

As a graduate student in the Boston area, I once encountered a stray sheet of paper in a library, the blank side of which I wished to use for notes. It was a photocopy of a handwritten page from an archived document of 1833, which mentioned the impending visit of the famous Unitarian from India to Salem, Massachusetts, Raja Rammohun Roy (1772–1833), who was currently visiting Bristol. In preparation for his visit, the Unitarians were circulating a locket with a curl of his hair in it. I was taken aback, because, as an Indian, I had known of Roy as the founder of the reformist Hindu Brahmo Samaj, a deist and the 'father of modern India'; I also knew that he had visited England, but had no idea of his planned visit to the United States or that he was even known there, let alone the reverence with which he was held by some. Roy died in Bristol in 1833 and so never did step on the shores of Salem, although his ideas and a lock of hair had represented him there.

Over the years, I picked up other scattered pieces of information that began to coalesce into a remarkable history of circulations. For one thing, the New England Transcendentalists, particularly, Henry David Thoreau and Ralph Waldo Emerson, read Roy's translations of the Upanishads and the principal Vedas, texts they deeply admired and cited profusely. They were doubtless familiar with the exchanges between Roy and the British Unitarians, which were published in 1824.[1]

The American Transcendentalists would come to influence a wide range of ideas and practices in America and the world, including abolitionism, proto-environmentalism and civil disobedience founded upon

---

[1] For the influence of Roy on the Transcendentalists, see Carl T. Jackson, *Vedanta for the West: The Ramakrishna Movement in the United States* (Bloomington, IN: Indiana University Press, 1994), pp. 8–9; for more details, see Yvonne Aburrow, "The Day-Star of Approaching Morn: The Relationship Between the Unitarians and the Brahmo Samaj" (http://bristolunitarians.blogspot.sg/2013/08/the-rammohun-roy-connection.html). For an interpretation of *Walden* as framed by ideas of the Samkhya-Yoga tradition, see William Bysshe Stein, "The Hindu Matrix of *Walden*: The King's Son," *Comparative Literature*, 22(4) (1970): 303–18.

Transcendentalist conceptions of the self-cultivation of the powers of the mind and the consciousness of ultimate reality. In 1849, Thoreau published *Civil Disobedience*; it became deeply influential and affected many great writers like Leo Tolstoy and the worldwide spirituality movement by the late nineteenth century. Mahatma Gandhi, who was experimenting with his ideas of non-violent resistance (*satyagraha* or truth force) from his days in South Africa in the 1890s, became profoundly impressed by Thoreau's (and Tolstoy's) philosophical and moral ideas upon reading *Civil Disobedience* and *Walden*. He adopted the phrase 'civil disobedience' as the English term for his own project.[2]

What we have here is the circulation, or rather, the circulatory nature of historical ideas and practices over a hundred years, emerging from one part of the world, India, traversing continents and visited by various transformations while still retaining recognizable connections with its sources, and then returning to India enriched and made usable for a new era. The story, of course, hardly ends there, as Gandhi is viewed as the patron saint of the Civil Rights movement in the United States rather than Thoreau. Moreover, the circulation was not only intellectual. From the late eighteenth until the mid-nineteenth century, several Boston families maintained commercial and artistic relationships with their counterparts in Bengal.[3] It would probably be fruitful to track any interweaving between these concurrent circulations, but I have brought up this episode merely to illustrate the theme of this chapter of circulatory versus linear, tunneled histories, and not to examine its details, which are best left to the specialists.

The argument I will be making in this book depends on recognizing that histories are not the exclusive property of a single community or entity since questions of sovereignty and identity are closely linked to history. The historical profile of a community is crisscrossed and shaped – for good or bad – by numerous scales of interactions with circulatory networks and forces.

[2] For the global influence of Thoreau's *Civil Disobedience* and, in particular, the influence on Tolstoy and Gandhi, see Joel Myerson, Sandra Harbert Petrulionis and Laura Dassow Walls, Eds., *The Oxford Handbook of Transcendentalism* (Oxford University Press, 2010), p. 633; see also Michael J. Frederick, *Transcendental Ethos: A Study of Thoreau's Social Philosophy and Its Consistency in Relation to Antebellum Reform* (Cambridge, MA: Harvard University Press, 1998) (http://thoreau.eserver.org/mjf/MJF3.html).

[3] Susan Bean, *Yankee India: American Commercial and Cultural Encounters with India in the Age of Sail, 1784–1860* (Salem, MA: Peabody Museum Press, 2001). See also Partha Mitter, "Mutual Perceptions in the Contact Zone: India and America," paper presented at the Smithsonian American Art Museum, Washington, DC, conference, "A Long and Tumultuous Relationship": East–West Interchanges in American Art, October 1–2, 2009.

Time, narrative and politics

All societies have diverse ways of conceptualizing the passage of time whether through natural cycles of the seasons, ritual or sacred times, and business cycles or through institutional rhythms. At the same time, certain conceptions of the past become dominant or hegemonic among different temporalities, such as the linear conception of time and history in the nineteenth and twentieth centuries. Indeed, our very notion of history as an irreversible movement is inseparably tied to the conception of time as a linear succession of some *bounded entity*. Although linear time represents the common sense of our notion of historical time, I want to identify its uniqueness and understand how it became dominant in the modern world, its functional relation to competitive states, and how we might build histories upon alternative temporalities. I propose that we replace the primacy of the linear history of nations with a circulatory, interactive and transformative history. Local, regional and national histories are by no means to be excluded, but the analytical priority in this optic would be given to how these histories interact and loop with circulatory transformations.

Benedict Anderson has popularized Walter Benjamin's conception of 'empty, homogeneous time' as the temporality of nations operating in a globally unified time-space (at least for nationalists and nation-makers). As such, it alerted attention to alternative conceptions of temporality. Time is understood not only as a given, linear, abstractly measured and neutral passage filled by activity but also by ways in which it is constituted through different social practices and by human experience. Historians are familiar with Ferdinand Braudel's differentiated conceptions of eventful time, the *longue durée*, cyclical time and geological time.[4]

The philosopher Paul Ricoeur regards time as it appears to humans – the phenomenology of time – not only as measured in abstract terms but also, crucially, as apprehended through narratives. The form of narrative addresses the human need to live in time, to express 'historicality', which refers to the urge to reach back into our past to change our future and see our life as a whole. Historicality, for Ricoeur, is the way we grasp our most basic potentialities as individuals and collectives by repetition or recollection that guides or sometimes propels us to the future in the form

---

[4] Benedict Anderson, *Imagined Communities: Reflections on the Origins and Spread of Nationalism* (London: Verso, 1991 (rev. and expanded version of 1983 text); Walter Benjamin, "Theses on the Philosophy of History," in *Illuminations* (New York: Schocken Books, 1969), pp. 253–64; Fernand Braudel, *The Mediterranean and the Mediterranean World in the Age of Philip II*, vol. I (Berkeley and Los Angeles, CA: University of California Press, 1995).

of personal fate or collective destiny. In other words, historicality is a mode of human temporal existence, and narrative is the most adequate means to express it.[5]

Hayden White expresses what I believe is a sympathetic critique of Ricoeur's ideas. He not only agrees with the necessity of narrative but also shows – by drawing on Lacan's analogy with the child who links her end to her remembered beginnings – that humans require narrative "to attest to an integrity which every individual must be supposed to possess if (s)he is to become subject to any system of law, morality or propriety." If Ricoeur is right about the need for narrative to represent time, White insists that Ricoeur's emphasis on narrative as "found" and not "constructed" avoids the necessarily political nature of narrative construction. "What is imaginary about narrative representation is the idea of a centered consciousness looking out on to the world and representing this world to itself as having the full coherency of narrativity itself."[6]

White's critique of Ricoeur's stress upon narrative as "found" rather than constructed is perhaps somewhat misplaced because in the latter's scheme the narrative is both homologous and pertinent to what is found, but not identical to it. Briefly, Ricoeur's scheme develops the theory of narrative as a threefold structure: its *prefiguration* or the happening of eventful activity, its *configuration* as a narrative with a plot by historians among others, and its *refiguration* or resignification of the narrative in the imaginative transformation by writers, artists or popular culture. As such, *configuration* or secondary narration has a constructionist element in it, but it is to be distinguished from the purely *refigurative* process in that it *purports and seeks* some pertinence in the events as they happened.

In the positivist view of history, this pertinence was converted into a strong claim of transparent representation. In weaker claims of narrative configuration, we may be able to include historical stories in mythological accounts which blur the differentiation between configuration and refiguration. Take the case of the historical Guandi (died 219 CE) from the era of the Three Kingdoms in China, who was first recorded historically and whose story was then circulated through several fictional romances and myths. He reappears as an important hero, model and god for secret societies, Buddhists, Daoists, merchants, soldiers and local communities,

---

[5] Paul Ricoeur develops Martin Heidegger's conceptions of time in this work on time and narrative. Historicality, for Ricoeur, is the second most authentic mode of temporality in the Heideggerian sense, located between the latter's within-timeness and deep temporality. See Paul Ricoeur, *Time and Narrative*, vol. III (University of Chicago Press, 1988); Paul Ricoeur, "Narrative Time," *Critical Inquiry*, 7(1) (1980): 169–90.

[6] Hayden White, *The Content of the Form* (Baltimore, MD: Johns Hopkins University Press, 1987), p. 36.

among others, throughout Chinese history. It is a consequence of this reconfiguration that he is deified as an imperial god during the Qing period. Yet, it is also possible to write an acceptable history of Guandi from contemporary sources.[7] Ricoeur's account sacrifices power, but it rescues the realistic and verifiable factors that mark academic history, however exaggerated some of those claims may be.

White, who is more concerned with the social function and ideology of history, frontally attacks the differentiation between mythic knowledge and historical knowledge because it is based on imperialism. It is a means to impose the imperialists' power of history upon the 'people without history'. All humans have a past however they represent it; modern historiography is as dependent on imagination as myth or ritual and other ways of giving meaning to the past. Narrativization is not only an act of historicality – it is simultaneously about power. However, in his important contribution about the ideological function of history, White tends to foreclose the possibilities of historical narratives as contested and reaching beyond a spatio-temporal fix.

The problem with White's understanding lies in his conception of narrative structures, which draws heavily and fatally, I believe, on structuralism. Thus, White wants to show that history and myth have important common elements in utilizing imaginative resources in their 'configuration', as it were, but both are also limited by the structural form of the narrative. Thus, White famously limited narratives to tragic, romantic, comedic, parodic, etc. These produce closures to ways of narrating history that we cannot agree with any longer. Historical narratives may be instruments of domination, but they can also be picked up, developed or improvised in other spaces and time with real effects. They are thus a political resource by which different groups seek to specify which potentials and resources are to be realized by whom and towards what future.[8]

---

[7] Prasenjit Duara, "Superscribing Symbols: The Myth of Guandi, Chinese God of War," *Journal of Asian Studies*, 47(4) (1988): 778–95.

[8] In some ways, Ricoeur, who is decidedly uninterested in the political dimensions of narrative, has more room for contestation through the philosophical notion of aporia or conceptual irreconcilability. Narrativity, for Ricoeur, represents aspects of time to form "continuity within a difference." See Mario J. Valdes, Ed., *Reflection and Imagination: A Paul Ricœur Reader* (University of Toronto Press, 1991), p. 25. The aporias of time reveal the gap between the necessary difference produced by the passage of time and the desire for continuity or what Derrida called the 'metaphysics of presence'. Jacques Derrida, *Of Grammatology*, Trans. Gayatri Chakravorty Spivak (Baltimore, MD: Johns Hopkins University Press, 1974), p. 49. For Ricoeur, the narrative has to address the aporia of temporal incoherence – White's 'imaginary' of 'centered consciousness' – but in a pertinent way, seeking to emphasize the connections rather than the gaps so beloved of

When a history is contested – whether in the academic or political world – the narrative is often simultaneously altered or inflected. So a tragedy can be converted into a parody – or a narrative of national heroism into the tragedy or satire of imperial domination. Indeed, a narrative may combine elements from these modes and from resources going beyond known tropes. At any rate, the meanings and politics of historical narratives are not foreclosed by their ultimate tropic structure; their significance lie in the possibilities that they embed in shaping the present and the future. Moreover, revisionist and contested accounts of dominant narratives, even when not immediately visible, often lie coiled near or within these accounts.

When we attend to how the effects of unfolding events (and concatenations) *disperse* over time *and* space. we can see how differently those who absorb or are affected by them can react to that process.[9] Similarly with narratives; if, as historians, we expand our view of events and processes as apprehended by those other than their immediate or powerful narrators, we can see how the human imagination not only moves forward in time but also returns to the event or concatenation as a loop to somewhere else, as a spiral developing other meanings from the same events and in other ways. Think of how heroic imperialist narratives of conquest – and the events and processes they refer to – have been circulated or recycled into a myriad of different ways, including anti-imperialist ones, of constituting people in different spaces and times.

Historicality, narrative and power represent the most basic concepts for understanding the role of history in the world – both as the *eventing* of the world as prefiguration and as the meaningful resignification of temporal processes. We may work with a conception of time as a process into which we never step twice. As such, history as event is a *worlding* process of which the key to understanding is spatial dispersion. An event disperses with rippling, layering and ramifying effects across unsuspected parts of the world. From a phenomenological or human perspective – as configured process – however, it is understood in a narrative which may be depicted as linear but which spirals, loops, revisits, and appropriates – such as with the Renaissance – and connects and disconnects. History as circulatory – both in the prefigured and configured versions – is a crucial missing term

---

deconstructionists. In my earlier work I have tried to utilize these temporal aporias to reveal historical and political contestation. For instance, in a society founded on the notion of linear and abstract time, the pervasive contestation between conservatives and progressives, or right and left in modern polities, can be understood in terms of preferences between 'continuity' and 'difference'.

[9] Of course, we cannot apprehend the unfolding of an event except through some cognitive structure, but we can attest to its unfolding by the common points of reference to the event by cognitively different accounts of it.

in the philosophical debate. Events simultaneously disperse across a variety of human and non-human borders, triggering and creating new events and processes. Historicality, narrative and power are, among other things, human modes of responding to this openness to time.

Cosmological and historical time

I endorse the common understanding that premodern, prenational societies were not dominated by a sense of linear history. But, in my understanding, the non-linear conception was *hegemonic* and not exclusive. While the cosmological values dominating time urged a return to the truths of a golden age or subordinated them to transcendent goals, there also existed other conceptions of time and history or histories in a minor key. There were incipient narratives of a bounded linear movement in time or ones that traced and justified the power of one worldly community over others. This has been clearly recorded for Greek and Chinese historical texts, which reveal many traits associated with the evidential history of modern times, and I will return to the Chinese case below. But, as Romila Thapar has recently argued, this is equally true for the most notorious exemplar of a non-historical culture, India.

Colonial administrators and scholars relied overwhelmingly on Brahmin views of Indian society and culture, in which the cosmology of Brahmanism had priority. Colonial and modern historians have tended to ignore the genealogies, chronicles, and dated inscriptions of events and grants in the Puranic tradition, as well as the histories of the Buddhists and the Jains, who sought to make many worldly claims, often in sectarian debates or disputations, by linking persons and events to the succession of monastic elders and the legitimacy of the Sangha. Thus, while, from a cosmological perspective, Hindu conceptions of time were cyclical (or spiral-like), there were also more measured versions of linear time associated largely with the claims or proof of legitimacy recorded in the various *samvats*, or Hindu calendrical systems.[10]

Chinese civilization possessed a sophisticated tradition of historical writing, and contemporary scholars have turned us away from the old shibboleths of this tradition. Among these is the view of imperial Chinese historiography as seeking a return to the ancient ideals of the sage-kings, or the view of the record of events as expressions of cyclical, cosmological patterns where human and supernatural agency was intertwined.

---

[10] Romila Thapar, "Was There Historical Writing in Early India?," in Cynthia Talbot, Ed., *Knowing India: Colonial and Modern Constructions of the Past: Essays in Honor of Thomas R. Trautmann* (New Delhi: Yoda Press, 2011), pp. 281–308.

Historical writing, such as that by the great Han dynasty historian, Sima Qian, was also characterized by a more contemporary conception of time, an urge to create new institutions for a new generation. Indeed, Sima Qian's *Shiji* depicts a kind of empty, homogeneous space-time. The chronology consists of "a series of years that proceed at a perfectly mechanical pace with events in the various states that made up China," revealing a space-time within which unrelated things could be contemporary.[11]

Indeed, Michael Puett has argued that in early Chinese history, during the period of the Warring States and the early Han period, strong claims were made for discontinuity, change and the creation of new institutions that were transgressive of the past and the divine; in other words, some Chinese statesmen advocated a conception of time as secular and innovative.[12] Indeed, the Qin emperor, founder of the imperial state in the early third century BCE, defied the mandate of Heaven and proposed to set up his own dynasty and moral order for eternity. He set off an institutional revolution that forever changed the face of Chinese politics. Nonetheless, even while later scholars like Sima Qian (*c.* 140–85 BCE) affirmed – however ambivalently – historical creation, the claim that came to dominate the empire was one of continuity with the patterns of the ancient sages and the normative order of Heaven. Linear temporality was seriously weakened, especially during the late imperial period (from around 1000 CE until 1911) when the tendency to "slight the present in order to favor the past" grew in importance.[13] Chinese historiography did not think of time in an evolutionary, developmental or progressive way where the future could be always made anew by humans, or, in other words, where future developments were an integral part of the entity called history. Still, I believe we can accept the contributions of Puett and Harbsmeier if we see the cyclical or return narrative as the *hegemonic representation* of time and history which obscures other perceptions, like the one Puett has excavated.

Observing the role of historical temporality in China and India, we may say then that there were coexisting temporalities in these historical

[11] Cristoph Harbsmeier, "Some Notions of Time and of History in China and in the West, with a Digression on the Anthropology of Writing," in Chun-chieh Huang and Erik Zücher, Eds., *Time and Space in Chinese Culture* (Leiden: E. J. Brill, 1995), pp. 49–71, at p. 57; Michael Puett, *The Ambivalence of Creation: Debates Concerning Innovation and Artifice in Early China* (Stanford University Press, 2001).
[12] Harbsmeier, "Some Notions of Time and of History," p. 61.
[13] Achim Mittag, "Historical Consciousness in China: Some Notes on Six Theses on Chinese Historiography and Historical Thought," in Paul Van Der Velde and Alex McKay, Eds., *New Developments in Asian Studies: An Introduction* (London: Kegan Paul, 1998), pp. 47–76, at pp. 51–2.

societies where one or more of these modalities were linear and utilized by rulers or groups to demonstrate, prove or confirm their legitimacy by successive written records. In some periods, particularly during moments of threat or anxiety about invaders, these records and perspectives could be bounded into a narrative of the community and mobilized by elites to rally defense of the community or empire. Such events were evident in the Mongol and Manchu invasions of China.[14] The point, however, is that these views did not become hegemonic as they did later in Europe and with nationalism in Asia. Rather, we are interested in their coexistence with more reversible and open-ended cosmological conceptions. This coexistence becomes more troubled when linear time itself became cosmologically hegemonic.

The account of the emergence in Europe of linear history and its epistemic condition, homogeneous and empty time-space, is a familiar one that I will briefly summarize below. My goal is not to dispute this account but to grasp: (1) what were the conditions in which this linear vision became institutionalized and hegemonic and (2) how linearity came to be about territorially or socially bounded histories within this time-space. In some ways, I suggest, this is a paradoxical development since this time-space is relatively unbounded.

In the classic account of J. G. A. Pocock, the disenchantment of cosmological time in Europe began with the European Renaissance. In *The Machiavellian Moment*, Pocock explores the Christian and Renaissance conceptions of time. Simply put, the 'Machiavellian moment' refers to the relationship of virtue to history. Both Christian and Renaissance humanist conceptions of time gave true meaning to the divine or rational virtue that existed outside time – outside the secular or temporal time of history. Pocock argues that while humanists, such as Machiavelli, believed that the citizen fulfilled himself through civic virtue rather than through ecclesiastical sacraments, they were still unable to develop a theory of history, or what Pocock calls historicism. Natural law was rational, unchanging and true; history was irrational, fickle and corrupting. The 'moment' consists of the deferral of the inevitable collapse or corruption of virtue in mundane time.[15] Pocock's insight into the Machiavellian moment has resonances with the conception of time in imperial China. The idea of the dynastic cycle embeds something very like the Machiavellian moment in the cycle of virtue and corruption, and the

---

[14] Prasenjit Duara, *Rescuing History from the Nation: Questioning Narratives of Modern China* (University of Chicago Press, 1995), ch. 2.
[15] J. G. A. Pocock, *The Machiavellian Moment: Florentine Thought and the Atlantic Republican Tradition* (Princeton University Press, 1975).

Tongzhi Restoration (1861) has been interpreted precisely as an effort to extend the regime of virtue in the face of impending collapse.[16]

Looping to Puritan America, Pocock shows us how this deferral was sustained by various strategies, such as imperialism and the spread of yeoman property ownership, which would continue to extend civic virtue. The Puritan extension of timeless grace into this temporal world ultimately had the effect of developing a secular history through the search for the kingdom of God on Earth – the city on the hill. But, although it transmutes into a modern history, Pocock argues that right through the nineteenth century this Old World preoccupation with virtue as a sacred, rational and timeless value persisted in America, and the vision of history as dynamic and creative in its "linear capacity to bring about incessant qualitative transformations of human life" struggled to emerge in pure form.[17] Thus, what we see is the coexistence, sometimes agonistic and sometimes interpenetrated, of two kinds of historical time or the past in a narrative in which the linear concept struggles to break free of Christian virtue. It was not until the eighteenth century in Europe that this relationship became inverted.

Thus, even while there may have been extraordinarily sophisticated evidentiary historians in the past such as Thucydides, Sima Qian or Ibn Khaldun, they understood the past in a radically different way from the moderns. In the view of Michel de Certeau, the very idea of the past as something 'dead' and subject, as it were, to laboratory analysis, does not really appear until the late eighteenth century in Europe.[18] In premodern histories, as Zachary Schiffman has recently shown, the past is episodic and even when causal relationships are seen, they are often deemed to be illustrative of a universal principle that is eternally present. That is the reason why the past can be seen to serve as the moral guide of the present and future. Modern historians, in contrast, evaluate past events in their contemporary spatial and relational context and regard their archival remains in another time as 'anachronisms' or sources to interpret the past.[19]

The European Renaissance was coeval with the failure of imperial consolidation in Latin Christendom, especially after 1300 CE when localism, commercialism and competitive warfare began to dominate

[16] Mary Clabaugh Wright, *The Last Stand of Chinese Conservatism: The T'ung-chih Restoration, 1862–1874* (Stanford University Press, 1967).

[17] Pocock, *Machiavellian Moment*, p. 551.

[18] Michel de Certeau, *The Writing of History*, Trans. Tom Conley (New York: Columbia University Press, 1988), esp. pp. 56–60.

[19] Zachary S. Schiffman, *The Birth of the Past* (Baltimore, MD: Johns Hopkins University Press, 2011), pp. 56, 72–4.

the region. Historians have dubbed the competition between effectively sovereign states in Western Europe from 1450 to about 1650 'fiscal militarism'. This period of constant warfare produced state indebtedness, which further accelerated warfare in order to garner greater revenues not only from landed territories but also from overseas. This kind of feedback loop between merchant or banking capital and political power also accelerated technological change and geographical expansion. During this period, McNeill writes, "even the mightiest European command structures became dependent on an international money and credit market for organizing military and other undertakings."[20]

Moreover, legitimate and illegitimate representatives of the overseas ventures of European monarchs frequently used the language of sovereignty and law to stake claims to their conquests, acquisitions and possessions in the emergent empires. Imperial expansion from the sixteenth century often entailed what we might call the 'sovereignty effect' within Europe. As royal-commission holders, adventurers and even pirates staked claims over territories and waters in the New World and in Africa and Asia against other European claimants, they made sovereignty claims in the name of the king in legal courts back home. Arguably, the notion of sovereignty within Europe, which was seen to be divided or lumpy before the modern period, became homogenized as a result of these 'effects' within both Europe and the early modern world.[21]

Antony Anghie goes still further to argue that sovereignty was developed in the confrontation with Indians in Spanish America. In his discussion of the sixteenth-century Spanish jurist, Francisco De Vitoria, Anghie argues that Vitoria justified extreme acts against American Indians by developing a form of power which defined the Indians as being so barbaric as to be beyond civilized organization and natural law, while simultaneously defining civilized sovereign power as the capacity to wage war and acquire title over territory and the alien, non-sovereign Indian. "Sovereignty doctrine acquired its character through the colonial encounter. This is the darker history of sovereignty which cannot be explored or understood by any account of sovereignty doctrine which assumes the existence of sovereign states."[22] Thus, not only did European state-building depend heavily on resources and technologies – such as silver, textiles, tea, spices

---

[20] William McNeill, *The Pursuit of Power* (University of Chicago Press, 1982).

[21] Lauren Benton, *A Search for Sovereignty: Law and Geography in European Empire, 1400–1900* (Cambridge University Press, 2010), pp. 280–1; Peter Borschberg, "From Self-Defence to an Instrument of War: Dutch Privateering Around the Malay Peninsula in the Early 17th Century," *Journal of Early Modern History*, 17 (2013): 35–52.

[22] Antony Anghie, "Francisco De Vitoria and the Colonial Origins of International Law," *Social Legal Studies*, 5 (1996): 321–36, at p. 332.

and gunpowder – from the rest of the world, but also these discursive practices contributed to state formation and sovereign territoriality in Europe. Territorial states and modern imperial power emerged from the competitive state system, which was subsequently consolidated as the Westphalian-Vatellian system of nation-states by the eighteenth century.

Under these conditions, secular conceptions of time since the Renaissance became serviceable for innovations and the capitalist revolution, which, however, ended up desacralizing all dimensions of the world and the commons as resources. The Renaissance was made possible not simply by a direct leap back to Greek antiquity but also by the contributions and circulations of Eurasian thought which had conserved and developed Greek knowledge as well as knowledge from Islamic, Chinese and Indian traditions.[23] Francisco Bethencourt argues that the Renaissance was an outcome of the major expansion of knowledge in fields such as natural history, geography, linguistics and political thought produced by the growing European interactions with other continents. At the same time, however, the conditions of the Renaissance enabled the successful institutionalization of secular knowledge for the long term.[24]

While Pocock shows us the continued importance and even intertwining of the two conceptions into the nineteenth century, Reinhart Koselleck brings the emergent Renaissance temporality up to eighteenth-century Europe, when the linear conception began to dominate European society. By the eighteenth century, Koselleck tells us, there was an increasing gap between the space of 'experience' and the horizon of 'expectation' in the dominant views of time. Whereas, up to this time, the bulk of the population in Western Europe had expected to live their lives as did their fathers and forefathers, the accelerating pace of change in their lives now caused their expectations to diverge from experience, and from this tension emerged the concept of historical time as we know it. Linear history was experienced and formulated as unique in that the past became distinct from the future, not simply in one case, but as a whole.[25]

By the time Hegel was lecturing on history in the 1820s, histories had already become the histories of nation-states, although Hegel's nation-state was considerably different from our own. He writes, " [I]n the history of the World, the *Individuals* we have to do with are *Peoples*. Totalities that

[23] Arun Bala, *The Dialogue of Civilizations in the Birth of Modern Science* (New York: Palgrave Macmillan, 2006).
[24] Francisco Bethencourt, "European Expansion and the New Order of Knowledge," in John Jeffries Martin and Albert Russell Ascoli, Eds., *The Renaissance World* (London: Routledge – Taylor & Francis Group, 2007), pp. 118–39.
[25] Reinhart Koselleck, *Futures Past: On the Semantics of Historical Time*, Trans. Keith Tribe (Cambridge, MA: MIT Press, 1985), pp. 276–81.

are States." In the Hegelian view, histories were expressed by particular nationalities but expressed through the records of the state which embodies reason. Thus, by this time, linear histories appear to be established (of course, for Hegel, it was not secular in the strict sense of the word). But what is less understood is how these histories became bound as they did.[26]

Modern times: disenchantment and global space-time

The transition from competitive states to nationalism and national histories inherited by the bulk of the world in the twentieth century was by no means automatic. The ideals of the secular state and popular sovereignty – both heralded by the French Revolution – were combined with the gritty realities of the competitive territorial state, and it is this mix that yielded the template adopted by twentieth-century states. The new form of national histories emerged to address the dual charge of undergirding the ideals of secular and popular sovereignty while developing the nation into a sleek, efficient body capable of competing for economic and strategic superiority: to emancipate and discipline for competition.[27]

National histories were cast in the common mold of an emerging national subject that joined an ancient past to a modern future, often by overcoming a dark middle age of disunity and foreign contamination. Note how this is fundamentally the trope of 'renaissance'. It allows you to disavow the present or immediate past and use a classical or ancient ideal as a motor to propel you into the future. Note also how, although there may be some continuities textually or archeologically with the ancient past, a particularly strong ownership claim is made on it, often by narrowing the optic that could view the wider cultural environment and the circulations in which that ancient past may have been engaged. This is an important means of binding the historical subject as exclusive and unifying territoriality, popular sovereignty and progress.

The new historical consciousness synthesized ideas of progress and popular sovereignty with claims to territorial sovereignty, three basic assumptions of nationalist thought. This relationship became the means

---

[26] See Hegel, *Philosophy of History*: III. Philosophic History (thesis 17) (www.marxists.org/reference/archive/hegel/works/hi/history3.htm). See also Douzinas Costas, "Identity, Recognition, Rights or What Can Hegel Teach Us About Human Rights?," *Journal of Law and Society*, 29(3) (2002): 379–405; Jürgen Lawrenz, "Hegel, Recognition and Rights: 'Anerkennung' as a Gridline of the Philosophy of Rights," *Cosmos and History: The Journal of Natural and Social Philosophy*, 3(2–3) (2007): 153–69.

[27] The next four paragraphs summarize my thesis in Duara, *Rescuing History from the Nation*, ch. 1.

of creating a historical agent or (often juridical) subject capable of making claims to sovereign statehood. A 'people' with a supposed unified self-consciousness developed a sovereign right to the territory they allegedly originally and/or continuously occupied.

The unity of territoriality, popular sovereignty and progress is not secured simply by a one-way, linear temporality. Crucial to academic histories located in the nation as much as to nationalist historiographies is the unit in which this history is framed, the national *subject* of history. How is it that different groups, conquerors, exterminators, people with a different sense of space, with no recognizable geographical knowledge or unity over millennia, come to be thought of as a single people with atavistic and primordial claims to the territory? In 1882, Ernest Renan solved this vexed problem of all national historiography with the idea that the nation is the daily 'plebiscite of the will'. He affirms the Spartan song, "We are what you were, we will be what you are," as the hymn of every *patrie*.[28] We may think of the nation as the machinery that produces the will to mythologize the historical unity of the nation.

Thus, the presumed subject of history – the nation – has to be seen as an unchanging subject: the intemporal kernel of time, the "non-modifiable nucleus of modification," in the words of Jacques Derrida.[29] In earlier periods, such a non-temporal being was none other than Heaven or God, from whom Machiavelli negotiated some secular extension. But if in prenational histories, 'real' time was sacred and eternal or belonged to the sage-kings, national histories sought the unchanging in the 'authentic'. The authentic referred to that which remains unchanged in the course of changing history.

The nation-state operates largely in a disenchanted system of states which presupposes an ontological plane of linear, secular time. As such, it does not usually appeal to God or the eternal real but to the authentic – the primordial and unchanging – subject that courses through history and realizes its goals in the progress, or end, of history. I have explored how a 'regime of authenticity' was developed around certain sacralized figures and institutions such as the family, the constitution, the chaste woman, the child, the aboriginal and others whose agency is often dependent on custodianship in the hands of the powerful. The regime of national

---

[28] Ernest Renan, "What Is a Nation?," in Homi Bhabha, Ed., *Nation and Narration* (New York: Routledge, 1990), pp. 8–22.

[29] Jacques Derrida, "Ousia and Gramme: Note on a Note from Being and Time," in Derrida, *Margins of Philosophy*, Trans. Alan Bass (University of Chicago Press, 1982), pp. 29–67.

authenticity is crucial to the internal and external sovereignty of the nation-state.

Why do nations have to establish their uniqueness? They do so because by the time of the transition to nation-states, the 'nation-form' itself is a circulatory global resource. Aspiring nationalists and states are busy importing all the norms, institutions and practices that will qualify them as nation-states. In part, nations are built from circulatory global resources – particularly from stronger states – because competition entails imitation, but, more importantly, as we will see in Chapter 3, because the secularization of the competitive political order as a whole (or its de-transcendentalization) generates a crisis of authority.

Regimes of eternity and regimes of authenticity

In Mircea Eliade's scheme, the cosmologies of premodern societies endorsed a view of true time as return to the eternal. As we have seen, premodern histories – binding together generations and events – of dynasts, aristocrats, sects or even threatened communities, such as Han or Hindu, generated by elite activists did exist, but in a minor key. Their significance was susceptible to being trumped by the sovereign transcendent, or what Eliade calls the "myth of eternal return." I prefer to call the authority underpinning eternal time 'regimes of eternal return', or, for short, 'regimes of eternity', which are produced and transmitted not only by the establishment clerisies or intellectuals (such as Brahmins, Catholic priests or Confucian thinkers) but also often by counter-establishment thinkers and prophets, who claim to derive a more just or alternative interpretation of the sovereign transcendent, thereby still sustaining the regime of the eternal.

The regime of authenticity may be seen as a late, even nineteenth-century, expression of the responses to the problems of transition from the Christian regime of the eternal, which shored up the power of the Holy Roman Empire. The anarchic conditions underlying the competition between multiple states produced several successive conceptions of sovereignty including Renaissance, divine-right and absolutist conceptions.[30] The regime of authenticity came to be established particularly after the French Revolution in the emergent nation-states, based upon ideas of disenchanted polity and popular sovereignty. Michael Freeman has said that in the French Revolution the nation was accorded a quasi-divine moral authority and the right of national self-determination has

---

[30] Jens Bartelsen, *A Genealogy of Sovereignty* (Cambridge University Press, 1995), pp. 208–12.

since then been in tension with the other idea of the rights of man (what we now call human rights).[31] As the nation-state staked its claim to sovereignty within and without on popular sovereignty, the idea of authenticity came to presuppose the unity of people, culture and state, and the regime of authenticity was deployed to deter the fractious components and multiple claimants, particularly in the face of external threat. As such, the national ideal has become entrenched and has largely subordinated the broader ideal of human rights.

Moreover, the regime of authenticity also seeks to reverse the erosion brought on, doubly, by disenchantment itself and the accelerating temporality of capitalism. This is represented in Paul Klee's painting *Angelus Novus* (Figure 2.1), described unforgettably by Walter Benjamin as the "Angel of History," a figure blown irresistibly by the storm of progress, facing backward, seeking fruitlessly to pick up the shards from the destruction left by this gale. Authenticity may be seen as this same angel turned forward towards the uncharted, leading the people and bearing the face of the chaste woman or the disempowered monarch or the natural aboriginal, telling us that we have salvaged something essential about us that will carry us through to our destiny at the end of history. The latter image represents a mobilizing call: this will happen only if we believe this, stay together, work hard and make sacrifices (Figure 2.2).

If the residue of the sacred, eternal and timeless still remains in modern histories, what differentiates the embodiment of authenticity from the regime of the eternal is that the former does not seek to trump history. It accepts the ineluctability of the passage of historical time, negotiates its status within it as the immanent timeless, and tries to promise progress. But, in so doing, authenticity produces its own form of politics: the politics of identity. Identity politics is premised upon a certain unchanging essence reflected in the mirror of a collection of people that seeks to constitute itself as the collective. The nation is the Ur-form of identity politics. As Renan tells us, it is the *will* (read *regime of authenticity*) to show daily that "We are what you were, we will be what you are."

We get a clearer sense of why identity politics is so much more central to modern history than it was to history in earlier times. Among the most significant historical functions of modern history – not necessarily of academic history – has been to produce identity, which in turn produces recognition and rights for a group so it may stake its claims and chart its destiny. Identity was important in prenational times, but it is only with the

---

[31] Michael Freeman, "The Right to National Self-Determination," in Clarke M. Desmond and Charles Jones, Eds., *The Rights of Nations: Nations and Nationalism in a Changing World* (New York: St. Martin's Press, 1999), pp. 47–50.

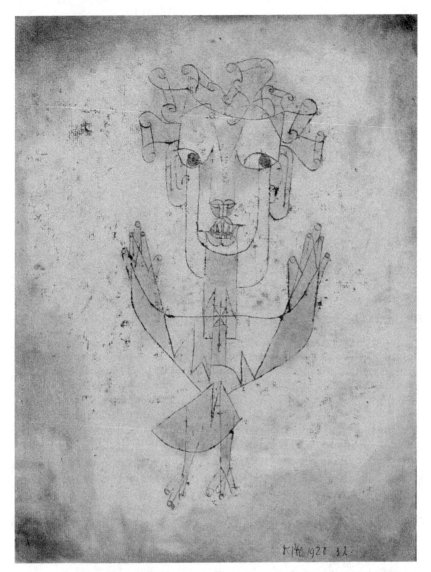

Figure 2.1 *Angelus Novus*, painting by Paul Klee (1920) (Source: © Israel Museum, Jerusalem). It "shows an angel ... His face is turned toward the past. Where we perceive a chain of events, he sees one single catastrophe which keeps piling wreckage upon wreckage and hurls it in front of his feet. The angel would like to stay, awaken the dead, and make whole what has been smashed. But a storm is blowing from Paradise; it has got caught in his wings with such violence that the angel can no longer close them. The storm irresistibly propels him into the future to which his back is turned, while the pile of debris before him grows skyward. This storm is what we call progress" (Benjamin, 1969, p. 249).

Figure 2.2 *American Progress*, painting by John Gast (1872), which illustrates the 'Manifest Destiny' of the United States to possess the whole of the continent of North America. It was widely disseminated as as color print (Source: Mary Evans / Library of Congress).

totalizing power of the fiscal-military state to mobilize the resources of the people, land and water in endless competition that this mode was catapulted to the hegemonic position. In our time, the claim of 'rights' attaching to a collectivity that can demonstrate that it should be 'recognized' as a historical entity is involuting and challenging the nation itself as new identity groups demand recognition, whether through nationalist or other identitarian claims.[32] My critique of national histories is, first, that identity function was enabled by the regime of authenticity which provided the basis of sovereign action in an anarchic condition, and, second, that the regime of authenticity reified and absolutized the history of one people or national community.

---

[32] Jürgen Lawrenz, "Hegel, Recognition and Rights: 'Anerkennung' as a Gridline of the Philosophy of Rights," *Cosmos and History: The Journal of Natural and Social Philosophy*, 3(2–3) (2007): 153–69. See also Clarke M. Desmond and Charles Jones, Eds., *The Right of Nations: Nations and Nationalism in a Changing World* (New York: St. Martin's Press, 1999).

Histories of circulatory transformations in early modern Eurasia

I have discussed authenticity in terms of the problem of time. There is, however, another very important way to understand the authenticity to which we have alluded in passing. Creating the authenticity of a historical people is also a way to expunge the real history of a community or space, which is based on multiple interactions and circulatory transformations. I have urged that the discussion of historicality, narrative and power be grasped in the wider context of circulatory histories. The eclipse of the latter precisely at the moment, historically, when they were becoming more and more forceful in the early modern world is testimony to the ideological power of bounded and identitarian histories that culminated in the hegemony of national histories in the nineteenth and twentieth centuries.

Histories ought not to be seen on the model of evolution whereby species develop through internal codes in order to interact with the local environment. Humans are the species, not historical institutions or cultures. Of course, institutions – especially in the territorially bounded state – are self-referential and depict their actions in iterative codes.[33] But the environments of the people who occupy the institutions are varied and multiscalar, and they are often influenced by remote ideas, practices, markets, technologies, microbes and networks. Jack Goody, David Pingree and others have demonstrated repeatedly that Eurasia has been basically unified since the onset of the Bronze Age. Pingree has declared that, as "a simple historical fact, scientific ideas have been transmitted for millennia from culture to culture, and transformed by each recipient culture into something new."[34] The early technological revolution enabled intensive agriculture that permitted surplus accumulation, class stratification, literacy, bureaucracy, urbanization and interlinked, city-based civilizations across the zone. Consequent upon these factors and depending on the changing circumstances of access in a particular region, the zone was connected by long-distance trade, warfare, technology, ideas, and organizational and institutional practices (including mass industrial production). Indeed, a recent interactive map of genetic mixing shows how human races have been migrating and mixing for over 4,000 years.[35]

---

[33] Niklas Luhmann, *Ecological Communication*, Trans. John Bednarz, Jr. (University of Chicago Press, 1989).

[34] David Pingree, "Hellenophilia Versus the History of Science," *Isis*, *83*(4) (1992): 554–63, at p. 563.

[35] Garrett Hellenthal, George B. J. Busby, Gavin Band, James F. Wilson, Cristian Capelli, Daniel Falush and Simon Myers, "Supplementary Materials for *A Genetic Atlas of Human Admixture History*," *Science*, *343* (2014): 747–51 (http://admixturemap.paintmychromo somes.com/).

In some of his recent works, Goody shows the ways in which European scholars have striven to disembed 'Western' history from its actual, interactive historical context, starting from antiquity to the present. Carthage, Phoenician traders, Persia, Egypt, India and, most of all, China and the Islamic world have played a much greater role in Western histories than even the most radical analysts have acknowledged. Thus, while it cannot be denied that the Industrial Revolution of the late eighteenth century was a northern European achievement, this revolution cannot be understood without the background of "industrialization, mechanization and mass-production developed ... in China with textiles, ceramics, and paper, in India with cotton, later taken up in Europe and the Near East." Goody also discusses the realm of institutions, particularly of knowledge production and values, including mathematics, medicine, humanism, democracy, individualism and romantic love. In none of these cases does he find European societies to be the exclusive proprietors of these institutions and values. Rather, the Europeans owed these traditions in a significant way to other societies, and, most notably, Islamic ones.[36]

At different times, different cities or regions in Eurasia – whether joined by trading, and religious and technological networks, or separated by empires, disease, political instability, piracy or climate change – created different nodes of absorption, innovation or isolation in this gradually expanding zone over the millennia. Seen in this wider canvas of changing zones of innovation, the capacity of some European social formations to institutionalize secular knowledge production and sustained economic growth over the last two centuries represents a very important but not unique achievement. Other societies were poised to learn the lessons from one part of the Eurasian world quickly enough – given the time scale of history – and it is unnecessary to identify the distinctive qualities of a region or nation as unifying all dimensions of life and reaching back into the mists of time – that is, unless that society has a competitive agenda.

I have urged that we should look at history from the *outside-in*, particularly from the late nineteenth century. Just as Foucault once asked us to focus not on 'causal' history but on 'effective' history – attending to the dispersed reception of an event – so, too, without denying the importance of internal institutional processes, I want us to shift our focus from internal processes to how those processes are themselves affected by

---

[36] Jack Goody, *The Theft of History* (New York: Cambridge University Press, 2006), p. 210.

myriad outside forces.[37] Such a shift not only redresses the imbalance in the understanding of historical forces but can also help to redistribute the sources of identity formation and lead to the recognition that the historical subject is never an entirely self-contained entity.

While major differences must be admitted, this also bears some resemblance to the various, often coexisting modes of apprehending time and history in premodern societies. More importantly, global conditions are particularly ripe for such a non-linear conception of history. Competitive capitalism is by no means less intense, but capitalism today is as much about interdependencies of nations and units as it is about competition between nationally or imperialistically unified entities. Today, there is a greater mismatch between our globality and national institutions than in the twentieth century.

A short chapter is hardly the place to demonstrate the nature and content of Eurasian historical connections, but we can try to identify a few routes and patterns over the last two millennia that joined east Asia to south and west Asia and beyond to the European cores. The famous Silk Route may be thought of as the name for a network of several different land routes linking east, south, central and west Asia with north and east Africa and the Mediterranean that became increasingly supplemented and was gradually exceeded in importance by the maritime routes linking these spaces, including southeast Asia (discussed in Chapter 7). The trading centers of south Asia were particularly important because they represented important nodes in both the land and sea routes.[38]

Among the most important connectors across Asia in the early period was Buddhism. It also exemplifies the mode of circulatory history in which ideas, practices and texts enter society or locale as one kind of thing and emerge from it considerably transformed to travel elsewhere even as it refers back, often narratively, to the initiating moment. Buddhist ideas spread from the Indian subcontinent to different parts of Asia by both maritime and land routes over the course of several centuries. Following trade routes, Buddhism was spread by traders, migrants, monks, envoys,

---

[37] Michel Foucault, "Nietzsche, Genealogy, History," in Donald F. Bouchard, Ed., *Language, Counter Memory, Practice*, Trans. Donald F. Bouchard and Sherry Simon (Ithaca, NY: Cornell University Press, 1977), pp. 139–64.

[38] This is reflected in Angus Maddison's statistical study, which shows that South Asia had the highest GDP in the world in the first millennium. It was overtaken by China in the second millennium, and the latter was overtaken by Europe only after 1820. Statistics on World Population, GDP and Per Capita GDP, 1–2008 AD (vertical file, copyright Angus Maddison, University of Groningen) (www.ggdc.net/maddison/oriindex.htm). Maddison's work also shows that per capital GDP in both China and India was relatively stagnant over the second millennium.

artisans and the royal patronage of kings, who saw in it a powerful instrument of legitimation, but it was rarely spread through warfare.

As Tansen Sen and others have shown, the circulation of Buddhism to China until the fourth century was not a linear movement of diffusion from the subcontinent, but involved different carriers from places such as the region that is now Iran, who made their own contributions to the faith. They included Indo-Scythian, Sogdian and Parthian merchants and monks, whose networks stretched from northwest India to many Chinese cities and ports. With the growing popularity of Buddhism in China, prominent missionaries from India, especially from the Gandhara-Kashmir region, begin arriving in large numbers between the fourth and fifth centuries CE. Their appearance led to massive, arduous and multiethnic collaborative projects of translation from Sanskrit into Chinese. These texts interwove important Buddhist doctrines, concepts and beliefs with Chinese ideas and culture over time, and Chinese Buddhism matured to generate the most important doctrines and practices of Mahayana Buddhism by the end of the first millennium.[39]

The routes and modes whereby Buddhism circulated across central and east Asia from China and from south Asia to southeast Asia after the middle of the first millennium are well established. While eventually several spheres of Buddhist doctrinal practices – including the Tibetan-south Asian, the Srilankan-southeast Asian and the east Asian – may be identified, the connections between them continue to the present day. Indeed, the travels of the earliest known Chinese Buddhist monk to India, Faxian, in the early fifth century CE, joined the land and sea routes. The most famous pilgrim monks from the Tang dynasty in the seventh century CE, Xuanzang and Yijing, took the land route and sea routes respectively. The powerful Buddhist kingdom of Srivijaya in Sumatra, which controlled the sea routes from the eighth to the twelfth century, was an important node linking east and southeast Asia to Nalanda and Vikramashila in south Asia. These monastic universities were also connected to Tibet, central Asia and China by the northern land routes.[40]

Among the most interesting modes of circulation is the way that the receiving cultures such as the Korean or Japanese, among others, sought to create ways of seeing themselves as centers of such a cosmopolis; this mode entailed circulatory involution. The monastic complex on

[39] Tansen Sen, "The Spread of Buddhism to China: A Re-Examination of the Buddhist Interactions Between Ancient India and China," *China Report*, 48 (2012): 11–27.
[40] Tansen Sen, "The Spread of Buddhism," in Benjamin Z. Kedar and Merry E. Wiesner-Hanks, Eds., *The Cambridge History of the World*, vol. V: *Expanding Webs of Exchange and Conquest, 500 CE – 1500 CE* (Cambridge University Press, in press).

Mt. Wutai in China's Shanxi province, which became a node linking the Chinese heartland with central Asia, particularly Tibetan Buddhism in the Tang dynasty (618–907 CE) (discussed further in Chapter 4), also represented a process that was transforming China into a sacred Buddhist land. Chinese Buddhists declared that the Snow Mountain on which the *Mahaparinirvana Sutra* prophesied that the Boddhisattva Manjusri would appear, was none other than Mt. Wutai.[41] In turn, Mt. Wutai was circulated by recreating or reinscribing it on the local landscapes of South Korea's Mt. Odae and Japan's Mt. Atago and Mt. Tonomine.[42] While this greatly enhanced the prestige of Mt. Wutai, it also allowed these 'borderland' societies to renegotiate their place in the Buddhist world. Indeed, one can see this development particularly in the Japanese Buddhist world. In an essay on the idea of India in Buddhist Japan, Fabio Rambelli shows how, by the seventeenth century, the centrality of India – or the idea of India – in the Japanese Buddhist imaginary became increasingly replaced by the idea that "Japan was the ultimate stalwart of Buddhism and, by extension ... [how] Indian wisdom after Buddhism had disappeared from India and had been marginalized in China and Korea."[43]

In the second millennium, the nineteenth-century narrative of China as self-sufficient and culturally self-centered was the result of, among other things, the preceding two-century exposure to the massively destabilizing forces and expenses of dealing with the effects of ungovernable maritime capitalism and piracy on the southwest Chinese coast. So, too, was Japan's seventeenth- to nineteenth-century adherence to *sakoku*, or isolationist policy. But China had long been a significant player in global circulations, especially in the Tang and Song periods. The succeeding Mongol (Yuan) dynasty, which ruled China during much of the thirteenth and fourteenth centuries, expanded considerably the ambit of Eurasian interactions with China by virtue of its being part of the wider Mongol Empire, which was the largest land-based empire the world has seen. Chinese ties to the Islamic empires, which had been interrupted during the political turmoil of the late Tang dynasty, were revived by the regional integration under

---

[41] Tansen Sen, *Buddhism, Diplomacy and Trade: The Realignment of Sino-Indian Relations, 600–1400* (Honolulu, HI: University of Hawaii Press, 2003), pp. 76–87.

[42] Richard D. McBride, II, *Domesticating the Dharma: Buddhist Cults and the Hwaŏm Synthesis in Silla Korea* (Honolulu, HI: University of Hawaii Press, 2008).

[43] Fabio Rambelli, "The Idea of India (Tenjiku) in Pre-Modern Japan: Issues of Signification and Representation in the Buddhist Translation of Cultures," in Tansen Sen, Ed., *Buddhism Across Asia: Networks of Material, Intellectual and Cultural Exchange* (Delhi: Manohar and Singapore: Institute of Southeast Asian Studies, 2014), vol. I, pp. 262–92, at p. 264.

the Mongols. For much of the century, Pax Mongolica guaranteed the relative openness of trade routes. China's position was crucial to this trade because it linked the overland with the overseas route, as evidenced, for instance, by the travels of Marco Polo.[44]

The legacy of connections with the Buddhist and Muslim societies of central and west Asia remained important for several centuries. The Ming dynasty (1368–1644), which followed the Mongols, was, in the early years, able to undertake the largest in scale and most powerful naval voyages of the time, in no small measure because of the cosmopolitanism of the earlier period. Zheng He, the Chinese admiral who famously reached the southern tip of Africa before the Portugese on his unprecedentedly large flotillas, in seven voyages between 1405–1433, exemplifies this cosmopolitanism.

Descended from central Asian Muslim governors of Yunnan during the Mongol period, Zheng He was captured and castrated by the Ming rulers as a boy. He subsequently became a famous general of the Ming and was commissioned to lead the voyages. Zheng recruited as his interpreter, Ma Huan, a Chinese Muslim from Zhejiang, who was proficient in Arabic, the lingua franca of sailors and merchants on the Indian Ocean. Moreover, while Zheng was born a Muslim, he was a practicing Buddhist and took a Buddhist name. Indeed, Chinese Buddhist pilgrimages – which circulated cosmological, medical and geographical knowledge – from China through central Asia, India and southeast Asia continued until the fifteenth century.[45]

A recent work by Victor Lieberman, 'Strange parallels': Southeast Asia in Global Context, c. 800–1830, is very relevant to our project. It is a monumental, comparative work on the Eurasian region over the last millennium. Lieberman seeks to explain the 'strange parallels' between different regions of Eurasia. He distinguishes two types of historical states in this region – namely, those in the 'protected zone' and those in the 'exposed zone'. Geographically, the latter included south Asia and China, which have large northern and northwestern areas exposed to inner Asian invasions, whereas the former zone included kingdoms in Burma, Thailand, Vietnam, Russia, France and Japan, which were relatively protected from direct massive predation. Maritime, or island, southeast Asia belatedly developed into an exposed zone, exposed to takeover by

---

[44] Janet L. Abu-Lughod, *Before European Hegemony: The World System AD 1250–1350* (Oxford University Press, 1989), p. 347. See also Hyunhee Park, *Mapping the Chinese and Islamic Worlds: Cross–Cultural Exchange in Pre–modern Asia* (New York: Cambridge University Press, 2012), p. 18.

[45] Edward L. Dreyer, *Zheng He: China and the Oceans in the Early Ming, 1405–1433*. Library of World Biography Series (New York: Pearson Longman, 2006).

the "white Inner Asians" from the sixteenth century. Historically, the two zones were separated by the presence in China and India of precocious civilizations, from which the protected kingdoms later crafted their own 'charter kingdoms' towards the latter part of the first millennium. In Frankish/Carolingian France, the charter state derived its ideas from the Roman Empire, whereas Kiev derived them from the Byzantine Empire.[46]

Lieberman sees two patterns over the millennium. The charter states in the protected zone facilitated a cycle of agrarian and population expansion, commercial growth, and development of new literate elites and charter religious ideologies of integration – in short, an early form of agrarian state-building. This pattern was also experienced in China and India, although, in these cases, new techniques and cultures of state-formation derived from inner Asian invasions – such as those by the Khitan, Jurchen, Tangut and Turks – combined with the older civilizational forms; these combinations created more hybrid forms rather than the civilizationally pure forms claimed, for instance, by Confucian and Hindu-Buddhist states in the protected zones. This hybridity might be considered ironic, though only from a national origins perspective.[47]

Lieberman argues that the causes of the rise of these states were global and had parallel effects. First among them was the global medieval climate anomaly, which had the effect of extending the growing season and arable lands, population adaptation to diseases (particularly smallpox), and long-distance trade between 830 and 1240 CE. The period of efflorescence was followed by the collapse of these polities in the protected zone, which occurred very roughly within the same period between 1240 and 1470. Just as with their rise, the decline of these states was coordinated by climate change – the relapse of the good but anomalous climactic conditions – the spread of bubonic plague and the impact of the Mongol Empire – whether directly through spread of disease, direct assault or indirect displacement of peoples such as the Tai, who then extended the invasive and disruptive process into other parts of Asia.[48]

A new cycle began around 1500, when stronger states consolidated in both zones. The new state-formation that we noted as 'fiscal militarism' in Europe appeared, albeit in different modes across Eurasia. Territorial expansion by the successor states was accompanied not only by deepening of administrative control and integration but also by the development of what Lieberman calls 'politicized ethnicities' – the horizontal and to some extent, vertical, social and cultural homogenization within these empires,

---

[46] Victor Lieberman, 'Strange Parallels': Southeast Asia in Global Context, c. 800–1830, vol. II (Cambridge University Press, 2009).
[47] Ibid., pp. 896–7.   [48] Ibid., pp. 160–4, 268–70.

which in turn created a majority group (who, presumably, become the dominant national core). Administrative and political technologies improved to the extent that political fragmentation during the interregna between centralized polities became shorter over the millennium in both zones.

Lieberman is not primarily interested in connections. Indeed, his goal is to see patterns of evolution to modernity, to observe the development (or at least parts of the development) of the modern centralizing state and the national community in different parts of the world over the *longue durée*. Thus, while his study is admirable and valuable for the extensive coverage and illumination of comparable 'early modernities' across several different parts of the world, the almost studied neglect of connections between these 'strange parallels' represents an important weakness. Indeed, the few global factors he mentions, such as the impact of the Mongol Empire and the bubonic plague are already well known and are not explored in depth, whereas the evidence for the impact of the medieval climate anomaly upon different parts of Eurasia appears not to be very strong. However, in other studies, the connections between these regions from the first millennium CE at the very least is very well developed, and Goody, Janet Lippman Abu-Lughod, Marshall Hodgson, Eric Wolf, Sanjay Subrahmanyam, David Christian and many others have put the connections in the second millennium CE at the center of their work, through both the land and sea routes.[49]

Synthesizing the growing literature on the early modern world and Europe, Jerry Bentley has shown that early modern Europe reflected, depended upon and contributed to an early modern *world*. The parallels that Lieberman observes were accompanied by the spread of global trade networks, the flow of bullion, migrations and the exchange of biological species in various different parts of Eurasia. European advantages were not overwhelming until the eighteenth century either in military technology or in economic strength. In both value and bulk terms, Asian merchants carried the majority of world trade until around 1750.[50]

---

[49] For a digest of some of these historical views on Eurasian connections and beyond, see David Christian, *Maps of Time: An Introduction to Big History* (Berkeley, CA: University of California Press, 2005), pp. 320–36; Tonio Andrade, "Beyond Guns, Germs, and Steel: European Expansion and Maritime Asia, 1400–1750," *Journal of Early Modern History*, *14* (2010): 165–86, at p. 170.

[50] Jerry H. Bentley, "Early Modern Europe and the Early Modern World," in Charles H. Parker and Jerry H. Bentley, Eds., *Between the Middle Ages and Modernity: Individual and Community in the Early Modern World* (Lanham, MD: Rowman & Littlefield, 2007), pp. 13–31.

It is estimated that in the second half of the sixteenth century, Ming China imported 43–46 tonnes of silver annually. Indeed, the role of imported silver was so great that its relative decline in the late Ming dynasty is said by some to have contributed to the fall of the Ming.[51] The Mughal Empire in India imported still greater sums – 85–131 tonnes of silver annually – during the late sixteeenth and seventeenth centuries. During this high Mughal period, this silver, imported mostly from the New World, enabled increased volumes and velocities of circulation in the interregional and intercontinental trade.[52]

In the vast Indian Ocean trade – the Indian Ocean Trade Ecumene or the Maritime Silk Route, as it is variously dubbed – of this period, European companies could rarely compete with Asian traders in any market, except when they could use force without fear of retaliation.[53] Over time, they were able to inflict greater violence to secure trade not because of vastly superior maritime technology and military power, but, rather, because the Europeans brought state power to maritime control. Most Asian states were landed powers and did not derive their revenues principally from maritime trade. Where certain Asian sea-trade-based powers did emerge, often in response to Portuguese and Dutch activities, as did the Yaruba Imamate in Oman (1650), they were able to oust the Portuguese. Cooperation between the Ottomans and the Gujarat sultan had earlier led to defeat of the Portuguese. Zheng Chenggong, considered a hero in Taiwan as its liberator, was able to defeat the Dutch in Taiwan as late as 1661.[54]

---

[51] Richard Von Glahn, *Fountain of Fortune: Money and Monetary Policy in China, 1000–1700* (Berkeley, CA: University of California Press, 1996), pp. 133–40. A later study by Atwell suggests higher levels of silver imports into China at a total of 7,000–11,000 tonnes from 1550 to 1645. William Atwell, "Another Look at Silver Imports into China, *ca.* 1635–1644," *Journal of World History*, 16(4) (2005): 467–89.

[52] Najaf Haider, "Precious Metal Flows and Currency Circulation in the Mughal Empire," *Journal of Economic and Social History of the Orient*, 39 (Special Issue, *Money in the Orient*) (1996): 298–364. See also Rosalind O'Hanlon and David Washbrook, "Religious Cultures in an Imperial Landscape," *South Asian History and Culture*, 2(2) (2011): 133–7, at p. 135.

[53] Sanjay Subrahmanyam, "Of Imarat and Tijarat: Asian Merchants and State Power in the Western Indian Ocean, 1400 to 1750," *Comparative Studies in Society and History*, 37(4) (1995): 750–80, at p. 753. As Janet Abu-Lughod says, trade was contained "within the interstices of a larger collaboration in which goods and merchants from many places were intermingled on each other's ships and where unwritten rules of reciprocity assured general compliance. This system was not decisively challenged until the sixteenth century, when the Portuguese men-of-war violated all the rules of the game." Abu-Lughod, *Before European Hegemony*, p. 11.

[54] Andrade, "Beyond Guns, Germs, and Steel," pp. 165–86; Giancarlo Casale, *The Ottoman Age of Exploration* (Oxford University Press, 2010).

More importantly, from our perspective, early modern practices, technologies and cultures were shared, especially in the maritime space. The scholar-novelist Amitav Ghosh, Hyun-hee Park, Engseng Ho, Barbara Andaya, Hugh Clark and others, riding on the shoulders of an earlier generation of Indian Ocean stalwarts such as K. N. Chaudhuri and Ashin Das Gupta, continue to reveal the extraordinary cosmopolitanism of the sailing community, including sailors, merchants and shipbuilders. Although seafaring was hardly devoid of violence, the demands of the ocean and the absence – in most cases – of accompanying military power to control the sea lanes made for cooperation and cultural exchange. Muslim sailors from the thirteenth century combined the technology of the Chinese magnetic compass with their own system of determing a ship's latitude by measuring the altitude of the stars, as did Zheng He's crew. Chinese and Islamic geographical knowledge was combined to produce coastal maps of the region. Vasco da Gama may not have been able to reach India if he had not been guided by the 'Moor of Gujarat'.[55]

Peter Shapinsky discusses the 'portolans', or pilot books – collections of written and diagrammed sailing instructions – in use among Japanese ships with multicultural, cosmopolitan crews before the Tokugawa restriction of maritime trade in the late 1630s. The nautical culture that developed in this maritime space was facilitated by cross-cultural brokers who assimilated Mediterranean navigation techniques with those of east Asian provenance, drawn from diverse sources including the Zheng He expeditionary charts of a century earlier and various Arab and Korean sources. Indeed, these Japanese portolans were sometime readopted by European cartographers in the late seventeenth century because they recognized the improved Japanese depictions of east Asia over the European ones.[56] By the eighteenth century, the situation had changed radically. Not only had the Indian Ocean become militarized, but cross-cultural relations became increasingly replaced by 'scientific' racial hierarchies about the capacities and functions of different groups.[57]

[55] Hyunhee Park, *Mapping the Chinese and Islamic Worlds: Cross-Cultural Exchange in Pre-Modern Asia* (New York: Cambridge University Press, 2012), pp. 174, 187; Casale, *Ottoman Age of Exploration*, p. 14; Barbara Watson Andaya, "Connecting Oceans and Multicultural Navies: A Historian's View on Challenges and Potential for Indian Ocean-Western Pacific Interaction," in N. Lenze and C. Schriwer, Eds., *Converging Regions: Global Perspectives on Asia and the Middle East* (Farnham: Ashgate, in press). See Amitav Ghosh, "The *Ibis* Chrestomathy" [the glossary of the cosmopolitan seafarer language], in Ghosh, *Sea of Poppies* (New York: Picador, 2008).

[56] Peter Shapinsky, "Polyvocal Portolans: Nautical Charts and Hybrid Maritime Cultures in Early Modern East Asia," *Early Modern Japan*, 14 (2006): 4–26, at pp. 13, 26.

[57] Andaya, "Connecting Oceans and Multicultural Navies," p. 13.

It was not only economic practices that joined this polycentric but shared world. Religious, intellectual and cultural factors were very important in connecting the different parts of Eurasia. Sanjay Subrahmanyam points to the massive expansion of cultures of travel outside Europe, which led to patterns of knowledge exchange across the regions and subregions, and the emergence of forums of debate between Christians, Muslims, Hindus, Confucians and others. Even though Buddhist pilgrim and teacher exchanges between China and India had begun to decline after reaching their height during the early centuries of the second millennium CE, exchanges among Buddhist monks, teachers and advisers continued between Srilanka and southeast Asian kingdoms. Millenarianism was a particularly powerful attractor for rulers and rebels and a connector between Christian and Islamic groups including those in southeast Asia, where the legend of Alexander, not only as a world conqueror but as a prophet and universal monarch, had become established by the seventeenth century.[58]

Modes of circular transformations: modern East Asia

Over the last decade there has been considerable writing on circulatory histories, particularly by historians of science and modern south Asia.[59] There is thus less need to present evidence of circulation from the nineteenth century when European imperialism dominated Asia. Instead I will present some materials from China and East Asia – my region of

---

[58] Sanjay Subrahmanyam, "Connected Histories: Notes Towards a Reconfiguration of Early Modern Eurasia," *Modern Asian Studies*, *31*(3) (Special Issue, *The Eurasian Context of the Early Modern History of Mainland South East Asia, 1400–1800*) (1997): 735–62.

[59] At an advanced stage of writing this book, I was alerted to a study of circulation in South Asia edited by Markovits, Pouchepadass and Subrahmanyam published several years ago. While limited to the study of South Asia, this work outlines some important ideas and methods with regard to circulation. Among the most fertile is the idea of 'circulatory regimes', by which they mean "circulation in all its temporal and geographical specificity, linking different parts of the subcontinent to one another and the subcontinent as a whole to the wider world"(p. 3). But perhaps the circulatory regime idea can be applied to another phenomenon suggested by the authors of the volume – that is, the ways in which circulatory forms are often under surveillance and policed by counter-circulatory forms of the state or other authorities. This dialectic can be particularly fruitful because it allows us to think of how either temporal or spatial circulatory modes could be leveraged in order, perhaps, to respond to or elude surveillance. Claude Markovits, Jacques Pouchepadass and Sanjay Subrahmanyam, "Introduction: Circulation and Society Under Colonial Rule," in Markovits *et al.*, Eds., *Society and Circulation: Mobile People and Itinerant Cultures in South Asia, 1750–1950* (Delhi: Permanent Black, 2003), pp. 1–22. For the history of science, see Kapil Raj, "Beyond Postcolonialism ... and Postpositivism: Circulation and the Global History of Science," *Isis*, *104*(2) (2013): 337–47.

specialty – to explore some ways of doing circulatory histories. In the first place, it is important conceptually to distinguish older theories of 'diffusion' from circulatory histories. Theories of diffusion tend to emphasize a one-way relationship, typically from a center to a periphery (in terms of the idea or process being diffused) and tend to become involved with political contestation over origins. Circulatory histories emphasize both the necessary forms of adaptation and the recreation of the circulatory form at the points of reception. To be sure, there may be multiple levels of recognition of the nodes or points of circulatory egress, from a reverential attitude towards 'the source' to a total denial of it. Much of the time, as we will see in later chapters, there are varied, differentiated and complex approaches towards the source. Nonetheless, we can recognize the common circulatory feature or item through a combination of references to the source and other objective elements.

Circulatory processes can often circulate back to the node of emanation, albeit in a necessarily modified form. I pointed to an instance at the beginning of the chapter with the flow of the Transcendental/Unitarian/civil disobedience chain from Roy to Martin Luther King, Jr. We have noted the complex ways in which Buddhism cycled around Asia (and the West) even as it had long disappeared in the south Asia locales (India and Nepal) where it had emerged. By the twentieth century, Buddhism had reappeared among certain elite intellectual circles in India through the efforts of regional Buddhist thinkers, the Theosophists and others. More dramatically, it was adopted by significant and politically aware leaders of the Dalit, or Untouchable, community under circumstances which I will explore in Chapter 6. Another case from the twentieth century is represented by Marxism in China. Marxist and other radical ideas entered China from the Soviet Union, France and Japan, among others, through various different channels. Although it finally came in from the Soviet Union as a coherent and developed doctrine, it was subsequently transformed very substantially by the peasant base of the revolution led by Mao. It subsequently egressed from China as the new Marxism-Leninism-Mao Zedong thought to penetrate other societies in Asia and the West itself.

An equally basic task is to map the pathways of ingress/egress and nodes through which circulatory forces generated transformations in society and reciprocally in those ingressing ideas, practices and processes. Geographical points of contact are, of course, the easiest to document. The treaty ports of Shanghai and Tianjin have been studied in considerable detail. Here the Chinese population learned to use and adapt new banking and economic practices, the modern press, educational institutions, and political ideologies and strategies of mobilization. Note that the Chinese Communist Party was founded in the French concession in Shanghai in 1921. Other points in the West and southwest (Xinjiang and Yunnan) were important for the transformation of Chinese Islam, whereas the northeast ushered in transformations in popular Chinese religions as did the spread of Taiping Christianity from the south in the nineteenth century

Shanghai has decisively captured the imagination as the node of transnational penetration into China, but Hong Kong probably played a more influential role for a much longer period as the entrepôt not only of goods but also ideas, discourses, political finance, organizations and much else until very recently. During the Maoist years (1949–79), Hong Kong became very important as one of the only conduits of information, knowledge, capital, markets and strategic goods from the capitalist world available to the PRC. It was also the channel through which the communists were able to reach out to various groups of the overseas Chinese, particularly in Southeast Asia, or Nanyang (literally, 'South Seas'). Hong Kong was the financial and communication hub for the Nanyang Chinese who responded to Deng Xiaoping's call in 1992 to invest and develop China; it was also from Hong Kong cinema that the *kung fu* and martial arts craze has spread both inside and outside China since the 1970s. This has been accompanied by the spiritual smorgasbord which covers the gamut from Chinese medicine, *taiqi* and *fengshui* to the more committed universalist, redemptive movements of the Taiwan-based Ciji Buddhist group and the banned Falun Gong, among many others.

Particular groups of people, whether because of their geographical, avocational or occupational dispositions, also serve as brokers, transmitters and enablers of circulatory change. The population of Nanyang Chinese has at various points initiated considerable change in Chinese history and carried Chinese influences abroad. There is perhaps no better figure to represent both Hong Kong and the diaspora as a major transcultural agency in the emergence of modern China than Sun Yat-sen, the Father of Modern China. Sun was born in south China but spent his most formative educational years in Hong Kong (and Honolulu), which also became the launching pad for his political uprising to topple the Qing dynasty and, later, the warlords. For Sun, Hong Kong became a major organizing and financing center of the 1911 republican revolution; indeed, the Nanyang Chinese even claimed – somewhat dubiously – that Sun had dubbed them the Mother of the Revolution. The effects of Nanyang Chinese activities on the republican revolution went much further than is often realized, although not necessarily in China itself. For instance, Wasana Wongsurawat has studied the impact of their activities on the political elites and the state in Thailand.[60]

Yet another influential segment included the students, intellectuals and professionals who studied abroad during the early years of the twentieth century. As self-reflective segments with a particular sensitivity to the indignities of imperialism, these groups went in large numbers, first to Japan and then to other metropolitan parts of the world from the 1920s. Rather than recount the familiar transformative activities they engaged in, it may be useful to probe ways in which they leveraged, although not necessarily self-consciously, the power of the circulating vocabulary of modernity – via Japan – to effect changes in the very discursive foundations of the Chinese language. The modernity that they transmitted to China involved thousands of new words coined to express the language of world culture, creating an entirely new subjectivity and consciousness for citizens and professionals. At the same time, many older words, belonging to an older cosmology – such as *fengjian* (decentralized polity) or *geming* (loss of the mandate of Heaven) – were resignified with meanings and functions drawn from Western conceptions of history as 'feudalism' and 'revolution', respectively, with radical implications. Thus, while the older Chinese term *fengjian* represented a native Chinese critique of autocracy, the new meaning represented the Other of everything modern.

Until just before the fall of the dynasty in the republican revolution of 1911, this political tradition of *fengjian* was often invoked to advocate modern, local self-government and was even married to ideas of civil society. But such a recourse to history did not last long because, as the new ideas of a progressive history began to flood the Chinese intellectual scene, *fengjian*, or feudalism, began to be construed in the Enlightenment mode as the Other of modernity – as the symbol of darkness and medievalism. Hence, in a way, Chinese intellectuals had Orientalized their own tradition. Among many nationalists, the idea of local autonomy began rapidly to be construed as a hindrance to the emergence of a strong nation-state, and the new meaning of *fengjian* with all its negative connotations was deployed against those who supported local autonomy. This included the federalist movement of the early 1920s where the idea of provincial autonomy was delegitimated significantly by this transformed meaning of *fengjian*. I have often cited this example of *fengjian*, but

---

[60] Huang Jianli, "Umbilical Ties: The Framing of the Overseas Chinese as the Mother of the Revolution," *Frontiers of History in China*, 6(2) (2011): 183–228; Wasana Wongsurawat, "Thailand and the Xinhai Revolution: Expectation, Reality and Inspiration," in Lee Lai To and Lee Hock Guan, Eds., *Sun Yat-sen, Nanyang and the 1911 Revolution* (Singapore: Institute of Southeast Asian Studies, 2011).

it seems a particularly subtle mode whereby an ingressing, hegemonic ideology transforms an older universe of meaning – by a chain of implications – without claiming to do so.[61]

Regional scales of historical circulations

Another dimension of circulatory histories worth noting is the scales of circulation. In the modern period, methodological nationalism has tended to obscure the region as the crucial transmission scale that has mediated and facilitated circulations between the world and the nation or locality. Although, as we have seen, China has participated in circulations with Southeast Asia and beyond, I focus here on the northeast Asian core of East Asia. Japan, Korea and China shared not only a common culture in Confucianism but also the range of popular ideas that derived from the substratum of Chinese and Buddhist cosmologies including syncretism and millenarianism. The imperial Chinese tribute trade system which framed economic relations between them joined these societies even when the Japanese were not formally part of it. These societies became still more tightly interconnected in every sphere of activity during the formative period of modern nationalism.

Much of the modern linguistic recreation of Chinese and Korean drew upon the earlier Japanese translations of modern concepts, which in turn drew upon classical Chinese words. During the first few decades of the twentieth century, Chinese and Korean ideas of gender, religion, citizenship, and many other modern institutions drew – whether consciously or not, albeit not exclusively – from recent Japanese models and ideas. The very form of national histories is an exemplary place to seek their wider provenance. To be sure, many historians recognized that they were affiliating with a universal history; certainly, their histories could not be recognized as national without the common narrative form. But the very idea of a collective subject of history born of common origins – or, as in East Asia, of founding ancestors – could hardly be recognized as an imported model. From a regional perspective, as noted above in the case of China, new historical paleonyms such as 'feudalism', 'restoration' (*isshin*) or 'religion' (*shūkyō, zongjiao*) concealed the new as the old.

By the early twentieth century in East Asia, for instance, the idea of the common origin of a people typically derived from a common ancestor,

---

[61] These materials on *fengjian* and for much of the next section may be found in Prasenjit Duara, "Historical Consciousness and National Identity," in Kam Louie, Ed., *The Cambridge Companion to Modern Chinese Culture* (Cambridge University Press, 2008), pp. 46–67.

such as the Yellow Emperor or the sage-kings of yore in China; Amaterasu as the divine ancestress of the Yamato people in Japan; or Tangun for the Korean people. Early Korean nationalists like Shin Chae-ho believed that the emergence of nationalist historiography was hindered by the strong tendency of Korean elites to see their state as a tributary of China and a mentality of subordination to it (*sadae*). Even while struggling to free themselves from Chinese hegemony, Korean nationalists were faced by Japanese colonialism, which sought to depict Koreans as lesser versions of the Japanese and tried ultimately to assimilate them. Writing in the early twentieth century, Shin Chae-ho struck out against both of these obstacles by transforming the myth of Tan'gun into the starting point of the history of the Korean people, or *minjok*, distinct from both the Chinese and the Japanese.[62] The semantics of the unique nation was expressed through the syntax of the circulating global mediated by the lexical and interactive pragmatics of the region.

Each of these societies sought to distinguish the authenticity of its nation, often by resignifying symbols from a circulatory historical reservoir. One such symbolic role was that of the 'self-sacrificing woman' (*xianqi liangmu, ryōsai kembo*), upon whose sacrifices for the home and nation the new citizen and modern society would be built. Similarly, historical practices of self-cultivation and discipline were evoked from Confucianism and Buddhism to produce new habits of citizenship, as in the New Life movement of the Kuomintang (KMT) (Chinese Nationalist Party; the name was later romanized as Guomindang) in China and later in Korea. In recognition of the relevance of this circulatory cultural sphere – especially beyond the relatively thin layer of nationalist intellectuals in the Chinese- and Korean-speaking empire – Japanese imperialism sought to build its regional hegemony by deploying and appropriating the still current intellectual and civilizational rhetoric of the Confucian universe.[63]

Manchukuo, the Japanese puppet state established in northeast China (1932–1945), exemplified an all too transparent effort to build a nation-state from these East Asian circulations. In the roughly 14 years of its existence, Manchukuo spanned an area almost four times the size of Japan with a population of 40 million (mostly Chinese inhabitants). Although characterized by brutal repression, it also attained levels of economic development and urbanization that were second only to Japan in all of

[62] Andre Schmid, *Korea Between Empires, 1895–1919* (New York: Columbia University Press, 2002), p. 183.
[63] Sven Saaler and J. Victor Koschmann, Eds., *Pan-Asianism in Modern Japanese History: Colonialism, Regionalism and Borders* (London and New York: Routledge, 2007), p. 12.

Asia. It was a composite 'nation-state' based on Japanese state-building experiences, Chinese conceptions of religion and culture, Soviet ideas of state ownership and party control, and much else from the region around it. Manchukuo's most unembarrassed import may have been the idea of a state of multiple nationalities from republican China.[64]

A republic based on the alliance of nationalities (the Republic of Five Nationalities) was established in China in 1912 before anywhere else in the world. European ideas of a nation of multiple nationalities (which fructified later in the Soviet Union), drawn from Bluntschli and others, entered China through Japanese translations, but its institutional expression in 1912 drew as much from Qing conceptions of an imperial federation and generated a hybrid innovation that has lasted into the twenty-first century. Manchukuo's founding ideals of a concordia of nationalities (*xiehe* or *kyōwa*) sought to appropriate this conception (with the later grafting of Soviet notions), and later Japanese ideas of an alliance of nationalities, particularly the East Asian Co-Prosperity Sphere, also developed this theme.

The effects of Manchukuo were felt long after it was dismantled and returned to China. Its heavy industrial base and automobile and film industry became an important part of the postwar Chinese nation-state. Its impact on postwar Japan was felt through several generations of returning migrants and technical experts. In South Korea, the Cold War military leadership emerged from the Manchukuo military elite while the revolutionary leadership of North Korea was forged in the guerilla warfare against the puppet state. Most of all, Manchukuo was perhaps the first model of the developmental state that subsequently became so important in postwar East Asia and elsewhere.

To return to Lieberman, in light of the circulatory histories we have referenced and discussed, his contributions that reveal the *contemporaneity* of widely separated parts of Eurasia are limited by the nationalist-modernization paradigm to which he appears to subscribe. This paradigm functions with a rather tunnel-vision of national histories projected back in time. His narrative is in some ways, of a piece, with the very important discoveries of the mid-twentieth century decolonizing historians of China and India – for example, Xu Dixin and Wu Chengming's *Chinese Capitalism, 1522–1840* (1990) and Irfan Habib's "Potentialities of Capitalistic Development in the Economy of Mughal India" (*Journal of Economic History*, 1969), among many others. These studies also sought to

---

[64] Prasenjit Duara, *Sovereignty and Authenticity: Manchukuo and the East Asian Modern* (Lanham, MD: Rowman & Littlefield, 2003).

show how developments in each of their societies reflected sprouts of capitalist or proto-modern formations.

Much of this work was conducted within the framework of anti-imperialist theories, particularly Leninist theories. Indeed, Japanese Marxist scholarship (and the Needham project on Chinese science at Cambridge University) during the postwar years made enormous contributions to our understanding of the highly developed state of imperial Chinese society that we now take for granted. Mark Elvin's celebrated work, published in 1973, *The Pattern of the Chinese Past*, which documented the economic revolution from the eighth to the twelfth centuries CE, would not have been possible without this contribution.

At the same time, the Marxist/anti-imperialist framework of the Asian scholars frequently obscured the other, nationalist framing which was just as important in these works. The theory of modes of production became lodged within certain national or regional boundaries that were not immediately evident until they became signifiers of difference and identity. Take, for example, the case of the 'sprouts of capitalism' argument made in China in the 1950s and 1960s. It gained salience during a time when Soviet historians insisted on consigning Chinese history to a stagnant 'Asiatic mode of production' and thus logically one more primitive than even the slave mode of production. Chinese Marxists identified their own historical system as a feudal mode (semifeudal, semicolonial) and were eager to demonstrate that China almost made the breakthrough to capitalism through the idea of the 'sprouts'.[65] The falling away of the Marxist goals has led to the celebration of civilizational achievements in nation-states like China and India solely as elements of nationalist pride and privilege.

The question that has dominated the history of science and modernity among both Western and non-Western scholars has been, "Why is it that the West is the only society that broke into modernity?" Sometimes when the question is asked by non-Westerners, they seek to assimilate their own society into the Western club that exceptionally broke into modernity. Can we extricate the wider Eurasian developments from the teleological paradigm of national modernization histories and see them instead in a paradigm of early modernity? Admittedly, since what we call early modernity can now be seen as a polycentric global phenomenon, and the moderns appropriated the earlier cosmopolitan period to the name of modernity, the term itself may be a malapropism. But let us bracket that problem for the moment. If the *telos* of early modernity is not modernity as

---

[65] Q. Edward Wang, "Between Marxism and Nationalism: Chinese Historiography and the Soviet Influence, 1949–1963," *Journal of Contemporary China*, 9(23) (2000): 95–111.

we know it and modernity catalyzed only some aspects of early modern forms, what other aspects may be catalyzed or developed in this global-ized era?

I believe a profoundly significant dimension of 'early modernity' was precisely the deepening circulations, interconnections and interdepend-ence, especially from 1500 onwards. The historical reality of the early modern world as a collective heritage that was interactive and polycentric has been systemically obscured by the dominance of linear narratives of historical process. Exclusive histories of nations and civilizations under-pinned unequal relationships in the capitalist world even as capitalist relations were integrating the basis of historical developments globally as never before in the nineteenth and twentieth centuries. The misrecogni-tion of historical flows tied to goods, ideas, microbes, finances and net-works has finally become unsustainable as the consequences of these real flows can no longer be controlled by a self-sufficient nation-state.

Conclusion

This chapter has sought to highlight a crucial dimension of history that has been conceptually and methodologically – if not empirically – neglected in professional and popular historical writing. Much of the writing in world and comparative history, and even that of transnational flows, has largely accepted the terms of methodological nationalism, partly no doubt because the apparently stable institutionalized entities in possession of indispensable archives predispose the historian to miss the powerful role of circulatory flows. I have also adduced the ideological force – via the regime of authenticity – of the misrecognition of circulatory or 'foreign' sources of national systems, history, institutions and values as a related factor. To be sure, rejection and misrecognition of circulatory forces are hardly unique to the modern nation, and I will try to locate the particular role of the nation-state and capitalism in relation to culture and transcendence in Chapter 3.

It is undeniable that premodern imperial states, civilizational or religious elites, and even populations also rejected and misrecognized circulatory forms with different degrees of vehemence and violence depending on the source and time. But these societies were structurally more differentiated and porous, in large part because they were not bounded territorially, historically and temporally. While this may have had to do with weak institutional and mobilizational capacities, they also functioned within a cosmology where it would be hard to imagine the community or nation as the end in itself. For the most part, these cosmologies recognized powers and goals higher than those of mortal humans and the physical world. The disenchantment of the world may have led to a more scientific view of reality, but it also promoted the hubris of a human-centric – mediated by a nation-centric – view of the world.

While premodern societies did permit the coexistence of different temporalities under the regimes of eternal return, they probably had little sense of the circulatory forces, particularly as we understand them in social scientific terms. The parallel with our time lies in the fact that we too live in a world of multiple temporalities, scales and histories that shape our subjectivities though not necessarily how we identify ourselves. The necessity of recognizing the multiplicity of the sources of our subjecthood is increasingly urgent because of the yawning mismatch between the nation as a sovereign unit and the global forces that shape the destinies of people in those nations.

In order to develop histories that are adequate to this challenge, we have to learn to link our existing subjecthood – the *I* of history – in many different scales and temporalities, from natural and geological ones to those of local ecologies; from changing capitalist production cycles to rhythms of sustainable institutions, practices and modes of life, and their intersections. We need the weak exclusivity of premodern or early modern histories if only because national societies are now increasingly unable to exclusively manage the escalating crises generated by the 'counter-finalities' of modern nations.[66]

---

[66] Jean-Paul Sartre, *Critique of Dialectical Reason: Theory of Practical Ensembles*, Trans. Alan Sheridan-Smith, Ed. Jonathan Rée (London: Verso, 1976). See also Ulrich Beck and Edgar Grande, "Varieties of Second Modernity: The Cosmopolitan Turn in Social and Political Theory and Research," *British Journal of Sociology*, *61*(3) (2010): 409–43.

3   The historical logics of global modernity

In this chapter, I will develop the analytics to grasp what I am calling global modernity and in particular to grasp the crisis of sustainability that it has produced. At the same time, by viewing modernity in a wider global and historical framework, I will explore the conceptual grounds for a more sustainable modernity. Analysts of modernity from at least Hegel through the modernization theorists have explored the philosophical and socio-logical conditions of rational approaches that promise material and spiritual emancipation. Yet, these approaches have not only had exorbitant historical costs, but they have also generated counter-finalities – Jean-Paul Sartre's term – and what Ulrich Beck specifies as 'reflexive' or 'second' modernity to refer to the modernity of advanced capitalist societies. 'Second' modernity is no longer concerned with development per se but with management of the risks that are typically compounded by earlier modernization achievements (such as the nuclear fallout from the Japanese tsunami). Today the counter-finality stares us in the face as the crisis of planetary sustainability in the Anthropocene.[1]

By exploring the global and historical underside of modernity, we can gain a more comprehensive view of our situation today when the rest of the world is seeking to catch up with the North Atlantic model of life. Further, I want to show how an alternative set of dynamic concepts can lead us to recover a relatively neglected source of historical transformations that may be critical to achieving a sustainable modernity. Among these concepts is the notion of 'transcendence', which, in my view, works – among its other functions – to control, direct and channel the ceaseless circulatory networks that transform society. To anticipate a principal theme of the

---

[1] Jean-Paul Sartre, *Critique of Dialectical Reason: Theory of Practical Ensembles*, Trans. Alan Sheridan-Smith, Ed. Jonathan Rée (London: Verso, 1976). See p. 164: "*[I]n* and *through* labour Nature becomes both a new source of tools and a new threat. In being realized, human ends define a field of counter-finality around themselves." See also Ulrich Beck and Edgar Grande, "Varieties of Second Modernity: The Cosmopolitan Turn in Social and Political Theory and Research," *British Journal of Sociology*, 61(3) (2010): 409–43.

chapter, the 'high Culture' of transcendent ideas seeks to anchor, sub-ordinate and deploy the 'small culture' of circulatory transformations to its own projects and purposes. What differentiates modernity from such earlier modes is not merely the accelerating transformations of capitalism, but also the disenchanted cosmology of linear time that brooks no limits to the human conquest of nature.

Historians tend not to favor large and constraining terms like 'modernity' or 'capitalism', finding them not very useful in their studies. Yet, we do presuppose such categories, if in no other way than in our acceptance of periods and, by extension, the philosophy of history that informs period-ization. If this is the case, it is somewhat risky for historians to leave this more abstract level of analysis entirely to social theorists, who have tended to be much more structural, or at least synchronic, in their conceptualiza-tion of society.[2] Recently, though, historians have been engaged in 'big history', perhaps not only reflecting the effort to reclaim the conceptual-ization of dynamic trends but also signaling the advent of epochal changes such as the move away from Western centrality and the crisis of sustain-able development. Like some of these historians, I seek my intellectual foundations in 'complexity theory', a loosely defined paradigm that eschews simple, reductionist laws of explanation for complex interdepen-dencies among phenomena that continue to unfold in directions that are not entirely predictable.

One important contribution of complexity theorists, particularly in relation to evolutionary theory, is the view of the basic domains of the world and life – e.g., physical, biological, human – as having their own emergent rules of transformation. To be sure, biological life cannot be understood apart from the phenomena of physics, but biology has emer-gent rules of transformation that cannot be reduced to physics – namely, natural selection and self-organization. Similarly, human society respects physical and biological laws, but the emergent principle of human con-sciousness is creativity performed through meaningful acts of symbol-ization, including language, thought and experimentation, albeit under contingent and often unanticipated circumstances.[3]

---

[2] I refer not merely to structural functionalists like Talcott Parsons and those we may call 'functional structuralists' like Niklas Luhmann or Pierre Bourdieu, but also Michel Foucault and the Marxists. In their search for hard continuities, they lose sight of questions of change, change that is meaningful not only on a human scale, but also regarding different temporal scales suggested by counter-finalities.

[3] Stuart A. Kauffman, *Reinventing the Sacred: A New View of Science, Reason and Religion* (New York: Basic Books, 2008), pp. 11–12. See also David Christian, *Maps of Time: An Introduction to Big History* (Berkeley, CA: University of California Press, 2005), pp. 123, 183, 251. For a reasoned account of how rationality and values cannot be fully reduced to a

The evolutionary trend of human societies has been to enlarge information networks through exchange, circulation and complex feedback loops – the matrix of circulatory history, we might say – in order to stimulate cycles of innovation and expansion. They are cycles because complexity theory argues not only that expansion has no *telos* or goal beyond expansion itself but also that it tends towards entropy and chaos.[4] Among the emergent rules of human activity is the creation of a normative order required to manage complex interactions and stall the slippage towards entropy.

For my purposes, I define modernity as the worldview constituting the space-time when the principal institutions governing human behavior are seen to be shaped by secular time and history. The worldview of temporal disenchantment underlies all major theories of modernity whether it is the Enlightenment ideal of the conditions to actualize rational human agency and justice, Weberian ideas of rationalization and differentiation (of institutions and functions), or classical economics' core doctrine of property regimes as enablers of capital accumulation and material progress.

As the vision of disenchantment became politically institutionalized through the revolutions and transformations that yielded the nation-state between the late eighteenth and twentieth centuries, the hegemony of transcendent cosmologies was dealt a body blow. The idea of institutions, property and humans themselves as developing, if not progressing, by human effort alone unconstrained by transcendent or cyclical returns represents the historical condition of modernity. Innovation, expansion and destruction occur with relative freedom. At the same time, however, the notion of linear time is itself hegemonic and not fully constitutive or exhaustive of humans in all their aspects. As we will see, the older transcendent view paradoxically continues to function as a kind of supplement: extraneous to the self-definition of the modern formation, but necessary for its existence.

Following the ideas of complexity theory, I demarcate the main domains of human activity as organized by three logics of power which are deeply interdependent but also relatively *autonomous* from each other. I consider three 'logics' – of economics (exchange and control of resources), politics (management of violence and rule) and culture (ordering of symbolization and meaning). All institutions and practices contain some combination of the three. Modernity can be analyzed as a specification or

Darwinian biological model, see Thomas Nagel, *Mind and Cosmos: Why the Materialist Neo-Darwinian Conception of Nature Is Almost Certainly False* (Oxford University Press, 2012), ch. 5, pp. 110–16.

[4] For instance, when population expansion overtakes the innovation required to feed more mouths. Christian, *Maps of Time*, pp. 310–15, 506–10.

configuration of the three logics in which *innovation and resource expansion are accelerated particularly by changes in the relationship of economics with culture and politics* (especially as weak transcendence claims fail to brake unrestrained resource expansion).

In this chapter, I try to understand modernity historically by exploring the logics which also serve as the factors of the narrative production of modernity. This narrative must not only be able to foreground process but also to reveal the wider ambit of modernity – namely, the non-Western world or the 'south'. In theories of modernization, these societies have largely been seen as lagging or lacking modernity. The present conjuncture is significant because it reveals that a kind of 'catching-up and a slipping-down' is taking place in the world. But some of the most fundamental features of modernity – namely, capitalist processes – dominated these societies from the start, albeit unevenly. In other words, I attempt here to articulate the historical logics of modernity which apply to a much wider base than the Western historical experience.

We are at a historical juncture where *modernization* theory has been discredited, largely because it presupposed that the rest of the world would come to look like the extant model of the modern West. As such, it failed to distinguish what was uniquely or historically Western from the more enduring circulatory or universalizable properties of *modernity*.[5] While the transition from the paradigm of modernization to modernity has been intellectually useful to understand the rise of the rest, there is hardly any consensus on how to characterize the present form of the modern, or even whether we should call it the modern instead of capitalism or empire. Some have even argued that "we have never been modern," that we have confused self-representation for real process.[6] While agreeing with several of these critics, I continue to believe that modernity is still serviceable as the hegemonic cosmology that shapes the dominant institutions of our world.

The period of my inquiry runs back 150 years to the 1860s or thereabouts with the conclusion of such events as the Taiping Rebellion (1850–64), the Rebellion in India in 1857, and the Meiji Restoration of 1868, among other global developments which retrospectively appear to mark

---

[5] Björn Wittrock, "The Meaning of the Axial Age," in Johann P. Arnason, S. N. Eisenstadt and Björn Wittrock, Eds., *Axial Civilizations and World History* (Leiden: Brill, 2005), pp. 51–86, at p. 58.

[6] Bruno Latour, *We Have Never Been Modern*, Trans. Catherine Porter (Cambridge, MA: Harvard University Press), 1993. I agree with Latour's analytical separation of the constitution of modernity (as ideology) from mediation and translation of the different spheres of activity, and I utilize his ideas to an extent in Chapter 7 below. But the situation is more complex because the constitutional division itself becomes embedded in the networks, and the distinction therefore is more porous than Latour allows.

the beginning of the ascendancy of modern forces in vast parts of the world beyond the West.[7] During this period, the world economy also became integrated, albeit very unevenly, not merely by the spread of capital through banks, industries and railroads but also by the activities of legions of petty agents who fanned out across the colonial and semi-colonial world to collect information and supply reports on local currencies, weights, measures, administrative practices, levies and the like, in order to ultimately create measurable, commensurable, standardized and marketable objects of exchange – creating vast circuits of exchange between such places as Tianjin and Rio de Janeiro.

The focus of my analysis of the logics of history, however, goes beyond the economic system to politics and culture: the territorial system of nation-states and the aspirational and mobilizing cultural forces in history. I seek to develop a more distinctive approach to the political and cultural logics in order to develop a more holistic understanding of the period. Both the nation-state system and the cultural-ideological force are often reactions to the dynamic of global capitalism, but they also have autonomous roots and cannot be fully assimilated or reduced to the latter. Much historical change takes place precisely in and through the interactions and tensions between these logics.

These logics embed certain enduring dualities and tensions which reference the dynamic relationship between transcendence and circulatory history discussed above. At different moments and in different spaces, the nature and modalities of these tensile relationships may change with cascading effects at various scales of society and the world. I prefer the term *logic* to *structure* because while *logic* carries a certain sense of endurance and deductivity, it is non-unitary and more open-ended than *structure*. As such, it gives us some freedom from structural analyses of dynamic trends. Steps can be inferred from initial conditions, but logics also operate within different (discursive) environments and interact variably with each other in producing historical changes. Every subperiod of modernity has a 'punctuated equilibrium' among logics with gradual changes that accelerate periodically and rearrange the relationship. I identify certain tensions in these logics and seek to show how, both by way of example and to understand the present, the relationship among these logics was radically reconfigured during the late stages of the Cold War.[8]

---

[7] See C. A. Bayly, *The Birth of the Modern World, 1780–1914* (Oxford: Blackwell Publishing, 2004). See also Michael Geyer and Charles Bright, "World History in a Global Age," *American Historical Review*, 100(4) (1995): 1034–60.

[8] While I have gained greatly from my discussions with my former University of Chicago colleague William Sewell, my own conception of the term 'historical logics' is quite different from his, which he describes as "the semantics, the technologies, the

The logic of capital

I find that the world systems theorization of global capitalism remains useful for my purposes in its following tenets: (1) that the thrust of capital is largely deterritorializing even though it is enabled by deploying state power;[9] (2) that the long-term systemic processes of integration of the world economy take place in an uneven and unequal capitalist system; and (3) that the nation-state and nationalism are the means whereby a state or social formation has historically sought not only to become competitive but also to leverage its way out of the periphery of the world system into the core. At the same time, I seek to develop a more autonomous, if interrelated, role for the political and cultural logics at work in history than world systems theorists concede.[10]

The leveraging strategies of the newer nation-states have begun to rebalance the North–South zonal divide of cores and peripheries in the world system. Capital formation, organizational systems and, particularly, the emphasis on innovation so central to the capitalist logic of creative destruction is no longer centrally focused in the West, as new technologies, patent numbers, reverse engineering, bottom of the pyramid, and new organizational patterns emerge in the newer capitalist societies such as Brazil, China, India, South Africa and others. Here innovations are appearing also in the wider economy, political systems, civil society and media, and cultural production including the production of history. Whether or not this will amount to a more inclusive form of capitalism beyond the neo-liberal model of the Washington Consensus, however, remains to be seen.

The effects of non-Western capitalism on the world scene have now become evident. The United Nations Development Program (UNDP) report of 2013 declares that for the first time in 150 years, the combined output of the developing world's leading economies – Brazil, China and India – which represented only 10% of the world output in 1950, is now about equal to the combined GDP of the six leading industrial economies

conventions – in brief the logics – that characterize the world in which the action takes place." William H. Sewell, Jr., *The Logics of History: Social Theory and Social Transformation* (University of Chicago Press, 2005), p. 10. For 'punctuated equilibrium', see Sylvia Walby, "Complexity Theory, Globalization and Diversity," paper presented to conference on British Sociological Association, University of York, April 2003, p. 12.

[9] Although Arrighi grants more of a role to territorial control, it is ultimately for the sake of enhancing strategies of accumulation. See his comment on "the capture of mobile capital for territorial and population control, and the control of territories and people for the purposes of mobile capital," Giovanni Arrighi, *The Long Twentieth Century: Money, Power, and the Origins of Our Times* (New York: Verso, 1994), pp. 32–3.

[10] Immanuel Wallerstein, "The Construction of Peoplehood: Racism, Nationalism, Ethnicity," in *Race, Nation, Class: Ambiguous Identities*, Ed. Etienne Balibar and Immanuel Wallerstein (London: Verso, 1991), pp. 81–2.

of the North Atlantic. This growth has been particularly apparent over the last 10 years and more pronounced since the financial and economic crisis in the West from 2008. In just over 10 years, from 1999 until 2010, the share of developing economies in global GDP has risen from 21% to 36%. Moreover, imports into the developing world are growing rapidly and accounted for more than half the increase in world import demand since 2000. Since the onset of the financial crisis in 2007–8, the BRIC countries (Brazil, Russia, India and China) have provided 45% of economic growth worldwide. By 2050, the combined output of three of these economies (Brazil, China and India) is expected to account for 40% of global output, far surpassing the projected combined production of the Group of Seven bloc.[11]

While there is rebalancing at aggregate national levels, the concept of global modernity rejects the idea that the peripheries of global capitalism over the last 200 years have been outside the modern system – a view widely accepted and represented by theories of modern civilization, not just modernization theory. These theories and discourses have depicted the premodern and the barbarian as outside the system, but from a political economic perspective the latter have been crucial to the functioning of capitalism, which incorporated or subordinated non-capitalist forms of resource extraction and labor use to its strategies of accumulation.

These peripheries were also often laboratories of colonial modernity, experimenting, for example, with new forms of plantation organizations and labor mobilization; new systems of classification, incarceration and surveillance (e.g., fingerprinting); pedagogical instruction in a lingua franca (e.g., English language); tropical sciences; etc., that later became more universal. If capitalism is crucial to modernity in the West, its modes of organization, extraction, surveillance, and pacification have also constituted modernity, albeit in its unsavory underside in the South.

Modernization theory did not grasp this logic of capital. Economic expansion was identified with the idea of self-sustained growth within nations, not viewed from the changing roles of center and periphery at the global level. Formulated during the era of theoretically sovereign nation-states in accordance with the United Nations (UN) vision of the world, modernization theory largely ignored the global scale and deterritorialized basis of capital accumulation in history. At this fundamental

---

[11] Human Development Report 2013 Summary, *The Rise of the South: Human Progress in a Diverse World*. United Nations Development Programme (New York: UN, 2013), pp. 1–2. See also Jan Nederveen Pieterse, "Global Rebalancing: Crisis and the East-South Turn," *Development and Change*, 42(1) (2011): 22–48, at p. 23.

level, methodological nationalism and modernization theory reinforced each other to generate a national modernization paradigm that dominated knowledge during the second half of the twentieth century.

The logic of capital is primarily deterritorializing because it seeks the most cost-effective strategies for capital accumulation across political, legal and territorial boundaries. At the same time, however, the deterritorializing logic does not mean that it creates or prefers an even playing field or space – the much touted 'flat world'. Deterritorialization is accompanied by a counter-logic of uneven integration that produces cores and peripheries differentiating the principal functions of capitalism. The logic of capital as deterritorializing but functionally and redistributionally differentiating has operated on a global scale since the appearance of the Atlantic exchange that joined the Americas with Africa and Eurasia from the sixteenth century. In recent decades the counter-logic of uneven integration has taken the form of graduated sovereignties discussed below.

During the colonial period in the history of modern capitalism, the core/periphery distinction roughly overlapped with that between territorial or sovereign states in the core – where imperialist countries and their allies were located – and the colonies and semicolonies in the peripheries. Imperialist power enabled the deterritorializing imperative insofar as it could overcome rivals. In the contemporary period, there is no longer a strict correspondence between cores and sovereign territorial units.

Cores and peripheries are no longer zonal or macroregional in the way described by the world-system theorists, and they do not only exist between the First and Third worlds. Rather, unevenness is accentuating within nations in the developing and developed world. In the rising capitalist states of China, India, Southeast Asia, Latin America and Africa, capital accumulation and modernity are being built on the backs of tribal people, migrant labor, the rural dispossessed and their sources of livelihood in the lands, waters and forests. At the same time, declining middle classes, riotous consumers, sweatshops and rights-less pools of migrant labor are becoming common in the West. This axis of accumulation cuts across national boundaries, and the capitalist centers no longer reside in the West. The capitalist class is only now becoming genuinely global, and the peripheries are internal to sovereign nations whether domestic or foreign.

Global capital now has to deterritorialize – in other words, subvert or overcome existing laws in sovereign territories – by means other than imperialism and neoimperialism. Multinational companies whether from the West or Asia engage in 'institutional arbitrage' whereby they deploy a variety of different arrangements within and between countries and zones within nations. They often allocate their activities where they can play to the available institutional strengths and weaknesses – whether these are to be found in special economic zones, tax shelters, weak labor laws, employment protection or collective bargaining capacities, high education and low occupational training, environmental laws and protection capabilities, or, of course, susceptible political institutions. Their actions are both conditioned by and condition state institutions, as was evident by the adaptation of many countries to the neoliberal policies of the Washington Consensus.[12]

Indeed, Aihwa Ong and others have argued for the idea of 'graduated sovereignties' in several countries in Southeast Asia and elsewhere. Graduated sovereignties have different types of boundaries within or across two national territories, such as legal, police, military, and economic boundaries for different groups of people with different relations to capital and state. These diverse regulatory regimes may be found in special economic zones, lower tax zones, tourism zones, gambling zones, and various types of enclaves and exclaves where management and disciplined labor may be permitted, but not unruly squatters, or where consumers can escape national regulations. Increasingly, core regions within nations, such as the megacities of Mumbai, Hong Kong-Shenzhen or Beijing-Tianjin, are becoming linked to other megacities and disembedding from the wider hinterlands, or separating their hinterlands between those that are city- and export-oriented and those that are not.[13]

Risk management, the hallmark of the second wave of modernity, has inescapable global dimensions. Economic globalization and financialization have compounded the effects of disasters in one realm with many others. For instance, it is estimated that the Thai floods of 2011 caused US$45.7 billion in economic loss because of severe damage to seven large industrial estates and consequently to the global supply chain. This was among the top ten global insured losses by value and represented almost half the total property insurance premiums paid in southern Asia and East Asia in 2010.[14]

---

[12] James D. Sidaway, "Spaces of Postdevelopment," *Progress in Human Geography, 31* (2007): 345–61. See also Warwick E. Murray, "Neo-Liberalism Is Dead, Long Live Neo-Liberalism? Neo-Structuralism and the International Aid Regime of the 2000s," *Progress in Development Studies, 11*(4) (2011): 307–19.

[13] Aihwa Ong, "Graduated Sovereignty in South-East Asia," *Theory, Culture & Society,* *17*(4) (2000): 55–75.

[14] "Achieving a Viable Approach to Flood Insurance in Thailand," Swiss Re group (www. swissre.com/reinsurance/insurers/property_specialty/Achieving_a_viable_approach_to_ flood_insurance_in_Thailand_anz.html); "New Swiss Re Sigma Study 'World Insurance in 2010' Reveals Growth in Global Premium Volume and Capital," July 6, 2011, Zurich (www.swissre.com/media/news_releases/nr_20110706_World_insurance_ in_2010.html).

These modes of reterritorialization which reflect new convergences or intersections between the logics of capital and politics also represent greater threats to the responsible use of planetary resources. Institutions that perform regulatory, supervisory and justiciable functions tend to be within jurisdictions of national sovereignty and often cannot reach these global zones of graduated sovereignty or spaces of institutional arbitrage. Furthermore, accelerating globalization, which has created much greater interdependency among different national economies and forms of economic circulation, has also multiplied the risks and dangers to people and institutions that may be geographically distant from each other.

The reterritorialization resulting from the expanding scale of capital requires new kinds of responses in politics and culture. People's movements, civil-society groups, and transnational agencies and NGOs in the new media landscape are the weak forces with a presence in these spheres. Even so, as we will see in later chapters, these non-state and quasi-state actors are beginning to project alternative sources of authority, legitimacy and the reconfiguration of sovereignty.[15]

Political logic: circulation and misrecognition of nations

The contemporary nation form has been replicated across the world in the last 150 years. According to John Meyer and his associates, nations have been constituted by norms and practices deriving not only from the system of nation-states but also from a 'world culture' which has accompanied this system since the late nineteenth century. World culture may be thought of as a wider system that circulates and disseminates authoritative standards, norms and institutions among nations. This group of sociologists has tracked the dissemination of 'world culture' in several different parts of the world. It is not merely standard technical units like the *hertz* which were adopted internationally; norms for society and culture were also disseminated. For instance, the notion of the 'child' has become increasingly standardized as the institutional rules governing childhood were diffused to all types of nation-states over the last hundred years.[16] Even the format of historical pedagogy of the nation-state came to be divided into ancient, medieval and modern periods (frequently accompanied by a renaissance joining the medieval to the modern), following a similar pattern. What is circulated and often unquestioningly

---

[15] Karen T. Litfin, "Sovereignty in World Ecopolitics," *Mershon International Studies Review*, *41*(2) (1997): 167–204, at pp. 175–6.

[16] John Boli-Bennet and John W. Meyer, "The Ideology of Childhood and the State: Rules Distinguishing Children in National Constitutions, 1870–1970," *American Sociological Review*, *43* (1978): 797–812.

accepted are the epistemological and cognitive principles underlying the models, norms, laws, rules and standards in each national society.

To be sure the circulation of the culture of the nation-state was, and, to a considerable extent, still remains, a highly uneven process, shaped significantly by processes emanating from the developed nation-states and capitalist cores, which often found it useful not to have strong nation-states in the peripheries. Over the course of the twentieth century, the decolonizing nations with their goal of building strong nation-states in the periphery did succeed, in significant part, in shifting the balance of power away from the older Western capitalist core. Both culture and politics were critical to that transition in their ability to leverage economic and demographic advantages.

Thus, a critical dimension of the globalization of the nation-state refers not only to the visible structures – such as international conventions or the UN and its affiliated bodies in the postwar period – but also to the more invisible dynamic: the relatively unacknowledged or unreflexive adoption of global norms through which nations have been constituted and effectively recognized in the system. This less visible dynamic is enabled by a *misrecognition* of that constitution by individual nation-states which claim a distinctive or unique history of their land and people. Thus, for instance, both China and Japan were able to undo the Unequal Treaties only when there was international recognition of their modern 'civilized' legal systems;[17] yet, the nationalist textbooks and rhetoric hardly recognize this institutional and cosmological overhaul as the basis of the nation, and they emphasize historical continuities and the injustice of the Unequal Treaties. This misrecognition is systemic in the nation-state because it addresses the problem of sovereignty.

The advent of nationalism as a world ideology from the late nineteenth century tended to identify sovereignty solely within the people and culture of the primordial nation. Sustaining such an immanent and internalist conception of sovereignty presupposes a misrecognition of the systemic or wider source and impetus of many national developments and of the ideas, techniques and practices of nation formation. Symbols like the national flag, the national anthem, war memorials and the civic rituals accompanying them are good, if obvious, examples. Elsewhere, I have analyzed a set of human symbols across most nations, such as the aboriginal, the housewife, the child, the yeoman and the martyr, who, because of their dependent or absent agency, become objects of the regime of national authenticity. As such, they serve up lessons from an allegedly

---

[17] See Gerrit W. Gong, *The Standard of "Civilization" in International Society* (Oxford: Clarendon, 1984).

primordial national tradition for citizens to behave like model national citizens elsewhere in the world. In their history, form, design and usage, these symbols are truly emblematic of the circulatory process, yet they can evoke powerful emotions as symbols of the *primordial* nation.[18]

Fundamentally, nations do not possess the enduring inside and outside that are so basic to their self-recognition in politics and scholarship. Rather, the nation is constituted by the volatile tension between its globality and its nationness. Let me cite a simple example. In the developing world, the second half of the twentieth century saw a great number of anti-American and anti-imperialist demonstrations on the streets and in the media protesting the encroachment or violation of national sovereignty. Yet, the very demonstrators who were raising banners and hurling stones could be found the very next day applying for visas to study at US universities. Moreover, many of these would go on to become US citizens and live their lives as American nationals. I do not bring up this case to point up any personal hypocrisy. If hypocrisy is involved, it is a systemic one. World culture, or what I prefer to call 'cognitive globalization' (or unreflexive globalization), shapes every national who has the opportunity to be exposed to it. Yet, the regime of national authenticity systematically misrecognizes or devalues this constitutive element of globalization.

Functionally, national boundedness, or the misrecognition of sovereignty, is critical to the management of a fundamentally anarchic global condition in which circulating global resources – material and cultural – are appropriated differentially between and within cores and peripheries. With the collapse of transcendent sovereignty in Europe, most proximately represented by the Holy Roman Empire, sovereignty was relocated in states and nations without a Hobbesian Leviathan to order the competitive relations between them. We have noted how the modern theory of sovereignty was incrementally developed by early modern states in Chapter 1. For European states in their quest for dominance and control of global resources, the Westphalian-Vatellian system emerged to maintain some stability but not sufficiently to prevent centuries of warfare globally, culminating in the two world wars of the twentieth century. Moreover, the Westphalian system did not apply to the new and non-nation-states outside the West.

The sovereignty of the nation-state allowed it to territorially limit the deterritorializing and often destructive force of capital expansion driven by imperialist states (that were also nation-states). The sovereign state

---

[18] See Prasenjit Duara, *Sovereignty and Authenticity: Manchukuo and the East Asian Modern* (Lanham, MD: Rowman & Littlefield, 2003), ch. 1.

typically authorized a space for polities to rehaul and reorganize themselves as nations in order to be competitive in this global condition. As is well known, this process of transformation known as modernization and nation-building has been and remains a difficult, alien and alienating process for much of the world. The principal ideological means by which the state secures its sovereign authority to manage this transformation within the heterogeneous domestic space is the promise of modernity combined and balanced by a regime of authenticity whereby the state represents itself as the custodian of the land and people who have a primordial and ancestral claim to it. The narrative of national history, I have argued in Chapter 1, had captured these two authorizing moments for most of the twentieth century; it is an exemplary place to observe the relationship between recognition and misrecognition.[19]

The idea of a national subject gathering or recovering awareness over historical time presupposed both features. First, this history identified an ancient subject represented by a present or would-be nation-state; second, the subject's very existence in a universal, linear historical trajectory set it on a track – powered by a discourse of rights – to a modern future occupied by advanced nation-states. While the future orientation secured the legitimacy of the nation-state in its ability to propel the nation towards a globally recognized ideal of progress, the past orientation tended to ground sovereignty in the misrecognition of history as the evolving primordial subject dominated by authentic racial, linguistic or cultural characteristics. The tension between circulation and misrecognition is the political logic of the modernity of nation-states.

It is not clear, however, whether the regime of authenticity can adequately contain the corrosion of identity or basic values caused by the intensifying velocity of circulatory change during much of the modern and, especially, the contemporary period. Indeed, the representations or symbols of authenticity are themselves inconstant, changing frequently to adapt to new needs and forces. Think, for instance, of the 'pure woman/ ideal mother of citizens' as the embodiment of national authenticity in a feminist age, or royalty in the commercial and political context of the UK, Thailand, Nepal or the Middle East. The aspiration for change and the pull of identity: this is the most concrete expression of the aporia of modern temporality. Much of modern history is secreted from this tension, particularly as it is entangled with changing economic and political forces.

---

[19] Prasenjit Duara, *Rescuing History from the Nation: Questioning Narratives of Modern China* (University of Chicago Press, 1995); see also Duara, *Sovereignty and Authenticity*.

The historical logic of culture

The logic of culture is informed by a duality in cultural processes. With a lowercase *c*, *culture* refers to the meanings and significances which people give to events, practices, customs and institutions that enable everyday activity, interpersonal relationships, career and life courses, and the like. In both modern and premodern societies, this culture was formed from many different impetuses and sources, including contemporary ideas of exchange and market relations, technologies of communication, local and foreign horizons of aspirations, subaltern and elite perceptions of institutions, and old and new conceptions of the family, personhood, gender, etc. These norms, values and morals are pragmatic, hybrid and variable. While there is considerable overlap between this realm of lowercase 'culture' and circulatory processes, this culture also often internalizes civilizational norms and anticirculatory ideals. It tends, however, to be much less self-reflexive than the other kind.

We can designate this other form, *Culture* with a capital *C*. Typically, this is the form we associate with 'high Culture', the Culture of civilization, authenticity and transcendence authorized by classical traditions, religions, and foundational revolutions and events. This Culture is often rationalized, systematized and institutionalized, and it informs the lowercase *c* 'culture', but only partially. Unlike the relatively unreflexive and hybrid culture of everyday practices, this is a self-conscious and highly self-regarding Culture. It is embedded in foundational doctrines of states and religions and presents a set of rationalized ethical values and program of self-cultivation for individuals and groups. Periodically through human history, this Culture generates movements of purification to return to its true values and ethics either as establishment or antiestablishment ideology, and its target for purification is often culture with a lowercase *c*. In other words, Culture is a *representation* that contributes to ideas of distinctiveness and authenticity and produces the image of a continuous culture and society (of which national authenticity is a subset). Note, however, that the transcendent may appear from either culture or Culture.[20]

We may think of the relatively unreflexive globalization of the national model in the world alluded to above as the seeping of foreign ideas and norms mixing with local perceptions to shape institutions and people in a given society. In relation to this lowercase *c* culture, the regime of

---

[20] My difficulty with identifying culture with ideology is that the conceptualizations of the latter do not properly acknowledge the meaningful, regenerative and oppositional capacity of transcendent authority, whereas civilization is at present too contaminated by nationalist and conservative appropriations. Hence my awkward dualism of 'high Culture'/culture!

authenticity represents the allegedly continuous and coherent civilization of the nation. We may also think of modernization theory as advocating an idealized model, while the practical circulation of capitalist or other modern activities generates what Arjun Appadurai has called "modernity at large." By modernization theory, I do not mean only academic theory but also the universal history of progress embodied in 5-year plans and so on that emphasizes the emancipatory and promissory aspects of state modernity. On the other hand, the circulation of modern practices may involve deepening stratification, ethnicization, new modes of dependency, resistance and so on.

The complex relationships of the dual logic of culture are developed in later chapters. Theories of modernity by Weber and Axial Age scholarship have explicitly acknowledged the necessity of transcendence, even as late as in Calvinism, which ushered in a disciplinary revolution, as a condition of modernity. While I fully recognize the importance of transcendent aspirations, I also hope to show that there are different modes of coexistence and co-referentiality between C and c cultures that need not accord with the singular notion of transcendence often assumed in this theory.

To recapitulate from the Introduction, Axial Age theories refer to Eurasian developments from the sixth century BCE in the areas where Judaic, Hellenic, Chinese, Buddhist and Vedantic thought flourished. A transcendent and synoptic vision of the world beyond the here and now emerged, underpinned by sacred and moral authority. The authority of the transcendent, be it God, Heaven or *dharma*, was institutionalized by the world religions and spread across much of Eurasia during the next two and a half millennia. While the transcendent realm was discontinuous with the human world, and no humans – including the state – could fully realize its goals or will in this world, humans were expected to aspire to the realization of these goals. As the vision became institutionalized, the transcendent realm became a new philosophical basis for universal ethics in these religions. Ethical conduct included better ways of organizing society and demands for self-sacrifice.

The dichotomy between the transcendent and the immanent is important in Axial Age theorizing because it secured the separation of moral authority from immanent, state or social power and produced a gap between the *telos*, or ideals, and the realities of the day. Critical to the notion of transcendence is the emergence of an impersonal, moral world order sanctioned by a locus beyond the world and fundamentally unknowable. In this sense, transcendence could have this-worldly or other-worldly effects. For Weber, it was the this-worldly asceticism of the Protestant ethic that held the key to modernity. Later I will explore the various possibilities that may not have been crucial to Weber's conception but may be important for sustainable modernity.

Axial Age theory has recently become important once again in historical sociology. The most recent revisions recognize different expressions of transcendence, as, for instance, in Eisenstadt's recognition of the this-worldly orientation of ethical transcendence in Chinese Confucian think-ing and David Shulman's formulation of the Indian case where he argues that there may be something distinctive about the South Asian modes of reflexivity. These modes posit no Archimedean point from outside the system; rather, the reflexive move is somewhere inside but also entails the removal of the viewer's frame.[21]

Other recent revisions emphasize the contestatory role generated by the transcendent authority. The new horizons of meaning did not merely justify the establishment but also questioned existing institutions. Even though transcendent moral authority was often institutionalized by pro-fessional groups, such as the Church, priests, monks or the *ulama*, who co-constituted the establishment, this authority, in most cases, remained institutionally separate from state power or in tension with it. Indeed, the moral authority of transcendence endowed the counter-establishment in these societies with a powerful historical motor to periodically challenge the existing order and seek new means of personal and institutional change. Reform movements targeting the established clerisy or state in Abrahamic, Chinese and Hindu-Buddhist traditions (by Franciscans, Protestants, Buddhists, Daoists, neo-Confucians, Sufis, Bhakti and others) evoked the transcendent in defying authority to recreate a new order that more truthfully represented the transcendent ideals.[22]

Finally, the revised views also acknowledge that transcendent visions generated a multiplicity of mutually impinging world civilizations – each trying to reconstruct the world according to its premises and bearing an attitude of tolerance, exclusion or denial of the others – but each was most certainly influenced by the others, however it may deny it. Indeed, even Jaspers himself was motivated by the urge to see the 'enigma' of parallel developments in ancient China, India and the Graeco-Roman world in terms of the unity of mankind or as 'three independent roots of one history'. More significantly, he saw these developments, albeit through rose-colored lenses, as a ramified historical process that led to profound

---

[21] See David Shulman, "Axial Grammar," in J. P. Arnason, S. N. Eisenstadt and B. Wittrock, Eds., *Axial Civilizations and World History* (Leiden: Brill, 2005), pp. 369–94; Johann P. Arnason, "The Axial Age and Its Interpreters: Re-Opening a Debate," in Arnason *et al.*, *Axial Civilizations and World History*, pp. 19–50. For an earlier version, see Shmuel Eisenstadt, Ed., *The Origins and Diversity of Axial Age Civilizations* (Albany, NY: State University of New York Press, 1986).

[22] See Armando Salvatore, *The Public Sphere: Liberal Modernity, Catholicism and Islam* (New York: Palgrave Macmillan, 2007).

mutual comprehension when these cultures met. Or as Eisenstadt puts it, "In any case, the interrelations, contacts, and confrontations between different Axial and between Axial and non-Axial civilizations constituted a fundamental aspect of their dynamics."[23]

Thus, one of the problems of Axial Age theory pointed out by its critics, that it is far too long and meaningless to think of at least two thousand years of history as a period[24] – tends to dissolve if we think of it from the perspective of circulatory history, and not as a parallel period in different histories. The logic of culture, at least since the age of agrarian empires, presupposes a human urge – if not yearning – to identify a transcendent source of authority that occasionally coincides with revolutionary potential in different times and places. Like nations, albeit much more glacially, the transcendent in these societies was at least partially and recurrently shaped and reshaped by circulatory ideas. At the same time, the transcendent also represented the authoritative instrument to order and organize circulatory flows. Historically, we can observe transcendent Culture periodically clashing with elements of the culture of everyday life, which were seen to be either corrupt or contaminating true Culture.[25]

Karl Polanyi, among the few modern economists who continued to study capitalist economy in relation to larger social, political and moral forces, described a similar process. He wrote famously about a dual movement of alternation between capitalist expansion and a closing of the national economy by "the principle of social protection aiming at the conservation of man and nature as well as productive organizations, relying on the varying support of those most immediately affected by the deleterious action of the market."[26] I argue that the dual movement that can be expressed not only in territorially bounded spaces precedes capitalist globalization. Circulation across boundaries is expressed in the movements of goods, ideas, people and cultures, whereas the pullback is often historically expressed through high Cultures or civilizational discourses of

---

[23] Karl Jaspers, *The Origin and Goal of History* (New Haven, CT and London: Yale University Press, 1953), pp. 8–20; Shmuel N. Eisenstadt, "The Axial Conundrum Between Transcendental Visions and Vicissitudes of Their Institutionalizations: Constructive and Destructive Possibilities," unpublished paper, May 26, 2009 (and personal communication).

[24] Antony Black, "The 'Axial Period': What Was It and What Does It Signify?," *Review of Politics*, 70(1) (2008): 23–39.

[25] The specificity of the modes of ordering and organizing difference and exclusion is certainly germane in premodern civilizations, but these differences may not have been determining or essential. Moreover, unlike nations and the modern worldview, these modes mostly did not seek to replace the 'ultimate beyond' with man.

[26] Karl Polanyi, *The Great Transformation: The Political and Economic Origins of Our Time*. Introduction by R. M. MacIver (Boston: Beacon Press, 1957), p. 132.

purity and exclusivity, often with political, social and economic consequences. In modern societies, the pullback is authorized by ideals of
popular and national sovereignty, grounded, as I have shown, in the
immanent regime of authenticity.

To return to Axial Age theories, there continues to be a lingering theo-
retical vision of transcendence that presents a starkly oppositional character
to the immanent sphere – a radical opposition that may not be a necessary
condition for transcendence to fulfill its ethical role in society. While this
radicalism may have characterized the Protestant revolution in Europe, the
case of Buddhism and, at different times, Christianity and Islam suggest
that major social transformations were not necessarily accompanied by the
totalistic negation of existing social and cultural practices. In my view,
transcendence is a historically structured *meta-epistemological space* from
which a charismatic moral authority can issue with the power to persuade
and transform. Indeed, this transcendence has to resonate with aspirations
and realities as much as it has to distance itself from them. What is essential
in this conceptualization is the perceived separation of transcendent authority from worldly powers and its historical capacity for regeneration, not the
capacity to totalize from the conviction of absolute truth.

While the logic of culture embodied in the relationship of the two cultures
represents a wider historical logic, the modern logic of culture represents an
important modification or specification. As recounted above, a fundamental
factor in the modern transformation is the cosmological one, whereby
history is no longer trumped by or subordinated to the sovereign transcendent, or to what Mircea Eliade called the 'myth of eternal return', at least in
its role in the foundation of modern states. As we have seen, linear, progressive history is the temporal plane of national existence. The modern
discovery of 'historical man', according to Eliade, posits "the man who *is*
insofar as he *makes himself, within history*."[27] How then does the regime of
timeless authenticity accommodate itself with the primacy of linear history?

---

[27] Mircea Eliade, *The Myth of Eternal Return*, with a new introduction by Jonathan Z. Smith
(Princeton University Press, 2005/1954), p. xxiii. To be sure, there has long been a critique
of Eliade, most recently made by Tomoko Masuzawa, *In Search of Dreamtime: The Quest for
the Origin of Religion* (University of Chicago Press, 1993). Such critiques often dwell on the
'sacred' or 'dreamtime' as all-pervasive – even ontological – in premodern societies in the
writings of earlier scholars. While this is probably an accurate reflection on this first
generation of social scientists eager to differentiate modern from non-modern societies, it
should be kept in mind that my approach to their constructs of the sacred is to view them as
hegemonic or dominant, and not ontological. In other words, Eliade's or Durkheim's notion
of the sacred reproduces to some extent the obscuring function of these hegemonic constructs; they are also not aware of their often covert – and probably overt – contestation by
alternative temporal practices, as, for instance, by women. See Masuzawa's analysis of Munn
on dreamtime, pp. 170–1.

I have argued above that the disenchanted polity cannot cope with the loss of certitude brought on, doubly, by disenchantment itself and the accelerating temporality of capitalism. It requires anchors of timelessness, but it cannot accept the transcendent timeless, the regime of sacrality. Consequently, the regime of authenticity, the centrality of identity in modern nationalism, represents an immanent timelessness that negotiates its status in progressive history. The aporia between the ever-changing progress of history and the timeless historical subject is rarely acknowledged overtly, and historical narrative strategies work to reconcile the rupture when it becomes too obvious. Chinese national historians, for instance, have focused much attention on the Eastern Jin (fourth century CE), the tiny rump state that was seen by them to preserve Chinese traditions and values when the rest of the region was overrun by barbarians for hundreds of years.[28] Benedict Anderson calls it the 'necessary forgetting' of ruptures and disunity so important for national histories.[29]

In one sense, the regime of authenticity also occupies a transcendent position in history. It is able to generate a sense of duty and loyalty beyond the here and now of kinship and community to a larger cause; that is, the nation. But this is a deeply limited transcendence that in no sense resembles the universal ethics of earlier or religious transcendent thought. The transcendence of the nation permits it to affiliate the 'eternal spirit of the nation' with a range of religious imagery, but the nation's transcendence is deployed for its tribalist goals: to constitute a coherent and bonded 'We' – to be sure, this is for the advancement of the people, but also to be able to compete in a non-ethical world. As Lord Acton shrewdly observed in 1862, "[T]he greatest adversary of rights of nationality is the theory of nationality."[30]

More significantly, however, the regime of authenticity plays a very different role than did the transcendent. Where the transcendent position sustained a separation between political power and sacred authority, this separation is significantly obscured by the regime of authenticity because of the centrality of the nation-state in the conception of the nation. To be sure, the ideas of national justice may also be used by cosmopolitan nationals to build alliances – for instance, in the anti-imperialist movement – but the very purpose of nationalism remains to advance the national interest through the medium of the nation-state. There are also

[28] Duara, *Rescuing History*, p. 38.
[29] Benedict Anderson, *Imagined Communities: Reflections on the Origin and Spread of Nationalism*, Preface, 2nd edn. (London: Verso, 1991), p. xii.
[30] John E. E. D. Acton, *Essays in the Liberal Interpretation of History by Lord Acton*, Ed. with introduction by William H. McNeill (University of Chicago Press, 1967), p. 157.

surviving and reshaped ideals of transcendence, including such notions as human rights, that continue to furnish the basis of opposition to state power, but nationalism is potentially a form of absolutism, as we have often seen in the past.

The historical logics in the Cold War and after

Of the three historical logics viewed in this macrohistorical scale, the distinctive features of the Cold War – or its equilibrium – were shaped largely by political logic. As a historical period, the Cold War may be defined as a rivalry between two nuclear superpowers or hegemons that threatened global destruction. The importance of the political logic stemmed in great part from the rivalry in which each side sought to contain the politically destabilizing logic of economic and cultural forces that could benefit the other. At the same time, although the differences between the two camps were touted by the leadership, the competitive dimension of the rivalry provided the framework for a political order within which there were many circulatory similarities between the two camps, including the territorial national state, models of industrial and urban development, structures of clientage, designs of imperial or super-power enlightenment, and even many gender and racial-cultural relationships.[31]

All in all, the deterritorializing force of capital was, speaking relative to the period before and after the Cold War, considerably constrained by the territorial nation-state, as were also the forces of culture and religion transcending the nation. The Bretton Woods system, instituted in part because of the destabilizing force of the Great Depression, regulated exchange rates between the major national currencies until the early 1970s. The primacy of politics also entailed greater state power. Most developing societies in both camps were democratic mainly in name and rhetoric and were ruled by military, party and authoritarian regimes backed by the superpowers who were themselves afraid that any change in the client state might strengthen the other side.

While the UN principle of the nation-state as the only legitimate model of governance sustained the ideal of sovereign nation-states, the actual existing nation-state in each camp often expressed a form of misrecog-nized sovereignty sanctioned by the superpower. The territorial bounda-ries and institutional arrangements established to the superpower's advantage in the new nation-states typically had its military support.

---

[31] See Prasenjit Duara, "The Cold War as a Historical Period: An Interpretive Essay," *Journal of Global History*, 6(3) (2011): 457–80.

Indeed, the sale of armaments by the superpower to its client states may itself have been sufficient to bolster the arrangement. According to Charles Tilly, while per capita military expenditure in the world increased by almost 150%, GNP per capita rose by only about 60% between 1960 and 1987. The developing world's expenditure on defense (purchases) increased from 3.6% to 5.6% of GNP.[32] Indeed, in some ways, the competitive fiscal military state of the late Renaissance period that evolved into the nation-state became telescoped and replicated in the developing world, with the obvious differences being that: (1) the competition was focused on territorial control rather than resources abroad, and (2) the state operated in a wider environment shaped by the superpowers.

The unraveling of the Cold War order provides a revealing instance of how the three macrologics became implicated in causal interactions. The fall of the Soviet bloc is typically attributed to the outspending of the Soviet Union by the US regime on armaments build-up, especially during the Reagan administration in the 1980s. This further reduced the availability of capital for the consumer industry and spending in the Soviet bloc which, combined with glasnost and perestroika reforms, led to the final collapse. Yet, I have argued that this is a very short-term understanding, and we need a deeper global perspective that considers the cultural logic as well. In the latter perspective, the roles of the Chinese and Islamic revolutionary ideology are crucial factors.

Most significant to this narrative is the fact that the Soviet bloc was grievously weakened by the Sino-Soviet split and by China's development of the atom bomb in 1964. By 1969, Sino-Soviet hostilities had become so pronounced that the PRC, fearing a Soviet nuclear attack, was prepared to deal with the United States in what became the famous US-Chinese rapprochement of 1972. The Reagan administration was emboldened by the neutralization of China to recommence the arms race with the Soviets at a much more advanced level with 'Star Wars', or the Strategic Defense Initiative (SDI). Meanwhile, its sales of nuclear reactors and high-technology weapons and equipment to China between 1984 and 1987 suggests that the balance of power had clearly moved back from a three-way to a two-way contest, made newly and highly asymmetrical by the China factor.[33]

---

[32] Charles Tilly, *Coercion, Capital and European States, AD 990–1992* (Oxford: Blackwell, 1992), pp. 209, 221. For some examples from Southeast Asia, see Anthony Reid, *Imperial Alchemy: Nationalism and Political Identity in Southeast Asia* (Cambridge University Press, 2009).

[33] Shirley Kan, *U.S.–China Military Contacts: Issues for Congress.* Updated May 10, 2005, CRS Report for Congress, Congressional Research Service. Library of Congress, Washington, DC. Order Code RL32496 (http://fpc.state.gov/documents/organization/48835.pdf), p. 1. For the effects of the arms race and the Strategic Defense Initiative on the Soviet Union, see Eric Ringmar, "The Recognition Game: Soviet Russia Against

The second factor was the globalization of political Islam, which is not simply a post-Cold War phenomenon. In many ways it was a result of, even a backlash against, the Cold War order. The Iranian revolution of 1978–9, caused by many political and economic factors, represented the opposition of political Islam to Cold War ideals. At the same time, from the early 1980s, the *mujahidin*, militarily supported by the United States and its Muslim allies, played a major role in increasing the costs of the war to the Soviets, driving them out of Afghanistan and bringing the Taliban to power. The *mujahidin* and political Islam had been encouraged by the success of the Islamic revolution in Iran, and it did not take long for them to turn their ire against the US camp. These two events, it should be noted, represented disenchantment with the two Western options of capitalist and socialist modernity and thus also catalyzed the end of the Cold War in a way that has not been sufficiently recognized.[34]

While the case of radical Islam may represent the role of a transcendent vision mobilizing against the world order, to what extent does the China factor represent anything more than a balance of power game? Nuclear power was certainly a necessary factor, but not a sufficient one. The Chinese revolution, which was independent of the Soviet pattern, produced a mighty party-state and revolutionary ideology that enabled it to break away early from Soviet dependence. This was the sufficient factor as well as the precondition driving China to acquire the bomb and for the emergence of one of the crucial disequilibrating factors in the Cold War.

Even the great pragmatist Deng Xiaoping, who is said to have reversed the direction of China's historical course from revolutionary socialism to capitalism, saw capitalism largely as strategic policy. While Deng attacked the Gang of Four for preaching 'poor communism' (i.e., where communist ideals were more important than alleviating poverty), and thus elevating the spiritual over the material, he remained convinced that, whatever else it could do, capitalism could not eliminate the fundamental problems of exploitation and plundering. It could not generate the common ideals and moral standards that were so necessary for human justice. Deng appeared to have underestimated the Faustian bargain that neo-liberal capitalism strikes once the spiritual forces become systematically weakened.[35]

the West," *Cooperation and Conflict*, 37(2) (2002): 115–36, at p. 130. See also J. M. Hanhimaki and O. A. Westad, *The Cold War: A History in Documents and Eyewitness Accounts* (Oxford University Press, 2004), pp. 274–5.

[34] Steve Coll, *Ghost Wars: The Secret History of the CIA, Afghanistan, and Bin Laden, from the Soviet Invasion to September 10, 2001* (New York: Penguin Press, 2004).

[35] Cited in Yuen-ching Bellette Lee, "Development as Governing Tactics – the Three Gorges Dam and the Reproduction and Transformation of State Power in Dengist

Agency in the Cold War emerged not only from the attractive power of consumer capitalism but also from alternative and momentous historical developments. The revolutionary and religious power, including the Polish Solidarity movement, that emerged in different regions of the world was able to gain agency from its historical pathways, whether progressive or transcendence-oriented. Maoist, world-defying, revolutionary agency in the modern period may not seem immediately connected to the power of transcendence in history. But it does not take much to show that the Maoist vision of universal revolution expressed a transcendent faith in the deferred utopia, a powerful source of self-formation and self-sacrifice, even when it became part of the party's routinized propagation of this promise.

This analysis has sought to stress the role of the non-West in the ending of the Cold War through an expanded notion of modernity. Admittedly, Maoist revolutionary energy can be seen as an expression of Enlightenment ideals that may be found from Kant to Marx, although, as a peasant revolution, Maoism stood that theory on its head. More complicated is the understanding of radical Islam. Recently, arguments have emerged that despite its avowed denunciation of secularism, by participating in and utilizing the circulatory institutions, communications and technology of modernity, radical Islamists reinforce the unwritten rules which secure the autonomy of the political and social spheres from religion. In the process, some believe that they have evacuated the transcendent function and become identified with power. However, Humeira Iqtidar argues that transcendence is changed – "not erased but consciously sought through a modeling of subjectivities, behaviors, and praxis."[36]

Iqtidar's work reveals the extent to which the transcendent vision is justified by organizations, activities and programs often modeled on leftist agendas, including land reform, union activity, and antifeudal and anti-imperialist campaigns (articulated with Muslim holy activities, of course). This notion of transcendence has accommodated itself to a linear history of improvement and success even as it seeks ultimate truth in the holy life. Indeed, Iqtidar shows how transcendence itself comes to sanction equality, individuality, rationalization and other modern values. As such, it remains within the modern dialectic of Culture/culture; but, by articulating a most pronounced role for religious transcendence in modern culture, it probes the limits of hegemonic modernity as we have known it.[37]

China," Ph.D. dissertation, University of Chicago, 2013. See also Deng Xiaoping, "Uphold the Four Cardinal Principles," *Selected Works* (1975–82) (Beijing: Foreign Languages Press, 1984), p. 175.

[36] Humeira Iqtidar, *Secularizing Islamists? Jama'at-e-Islami and Jama'at-ud-Dawa in Urban Pakistan* (University of Chicago Press, 2011), p. 23.

[37] *Ibid.*, 23–5.

In China, and in much of the rest of the world, the contemporary nullification of revolutionary transcendence and its replacement by consumer capitalism probably comes as a relief to many. But the logic of cultural transcendence has by no means been exhausted in the world. I refer neither to revolutionary transcendence nor exclusively to the reglobalization of religious entities and communities, but to the emergent global ideal of sustainability. Sustainability requires transcendence not only of the dominant practice (culture) of accelerating consumption with the accompanying destruction and obsolescence, but also of the entrenched ideology of nationalism (Culture of misrecognized authenticity) and its exclusive sovereignty claims. Whereas changing the behavior of individuals and collectives depends upon the mobilization of ideals and principles that shape self-formation and self-discipline, the institutional underpinnings of these changes involve an ideal of shared sovereignty.[38]

Since the end of the Cold War, the logic of economic deterritorialization has been salient and has altered the structural relationship between the nation-state and globalization. The rationale of the nation-state is no longer exclusively or overwhelmingly based on the protection of national sovereignty. Indeed, the state has aligned itself more closely with multi- and transnational interests, and the neo-liberal economic order has spelt out an agenda of state withdrawal and privatization or corporatization of the provisioning of national public goods. Consequently, the globalism of the national order is no longer as covert or misrecognized as it once was. Moreover, the ideology of nationalism has also tended to transmute with these changes. While national leaders can scarcely abandon it, nationalism is less dependent on state direction than it is on an unreflexive reaction by the populace to the dangers and threats posed by overt globalization to stability, community and the promise of citizenship.[39]

The realignment in much of the world presents, in some ways, a still greater incongruity between our globality and national institutions. Not only is there a deeper embeddedness in, and dependence of the nation on, the world, but many of the effects of globalization on society are no longer shielded by state institutions as they were previously. National and local institutions of governance and delivery are ambiguously committed to projects of development, as they are also diverted by neo-liberal goals of profit maximization. Perhaps most significantly, the profit-maximizing drive of economic globalization has generated environmental degradation

---

[38] Or even dialogical sovereignty, if that paradox can be sustained.
[39] For the more detailed argument of this paragraph, see Prasenjit Duara, "Historical Narratives and Transnationalism in East Asia," in *The Global and Regional in China's Nation Formation*, ch. 3 (London: Routledge, 2009), pp. 60–76.

across the world that can no longer be addressed only by national policies. Ecological instabilities have effects on global resources such as water and climate that do not respect national boundaries. National wealth and national problems are generated on the global scale, but the institutions of remediation and justice function at national and local levels. In order to address this mismatch, nation-states will have not only to coordinate but also to share sovereignty with regional and global entities.

Sustainable modernity and the logics of history

This chapter has allowed us to identify modernity as a global phenomenon that is not only charged with the promise of progress but also carries the costs and burdens of the past and an unsustainable future. It has also developed a set of categories – or logics – that allows us to grasp the historical dynamics of modernity and its current crisis. They can lead us to recover a relatively neglected source of historical transformations – the logic of culture – which may be critical to achieving a sustainable modernity by rebalancing the relations in human society and of humans to the world. The remainder of the book will elaborate upon the various dimensions of these propositions.

The political and cultural logics of global modernity not only flesh out the non-economic dimensions of the system, but they also indicate the limits of the regimes of global accumulation. For instance, while the world-systems theorists would see global capital and the nation-state as intrinsically collusive – and perhaps they have rarely been more so than in the present era – the notion of misrecognized sovereignty allows us to see the strategies and consequences, as well as the limiting functions, of the state with regard to the deterritorializing impetus of capital. By appealing to an autonomous or transcendent source of justice, Cultural forces have often provided the inspiration and energy to limit or reshape political-economic formations, whether on a local or wider scale.[40]

The logic of culture framed by the duality and tension of Culture/culture and the logic of politics framed by the paradox of recognition/misrecognition are among the most basic forces in modern history and possibly come as close to structural forms as may be found for the historian and analyst who seeks to foreground process. In this respect, these logics evade the pitfalls of methodological nationalism even while they allow talk about national developments, because the logic of politics incorporates the very mode of constituting the nation through the

---

[40] This is by no means meant to justify all cultural movements; consider the disastrous consequences of the Cultural Revolution or Islamic fundamentalism.

recognition/misrecognition logic. The bifurcation of culture into Culture and culture allows us to see Culture as a *representation* that may be important as much for the self-formation and resistance of people as for its capacity to bolster the hegemony of establishment powers. As an ethical system, it is often in tension with circulatory culture, as represented, for instance, by untrammeled consumerism or new sexual mores, or with entrenched practices of "superstitious worship" or bonded labor.

Over the last 150 years, world culture has been circulating and rapidly mixing with the local through formal and informal, legal and illegal, recognized and misrecognized means. Representational Cultural forces – which have been deeply important for the regeneration of human agency and reshaping of politico-economic formations – have, of course, also circulated and been transformed in the process. Central to this circulation has been the Enlightenment discourse of rights expressed in revolutionary or reformist social movements, which have often combined with indigenous or foreign, transcendent – e.g., Christian or Islamic – movements. Historically, it is even doubtful whether rights movements have been able to sustain themselves over the long term without the moral authority, universalism and symbolism of – or akin to – transcendent movements. This has been witnessed since the abolitionist movement in the early nineteenth century to contemporary environmental and Gandhian movements.[41]

Let me briefly try to locate my understanding of the logics of modernity in relation to some of the more recent theories of modernity. As suggested, modernization theory has been able to provide some indices of modernity across different parts of the world. But its explanatory variables and schemes are limited especially by the national frame of reference and neglect of the systemic dynamics of competitive capitalism and the changeable – and now very volatile – relationships between cores, semi-cores and peripheries, extending within nations and regions, and across the world. Moreover, in generalizing the conditions of an idealized West during a limited period, the theory was unable to identify shifting roles – for instance, those of the state, social movements or secularism. As indicated, I have drawn greatly from world-systems analysis, especially

---

[41] Owen Whooley, "Locating Masterframes in History: An Analysis of the Religious Masterframe of the Abolition Movement and Its Influence on Movement Trajectory," *Journal of Historical Sociology*, *17* (2004): 490–516. See also Samuel Moyn, who discusses the first historian of 'human rights', Gerhard Ritter. Ritter was persuaded that the moral ideal of human rights derived from the 'Christian-Occidental culture' to provide limits on state power that once came from God. Samuel Moyn, "The Last Utopia: Human Rights in History," *American Historical Review*, *116*(1) (2011): 58–79. See also Chapter 6 in this book.

for my analysis of economic logic; but it, too, has a limited or reductive understanding of political and cultural forces.

Theories of post-modernity or post-colonialism represent significant deconstructive strategies but present no alternatives. Other recent correctives, such as the notion of multiple modernities, do seek to address the problems resulting from the overgeneralization of the Western model. This school pays particular attention to the 'proto-modern principles' (my term) embedded in other cultures, especially associated with Axial Age traditions of transcendence. While, as it should be clear, I hold to an important historical role for the epistemology of transcendence, I believe the advocates of multiple modernities tend to extrapolate contemporary nations or peoples (even races) back in time to premodern eras along the model of Western civilization evolving from classical times in a linear, bounded fashion. As such, they extend the scope of the essentialist principle of methodological nationalism, underestimating the role of global circulations over millennia.

Ulrich Beck and Edgar Grande's recent work on second modernity and methodological cosmopolitanism is more useful in that it is aware of the counter-finality entailed by modernization. They also differentiate modernities not strictly by nations or cultures but also by stages and types, such as the statist modernity of China or 'failed modernities'.[42] Sudipta Kaviraj's view that the *forms* of modernity differ because of historical differences in timing and sequencing of the appearance of various functions associated with the modern allows us to see the temporal differentiation of the singular. Thus, Indian modernity – and other newly independent states – had to manage democracy when only 30 percent of its population was literate in 1947, whereas most Western democracies had already industrialized by the time of universal suffrage.[43]

Most of all, for any theory of modernity to work, it will need to grasp the deep historical interdependencies and porosities of capitalism, the nation-state, 'world culture' and compounded and multiscale effects of crises. Even if we consider these modernities to be resilient subsystems, such as Anglo-American forms of capitalism versus Chinese or German ones, we still need to grasp how they adapt and cope with the pressures of globalization upon their activities, including the inchoate social and aspirational movements spreading across the world. The theory will have to comprehend how social and national systems manage or police their inside from the outside.

---

[42] Ulrich Beck and Edgar Grande, "Varieties of Second Modernity."
[43] Sudipta Kaviraj, "An Outline of a Revisionist Theory of Modernity," *Archives européennes de sociologie, 46* (2005): 497–526.

My analysis suggests that modernity refers to a single phenomenon that joins the globe but does not exhaust it; there are other ways of perceiving and being in the world. Rather, modernity is a hegemonic formation based upon a dominant concept of time and history as linear, measurable and unfolding. This is the temporal plane upon which capitalism and political systems and the institutions dependent upon them function. In nature and for many people and communities, time is relevant and apprehended in many different ways, as discussed, for instance, by geologists and climatologists on the one hand, and community activists, anthropologists or phenomenologists on the other hand. Seeing time as a hegemonic condition allows us to apprehend how natural events or a vision of transcendent temporality shapes and disrupts the social formation.

Within a social formation, the advent of modernity came with the promise of a more just and materially better future in the Enlightenment. But it was accompanied by a range of material and practical iniquities and the unrestrained exploitation of nature. The promise of Enlightenment modernity represented by its rhetoric of equality, justice and freedom still holds value for most of the world because the universality of these ideals has become meaningful. Testimony to this is the manner in which the new nations have mobilized and leveraged the modern logics of politics, economics and culture to achieve those ideals. What this has done is to exacerbate the underside of Enlightenment modernity – chiefly the freedom to treat nature and the world as objects and resources for man – leading to its unsustainability.

The question is not whether we need to jettison modernity as a value system in order to sustain the planet and its creatures. Rather, modernity has to be understood in terms of the logics of human evolution, particularly its emergent property – the quintessentially human logic of culture, reflexivity and ethics. The paradigm in the academic world remains some form of national modernization. We are judged not only by growth rates but also by the habits and practices of the individual which contribute to the ideal of material progress. A paradigm of sustainable modernity is needed to forge once again an equilibrium among the logics to restore the balance between humans and the world.

4   Dialogical and radical transcendence

But did we kill God when we put man in his place and kept the most important thing, which is the place?

Gilles Deleuze, *Pure Immanence: Essays on a Life*, p. 71

The true philosophical question is, How can concrete fact exhibit entities abstract from itself and yet participated in by its own nature? . . . Each fact is more than its forms, and each form participates throughout the world of facts. The definiteness of fact is due to its forms; but the individual fact is a creature, and creativity is the ultimate behind all forms, inexplicable by forms, and conditioned by its creatures.

Alfred North Whitehead, *Process and Reality*, p. 20

If both action and agent are non-existent, where could there be the fruit born of action? Where there is no fruit, where can there be an experience? (MKVP 328, 329)

Just as a teacher, through psycho-kinetic power, were to create a figure, and this created figure to create another, that in turn would be a created.

In the same way, an agent is like a created form and his action is like his creation. It is like the created form created by another who is created. (MKVP 330)   Nagarjuna, *c.* 150–250 CE

This and the following two chapters deal centrally with the theme of religion, spirituality and transcendence in China, India and other parts of Asia from a historical perspective. In terms of the conceptual framework of the book, this part foregrounds the logic of C/culture in the non-Abrahamic traditions in relation to political, and more distantly, economic logics. As such, a principal goal of this chapter is to explore the relationships between circulatory historical ideas and practices and Cultural anchors of transcendence.

The high Cultures in these societies – Confucianism, Hinduism, Buddhism, Daoism, and others – seek, as do the Abrahamic high Cultures, to specify, authorize and institutionalize their ideals and prescriptions of the proper life. They usually define their worldview as the only legitimate vision of the universe even though their ideas and practices have been a part of circulatory transformations for millennia. Nor have

119

they fully escaped the most recent circulation of Protestantized ideas of religion and secularism in their remaking since the nineteenth century, as we will have occasion to reference in the later chapters. Nonetheless, the entrenched pathways as well as the continuing plurality of these ideas and practices in local and popular society have managed to sustain alternative visions of life, the world and transcendence in these societies, frequently in conversation with other circulatory fragments.

In this chapter, I distinguish two traditions of transcendence in Eurasia: the radical transcendence, or strict dualism, and the more dialogical religious traditions, where transcendence is interwoven with immanent, polytheistic, pantheistic and plural religious practices. Although radical transcendence is often associated with the Abrahamic religions, I hope to avoid an East versus West essentialization by distinguishing the two traditions in order to allow us to see dialogical trends and sects within the Abrahamic traditions as well as radical tendencies in non-Abrahamic ideas of transcendence. The analysis subsequently focuses on historical and institutional contexts in which these tendencies develop without ignoring the philosophical and doctrinal features that dispose them in certain directions.

Although mine is principally a historical study, and the goal of this chapter is to understand the dispositions and consequences of adopting a certain view of transcendence, it is difficult to avoid some discussion of the truth claims of these positions. Many of the Asian expressions of dialogical transcendence bear a resemblance to philosophical ideas of complexity today. Some schools of complexity theory, inspired, for instance, by A. N. Whitehead, entail a relationship between abstract principles of knowledge and the circumstances and conditions – including affective, attitudinal and ethical conditions – for their realization. As different expressions of dialogical transcendence, the juxtaposition may be helpful in understanding these related positions.

Transcendence: radical and dialogical

Jan Assmann, Arnaldo Momigliano and others have shown that the contestation between monotheism and polytheism dominated the religions of antiquity in the Mediterranean and the Middle East region until the Christianization of the Roman Empire in the fourth century CE. What Assmann calls 'revolutionary monotheism' and distinguishes from polytheism and 'evolutionary monotheism' (where 'all gods are one') had appeared with the theologization of history or *historia sacra* in the Judeo-Christian tradition. This historical vision challenged the polytheistic idea of the world suffused with divinity with one which is merely the creation of a single God in whom truth resides. Time in this world – since the fall of Adam and Eve from grace through the revelations of the prophets and until the Second Coming or Judgment Day – is a period of waiting and preparation. Events in this temporality gain significance only in relation to salvation. History in the Abrahamic traditions is thus the stage for the unfolding of a divine message revealed by the prophecies of the messiah or prophet and recorded in sacred text. The community of the chosen or the believers are expected to lead a life of faith and godly conduct in the expectation of salvation in the kingdom of Heaven, whether in later generations or in the afterlife.[1]

Tracking the centuries-long literature since Edward Gibbon on the origins of Christian intolerance and violence towards pagans and others in late antiquity, Guy Stroumsa provides further background for the emergence of monotheism. The region occupied by the myriad communities across the Byzantine and the Sassanian empires in late antiquity generated a new axial development, a novel conception of religion based not only on the religions of the Book and monotheism but also on the interiorization and personalization of faith, and the shift from civic religion to communitarian religious *identity*. After the destruction of the Temple in 70 CE, Judaism became the laboratory and the model for several of these ideas, such as the sacrality of the Book, revelation and *historia sacra*, for these communities which spread across the region. Among them were many confessional communities who claimed their own prophetic revelation or story of the truth – modeled on the same *historia sacra* – to be authoritative. While they may have done so largely to distinguish themselves from each other, their contestations led to a highly competitive and often intolerant environment.[2]

Among the most important studies of the emergence of Islam in the circulatory socioreligious context of this region, albeit at a later point, is John Wansbrough's aptly titled *The Sectarian Milieu*. Wansbrough makes a strong claim that the doctrines of Islam evolved from debates with Jews and Jewish Christians. In the sectarian milieu of hardly distinguishable religious groups – including, as Al Makin has shown, those among local Arab communities of the seventh century – the theology sought to establish an identity for Islam distinguished quite sharply from its religious

---

[1] Jan Assmann, "Monotheism and Polytheism," in Sarah Iles Johnston, Ed., *Religions of the Ancient World: A Guide* (Cambridge, MA: The Belknap Press of Harvard University Press, 2004), pp. 17–31; Arnaldo Momigliano, "The Disadvantages of Monotheism for a Universal State," in Arnaldo Momigliano, *On Pagans, Jews, and Christians* (Middletown, CT: Wesleyan University Press, 1987), p. 152.

[2] Guy G. Stroumsa, *The End of Sacrifice: Religious Transformations in Late Antiquity*, Trans. Susan Emanuel (University of Chicago Press, 2009), p. 104; cf. pp. 95–107.

rivals. The similarities among the monotheistic religions and their claim of a common religious ancestry made the quest for identity all the more urgent.[3]

The thickets of controversy surrounding Wansbrough's claims pertain to the extent to which Islam borrowed from the Jewish tradition and the originality of its own synthesis. These debates need not detain us here. For our purposes, the biblical tradition of salvation history (*historia sacra*) reveals certain common features among the major religious traditions of this area: the acceptance of a body of material as *sacred scripture*, a *doctrine of prophecy strongly influenced by the Mosaic pattern* and a *sacred language*. History, then, is 'kerygmatic': it is the proclamation of a message of divine significance. There are, of course, several other distinctive features among the Abrahamic faiths, and we will return to the relationship of the community and doctrine to the state in the next chapter.[4]

As we know from similar environments of religious competitiveness in different periods and different parts of the world (such as South or East Asia), competition based on the belief in truth did not necessarily lead to large-scale elimination of the Other, in and of itself. Indeed, Stroumsa argues that, despite providing many of the fundamental characteristics of the new religiosity of late antiquity, Jewish exclusivism and insistence on the boundaries of collective identity remained within the framework of the civic religion and were indifferent to the Other. It was only when the collectivity of believers in a single universal truth fired with an imperative to proselytize came to control state power that there developed a systematic "intolerance for those who refused to accept the message of love."[5]

Thus, a significant characteristic of the later Abrahamic societies, Christianity and Islam, is the proselytizing injunction that takes them "beyond the community paradigms of the first axial breakthrough associated with Jewish and Greek models."[6] Once Christianity became identified with political power in the Roman Empire in the fourth century, the polytheistic, civic religion model of the early empire gave way to

---

[3] John Wansbrough, *The Sectarian Milieu: Contest and Composition of Islamic Salvation History* (New York: Prometheus Books, 2006/1978), pp. 40, 98–9; Al Makin, *Representing the Enemy: Musaylima in Muslim Literature* (Frankfurt am Main and New York: Peter Lang 2010), esp. ch. 1.

[4] Charles Adams, "Reflections on the Work of John Wansbrough," *Method and Theory in the study of Religion*, 9(1) (1997): 75–90.

[5] Stroumsa, *The End of Sacrifice*, p. 104; cf. pp. 95–107. Christians in fourth-century Rome believed that the reduction of diversity was the best preparation for the coming of the Savior; they constructed their interpretation of the Roman Empire as the providential instrument for the Church.

[6] Armando Salvatore, *The Public Sphere: Liberal Modernity, Catholicism and Islam* (New York: Palgrave Macmillan, 2007), p. 100.

community churches of the chosen, who were defined by shared belief. Good and evil become associated with obedience or disobedience to a single God and the divine law. The attainment of salvation was based not only on prescribed duties, rituals and other orthodox practices; in this new model, the faith and piety of those who were converted or baptized was more important than ritual practice. It was imperative to win over those who lived among false gods to live a life and a social bond based on a fellowship of faith.[7]

At the same time, it is equally clear that there are significant differences between the three Abrahamic faiths. As mentioned, unlike the later Abrahamic faiths, Judaism has no conception of proselytism among those not in the fold or of notions of the heathen or *kafir*. The sinfulness of people and the dire need for salvation in Christianity that can be met only by the human incarnation of God suffering the agony of crucifixion has no counterpart in the Muslim view of the world. Moreover, while Christianity demonstrated, particularly early on, some ambivalence towards the political sphere, in Islam, the political foundation for the *umma* of believers was important from the start.[8]

Whereas the radical transcendence of these faiths predisposes them to communitarian distinctiveness and often to intolerance, they also generated vast movements and efforts to bridge the chasm with the non-believers, whether by policies or activities from above or movements from below. Many Islamic and Christian courts – for instance, the court of the Mogul emperor Akbar (reigned 1556–1605) or Roger II of Sicily in the twelfth century – fostered debate and dialog among the different faiths. Within Sunni thought, for instance, the Andalusian debates about free will and God which later fed into the European Enlightenment, revealed a capaciousness among some of its most radical thinkers, such as the mystic Ibn 'Arabi, who was able to dismantle the transcendence–immanence dichotomy.[9] Just as important were the movements outlined by Armando Salvatore that developed periodically among Christian monastic movements – such as the Franciscans – and the Sufi mystic brotherhoods which sought to extend the social bond in the public

---

[7] Stroumsa, *The End of Sacrifice*; see also Salvatore, *The Public Sphere*, pp. 100–1.

[8] Charles J. Adams, "Reflections on the Work of John Wansbrough," p. 89; Stroumsa, *The End of Sacrifice*, p. 107.

[9] See Nazry Bahrawi, "The Andalusi Secular," in Ziauddin Sardar and Robin Yassin-Kassab, Eds., *Critical Muslim 06: Reclaiming Al-Andalus* (London: Hurst, 2013), pp. 47–56. Note how it was also in Andalusia that the mission of the Crusades was developed in relation to a *jihadi* movement. For the relationship of the *Reconquista* in Andalusia to the Crusades, see Roberto Marin-Guzman, "Crusade in Al-Andalus: The Eleventh Century Formation of the *Reconquista* as an Ideology," *Islamic Studies, 31*(3) (1992): 287–318.

sphere through traditions of interfaith understandings, a phenomenon we will revisit in Chapter 5.[10]

Finally, there were also several different religious groupings in non-Abrahamic societies that were monotheistic or had ideas of radical transcendence, but few ever came to dominate the society or region (Sikhism may have been the closest in recent centuries). The later Abrahamic religions were dynamic, transcendent faiths that expanded through various modes of proselytism, including persuasion, trade, politics and violence. Analytically, there were two factors behind the expansionism: theology and political circumstances. Both were necessary but neither was sufficient by itself. The theological imperative to expand the community of believers and dispel non-belief was possible and did occur through trade and missionizing, but it was most efficiently achieved through state violence – or its threat – against non-believers, particularly, when the non-theological ambitions of rulers could also be satisfied.

Comparing the situation with Buddhist conversions, which were rarely accompanied by state violence, Steve Collins makes the following observation. He argues for two types of salvation: (1) where everyone can and should undertake the path; and (2) where everyone is permitted to undertake the path (if individually capable), but no one is required to do it. The first corresponds to Christianity and Islam and the second to Buddhism, especially Theravada Buddhism. Indeed, we can argue that not only in Buddhism but also in most versions of Hinduism, Daoism and Confucianism – whether or not their subsects engage in conversion or bring others into the fold – the path of salvation is open to all (although often very unequally, especially in Hinduism, where it may take well over a million lifetimes). But it is not required of everyone to follow the path strictly and, indeed, only the virtuosos may in fact achieve the *Dao*, sagehood, *moksha* or *Nirvana*.[11]

We can extrapolate Collins' insight further into the nature of the *sovereign subject position* among human communities. Transcendent states and beings frequently authorize sovereign positions, but the nature of this inscrutable position is also important. If it is cognized as an all-powerful, all-knowing and punishing God, it is a position that can be delegated to or inherited by the human subject as the new sovereign. If, on the other hand, authoritative sources in society cognize it as empty or essentially inscrutable – as do Buddhist or Confucian positions – the sovereign subject among humans may also be denied that absolute position.

---

[10] Salvatore, *The Public Sphere.*
[11] Steve Collins, *Nirvana and Other Buddhist Felicities: Utopias of the Pali Imaginaire* (Cambridge University Press, 2003), p. 34.

While the theological disposition may have had a certain logic, histor- ically, there were also political and institutional constraints upon violent conversion or elimination. Particularly in empires, there were important reasons of state to restrain the lethal combination between missionizing and state expansion or plunder. Yet, that combination surfaced periodically – for instance, during the war of religions – in sixteenth- and seventeenth- century Europe, which was stabilized by the Treaty of Westphalia in 1648. However, the spread of confessional religions accompanying imperialism beyond the European states into the New World, Africa and Asia did not result in any such restraint for a long period.

Transcendence and circulation across the Sinosphere

While it is easy to overgeneralize about the non-Abrahamic traditions, there are several points of convergence in the major traditions of Hinduism, Buddhism, Confucianism and Daoism, as well as significant differences between them and the non-Abrahamic religions regarding transcendence, belief and faith. In these traditions, the conceptions of transcendence are often not radically separated from the immanent. Transcendence, however, remains extremely important to them and as a *historical* concept, but it needs to be salvaged from the Abrahamic frame- work. As indicated in Chapter 2, with reference to its epistemological status, transcendence is a *locus* from which the Axial Age religions "sought to take a synoptic view of the world ... and to distinguish the flood of phenomena from the underlying essences."[12] We may think of this locus as the source of reflexivity on consciousness as a whole that is endowed with a powerful moral authority. In turn, this moral authority serves as a historical motor to empower the quest for justice and its ideal of a better world. Indeed, one could also think of the transcendent as an inviolable (sacred) moral space that may not be fundamentally religious but may be a condition for human aspirations, as some would argue is the case of Confucianism. Most fundamentally, it issues in and requires a space that is autonomous from worldly powers. Needless to say, this autonomy is constantly being encroached upon or violated by these powers – whether political, clerical, ideological or even scientific. The Sinosphere, as we will see, reveals its own historical patterns of encroachment.

The field of Chinese religion has long been dominated by the question of whether it was a single integrated entity or whether there were several different traditions that, needless to say, interacted with each other and

---

[12] Jurgen Habermas, *An Awareness of What Is Missing: Faith and Reason in a Post-Secular Age,* Trans. Ciaran Cronin (Cambridge: Polity Press, 2010), pp. 17–18.

with beliefs and practices from outside the state and linguistic space.[13] At present, Western scholarship leans strongly towards the side of pluralism but acknowledges the importance of shared cosmological notions which both influenced and were in turn shaped by plural religions, most notably Manichaeism, Buddhism, Islam and Christianity. These cosmological ideas hold that the universe is a dynamic, organic unity of humans, earthly nature and Heaven operating under the principles of yin/yang forces, the five phases and the eight trigrams. Under these conditions, the different beings have more or less spiritual power (*ling*) – which Palmer and Goossaert gloss as efficacy and charisma – which can also be expressed after death in the form of ancestors, gods and ghosts.[14]

Together with these pluralistic and quite immanent expressions of cosmological power, the conception of Heaven (*Tian*) was widely under-stood as the dominant and encompassing cosmological authority impact-ing the temporal and political world. The Zhou dynasty (1046–256 BCE), which overthrew the Shang, established its legitimacy by elevating the patterned power of Heaven's will – or what David Pankenier calls the 'cosmic imperative'– over the preceding Shang's neglect of Heaven in favor of its 'superstitious' reverence for its ancestors and lesser gods (*shangdi*). Thus, at the beginning of the first millennium BCE, the Shang–Zhou transition marked the change in the basis of kingship from the principle of dynastic continuity to one of emulating Heaven as the paradigm of order and harmony.[15] But as we will see, this was not merely transitional; there remained a dialectic of tension and accommodation between immanent and transcendent cosmic power in Chinese religious and political authority.

I will pursue the Chinese political-religious context – particularly as it deals with neo-Confucianism and the redemptive societies – more closely in the next chapter. Let me make a few preliminary comments about Confucianism and Daoism in relation to the transcendence–immanence dialectic here. Daoism is an enormously pervasive spiritual influence in China which is as difficult to pin down as it is important. James Miller

[13] The historicization of 'traditions' in recent decades requires us to specify what we mean by them. Tradition, such as Confucianism, refers to a self-proclaimed interpretive commun-ity whose concerns and assumptions undoubtedly change over time. Yet, there is an intrareferentiality that is both temporal and spatial and that is frequently focused on questions and points of contention in the tradition. Some of the assumptions in the posing of these points or questions can be shared over a significant period of time, although they, too, evolve.

[14] Vincent Goossaert and David A. Palmer, *The Religion Question in Modern China* (University of Chicago Press, 2011), pp. 20–1.

[15] David W. Pankenier, "The Cosmo-Political Background of Heaven's Mandate," *Early China*, 20 (1995): 121–76, at pp. 172, 174.

reminds us that there are at least four ways to think of Daoism: as an intellectual alternative to Confucianism for the literati, as a mystical philosophy focused on attaining unity with the Dao, as a force in popular culture and as an organized religious tradition.[16]

Daoism shares with Confucianism the wider Sinitic cosmology of the Way (Dao) of Heaven and Earth as a dynamic, evolving, organic process. Yet, for Daoists, the Confucian version of the *Dao* as principally an ethical path was entirely inadequate since it belittled the supreme importance of nature, which embedded the cosmological principles and sacred revelations of Heaven. Moreover, nature – which includes the human body – revealed the principle of dynamic creativity; human actions needed to be judged in relation to their accord with this ceaseless flow of nature. The Confucian preoccupation with civilization and morality was secondary and artificial, prompting humans to overreach themselves and produce aggressiveness. More than ritual, the individual had to turn within to cultivate his own virtue or the *de* that was received from the *Dao* – the *Dao* of which we cannot speak – the *Dao* that points beyond.

Even while it sustained some of these early ideals, Daoism was many other things over history. In the ancient texts, Daoism advocated a "doctrine of liberation through submission, of control by means of non-interference, and of transcendence as a result of physiological and mental regimens."[17] The famed renewal of the covenant between the spirit of Laozi and his followers in the mid-second century CE, which led to the founding of the Way of the Celestial Masters in Sichuan, conferred the charge to reform and supersede the existing order. Subsequently, Daoist groups became associated with utopianism, messianism and periodic insurgency.

Anna Seidel first emphasized the image of the messiah and apocalyptic thought in Daoism. To be sure, the apocalypse was not expected to usher in an absolute beginning but rather the end of one cycle and the beginning of a new cycle of time. Human history proper is a story of decline of human virtues capable of maintaining the harmony of the 'three Heavens'; and so, from time to time, the Dao dispatches a revelatory sage, who establishes sagely rule for a time. Stephen Bokenkamp discusses how, in the first millennium, the founders of the Sui and the Tang dynasties sought to respond to these popular yearnings for the sage-ruler by enlisting the rituals and symbolisms of the by-now interfluent Buddhist and Daoist religions to establish themselves as such. But not long after the

---

[16] James Miller, "Daoism and Nature," Notes for a lecture delivered to the Royal Asiatic Society, Shanghai, on January 8, 2008 (personal communication).

[17] Franciscus Verellen, "Taoism," *Journal of Asian Studies*, 54(2) (1995): 322–46, at p. 322.

establishment of the rule, apocalyptic expectations once again rose fast and furious; and the pattern was repeated long after Tang rule.[18] It is notable that one of the most influential redemptive societies in republican China, the Daoyuan, also predicted the coming of Laozi to usher in a new era just prior to the Japanese military coup in 1931 that established Manchukuo in northeast China. The de facto Japanese rulers made common cause with these societies by utilizing their historical vocabulary and pledging to bring about a Chinese or Asiatic modernity.

The Daoists jockeyed with the Confucians and Buddhists to secure court patronage and legitimate imperial power. Particularly during the so-called Chinese dynasties – the Tang, Song and Ming – the Daoists provided important liturgical services to the court. In the second millennium, Daoist rituals penetrated the interior and peripheries of the empire, where they mimicked the rituals of the court and introduced the 'imperial metaphor' into rural society. But this mimicry took on a life of its own, becoming a source of power in its own right. As John Lagerway says, "[T]here are two religions in China, that of the state-church and that of local society... The state plays God, but it can only do so because local society is a god-producing machine whose prodigious inventiveness still today keeps the state hopping..."[19]

By the Qing period (1644–1911), the Confucianists re-established their centrality in the imperial order, and both organized Buddhism and Daoism were assigned a niche role as monastic institutions subordinated to the imperial ritual order; they were expected to provide specialized services to popular society and the imperial court. But more than in the court or through their clerical organizations, it is in popular society that we see Buddhism and Daoism play a powerful role long before the Qing period. Indeed, since at least the penetration of Buddhism into Chinese society, there have been acknowledged and unacknowledged 'civilizational exchanges' and circulations that have not only been reforming these religions but also producing new syntheses and syncretisms that created the foundations of popular religiosity, in both its transcendent and immanent forms.

The sea change introduced by Buddhism into Chinese culture during the first millennium CE – the Indianization of China, as Dr. Hu Shi put it

---

[18] Stephen R. Bokenkamp, "Time after Time: Taoist Apocalyptic History and the Founding of the T'ang Dynasty," *Asia Major*, 3rd series, 7(1) (1994): 59–88.

[19] John Lagerway, *China: A Religious State* (Hong Kong University Press, 2010), p. 54. See also Kenneth Dean, "The Daoist Difference: Alternatives to Imperial Power and Visions of a Unified Civilisation," *Asia Pacific Journal of Anthropology*, 13(2) (2012): 128–41. For 'imperial metaphor', see Stephan Feuchtwang, *Popular Religion in China: The Imperial Metaphor* (London: Routledge Curzon, 2001).

in the 1930s – has been well recorded. Several decades ago, Eric Zürcher showed how Daoism developed its theological identity chiefly in response to Buddhism, particularly in the areas of the conception of ritual space, Mahayana universalism, and ideas of *karma* and sin. Zürcher admitted that he had not had the chance to study influences in the other direction; in other words, to grasp the circulatory nature of these civilizational influences.[20] Recently, Christine Mollier has fulfilled this incomplete task. By probing the apocryphal Buddhist texts from the Dunhuang collections of *c.* 1000 CE, she shows that there was a two-way flow of influence, particularly since the Buddhists also needed to adapt to the rather different social and cultural conventions in China.

What Mollier reveals in the second half of the first millennium is a feverish traffic between the Daoists and the Buddhists of mutual appropriations, falsifications, denials, excisions of telltale signs or 'cut and paste', and reformatting in the competitive environment of court and society. Thus, an apocryphal sutra has the Buddha preach that life can be prolonged by worship of the Big Dipper, which is none other than the abode of the One supreme, the Dao. Indeed, the Buddhist disguise of the Daoist idea enabled it to circulate not only in Chinese, Korean and Japanese but also through Buddhist central Asia in Uighur, Mongolian and Tibetan recensions. Conversely, the Daoist Guan Yin or Avolokitesvara, Jiuku tianzun, was evidently introduced because the novel savior figure had become too popular for the Daoists to ignore. Visual representations – for instance, in tomb paintings or architectural expressions, various motifs of which have been traced by Tansen Sen and others – often reveal insights into the ways in which symbols from different traditions, often favored by the populace, fuse to serve functional or aesthetic choices, thus pushing back high Culture's predilection for purity even while the representations absorbed new ideals of transcendence.[21]

Indeed, such was the velocity of the traffic that much of theology, imagery, ritual and other practices between the two began to blur. Zürcher had concluded his seminal essay with the image of twin pyramid peaks which merged at the lower levels "into a much less differentiated lay religion, and at the very base both systems largely dissolved into an indistinct mass of popular beliefs and practices"; the two teachings became "branches springing from a single trunk." Mollier suggests that

[20] Erik Zürcher, "Buddhist Influence on Early Taoism: A Survey of Scriptural Evidence," *T'oung Pao*, 46(1–3) (1980): 84–147, at p. 142.
[21] Christine Mollier's *Buddhism and Taoism Face to Face: Scripture, Ritual, and Iconographic Exchange in Medieval China* (Honolulu, HI: University of Hawaii Press, 2009), pp. 136–7, 185; Tansen Sen, "Ancestral Tomb-Paintings from Xuanhua: Mandalas?," *Ars Orientalis*, 29 (1999): 29–54.

the image may be unfortunate because these ideas did not just descend into a mass of superstitions but were picked up by new types of quite sophisticated ritual and scriptural specialists who emerged from the cross-roads, constituting a kind of third party enlivening the religious market-place of medieval China.[22] My sense is that these were the progenitors of the founders and leaders of the redemptive and sectarian societies – charismatic figures with complex and hybrid scriptural knowledge – who spread rapidly during the Ming, Qing and republican periods. As in these later traditions, the transcendent and world-renewing dimension of these doctrinal religions coexisted with their popular and desiring expressions.

With regard to Confucianism, a question that is as stubborn as the one regarding the plurality of religions is whether or not Confucianism is a religion. The question is somewhat misplaced, particularly since, as we will see, the notion of religion has itself significantly come to be shaped by the radical Abrahamic conception. Although Confucian thinkers were not preoccupied with the question of divinity compared to other major civi-lizational traditions, we can identify the notion of Heaven, first as a "God-like deity" but transformed into the Ultimate Principle, as a religious idea throughout Chinese history. This does not mean that there are no agnos-tics or even atheists in the Confucian tradition similar to those we will see in the Indian traditions.[23]

The conception of transcendence or the transcendent factor in the Confucian tradition was not identical over time or for different groups. With Confucius and the early Confucians, Heaven and Earth were meta-phorized as Father and Mother of the myriad creatures, and man was regarded as the most highly endowed of these. For Confucius, Heaven could be considered a deity whose will (*tianming*) is to be realized by man, who has the capacity to harmonize the correspondence between heavenly order and human one. The motive force for transformative harmonization by man derives from the commission of Heaven, or the 'cosmic imper-ative'. The imperatives of the Way: the love, righteousness, virtue and propriety (or rites) which guide the sage (*shengren*) or gentleman (*junzi*) are governing principles of Heaven. For the Confucian gentleman, there is no thought of paradise or hell. Virtue is its own reward and the inner satisfaction of being in accord with Heaven's will.[24]

---

[22] Zürcher, "Buddhist Influence on Early Taoism," p. 146; Mollier, *Buddhism and Taoism Face to Face*, pp. 209–12.

[23] Julia Ching, "The Problem of God in Confucianism," *International Philosophical Quarterly*, *17*(1) (1977): 3–32.

[24] D. Howard Smith, "The Significance of Confucius for Religion," *History of Religions*, 2(2) (1963): 242–55.

Transcendence here may seem relatively weak except that the authentic possibility of the unity of man and Heaven was always elusive and so the gentleman – not to mention the sage – constantly needed to maintain a critical posture towards moral debasement and abuse by power. In other words, the source of ethics in Confucian thought remained outside the realm of worldly institutions even though Confucians sought to realize them in this world. According to Tu Wei-ming, even Dong Zhongshu, the Han dynasty scholar identified as the architect of official Confucianism, predicated his theory of cosmic correlation with earthly events on the assumption that the emperor harmonized his rule morally and ritually with the cosmic process. Outer kingliness could not be achieved without inner sageliness.[25]

The idea of transcendence became clarified once again with the development of neo-Confucianism in the second millennium CE. Instigated by Buddhist religious philosophy – which the neo-Confucians overtly tended to denounce as rejecting human society and the world – the neo-Confucian idea of Heaven expressed as the Heavenly Principle (*tianli*) or the Great Ultimate (*taiji*) was articulated as the First Principle, the Ultimate which is above all limits of space, form and time. According to Zhu Xi, the Heavenly Principle is the principle of both being and becoming as well as of moral goodness (*ren*).[26]

For the heart/mind (*xinxue*) or Wang Yangming school of neo-Confucianism, the Ultimate can only be realized through the self, which has a fundamental, though often unrealized, unity with the universe. Self-realization takes place through the purification of the egotistic desires and moral resolve of the inner subject to act upon the world. Thus, for the neo-Confucianists, the principle is both immanent and transcendent. Everything in the universe has in itself the Ultimate, but the Ultimate is not exhausted by them. Note also how it is the transcendent principle that empowers the individual to (relatively) autonomous moral action, for

[25] Tu Wei-ming, "The Structure and Function of the Confucian Intellectual in Ancient China," in S. N. Eisenstadt, Ed., *The Origins and Diversity of Axial Age Civilizations* (Albany, NY: State University of New York Press, 1986), pp. 360–74, at p. 368. Thomas Metzger refers to this elusiveness as 'elusive immanence'; thus, while there may have been nothing as radically transcendent as the Abrahamic God, the striving and difficulty of finding 'perfection' represented the kind of tension between an ideal order and an imperfect reality that we encounter in Axial civilizations. Thomas A. Metzger, *Escape from Predicament: Neo-Confucianism and China's Evolving Political Culture* (New York: Columbia University Press, 1977). See also the symposium about this book in the *Journal of Asian Studies*, especially Hao Chang, "Neo-Confucian Moral Thought and Its Modern Legacy," *Journal of Asian Studies*, 39(2) (1980): 259–72.

[26] Youngmin Kim, "Political Unity in Neo-Confucianism: The Debate Between Wang Yangming and Zhan Ruoshui," *Philosophy East and West*, 62(2) (2012): 246–63, at p. 256.

ultimate authority resides in those who realize *li*. Indeed, as Youngmin Kim has said, "[T]he moral perfection of the individual self or the perfection of one's own community is not so much an *aspect* of politics; in a sense, it *is* politics."[27]

Transcendence–immanence dialectic in the Indosphere

As in the Sinosphere, the Indic religions tend to be bound not by any single truth or doctrine, but by a set of assumptions and questions. The Vedas and the Upanishads do not specify true propositions, but rather work as foundational texts that shape and govern discourse and debate. To be sure, as the parties to debate and schools of interpretation carry forward the tradition, these traditions themselves change.[28] But as the interpreter reaches back to the text, he also renews the links to the textual tradition, creating an interpretive, interactive bridge between present and past, the subjective and the objective, circulation and reification.

The highest good in Vedic religion was identified with the total harmony of the cosmic order; the social and moral worlds were seen as correlates of the natural order, which in turn reflected an inner order of the universe. The post-Vedic, Axial Age of classical Hinduism, Buddhism, Jainism and other systems of thought developed the moral concept of *dharma* as an abstract, authoritative and autonomous notion, but *dharma* itself was expected to preserve the organic unity of beinghood.[29] Most of these traditions also accepted that phenomenal life (*samsara*) is ultimately suffering and there is an endless cycle of rebirths, that we harvest the fruits of our past acts (*karma*) and that some kind of liberation from this cycle of rebirth (*moksha* or *Nirvana*) can be obtained, even in this life.[30]

Beyond these assumptions, the Indosphere reveals a great variety in conceptions of transcendence and the kinds of relations of the self to the transcendence–immanence framework. Thus, Buddhist doctrine denies not only God but also a notion of Being beyond the universe. For this doctrine, transcendence is to be found in a permanent *state* (*Nirvana*), in contrast to the impermanent states of empirical existence. Like Buddhism, many other Indic traditions historically deny the ideal of the divine Being or an 'eternal soul' (*paramatman*) – and some, like Jainism, continue to deny

---

[27] *Ibid.*, p. 249; Julia Ching, "The Problem of God," pp. 20–3.
[28] J. N. Mohanty, "Some Thoughts on Daya Krishna's 'Three Myths'," in Daya Krishna, Ed., *Indian Philosophy: A Counter-Perspective* (Delhi: Oxford University Press, 1991), pp. 52–3.
[29] Purushottama Bilimoria, "Environmental Ethics of Indian Religious Traditions," paper presented at symposium on "Religion and Ecology," American Academy of Religion Annual Conference, San Francisco, November 1997, p. 4.
[30] Mohanty, "Some Thoughts on Daya Krishna," p. 54.

it – which is accepted by mainstream Hindu traditions.[31] While God or gods may be irrelevant to Theravada doctrine, it does conceive a path to liberation which is to free oneself from the cycle of rebirth. One does so by ethically following the Eightfold Path, which culminates in the highly concentrated meditation, or *dhyana*, a form of yogic cultivation.[32]

The various medieval Hindu conceptions of the self's relation to transcendence have, in the forms of dynamic traditions described above, come down to the modern age. I identify them here with their principal thinkers not to suggest that they have been unchanging since their founding but to clarify the self-identification of the tradition. They are principally affiliated with the post-Vedic philosophical texts known as the Upanishads or Vedanta. The different Vedantic schools have different answers to the relation between the finite self (*jiva*) and *paramatman* (the highest self).

The dualism (*dvaita*) of Madhava (*c.* 1238–1317 CE) treats the souls of individuals as distinct from the supreme God and remains so even in the highest kind of contemplation. Madhava's dualism thus comes closest to Abrahamic theism where the salvation of the worshipper (or *bhakta*) is utterly dependent on the grace of the supreme God, Vishnu, although there are lesser gods subordinate to him. Madhava is also among the very rare Hindu thinkers who hold that there are a class of souls who are eternally damned. Most other sects believe in universal salvation (although possibly after millions of rebirths). At the opposite end of the Vedanta spectrum from Madhava's dualism is Shankara's (*c.* 788–820 CE) monism, or Advaita, in which the eternal self within the individual is basically identical with Brahman, the absolute reality (*paramatman*) that is the ground of all being. The individual needs to undertake ethical, devotional, yogic and meditative practices to overcome the deceptive or illusory world of human perception in order to realize the inner existential bonds with Brahman.

A third tradition is represented by the eleventh-century theologian and philosopher Ramanuja's 'qualified non-dualism', or Vashishta Advaita. As Minkowski puts it, to the question, "Was the Ultimate different from the individual soul? The Advaitins thought ultimately not; the Dvaitins though ultimately so, as the Ultimate was just God; the qualified nondualists ... thought the Ultimate was different from the soul in one sense but not different in another" (Minkowski, 2011: 211). A mere dualism cannot explain the creaturely dependence of all things on God. Nor does

---

[31] Ninian Smart, *The Yogi and the Devotee: The Interplay Between the Upanishads and Catholic Theology* (London: George Allen and Unwin, 1968), pp. 20–3.
[32] Daya Krishna, "Three Conceptions of Indian Philosophy," in Daya Krishna, Ed., *Indian Philosophy: A Counter-Perspective* (Delhi: Oxford University Press, 1991), pp. 5–12.

the rigorous monism of Shankara admit of the reality of this pluralistic world (at least in theory), which is also part of Brahman's nature and not merely illusory. Ramanuja's Brahman is a personal god and ruler of the real world, which is also permeated by his spirit. For Ramanuja, God is both creator and the everlastingness of the cosmos; he is beyond the universe and also emerges within it. Meditation, or *dhyana* as a means of liberation, or *moksha* so important in Shankara's philosophy is not as important for Ramanuja as devotion.[33]

There was considerable interaction and circulation within these traditions through the second millennium. Indeed, Shankara himself created space for difference when he suggested that, while the highest level of realization of one's true identity is with Brahman, for ordinary (or ignorant) people, it was of some merit to identify with and worship lower levels of reality such as a creator God. The highest levels of truth or liberation could be achieved through meditation in its many forms, including yogic practice, and were thus reserved for monks or virtuosos. But there was room for other forms of worship, whether through devotional practices (Shankara himself composed Bhakti hymns) or merit-making and faith in the Bodhisattva. What Ninian Smart calls a 'double-decker' religiosity is none other than an expression of dialogical transcendence representing a kind of capaciousness across Asian traditions. We will find it at work in the modern Hindu reformers of the early twentieth century as well as among overseas Chinese reformers like Kwee Tek Hoay.

Just as neo-Confucianism owed much to Mahayana Buddhist metaphysics, so, too, did Shankara's Advaita, albeit in different ways. Shankara owed the idea of the illusory world partly to the doctrine of the Void (*sunyata*) of Nagarjuna (*c.* second century CE), who was arguably the most important Buddhist philosopher since the Buddha.[34] Nagarjuna's non-dualist ideas were interpreted and adapted, overtly and covertly, by many different – particularly, Indic, Tibetan and Sinitic – traditions. As such, it is important to focus on his ideas, although I admit I will not be able to do justice to them. According to Nagarjuna, phenomena – not just sentient beings – have no fixed substance or essence. Things arise not of their own power but through their conditioned and causal interdependence. Indeed, transformation (becoming) is possible only because of the lack of immutable being. "The Buddha himself was only transformed

---

[33] See also Swami Sivananda, "Advaita and Vishishtadvaita" (www.sivanandaonline.org/public_html/?cmd=displaysection&section_id=704).
[34] Smart, *The Yogi and the Devotee*, pp. 43–4.

because of interdependence and emptiness, and so, Nagarjuna infers, 'the nature of *Tathagata* is the very nature of the world.'"[35]

Nagarjuna developed the foundations of the Mahayana resolution of the role of *sunyata* (emptiness) or *nirodha* (negation). However, while indeterminate reality is the ground of determinate entities, he argues that the former is only the ultimate nature of the latter themselves and not another entity apart from them. Nagarjuna emphasizes the concreteness of becoming and meaningfulness of the sense of self-hood; but it is still essential to show that mundane truth is not the ultimate truth. The Bodhisattvas and the Buddhas derive their all-embracing compassion from this comprehensive understanding – at both levels – of the interrelatedness of the self with the world. This world is Nirvana itself when seen correctly.[36]

Among the more important practitioners of non-dualism in the contemporary world is the Vajrayana Nyingma (Red Hat) school of Tibetan Buddhism. In Dzogchen Rinpoche's words, "Holding to both the oneness and multiplicity of existence takes greater spiritual maturity; it requires being present with the moment with all its paradox and radicalness. Experiencing both the bliss and sorrow of existence takes greater spiritual maturity; it requires us to be present to the entire situation of existence, our own and all others. In terms of our tradition, we describe this as the dance between emptiness and form and our path as the willingness to experience both and their mutuality."[37] In Nagarjuna, the imperative to be "present to the entire situation of existence, our own and all others" is thus expressed:

> Some he (the Buddha) urges to refrain from sins, others to do good,
> Some to rely on dualism, others on non-dualism;

[35] Douglas Berger, "Nagarjuna (*c*.150–*c*.250)," *Internet Encyclopedia of Philosophy*. See also the relevant verse in the *Mulamadhyamakakarika of Nagarjuna: The Philosophy of the Middle Way*, Trans. and Annotated David J. Kalupahana (Delhi: Motilal Banarsidass Publishers, 1991), p. 310.

[36] K. Venkata Ramanan, *Nagarjuna's Philosophy as Presented in the Maha-Prajnaparamita-Sastra* (Delhi: Motilal Banarsidass Publishers, 2011/1966), pp. 62–3, 68–9. See also *Nagarjuna: A Translation of His Mulamadhyamakarika*, with Introductory Essay by Kenneth K. Inada (Delhi: Shree Satguru Publications, 1993).

[37] (http://ngakpa.org/library/not-duality-is-not-non-duality/). Note that the website is not clear as to whether this quotation is from Dzogchen Rinpoche or Ngakma Lama Troma Rinpoche. See, however, similar ideas in Dzogchen Rinpoche, "Taming the Mindstream," in Doris Wolter, *Losing the Clouds, Gaining the Sky: Buddhism and the Natural Mind* (Somerville, MA: Wisdom Publications, 2007), pp. 82–91, at pp. 83, 89: "The heart of our practice is the use of the relative truth of interdependence to arrive at our ultimate nature... Ideally, a practitioner proceeds from the lower levels of practice to the higher levels, and then to the summit. This does not mean that the lower levels of practice are to be disparaged or ignored. We should not focus on the higher paths at the expense of the lower paths."

> And to some he teaches the profound,
> The terrifying, the practice of enlightenment,
> Whose essence is emptiness that is compassion.[38]

At a mundane level of truth, through the recognition of emptiness, the self can be rid of the conviction that it is an essential and autonomous substance. But, in his debates with the Brahmin skeptics, Nagarjuna recognizes that the claim of emptiness itself cannot be absolute because it would be self-contradictory (the *sunyata* of *sunyata*). Since all theories of reality are self-contradictory, the best way to indicate reality is with terms such as 'voidness' or 'suchness' which indicate the indescribability of the ultimate reality and adopt a non-absolute posture. "Without relying upon convention, the ultimate fruit is not taught. Without understanding the ultimate fruit, freedom is not attained." Thus, the emptiness of the world did not prevent the different levels of phenomenalization of the void – such as by the life of Buddha.[39]

In his discussion of Nirvana and Buddhist utopias, Steve Collins has argued that transcendence doctrines are 'machines' for generating the presence–absence discourse. From a sociological perspective, if transcendence is entirely unapproachable for living humans, this would lead to its irrelevance and disappearance – as may be argued from the case of radical Protestantism (see Chapter 5). So, even the most abstracted expression of Buddhahood as a state of non-being is expressed in the present or future world as a focus of anticipation and hope. Through imagery, relics, festivals for the future Buddha, and even the Pali language, as something that exists at the point where eternity meets history, transcendence is linked not only to the immanent but also even to human flourishing.

To be sure, in Theravada Buddhism, not everyone can approach Buddhahood or see the future Buddha when he comes. There is a moral hierarchy which places celibacy and world renunciation (as well as those who practice charity and keep vows) closer to the top than the others. But those closer to transcendence are, by the principle of renunciation, kept apart from worldly power. Since Theravada Buddhism is not theistic in any conventional sense, monks do not regard a ruler or polity as the ultimate sovereign; rather, the true ruler is one who upholds the *dhamma*

---

[38] http://blog.gaiam.com/quotes/authors/nagarjuna Or see *Mulamadhyamakakarika of Nagarjuna*, pp. 331–3: "The teaching of the doctrine by the Buddhas is based upon two truths: truth in relating to worldly convention and truth in terms of ultimate fruit."
[39] *Mulamadhyamakakarika of Nagarjuna*, pp. 331–3.

(*dharma*).[40] Monks and nuns are structurally located so they may engage in a socially sanctioned evaluation and critique of power and the moral order from their epistemic closeness to the *dhamma*. Many monks in authoritarian societies of Asia, whether in Tibet, Myanmar or the rest of Southeast Asia, continue to exercise this role in society, although, in many cases, they have also adapted to the politics of religious nationalism. Since the appearance of transcendent traditions in Southeast Asia, charismatic leaders of peasant movements – including, but not only millenarian rebellions – have, as Rey Ileto and others have shown, authorized their locally based experience of grievance and injustice by developing fragments and even theories from these various philosophies of transcendence. In this way, they have been able to enlarge, if not universalize, their ideal of justice.[41]

The relationship between Buddhism and Hinduism – or rather Vedic religion in early India – is a story of mutual appropriations similar to those we find in the Mediterranean and Middle East, or between Buddhism and Daoism or Confucianism in China. Buddhism emerged as a major challenge to the Vedic sacrificial religion during the Axial Age. According to Sheldon Pollock, Buddhism "transvaluates Vedic Hinduism by semantic appropriation."[42] *Dharma* had been a central concept in Vedic sacrifice and ritualism, which Buddhism turned on its head, developing an entirely new philosophy of rational agency involving the Four Noble Truths, the theory of karmic conditioning, and the necessity of a new self beyond ascribed roles of society. In reply, Vedic Hinduism developed its own transcendent response – an important version of which we have seen in the philosophy of Shankara in the eighth century CE and his interpretations of the Upanishads and the Vedic canon. In a parallel study, Pollock also demonstrates how the Buddhists who had initially renounced Sanskrit for the local languages had gradually adopted it – e.g., Nagarjuna – and its accompanying cosmological status by the early first millennium.[43]

[40] For an example of the modern adaptation of this sense of righteous autonomy in the war-ravaged Cambodia of the mid century, see Ian Harris, "The Monk and the King: Khieu Chum and Regime Change in Cambodia," *Udaya: Journal of Khmer Studies*, 9 (2008): 81–112.

[41] Ray Ileto, "Religion and Anti-Colonial Movements," in Nicholas Tarling, Ed., *Cambridge History of Southeast Asia*, vol. II: *The Nineteenth and Twentieth Centuries* (Cambridge University Press, 1992), pp. 197–248.

[42] Sheldon Pollock, "Axialism and Empire," in Johann P. Arnason, S. N. Eisenstadt and Björn Wittrock, Eds., *Axial Civilizations and World History* (Leiden: Brill, 2005), pp. 397–450, at p. 402.

[43] Sheldon Pollock, *The Language of the Gods in the World of Men: Sanskrit, Culture and Power in Premodern India* (Berkeley, CA: University of California Press, 2006), pp. 53–5.

Bringing up the social history of South Asian religions to the early modern period (*c.* 1500–1800), we can see several parallels with other parts of Asia and Europe at the time. Radical devotional movements among Sufis and Bhakti sectarians intensified their questioning of the hierarchy of the religious establishment on the basis of transcendent authority. At the same time, however, states and elites intensified their power and learned to gradually incorporate these challenges, although not without effecting changes in their power and ideological structures. Both tendencies were of a piece with developments in the rest of the early modern world; post-Reformation Europe may have represented a *particular* culmination of these trends.[44]

Popular challenges and elite responses in South Asia led to reconfigurations of Advaita or non-dualist philosophy, which was, to be sure, also influenced by the Islamic political presence. The Advaita school developed into the 'big tent' of Hinduism, a pluralism in which many views are allowed to coexist because of their common goal or aspiration (recall Assman's 'evolutionary monotheism', Smart's 'double decker' model and the philosophy of Nagarjuna). Combining scriptural, philosophical and devotional religion, it secured its cultural capital in the ancient city of Benares and consolidated its role as the principal spokesman of 'Hindus' to the Mughals. Indeed, this school continued this role into the early twentieth century when Hindu nationalist leaders, such as Vivekananda or Aurobindo, offered a reformed or 'Protestantized' version of this religious philosophy as a model of self-formation and spiritual citizenship for the Indian nation.[45]

The tradition of debate and polemics between different Hindu sectarians during the early modern centuries appears to have been pursued with considerable intensity. The polemical targets of the Advaitins appear not to have been Islam or popular religiosity as much as the dualism of Madhava and his Bhakti successors. As in many such exchanges, despite their ferocity, there was often a mutual reshaping and even efforts to construct new syntheses on the part of dualists and non-dualists. Thus, for instance, the (dualist) Bhakti saint Chaitanya, who introduced what the Benares Advaitins viewed as 'sentimentalist' devotionalism into Bengal, was also said to have been inducted into the Advaita monastic order. At the same time, Jiva Gosvamin sought to establish a strong foundation for Caitanya devotionalism by drawing imaginatively on a

---

[44] Rosalind O'Hanlon and David Washbrook, "Religious Cultures in an Imperial Landscape," *South Asian History and Culture*, 2(2) (2011): 133–4.
[45] *Ibid.*, pp. 136–7.

multiplicity of Vedanta traditions, including Ramanuja and Shankara. On the other side, perhaps the most important late Advaitin of this period – whose popular fame comes from participating in the debates at the court of Akbar – Madhusudana, fundamentally transformed Advaita. By endorsing the pursuit of Bhakti as a valid path independent of Vedantic philosophy while rejecting the dualist *doctrinal* position, he opened up a new era in "the life of the doctrine of undivided Being."[46]

Nor was this accommodating if highly contentious dialogic restricted to Hindu sects. Indeed, debate and exchange was, if anything, sharpened by the ascendancy of Mughal power especially from the mid-sixteenth to the mid-seventeenth centuries under the ecumenical rule of Akbar, Jahangir and Shah Jehan (and Prince Dara Shikoh, who commissioned the translation of the Upanishads and other Sanskrit texts).[47] These rulers rejected the influence of the Naqshbandiyas, who had accompanied their forebears from central Asia and who represented a relatively intolerant Sufi view, in favor of the more homegrown Sufis of the Chishti sect. Recovering the now forgotten though vastly influential work of the seventeenth-century Chishti Sufi 'Abd al-Rahman Chishti and that Sufi tradition, Muzaffar Alam reveals how Chishti rejected the conservative Naqshbandi emphasis on a narrowly construed jurisprudence and offered an alternative vision of tolerance (the *sulh-i-kul*, or 'peace with all', policy of Akbar) in the Mughal imperium under these emperors. Thinkers like Chishti must have been strengthened in their conviction of ecumenical or imperial Islam through the works of not only famed poet-scholars of the earlier period, such as the Persians, Rumi and Hafez, but also contemporaries such as the Egyptian scholar al-Sharani writing in the Ottoman empire, who went so far as to even imply the fundamental unity not only of different sects but also of different religions.[48]

One of the most influential writings of Hinduism in this period, the *Ramcharitmanas* (1574 CE) of the saint, Tulsidas, was created in the language of the Avadh region of north India. Although it is today among the most revered texts for the contemporary Hindutva movement, the *Ramcharitamanas*, as a literary work, was a product of the "exchange of cultural symbols and practices between Hindus and Muslims." It belongs to the literary genre developed by Indian Sufi poets, who transformed older Indian narratives into mystical romances in the Avadhi language.

[46] Christopher Minkowski, "Advaita Vedānta in Early Modern History," *South Asian History and Culture*, 2(2) (2011): 205–31, at pp. 222–3.

[47] *Ibid.*, p. 218.

[48] Muzaffar Alam, "The Debate Within: A Sufi Critique of Religious Law, Tasawwuf and Politics in Mughal India," *South Asian History and Culture*, 2(2) (2011): 138–59, at p. 145.

Thomas de Bruijn seeks to show that this kind of interchange – for instance, of a Sufi genre utilized by a Bhakti poet or, conversely, the intertext of the Ramayana within a Sufi narrative – reveals not necessarily a syncretism but rather a polyphony "defined by the dialogical nature of the traditions involved."[49]

These kinds of early modern works developed in dialog and did not represent fixed religious texts or precepts. However, with the communalization and ethnicization of these works in the colonial public sphere – considerably aided by the rapid circulation of print media – in the late nineteenth and early twentieth centuries, they were increasingly thought of as fixed emblems of fixed religious communities.[50]

But perhaps the most remarkable figure of religious synthesis was the poet-saint, Kabir (1440–1518). Born into a Muslim weaver family in Benares, Kabir remained a working householder through much of his life; he is regarded to this day as one of the greatest poet-saints of the Bhakti tradition. His poetry, which was first translated by Rabindranath Tagore into English in 1915, is widely dispersed in popular, classical and devotional music, and, according to *Wikipedia*, his contemporary followers number close to 10 million around the world.[51] Early twentieth-century discoverers of Kabir celebrated the pluralism and syncretism they found him to represent in the Indic tradition. Evelyn Underhill, who wrote the introduction to Tagore's translations of 1915, observed that Kabir "seems by turns Vedantist and Vaishnavite, Pantheist and Transcendentalist, Brahmin and Sufi." Hindu reformers often identified him with the 'qualified monism' of Ramanujan, but, as the scholarship of Charlotte Vaudeville has shown, Kabir is not easily fitted into the received categories of Bhakti devotionalism; nor was he a simple syncretist. He is profoundly irreverent towards both Islamic and Hindu beliefs, doctrines and clerics.

Hindu and Turk [Muslim] have but one Master
What is the Mulla doing? And what Shaykh?[52]

---

[49] Thomas de Bruijn, "Many Roads Lead to Lanka: The Intercultural Semantics of Rama's Quest," *Contemporary South Asia*, *14*(1) (2005): 39–53, at p. 40.

[50] Note also the observations of Nile Green on the similar transformation of Sufi and Yoga techniques of physical and spiritual cultivation from face-to-face, living and variable forms of knowledge production and instruction to their 'traditionalization' as authentic emblems of cultural, ethnic and national identities. Nile Green, "Breathing in India, *c.* 1890," *Modern Asian Studies*, *42* (2008): 283–315.

[51] The 9.6 million devotees are spread within India and worldwide (http://en.wikipedia.org/wiki/Kabir).

[52] Charlotte Vaudeville, *A Weaver Named Kabir: Selected Verses with a Detailed Biographical and Historical Introduction* (New Delhi: Oxford University Press, 1993), p. 83.

His contempt for the hypocritical scholars and superstitious religious elites of Benares is profound:

I am the beast and you are the Shepherd who leads me from birth to birth,
But you have never been able to make me cross the Ocean of Existence:
   how then are you my master?
You are a Brahman, and I am only a weaver from Banaras:
Understand my own wisdom:
You go begging among kings and princes, and I think only of God![53]

According to Vaudeville, Kabir draws from a long, perhaps even pre-Buddhist tradition of nonconformism and protest in South Asia. She argues that a form of late Buddhism, mingled with Advaitin ideas and concepts of tantric yoga (see below) and magic, had profoundly penetrated the lower layers of Hindu society and many Sufi groups in north India. The kind of yoga practiced by these groups was more method than devotion or even religion. Its ideal of truth and quest for a superior reality or state of non-duality was not to be discovered, but 'realized' through bodily, breathing and sexual practices.[54]

Kabir came to be known as a *nirguna* (formless) Bhakti practitioner who combined Sufi ideas of the *tariqa* or path to God, which is a path of inevitable suffering and ultimate inaccessibility of his Beloved. "Kabīr's conception of divine love seems to be an original synthesis of the traditions of Yoga and of Sufīsm, the former exalting man's effort, the latter making of the yearnings, of the torments suffered by the exiled soul in its mortal condition, the necessary condition for every spiritual ascension. For Kabīr, Bhakti is no longer the 'easy path', but the precipitous path where the lover of God risks his life."[55]

The life and poems of Kabir represent not only an ideational and practical synthesis but also a dense point of convergence involving circulation and transcendence, practice and poetry, discipline and passion, abstraction and love. His poetry succeeds in rendering the most unfathomable, formless expression of God (both Sufi and Advaita) with a tender familiarity. He upholds the transcendent source of authority as intimate without, in the words of Underhill, "entailing the unrestricted cult of the Divine Personality" or the "soul destroying conclusion of monism."[56]

---

[53] Charlotte Vaudeville, "Kabir and Interior Religion," *History of Religions*, 3(1–2) (1963): 191–201. See also *Songs of Kabir*, Trans. Rabindranath Tagore, Introduction by Evelyn Underhill (New York: Macmillan [1915]).
[54] Vaudeville, "Kabir and Interior Religion," pp. 194–5. See also Vaudeville, *A Weaver Named Kabir*, pp. 96–8.
[55] Vaudeville, "Kabir and Interior Religion," p. 199.
[56] E. Underhill, "Introduction," *Songs of Kabir*, p. 27.

In the descriptions I have furnished above, transcendence and immanence are not separated, whether in theory or practice. Although Wang
Yangming and Kabir are worlds apart in many ways, for both, the ultimate
is both immanent and transcendent. Transcendence courses formlessly
through the cosmic process. Let me sum up some of the common characteristics of dialogical transcendence.

First, the two or more levels of truth are seen not as exclusive of each
other but as *negotiatory*. There is frequent acknowledgement that there are
different modes of accessing different levels of transcendent power often
for different goals, such as wish fulfilment, protection, salvation or oneness. The more immanent goals embedded in mundane exchanges
involve partial or relative expressions of the truth at best, but are tolerated.
These different levels do not habitually correspond to different levels of
the social or religious hierarchy, and people from the lower orders or
margins of society frequently contest the claims of the theological and
political establishment. These contestations are often not overtly conflic-
tual, but prophets or rebels from the lower social orders periodically arise
to challenge the betrayals of the self-appointed custodians of 'higher
truths'.

Second, the relationship is frequently one of encompassment.
Encompassing is an act of power as the higher subordinates the lower.[57]
There are different modes of subordination: thus, Brahmins encompass
lower castes by a very strong principle of hierarchy to the point of dehu-
manization. In the Chinese case, Confucian elites periodically deny the
right of alternative 'heterodox' traditions and practices to exist, an attitude
that carries over (or traffics) into modern attitudes against 'superstition'.
However, most of the time, large segments of the Confucian literati
themselves engaged in many of these 'heterodox' practices, thereby com-
partmentalizing them in relation to orthodoxy. By and large, there is a
stronger tradition of tolerance of different religions and practices and
inclusion of nature and creatures.

Third, access to the higher level of transcendence is more often than not
achieved by *practices* of cultivation and discipline (addressed in the final
section). Historically, it has often been adepts and the virtuosos who
undertake the strict disciplinary regimens of bodily and ethical activity
required to cultivate spiritual power and to access the power and moral
authority of the transcendent. Indeed, the practitioner frequently engages
in a procedure that Foucault once described, in a different context, as the
'games of truth', the process of 'subjectivation' or self-formation whereby

---

[57] I am adapting here Louis Dumont's famous idea of 'encompassment' in his *Homo
Hierarchicus: The Caste System and Its Implications* (University of Chicago Press, 1980).

the individual converts his or her experience into truth. In my view, the recognition of having attained the higher truth results in what Weber called charisma, which opens the truth to a broader social milieu.

Finally, immanence and circulation are, of course, analytically distinct categories in my study, but we can also see that dialogical transcendence is more capacious in its actual tolerance of plurality and circulatory histories, however misrecognized the latter may be. Thus, the significance of this dialectic emerges from not only a metaphysical perspective but also a sociological one.

Complexity and dialogical transcendence

In several ways, these philosophies are consonant with process philosophy – the philosophy of becoming – a relatively minor tradition in Western philosophy traceable to Heraclitus (c. 535–475 BCE), but one which counted many important continental philosophers in the twentieth century, including Henri Bergson, Martin Heidegger and Gilles Deleuze as well as the American pragmatists and some analytical philosophers. The great variety of different philosophical systems represented by these thinkers should not obscure the assumption among them that the primary ontological categories should be terms for *occurring* entities.[58]

Speaking *grosso modo*, process philosophy and most Asian traditions, as well as many aboriginal cosmologies, share a number of features. They tend to reject the bifurcation of nature into physical and mental domains, the dualism of concrete facts and abstract principles, and in relation to the philosophy of religion, the opposition between immanence and transcendence, as neither God nor the scientist is entirely outside nature. Rather, they view the universe, including ourselves, as part of interdependent, organic wholes filled with energy and creativity.[59]

In recent times, Alfred North Whitehead, the analytical philosopher of science, has emerged as a major source of inspiration for the scientific philosophy of complexity that is gaining ground in the twenty-first century. Whitehead has been rediscovered by a group of complexity theorists, such as Ilya Prigogine and Isabelle Stengers, particularly for his writings in *Process and Reality*. Whitehead reveals that emergent complexity is not

---

[58] Johanna Seibt, "Process Philosophy," in Edward N. Zalta, Ed., *Stanford Encyclopedia of Philosophy* (Winter 2012 Edition), p. 17. (http://plato.stanford.edu/archives/win2012/entries/process-philosophy/).

[59] See J. B. Callicott, *Earth's Insights: A Survey of Ecological Ethics from the Mediterranean Basin to the Australian Outback* (Berkeley and Los Angeles, CA: University of California Press, 1994), pp. 12, 52–80, and *passim*.

necessarily a directional process with a *telos*. His ideas probably did much to reverse the (one-way) subject-to-object vector so dominant since Kantian philosophy. Indeed, the purposive subject is understood to emerge from the past activity of the universe just as the objective universe is the product of creative subjects.[60] Moreover, ideas or, more accurately, 'conceptual feelings' in the higher organisms express the principle of creativity – or emergence – which for him is the ultimate principle (also known as God).

'Creativity' is the principle of *novelty*. An actual occasion is a novel entity diverse from any entity in the 'many' which it unifies. Thus 'creativity' introduces novelty into the content of the many, which are the universe disjunctively. The 'creative advance' is the application of this ultimate principle of creativity to each novel situation which it originates.[61]

Whitehead, who established his reputation as a philosopher of science and mathematics before turning to metaphysics and society, develops the idea of God through his philosophy of organisms, which bears remarkable similarities to several strains of Buddhist, Daoist and neo-Confucian philosophies. Processes modified by other processes are "immanent in the sense that they affect (by constraining and enabling) how the modified processes occur, but are transcendent in the sense that they are multiply realizable, that is, they are not themselves dependent on the particular spatio-temporal occurrences of the processes that realize them."[62] Creativity, the production of the world as novel, represents the ingression of 'eternal objects' which accompanies the determination of something new (the factual creature) that is not reducible to its physical or material properties. Compare Ninian Smart's statement, "We are co-creators with God in the ongoing dance of Shiva." The cosmic dance of Shiva is the self-expression of the deity which expresses creation and destruction over and over again.[63]

---

[60] Isabelle Stengers, *Thinking with Whitehead: A Free and Wild Creation of Concepts*, Trans. M. Chase (Cambridge, MA: Harvard University Press, 2011); see also Stengers, "Whitehead and Science: from Philosophy of Nature to Speculative Cosmology," n.d. (www.mcgill.ca/files/hpsc/Whitmontreal.pdf).

[61] Alfred North Whitehead, *Process and Reality: An Essay in Cosmology*, Ed. David Ray Griffin and Donald W. Sherburne (New York: Free Press, 1985), p. 21.

[62] Seibt, "Process Philosophy."

[63] According to Smart, Indic cosmology has tended to assume a pulsating cosmos – periodically collapsing into chaos and emerging from it at the beginning of the next cycle. Samkhya philosophy, in particular, delineated a dynamism within the cosmos to explain its evolution out of chaos. Alternatively, re-emergence has to be explained by a divine Being either because atoms require coordination and arrangement or if we suppose that the cosmos emanates from the fabric of Brahman and is periodically reabsorbed therein. Smart, *The Yogi and the Devotee*, pp. 110, 153.

Other contemporary philosophers such as Thomas Nagel, as well as several scientists, have argued for the 'creative emergence' of forms and values that cannot be reduced to physical or even biological processes or be predicted entirely from them.[64] Stuart A. Kauffman argues that natural selection does not create self-organization and self-propagation; rather, self-organization within the biosphere guides selection.[65] The popular idea that 'genes rule' misses the important point that genomes are, in the words of Goodenough and Deacon, "the handmaidens of emergent properties, not the other way around."[66]

Kauffman argues that "self-propagation creates forces that move the reproduction by a few degrees of difference" into what he calls "the *'adjacent possible'* thus creating incremental but genuine novelty."[67] We may gloss the 'adjacent possible' as an emergent path which conveys a contingency, in the sense of dependence or conditioning upon something else, but which is not predictable in advance. Interestingly, the logic of the 'adjacent possible' is not dissimilar to theories of language which attribute the production of meaning – arguably the most productive of emergences – to metaphor and metonymy. This value addition is what Whitehead calls the ingression of eternal objects whereby specific facts or forms acquire their ultimate determination.

Recognition of emergence and contingent determination alerts us to the context and process of scientific development. It tells us that there are circumstances and networks, à la Bruno Latour, which also go into the production of scientific results.[68] The scientist not only is the subject in command of the laws of nature but is also caught up in circumstances which equally shape the results – some of which have applicability and

---

[64] Thomas Nagel, *Mind and Cosmos: Why the Materialist Neo-Darwinian Conception of Nature Is Almost Certainly False* (see especially ch. 5, "Value") (Oxford University Press, 2012).

[65] Stuart A. Kauffman, *Reinventing the Sacred: A New View of Science, Reason and Religion* (New York: Basic Books, 2008), p. 119. Kauffman gives the interesting example of the heart. It is believed that the emergence of the heart for oxygen intake cannot be explained by physics alone – there are many creatures without hearts – but by natural selection. However, the heart also has other causal features (like its thumping sound) with possible selective significance for a different environment. The pumping function of the heart is selected by a self-organizing property because of the heritable variation that produced it in the first place. Moreover, its contemporary salience will predispose evolution in certain directions that are not explicable by natural selection alone but by the emergent principle of self-organization (pp. 86, 131). See also Kauffman's view of Buddhism, pp. 283–4.

[66] Ursula Goodenough and Terrence W. Deacon, "The Sacred Emergence of Nature," in Philip Clayton and Zachary Simpson, Eds., *The Oxford Handbook of Religion and Science* (Oxford University Press, 2006), pp. 853–71, at p. 866; see also see Bellah, *Religion in Human Evolution*, p. 48.

[67] Kauffman, *Reinventing the Sacred*, pp. 119, 266.

[68] Bruno Latour, *We Have Never Been Modern*, Trans. Catherine Porter (Cambridge, MA: Harvard University Press, 1993).

others of which are subject to further revisions. The subject/scientist does occupy a transcendent *positionality* (like the sage) but, dialogically, also requires recognition of her contingent involvement in the world. Among other results, this may generate a greater humility before the natural and social world around the subject; nature and society are, after all, co-producers and have their own requirements and limits.

The two levels of dialogical transcendence may be compared with the part and the whole in emergent complex processes. The two are not exclusive of each other but shape each other – the whole shapes the parts that shape it; moreover, the higher emergent level of the complex system – the transcendent view – encompasses the parts that forms it. The philosopher of religion Mark C. Taylor has made a similar argument about understanding God in relation to the idea of emergence in complexity theory. Even secular thinkers in the Judeo-Christian tradition find it difficult to accept the transcendence–immanence dialectic, perhaps because of the strong dualism in the tradition. For example, such thinkers as Freud and Marx are trapped by the dualism of the deep structure of truth versus surface appearances. Taylor argues that "transcendence is the outside that is inside the system and schema as its necessary condition."[69] The notion of dialogical transcendence I have discussed is closer than radical transcendence to this creative process discussed by Whitehead and Mark Taylor.

To be sure, there is disagreement about the status of the transcendent among the scientists and philosophers of complexity. Kauffman, for instance, avers that "God, a fully natural God, is the very creativity of the universe."[70] Ursula Goodenough and Terrence Deacon place humans at the center of the creative process without reducing the process to our capacities. They believe that human consciousness epitomizes the logic of emergent phenomenon in its very form. Yet, they urge, "Consciousness emerges as an incessant creation of something out of nothing, a process continually transcending itself." Goodenough and Deacon also spell out a religious ethics that flows from their position of thinking of transcendence as 'horizontal', ever opening to the future, which, they aver, should facilitate the deconstruction of the hubris

[69] Mark C. Taylor, *After God* (University of Chicago Press, 2007), p. 127. Deleuze sharpens the implications of the difference when he writes, "[T]here is a big difference between the virtuals that define the immanence of the transcendental field and the possible forms that actualize them and transform them into something transcendent." Gilles Deleuze, *Pure Immanence: Essays on a Life*, introduction by John Rajchman; trans. Anne Boyman (New York: Anne Boyman Zone Books, 2001), p. 31.

[70] Kauffman, *Reinventing the Sacred*, p. 6.

accompanying human ambitions.[71] Yet, without the understanding of the revered and sacred in history, such valuable scientific and philosophical contributions are unlikely to translate into enacted values.

There is also some uncertainty and debate as to how close Whitehead's eternal objects are to God in the religio-moral sense. Are eternal objects simply aspects of occasions having no status of their own? Whitehead is not entirely clear on this question.[72] Remarkably, this is also the question that Nagarjuna faced in the debates of the second century.[73] For Nagarjuna, knowledge of the emptiness of all things allows us to see 'conditioned arising' through the interconnectedness of the world. But in response to the question of whether there is an ultimate condition behind nothingness, he takes the position that this is unanswerable. It is a meta-epistemic issue. In the face of such a prospect, he is left to adopt the appropriate ethical stance from the mundane knowledge of interdependence (compassion) and knowledge that no knowledge can be absolute (humility and the middle way).[74] In the contemporary words of the Thai monk Buddhadasa, "One's realization of the interconnectedness of all things and life forms – which are transient and changeable – will help deflate one's ego, knowing that everyone is one and the same, being subject to the same natural laws."[75]

---

[71] Goodenough and Deacon, "Sacred Emergence," pp. 868–9.

[72] For some, 'eternal objects' are unnecessary in his philosophy; see his contemporary critic, Everett W. Hall, "Of What Use Are Whitehead's Eternal Objects?," *Journal of Philosophy*, 27(2) (1930): 29–44; see another critique in the next note. For others, 'eternal objects' are "pure potentials for the specific determinations of fact." See Victor Lowe, *Understanding Whitehead* (Baltimore, MD: Johns Hopkins University Press, 1962), p. 43.

[73] For the similarity and difference between Whitehead and Buddhist thought, see Sean Esbjörn-Hargens and Ken Wilber, "Toward a Comprehensive Integration of Science and Religion: A Post-Metaphysical Approach," in Philip Clayton and Zachary Simpson, Eds., *The Oxford Handbook of Religion and Science* (Oxford University Press, 2006), pp. 523–46. The authors argue in both the Whiteheadian and Buddhist notions there is the idea that each moment is a momentary, discrete, fleeting subject that apprehends *dharmas* or momentary, occasions. In their view of 'integral post-metaphysics', however, this is a third-person generalization of a first-person view of reality in a first person. Each moment is not a subject prehending an object; it is a perspective prehending a perspective. They are particularly critical of Whitehead's 'hidden monological metaphysics' (p. 538).

[74] For Nagarjuna, see Ramanan, *Nagarjuna's Philosophy*, p. 68; see also Douglas Berger, who writes, "Pretense of knowledge leads to ruin, while genuine skepsis can lead the human being to ultimate knowledge. Only the method of skepticism has to conform to the rules of conventional knowing, for as Nagarjuna famously asserts: 'Without depending on convention, the ultimate truth cannot be taught, and if the ultimate truth is not attained, nirvana will not be attained.'" Douglas Berger, "Nagarjuna (c.150–c.250)," in *Internet Encyclopedia of Philosophy: A Peer-Reviewed Academic Resource* (www.iep.utm.edu/nagarjun/).

[75] Quoted in Amare Tegbaru, "Local Environmentalism in Northeast Thailand," in Arne Kalland and Gerard Persoon, Eds., *Environmental Movements in Asia* (Richmond: Curzon Press, 1998), pp. 151–78, at p. 170.

This response furnishes us with the clue to the value of transcendence. The 'great ultimate', the Dao, Shiva's dance and eternal objects give possibilities in their flow and so we co-create. Humans have the capacity to recognize the transcendent source of the gift and revere it so as not to arrogantly abuse or destroy it. This recognition represents the moral dimensions of the human relation to the transcendent. Its absence leads to human overreach. Reverence is accompanied by inviolability, and, to be sure, this is often colored by what we call the sacred, tending to limit the application of reason to the inviolable. Whitehead thought it was possible to combine reason with reverence, as do many of the intellectual traditions of the East, more or less. But the interface between reason and the inviolable is hardly stable or certain; as a result, history as we know it does not end. Reason debates and fights over its limits; it is also often overcome by terror and hope.

Transcendence is precisely transcendent in that it is not fully knowable; hence, it is underspecified if not unspecified. *Tian*, Dao, Brahman and Nirvana are not active beings imposing and demanding belief, particularly of non-believers. As such, they are meta-epistemological concepts – or Simmel's bridge between the subjective and the objective – that have the capaciousness to accommodate lesser gods and beings required by the needs of human flourishing. To be sure, beliefs about gods and contracts with them are subordinated, relativized, encompassed or ordered by the more purist transcendent traditions. But although transcendence is not knowable or *fully* accessible, all of these traditions have highly developed means of access to it which are varied and multifarious. Indeed, one may think of these means as techniques or, more systematically, technologies to cultivate the mind and body. As such salvation or perfection tends to be more accessible to the virtuoso: the yogi, the meditator, the *qigong* master, the Daoist adept, the Arhat or Luohan, the Confucian sage and the renouncer-sanyasi who show the path or give guidance to the merely mortal.

Approaching the transcendent

Among neo-Confucians the debate about human access is between whether the 'great ultimate' can be approached through learning and ethical conduct (Zhu Xi school) or potentially by anyone able to ethically cultivate the mind through action (Wang Yangming). But in all of these traditions, the unanimously accepted attitude in approaching the ultimate is reverence or *jing*. The neo-Confucian is ideally infused with profound awe and respect for the ultimate, and this attitude is necessary to achieve identification with *tianli*. All things and events – especially in the human realm – are sacred and have to be honored. Kiril Thompson writes, "Cultivation then is a multifaceted process of interpersonal practice, attitude building and continuous learning whereby one seeks to fulfill one's inner 'mandate' and become a 'consummate person', socially involved and cosmically attuned."[76]

Other points of contact with the transcendent can be found, *inter alia*, in ritual, sacrifice, bodily cultivation practices and even language. Regarding language, for instance, David Shulman argues that it is a particularly important link to transcendence in the Hindu-Buddhist world. The goddess who inhabits speech may reveal herself only when the grammarian and the literatus master their materials in a highly disciplined and logical way. Similarly, the path to transcendence via the rationalities of cultivation, whether through yoga, music, astronomy or other rational arts, is particularly developed in the Indic forms. "Thus in India we might seek an axial moment of insight in the radical negation of any external frame and the restoration of a powerful, though continuously self-transforming, continuity in cosmic domains."[77]

With reference to ritual, the earlier scholarly arguments about its study in these societies revolved around whether participants engaged in ritual orthopraxy; in other words, whether it was enough for the people in these societies to go through unquestioned motions in the sacred realm conducted by clerics or ritual authorities. Implicit in the idea of orthopraxy is the narrative that while the virtuosos may lead lives of transcendentally sanctioned discipline, the masses thoughtlessly follow the didactics of ritual. Thus, the Protestant revolution which brought belief, sincerity and individuality to the masses in parts of the West was poised to engineer the transition to modernity.

The more recent contributions, particularly in a collectively edited volume by Adam B. Seligman *et al.*, entitled, *Ritual and Its Consequences* (2008), have shifted the ground of debate to argue that ritual praxis must be seen against the pressures brought on by Reformation ideas of truthfulness and sincerity. The older generation of scholars, they argue, have brought their own partiality or assumptions about the higher value of sincerity to the understanding of ritual, thus negating a valuable form of sociality that is missing in modern society.[78] Ritual may be needed once

---

[76] Kiril Thompson, "The Religious in Neo-Confucianism," *Asian Culture Quarterly*, *15*(4) (1990): 44–57, at p. 50.
[77] Shulman, "Axial Grammar," p. 381.
[78] Adam B. Seligman, Robert P. Weller, Michael J. Puett and Bennett Simon, *Ritual and Its Consequences: An Essay on the Limits of Sincerity* (Oxford University Press 2008).

again to restore a sense of the inviolability of our most treasured resources and values.

Indeed, for much of the world, ritual remains a vastly important domain that allows the common people to approach the transcendent in the present. In a discussion of recent ritual practices in southern China and Southeast Asia, Kenneth Dean shows how the ritual specialist often combines many different ritual technologies from the ambient traditions of Daoism, Buddhism, and syncretic and mediumistic practices. He illustrates how syncretic and Daoist ritual enables the communication and negotiation between different temporalities and worlds in these particular liminal moments. The ritual processes "make the body of the ritual specialist into a kind of membrane or Moebius strip linking inner worlds and the processes with the space of the altar, the temple, the courtyard, the village, and the entire ritual territory." The ritual master also reworks time. "The principal visualization of the Daoist ritual master involves a journey backwards through time to the Undifferentiated Dao. Meanwhile, the laying out of talismans and the reciting (re-revelation) of scriptures accelerate and complete cycles of cosmic time, generating merit for the community and the ritual master." In my view, this is none other than the performance of dialogical transcendence.[79]

Bodily practices remain extremely important modes of accessing the transcendent in Asian traditions. Tantricism represents perhaps the most developed tradition of yogic cultivation practices. Tantric beliefs and practices, which developed from the sixth century CE in opposition to Vedic norms and rituals – often relegating the latter to a lower or outer level of scriptural authority – were as developed in the various Hindu traditions in South and Southeast Asia as in Mahayana Buddhism. As Buddhist practice, they continue to hold their own with other expressions of Buddhism in Japan, and they are, of course, the predominant form of Tibetan Buddhism (Vajrayana). The common thread running through various tantric ideas is the divinization of the body. The body is part of a 'hierarchical and emanationist cosmology' in which lower levels emerge from higher ones: from refined matter to physicality. In their practice, the body recapitulates this structure by tracing a route back through the cosmos to the divine source from which it emerged before it became immured in materiality – often by utilizing the body's physicality. The body is thus both the map and the means of salvation.[80]

---

[79] Kenneth Dean, "The Daoist Difference: Alternatives to Imperial Power and Visions of a Unified Civilisation," *Asia Pacific Journal of Anthropology*, 13(2) (2012): 128–41, at p. 138.
[80] Gavin Flood, *The Secret Tradition of Hindu Religion* (London and New York: I. B. Taurus, 2006), pp. 29–30. See also Dominic Goodall and Harunaga Isaacson, "Tantric

Different strains of tantrism bear a different relation to orthodoxy, but, except for the extreme ascetic sects (such as the *atimarga* of Saivism), their transgressive qualities have often had the effect of reconfiguring orthodox or householder practices rather than replacing them. The emphasis on bodily cultivation as opposed to ascribed status permits a variety of people to seek pathways to salvation and also to omnipotence – that is, for both liberation and occult power. Thus, tantric notions are involved in or associated with devotional or Bhakti practices, powerful female deities, sexuality, magic, martial arts, and, not least, breath control, which is considered among the highest forms of meditation and physical cultivation even beyond tantrism.[81]

The control of breathing – 'as universal praxis and cosmic principle' – to be found in yoga and *qi* traditions has a special place in the traditions of dialogical transcendence in Asia, including Sufi practices. While textually elaborated theories explain how these techniques can produce a better life and enlightenment, the methods were developed within particular, sometimes secretive, face-to-face, living traditions handed down through particular schools or monasteries.[82] In precolonial South Asia, these practices and legends about breath control were often shared between yogis and the Sufi adepts. As Peter van der Veer has shown, these techniques were also cultivated by warrior ascetics in precolonial India, who combined their breathing techniques with martial arts.[83]

In China, the *qi* traditions – now better known as *qigong* and popularly associated with the martial arts – were also cultivated for a variety of other reasons associated with meditation, ethical action, improved health, medical practices, universal salvation and, especially, transcendent power. These practices spread among the populace in late imperial China; the networks of the practitioners were capable of scaling up to entire social movements directed against the establishment, as in the White Lotus uprisings of the eighteenth century, and among the Boxers (or Harmonious Fists) in their resistance to Christian missionizing in North China.[84]

Traditions," in Jessica Frazier, Ed., *Continuum Companion to Hindu Studies* (New York: Continuum, 2011), pp. 122–37. My thanks to Andrea Acri for opening up the field of Tantric studies to me.

[81] Alexis Sanderson, "Saivism and the Tantric Traditions," in S. Sutherland, L. Houlden, P. Clarke and F. Hardy, Eds., *The World's Religions* (London: Routledge and Kegan Paul, 1988), pp. 660–704, at pp. 661–6.

[82] Nile Green, "Breathing in India, *c.* 1890," *Modern Asian Studies*, 42 (2008): 283–315.

[83] Peter van der Veer, *Gods on Earth* (London: Athlone, 1988).

[84] Joseph Esherick, *The Boxer Uprising* (Berkeley and Los Angeles, CA: University of California Press, 1988); Paul A. Cohen, *History in Three Keys: The Boxers as Event, Experience, and Myth* (New York: Columbia University Press, 1998).

Contemporary scholarship seeks to historicize these bodily practices, observing how they have been used at various times for different purposes, cosmological and practical. In particular, the assumed closeness of these techniques of the self to textual traditions has been deconstructed. With the development of modern print culture and the emergence of national or confessional communities, the elites in these societies, who recognized and celebrated their value, sought to extricate these bodily techniques from the living cosmologies and environments in which they were embedded and insert them into textual traditions of modern spirituality and even science. For instance, Gandhi called himself a *karmayogi* – the yogi of action – and conducted his "experiments with truth" as a form of yoga.[85] Today, they are utilized by the middle classes for a variety of de-stressing programs. Nonetheless, the connection to the transcendent has not disappeared; nor have they been fully transformed into a cosmologically emptied modern spirituality.

David Palmer has explored the "*qigong* fever" that arose in China during the 1990s when the regime permitted and even supported the practice of traditional Chinese culture. Since the 1950s, the PRC had periodically promoted *qigong* (bodily and breathing practices designed to cultivate *qi* or life energy) as an aspect of traditional Chinese medicine and as a scientific practice (whose laws have still not been fully discovered by modern science). For a variety of reasons, including the perceived low-cost healing value of *qigong* and a "love affair between a part of China's scientific community and the charismatic masters and their political supporters," a veritable boom involving the activities of thousands of masters, over 100 million practitioners, and their organizations, networks, publications and publicity reached a peak in the late 1990s.[86] The Falun Gong, among several other groups, emerged as a significant force in this environment. More recently, Farquhar and Zhang have studied the emergence of a milder expression of cultivating and nurturing forms of everyday life – gentle exercise, simple food, fresh air, regular habits, etc. – known as *yangsheng*, which they regard as a living tradition that is being brought back to liveliness. More and more though, these practices look like principled expressions which search for their principles in the classics of Chinese tradition.[87]

---

[85]   van der Veer, *Gods on Earth*, p. 12.
[86]   David A. Palmer, *Qigong Fever: Body, Science, and Utopia in China* (New York: Columbia University Press, 2007), p. 300.
[87]   Judith Farquhar and Zhang Qicheng, *Ten Thousand Things: Nurturing Life in Contemporary Beijing* (New York: Zone Books, 2012), p. 234.

Returning to 1999, the Falun Gong's massive, highly placed and mobilized – albeit pacifist – following, rattled the regime and brought a sharp and violent end to this fever. Although it started out as a 'scientific' and secular practice, its meaningful pursuit was such that *qigong* could not be disembedded from the cosmological system whence it developed. As Palmer says, the body is the "'temple' of the sectarian adept," and the goal is to cultivate the energies of the body so it can discover the inner connection with the ultimate cosmic power.[88] Therefore, the modern state remains anachronistically locked into the old imperial paranoia about the power of the transcendent – a power which may be cultivated in the body of the citizen.

I must return in the end to 'belief', the idea that is so central to the Abrahamic faiths and which surely continues to exist among hundreds of millions in Asian societies. However, belief in the non-Abrahamic traditions – for instance, among the followers of Bhakti devotionalism (of Vishnu or Meera) or lay followers of Mahayana Buddhism – represents something quite different from belief in the confessional faiths. Confessionalism requires full and unconditional belief in the entirety of a religious teaching. Different interpretations of the story of revelation are not tolerated. For the bulk of the believers in Asian societies, there is often no exclusive loyalty to a single overpowering God or to the exclusive truthfulness of a single story. People may differentiate gods according to different needs or functions. In Singapore, a Chinese student may worship at not only the Chinese temples but also the proximate Indian ones to ensure success in the examinations. She may settle on one that may be most efficacious – for the moment. Yet, the sense of self may be shaped not only by these contractual relations with the gods and the clothes she wears, but also, perhaps in equal measure, by fragments of cosmic doctrines and ideas that she has heard, practiced and embodied in her habitus.

Conclusion

I began my understanding of transcendence as a meta-epistemic locus for the authoritative moral understanding of the world which inherently or ultimately tended to elude domination by worldly powers, even though the history of the world is the history of the attempt to dominate this locus. I tried to show how a dialogical notion of transcendence suggests something *real*, but not knowable precisely. It is the elusiveness

---

[88] Palmer, *Qigong Fever*, pp. 287, 291.

of this real – which has been depicted as the truth, eternal objects or the ultimate – that has drawn both the powerful and the powerless to it as a resource. We can understand it as real because it has ontological or creative *effects* not explicable by human agency or science alone. But precisely because it is metaphysical, it must remain for the analyst, an epistemic placeholder – a locus pointing to something beyond.

Recognition of transcendence not only acknowledges something greater that enables us to do what we do as humans; it also generates awareness that history is not simply the product of human activities but a co-production with the natural world and with 'eternal objects' beyond our understanding. The historical sense has to acknowledge these limits not by adopting irrational postures but by a renewed attitude of humility regarding the limits of human activity. More than most historians recognize, the subject–object dualism – 'the world picture' – informs our view of the autonomy of the human subject capable of world mastery. It is by recognizing the ways in which the transcendent has worked through history – through both the moral empowerment it has authorized historically and the limits it had set on human overreach – that a dialectics of transcendence can remain relevant to our world.

Unlike the Hegelian dialectic, the conception of dialogical transcendence is not one of synthesis, sublation and supercession (*aufheben*) of contradictions. Rather, in the mode of circulatory transformations, it is one of exchange, competition, coexistence and partial absorption often under the sign of denial. In later chapters we will also see further elaborations: instances of camouflage, partial accommodation and superscription. Even formulations of transcendence and associated notions of asceticism, discipline, sacrifice and transformation are shaped by these circulations, although their advocates may voice the shrillest denials. To be sure, this leads just as surely to tensions between the populace and those – clerics, Confucians, Brahmans or even rebels, among others – who seek to purify the tradition and rid it of the foreign, superstitious, heterodox or other circulatory phenomena. But these dominant or hegemonic traditions have never managed to establish exclusive power over the plurality, impose conversions, or restrict their vision to solely human concerns.

In part, this has to do with imperatives in the doctrine or canon, but it also has to do with the role of the state and the historical organization of social power, a subject to be considered in later chapters. We may also question whether the ideals of disciplined realization or transformation among the virtuosos or particular groups can be of general social significance unless it is mobilized by modern organizations and technologies – thereby eliminating the coexistence of plural traditions. We will take up this theme with the redemptive societies, Gandhi and others, but at the very least we can affirm that dialogical transcendence has remained relevant for many who seek guidance for moral transformation of self and society.

5   Dialogical transcendence and secular nationalism in the Sinosphere

When religious systems began to cease legitimating political structures over the last few hundred years, they were replaced, ultimately and in most cases, by secular nationalisms. After an extended period of religious wars in Europe from the sixteenth to the early eighteenth century, the Europeans, according to a broad understanding of secularism, brought religion under an enlarged state order and sought to protect minorities from majority religious groups, and, ideally, from the state itself. While much of this narrative may still hold, the complex and implication-laden history of the transition in its global context is still poorly understood. As we will see, nationalism inherited and reconfigured confessional polities rather than rejected or annulled religious politics in Latin Europe. As a kind of secularized confessionalism, the nation became an engine of conquest over peoples and nature.

Although the details of this transition are obscure, nationalists, reformers and leaders in Asian societies began to recognize the importance of both confessional nationalism and secularism in order to resist and compete with the Western powers from the late nineteenth century. In this chapter, I explore these processes in East Asia, where institutionalization was less affected by *direct* colonial rule than the rest of Asia (examined in Chapter 6). In order to track the impact of these forces, I will explore the changing relationship between state and religions in late imperial China, focusing mostly on the Qing period (1644–1911). I also examine the impact on segments and groups in Chinese popular religion who accommodated diversity by modes of dialogical transcendence. What became of the techniques of self-formation linking the self/body (*shen*) to the local and to universal ideals in late imperial China?

I argue that the Chinese case has largely escaped the conflicts among confessional communities through much of its history. It also largely escaped the late nineteenth- and early twentieth-century penetration of faith-based models of nationalism that appeared in Japan, which is discussed at the end of this chapter (it also appeared in India as discussed in the Chapter 6). But if the Chinese case escaped both these developments, it suppressed and continued to deal with another type of problem, a vertical division – state and elites versus popular religiosities – rather than a lateral competition in the realm of transcendence and faith in the modern transition.

Confessional communities and nation-states in Europe

Confessional communities, we have seen, carried within them the potential of national societies. While they differed from national societies in that they were not territorial states and did not possess modern technologies of integration, the identity of the believer *qua* believer in these confessional faiths was constitutive of the community. Indeed, we might think of them as *potentially* or *dispositionally* vertically integrated communities where state, church or clergy, and believer are one under God. Privilege and hierarchy within this community were doctrinally a secondary matter.

Moral authority in medieval Christian communities derived from the institutional and ideological power of the Church, which directly controlled the people and the state; the latter, in turn, also controlled the people. Max Weber identified hierocracies as political societies where the religious leader is the ruler or where the ruler acquired his legitimacy through religion.[1] The Judaic kingdom and the 'exemplary' Roman Empire and its various successor state forms in the Middle Ages represent the ideal form of hierocracy. Weber distinguished these polities from the Caesaropapist pattern which dominated the Eastern Christian Church from the sixth to the tenth centuries as well as the Russian, Turkish, Chinese and Persian systems.[2] In these empires, the emperor's legitimacy, based upon alternative traditions of royal charisma and sacrality, was relatively autonomous from that of the Church. At the same time, Weber claimed that "wherever religious charisma developed a doctrinal system and an organizational apparatus, the Caesaropapist state, too, contained a strong hierocratic admixture."[3]

---

[1] See this discussion in Max Weber, *Economy and Society: An Outline of Interpretive Sociology*, Ed. Guenther Roth and Claus Wittich (Berkeley and Los Angeles, CA: University of California Press, 1978), pp. 1158–67.

[2] Max Weber, "Sociology of Rulership and Religion," in *The Max Weber Dictionary: Keywords and Central Concepts*, Ed. Richard Swedberg and Ola Agevall (Stanford University Press, 2005), pp. 22–4 (www.cjsonline.ca/pdf/weberdict.pdf). Bendix and Roth believe that Weber linked both "hierocracy and caesaropapism in one historical model" where the former means the political domination of priests and the latter signifies the ruler's control over the priesthood. Reinhard Bendix and Guenther Roth, *Scholarship and Partisanship: Essays on Max Weber* (Berkeley and Los Angeles, CA: University of California Press, 1971), p. 124.

[3] Weber, "Sociology of Rulership and Religion." While Weber regarded the Chinese imperial system as Ceasaropapist in some sense, there was no institutionalized Church or *ulama*

A clear link between hierocracies and confessional societies – such as the Church – could realize the potential of vertical integration as a national model. But Weber did not link the state form to confessional communities. However, he did distinguish the congregational communities from Asian religious communities particularly in the ways they identify themselves. Weber recognized that once a congregational community is established by priestly doctrine or 'dogma', the community feels a "need to set it apart from alien, competing doctrines and maintain its superiority."[4] There are, of course, many other ways of marking out a congregational community from another, such as body-painting (or marking of the forehead as some Brahmin communities do), circumcision or choosing Friday instead of Saturday for worship and rest.

Weber was convinced that "Asiatic religions [on the other hand,] knew practically nothing of dogma as an instrumentality of differentiation."[5] According to him, even the great schism of the Second Buddhist Council (c. fourth century BCE) over the ten points involved 'mere' questions of monastic regulations. In India, theological and philosophical debate was contained within the schools of thought, who were permitted wide latitude by orthodoxy. In China, where Weber considered Confucianism to be dominated by bureaucratic rationality, its "ethic completely rejected all ties to metaphysical dogma, if only for the reason that magic and belief in spirits had to remain untouched in the interest of maintaining the cult of the ancestors." On the other hand, in the Abrahamic traditions, doctrine as constitutive of membership became more and more important. "For Islam, (Zoroastrians), Jews and particularly, Christians, dogmatic distinctions, both practical and theoretical, became more comprehensive as priests, community teachers, and even the community became bearers of the religion."[6]

While, in fact, there have been many cases of congregational and even confessional communities east of West Asia, none became politically dominant over any extended period, perhaps principally because of the absence of a centralized, church-like institution in these societies. As a

---

to restrain it. Although Caesaropapism was prevalent in the Russian Tsardom, John Meyendorff has vigorously contested the claim that it became an accepted principle in Byzantium. Not only did several saints resist the imperial power, but also, on several occasions, people of the Church, both laypeople and monks and priests, refused to accept orders and rules at variance with the Church's customs and beliefs. Meyendorff believes that these events demonstrate that the power over the Church really was in the hands of the Church itself – not the emperor. John Meyendorff, *Byzantine Theology: Historical Trends and Doctrinal Themes*, rev. 2nd edn. (New York: Fordham University Press, 1983), pp. 5–6. See also Swedberg and Agevall, *The Max Weber Dictionary*, p. 23.

[4] Max Weber, *The Sociology of Religion*, Trans. Ephraim Fischoff (Boston: Beacon Press, 1964), p. 70.

[5] *Ibid.*, pp. 71–2.   [6] *Ibid.*, pp. 72–3.

result, the above type of vertical integration was rarely achieved in China and India even when faith-based communities were generated within them. The Sikh faith in the eighteenth century under Maharaja Ranjit Singh may have come closest to such a community when they briefly held state power, but it was not committed to active proselytization.[7]

However, while there may have been a tendency for the confessional congregations or communities to align with the hierocratic state, even in the Holy Roman Empire and its successor states, the pre-Renaissance states did not exhibit the full overlap between state, community and religion/culture that I argue is the basis of the identitarian polities. As discussed above, the imperial principle, which requires a measure of internal autonomy and self-management of communities for the sake of the stability of the empire, in addition to the presence of Ceasaropapist elements (seeking alternative religiosacral or magical powers for kingship not dependent on Church or congregation), tended to counteract the emergence of the communitarian or identitarian polity. Such a political form emerges chiefly after the Reformation in western and northern Europe.

Even as the power of the Holy Roman Empire declined from the thirteenth century and Renaissance ideas began to take hold, the states in Europe still had considerable trouble claiming legitimate authority, which remained in the sphere of religion and the Church. Between the 1320s and the late seventeenth century, there were many experiments which sought to found normative authority outside the Church (see Chapter 1), but it was not until the Protestant Reformation and the ensuing religious wars of the sixteenth and seventeenth centuries that normative authority – the rightful application of force and violence – began the long journey of moving away from a religious framework.[8] Recent research has found that the shift began, perhaps not unsurprisingly given the argument I have been building, with a conflation of religious identity – more or less – with the new state structures. In other words, before the twentieth-century disavowals (however partial) by nationalism of religious affiliation, there was an intensification of confessional solidarity with the state in northern Europe.

Confessionalism in Europe from the sixteenth to the eighteenth centuries was a decisive factor in the emergence of modern states,

[7] T.N. Madan, "Religions of India: Plurality and Pluralism," in Jamal Malik and Helmut Reifeld, Eds., *Religious Pluralism in South Asia and Europe* (Oxford University Press, 2005), pp. 57–8, 71–2.
[8] Ingrid Creppell, "Secularization: Religion and the Roots of Innovation in the Political Sphere," in Ira Katznelson and Gareth Steadman Jones, Eds., *Religion and the Political Imagination* (Cambridge University Press, 2010), pp. 23–45.

identities, nationalism and what Heinz Schilling calls the "saddling up to modernity" (*Vorsattelzeit der Moderne*).[9] In the early years, it was Spain and Sweden that represented the 'most closed models' of confessional states. Spanish Catholic identity was based significantly on medieval self-assertion towards Muslim Arabs where the principle of the necessity of common religious belief (*religio vinculum societatis*) overlay the older doctrine of purity of blood (*limpieza de sangre*) and became the means to cleanse Spanish society. In Sweden, the Reformation met with little friction or opposition, and Lutheran confessionalization of the early modern state was key to the rise of Sweden as a great European power.[10]

In *Faith in Nation*, Anthony W. Marx argues that the religious wars following the Reformation in the sixteenth century were often – though by no means always – manipulated by monarchs and elites to further their own ends. The outpourings of religious passion laid the groundwork for identity and loyalty that could be utilized for purposes of regime and state strengthening.[11] The unity of religious belief was often accompanied by the standardization of the vernacular, and, in England, the use of English as the liturgical language played an important role in the creation of confessional identity.[12]

These passions were directed as much against minorities within as against enemies outside the state. Once states were able to mobilize the confessional passions, they sought to "solidify and enforce a religious sect as unitary, excluding others, as a basis for increasing cohesion." Many of these earlier divisions were later papered over by nationalist amnesia (or what Renan called the 'necessary forgetting'), although important vestiges remained as festering sores. "For instance, the crucial role of antagonism against the Irish Catholics in solidifying the English as a Protestant nation was later subordinated to the image of a United Kingdom, even if never fully abandoned."[13]

[9] Heinz Schilling, *Early Modern European Civilization and Its Political and Cultural Dynamism*. The Menahem Stern Jerusalem Lectures (Lebanon, NH: Brandeis University Press, University Press of New England, 2008), pp. 12–15.

[10] *Ibid.*, pp. 21–5.

[11] Anthony W. Marx, *Faith in Nation: Exclusionary Origins of Nationalism* (Oxford University Press, 2003), p. 29.

[12] Hagen Schulze, *States, Nations and Nationalism. From the Middle Ages to the Present* (Oxford: Blackwell, 1996), pp. 118–20. In Germany, although Martin Luther's translation of the Bible created the basis of German national unification, the battle between the confessions hung in a precarious balance, petrified by the territorial criterion of statehood: *cuius regio, eius religio*. Thus, the unification of the German nation was delayed until the Prussian state was able to unify it through state power (p. 130).

[13] Marx, *Faith in Nation*, pp. 29, 31.

Philip S. Gorski refers to the early modern period of the sixteenth and seventeenth centuries as the 'Mosaic moment' dominated by a 'Hebraic nationalism', particularly among the Dutch and the English and, later, the Scots, the Americans and the French.[14] The Dutch Republic (1588–1795) was founded largely by Calvinists and grounded in a biblical narrative which regarded the Netherlanders as a 'chosen people' bound to God by a holy covenant. According to Gorski, the 'Hebraicist program' pressed the goals of religious conformity and unity by suppressing non-orthodox and non-Calvinist groups, creating an autonomous Church and strong central government, and enforcing strict work and moral discipline.

State formation was closely tied to institutional and bureaucratic formation based on the education and training of personnel in the confessional churches and systems of surveillance and discipline in the formation of selves.[15] In another study, Gorski has shown how the ascetic ethos deriving from the new Protestant mode of faith in transcendence mobilized individual discipline and a disciplinary reform agenda for the collectivity.[16] In economic terms, what Schilling calls 'confessional migration' during these centuries was a major movement of skills, talents, and mercantile and banking wealth from persecuting societies to states of common faith or asylum.[17] The movement of Calvinists and Sephardic Jews from the south to the Netherlands, in particular, was highly significant. Needless to say, these virtues and resources were very important in securing the status of the Dutch as the rising naval and economic nation in the seventeenth-century world.

To be sure, scholars like Gorski do not only emphasize the Abrahamic dimension of this early modern nationalism; they also recognize several other narratives, such as that of ancient Batavia for the Dutch Republicans, or that of England as the new Rome. But the Protestant – indeed, Calvinist – element in both England and the Netherlands played a crucial role in the nationalisms of both societies. Both Gorski and Marx also feel that too strong an emphasis has been put on the revolutionary nature of French nationalism. It, too, was tied to Catholicism and there were levels of violence similar to those in Britain over religious differences which – in Anthony Marx' logic – created a coherent majority in France.[18]

---

[14] Philip S. Gorski, "The Mosaic Moment: An Early Modernist Critique of Modernist Theories of Nationalism," *American Journal of Sociology*, 105(5) (2000): 1428–68.
[15] Schilling, *Early Modern European Civilization*, pp. 22–3.
[16] Philip S. Gorski, *The Disciplinary Revolution: Calvinism and the Rise of the State in Early Modern Europe* (University of Chicago Press, 2003).
[17] Schilling, *Early Modern European Civilization*, pp. 45–55.
[18] Anthony W. Marx, *Faith in Nation*, p. 27.

Nonetheless, it is equally important to recognize the different type of nationalism ushered in by the French Revolution of 1789. It was based not on a religious covenant but on a social contract; popular sovereignty was not the same as being the chosen people. Without denying the religious basis of early modern national identity, Ingrid Crepell has explored the ways in which the political authority of the state gradually emerged as the guarantor of stability and tolerance towards minorities, and this was expressed as a kind of civic nationalism in the nineteenth century thereby absorbing into itself the normative authority that the Church had begun to lose many centuries before.[19]

This new scholarship on the transition from the early modern to the modern in Europe is refreshing in several ways, including the ways in which it takes into account the once-elided role of religion and identity in modern history. But it remains an internalist, Europeanist account of the vast changes taking place precisely at the time when European societies were encountering the world in an unprecedented way (as discussed in Chapter 1). I am not equipped to undertake this enormous research, but I would like to pose some questions that might justify placing this encounter at the center of the discussion. First, to what extent was the 'disciplinary revolution' and the underlying transcendent revolution in purpose and conduct important for the competitive, capitalist successes of the Dutch and the British on a global scale?

Second, to what extent is the sublimation of the faith-based nation into the civic nation a coherent and irreversible process? I have tried to show in several of the chapters that some measure of faith – the regime of authenticity – informs every nationalism, more or less. Historical circumstances have catalyzed highly intolerant nationalisms at different times, often with genocidal ferocity, as we saw in Nazi Germany. Indeed, my discussion of Carl Schmitt in the next chapter will reveal the extent to which he saw the friend–enemy relationship of nation-states exactly on the model of confessional nationalisms.

Periods of heightened national exclusivity are often tied not only to the circumstances of global competition but also to the particular ways in which nationalism became tied to imperialism. During the period in which I have specialized – the late nineteenth and early twentieth centuries – nationalism across the world was galvanized by imperialism,

---

[19] Ingrid Creppell, "Secularization: Religion and the Roots of Innovation in the Political Sphere," in Ira Katznelson and Gareth Steadman Jones, Eds., *Religion and the Political Imagination* (Cambridge University Press, 2010). Schilling, *Early Modern European Civilization*, believes that it is the legacy of Roman law and the older Christian idea of separation of church and state that finally gave protection to minorities (pp. 28–33).

creating a feedback loop that climaxed in the two World Wars.[20] The late-comer nations, Germany, Japan, Russia and others all sought to create a sleek, competitive nation with a highly mobilized and faithful population directed against internal and external enemies in order to gain the largest share of world resources. That process, I submit, began in the seventeenth century.

Transcendence and imperial authority in China

A quotation from a minister explicating cosmology to the king of Chu is recorded in the fourth-century BCE text *Guoyu*:

Anciently, men and spirits did not mingle ... [there were special men and women called *xi* and *wu*] who supervised the position of the spirits at the ceremonies, sacrificed to them, and otherwise handled religious matters... [But later] Men and spirits became intermingled, with each household indiscriminately perform-ing for itself the religious observances which had hitherto been conducted by the shamans. As a consequence, men lost their reverence for the spirits, the spirits violated the rules of men, and natural calamities arose. Hence the successor of Shaohao, Quanxu, charged Chong, Governor of the South, to handle the affairs of heaven in order to determine the proper places of the spirits, and Li, Governor of Fire, to handle the affairs of the Earth in order to determine the proper places of men. And such is what is meant by cutting the communication between Heaven and Earth.[21]

K. C. Chang notes that this myth is the most important reference to shamanism and its central role in ancient Chinese politics in early China. He argues that the king himself was the most important shaman, and he and his priests sought to monopolize access to the sacred authority of Heaven. In other words, the emperor aided by his ritual specialists claimed monopoly of communication with sacred power not only with regard to other clergy or churches but also with regard to the people. This modality of historical authority was very different from other so-called Axial Age civilizations.

Axial Age theory, it will be recalled, draws from a Weberian lineage and stresses the importance of transcendence for the intellectual capacity of rationality and abstraction as well as for ethical universalism. Both Weber and the early post-World War II Axial Age theorists were doubt-ful about whether Chinese civilization possessed a truly transcendent

---

[20] See Prasenjit Duara, *Sovereignty and Authenticity: Manchukuo and the East Asian Modern* (Lanham, MD: Rowman & Littlefield, 2003), ch. 1.

[21] K. C. Chang, "Shamanism and Politics," in Chang, *Art, Myth and Ritual: The Path to Political Authority in Ancient China* (Cambridge, MA: Harvard University Press, 1983), pp. 44–5.

perspective.[22] Eisenstadt and the more recent Axial Age theorists have revised the earlier views to suggest that transcendence in Chinese civilization had a this-worldly ethical orientation. But Weber's observations are worth revisiting. Weber suggested that China lacked transcendence because of the Caesaropapist character of the emperor and because the patrimonial bureaucracy, which he identified very closely with Confucianism, was opposed to any metaphysical idea that would challenge the ancestral cult or what we today call 'lineage ideology'.

Contemporary studies indicate that Weber got much right even though we cannot agree with his characterization of transcendence in China. Confucianism cannot be fully identified with bureaucratic rationality, and, while it was committed to lineage ideology, at different times and among different segments, it revealed a commitment to what I have called dialogical transcendence. More importantly, as indicated in Chapter 3 and explored further below, Chinese civilization is not exhausted by the imperial state and the bureaucracy. But, as the quotation from the *Guoyu* suggests, through the exertion of his Caesaropapist authority, the Chinese emperor sought not only to protect his shamanistic monopoly or charismatic legitimacy from other religious authorities but also to systematically preclude any other potential competitor. At the same time, the wider acceptance of the transcendent authority of Heaven necessarily introduced a 'strong hierocratic admixture', as indicated in the notion of the 'loss of the mandate of Heaven,' albeit without a priesthood.

In contrast to the vertically integrated, congregative Abrahamic societies, Chinese imperial society was thus vertically divided from the perspective of transcendence. Although the empire was constituted by the axiom of 'all under Heaven' (*tianxia*), only the emperor was permitted access to transcendent power. A panoply of gods, spirits and ancestors could be worshipped by the rest of the population to satisfy their desires for 'human flourishing'. The general ban on the worship of Heaven, however, is worth reconsidering: why was the ban enforced so fiercely unless it represented a significant symbolic source of cosmic authority? Indeed, the long history of popular uprisings challenging the mandate of Heaven is evidence of the immense power of this transcendent authority.

Cosmologically, imperial authority was forged not only through the concept of Heaven but also through a non-Axial Age tradition of sacred

---

[22] For a perspective from within the study of Chinese philosophy that categorically rejects any theory of transcendence in Confucianism, see Roger Ames, *Confucian Role Ethics: A Vocabulary*. Ch'ien Mu Lecture Series (Hong Kong: Chinese University Press, and Honolulu, HI: University of Hawaii Press). Note, however, that most postwar New Confucians, such as Mou Zongshan and Du Weiming, assert a view of Confucianism as closer to what I have termed 'dialogical transcendence'.

authority that may have even preceded Shang and Zhou China. Anthony Yu has clarified a body of scholarship that has suggested that there were two forms of religious authority in China: Heaven and the ancestor. The emperor made both kinds of claim for his absolute sovereignty. One was in the cosmic realm of the relations between Heaven and Earth, and the other was in the realm of human relations. The former derived from a transcendent Heaven and the latter from a non-transcendent but no less powerful cult of the imperial ancestor, who also had sacral potency. For instance, for punitive expeditions during the Shang period, the emperor had to receive the mandate from ancestor Di. It was this pre-Axial Age tradition of ancestor worship – or what Yu calls 'ancestor-making' whereby rituals transform a kinsman into a symbol of divine power – that authorized the emperor to trump or pre-empt the transcendent power of Heaven.[23]

Ritual was perhaps the most important expression of the imperial cosmological statement. As the axis of the cosmos, the emperor per-formed his unique role as the only human who could connect Heaven, Earth and man through the grand sacrifice to Heaven. At the same time, he also conducted the ancestral ritual which made him the exemplar of filial piety. As such, he was both the sage-king who embodied *wen* (Culture) and the human imperial son, the filial paragon (*xiao*). How the imperial institution negotiated the two statuses ritually is explored by Rawski in the imperial death rituals when the emperor, in mourning for his mother, had to delegate an official to perform the annual sacrifices at the official altars for the first hundred days.[24]

From the earliest times, the imperial state appears to have possessed the organizational capacity to prevent clergy and other religious authorities from developing an institutional independence, although it often patron-ized these religious authorities with an eye to their efficacy in magical matters as well as the spiritual authority they might command over the people. Mahayana Buddhism in China had reached out to the state as early as the fifth century CE to escape destruction by either a capricious ruler or competitive elites. The *Scripture for Humane Kings*, an apocryphal text attributed to the Buddha, was designed as a proposal for a Buddhism-

---

[23] Anthony Yu, *State and Religion in China: Historical and Textual Perspectives* (Chicago and Lasalle, IL: Open Court, 2005).

[24] Angela Zito, *Of Body and Brush: Grand Sacrifice as Text/Performance in Eighteenth-Century China* (University of Chicago Press, 1997); Wang Aihe, *Cosmology and Political Culture in Early China* (Cambridge University Press, 2000), pp. 206–8; Evelyn Rawski, "The Imperial Way of Death: Ming and Ch'ing Emperors and Death Rituals," in James Watson and Evelyn Rawski, Eds., *Death Ritual in Late Imperial and Modern China* (Berkeley, CA: University of California Press, 1988), pp. 233–5.

protecting model of emperorship and was subsequently transferred from Tang China to Korea and Japan. The principal idea of the text is that the state and Buddhists should serve each other.[25]

Charles Orzech undertakes a deft linguistic analysis to demonstrate how the Buddhists employed familiar Confucian vocabulary to identify the emperor as the sage-king who was equivalent to a Boddhisattva possessing the virtue of 'forbearance' (*ren*).[26] The true king and the Boddhisattva were part of the same continuum and cosmic order. The mid Tang monk at the imperial court, Bukong/Amoghavajra (eighth century CE) did much to institutionalize this Buddhist plan for the emperor for a period and create a kind of dual sovereignty. Bukong oversaw the building of a series of monastery complexes, such as those on the five peaks of Mt. Wutai, that became increasingly important, particularly as the non-Han dynasties performed their role as Boddhisattva, a model of Buddhist imperial rule directed towards the Tibeto-Mongol nomadic world.[27]

The emperor of the Mongol Yuan dynasty in China, Kublai Khan, was posthumously considered an incarnation of the Boddhisattva Manjusri on Mt. Wutai, and the Manchus portrayed themselves as reincarnations of Manjusri, worshipping frequently at Mt. Wutai. During the republic, Mt. Wutai re-emerged as a major site for the negotiations over the nature of the Chinese rule of Tibet. Indeed, by the time of the Qing dynasty in the seventeenth century, the Chinese emperor wore several different faces of sovereignty. To the Han Chinese populace and bureaucratic elites, he was the Son of Heaven as well as the exemplary descendant of the imperial ancestor, Di. Among Manchus and the tribespeople of the northeast, he patronized Manchu shamanism, and, for Buddhists, the emperor was the Boddhisattva, Manjusri.[28]

As the imperial patron of patrons, all religions flourished under imperial rule as long as there was no challenge to their authority, whether based on

---

[25] Charles D. Orzech, *Politics and Transcendent Wisdom: The Scripture for Humane Kings in the Creation of Chinese Buddhism* (University Park, PA: Pennsylvania State University Press, 1998).

[26] Charles D. Orzech, "Puns on the Humane King: Analogy and Application in an East Asian Apocryphon," *Journal of the American Oriental Society*, 109(1) (1989): 17–24, at p. 21.

[27] Charles D. Orzech, "Metaphor, Translation, and the Construction of Kingship in *The Scripture for Humane Kings* and the *Mahāmāyūrī Vidyārājñī Sūtra*," *Cahiers d'Extrême-Asie, 13* (2002): 55–83, at pp. 72–3.

[28] Susan Naquin and Evelyn S. Rawski, *Chinese Society in the Eighteenth Century* (New Haven, CT: Yale University Press, 1987), pp. 29, 145. See also Gray Tuttle, *Tibetan Buddhists in the Making of Modern China* (New York: Columbia University Press, 2005), pp. 88–92.

transcendence or other grounds. When Marco Polo sought to convert Kublai Khan to Christianity in the thirteenth century, Polo relates his response: "There are four great prophets who are reverenced and worshipped by the different classes of mankind. The Christians regard Jesus Christ as their divinity; the Saracens, Mahomet; the Jews, Moses; and the idolaters, Sogomombar Khan [Buddha], the most eminent among their idols. I do honour and show respect to all the four."[29]

The concerns of the Chinese emperor with regard to proselytizing religions were made abundantly clear by the Yongzheng emperor who famously told the Jesuit missionaries at his court in 1724: "You want all the Chinese to become Christians. I know well that this is something required by your religion. But if that happens what will we become? The subjects of your kings?" Later in the century, the governor of Fujian observed about the Christian community in the province, "From antiquity up to now, for example, the *dharma* of the Buddha and the Teachings of the Dao have been spreading in China, but [followers of those teachings] have never gone beyond diffusing their scriptures, charms, talismans, or *dharma* techniques, and having people believe in those things. They never went everywhere proselytizing."[30]

By the beginning of the second millennium, the imperial establishment had more or less succeeded in co-opting the organized religions of Buddhism and Daoism. The two religions were institutionally controlled by state licensing and surveillance. Tolerance and even support for these religions at the court and among the elites allowed for pluralistic scriptural development, building projects and cultural achievements. But this co-optation came at a cost. As Hubert Seiwert observes, the transformation of Confucianism, Daoism and Buddhism into orthodox religions implied their 'purification' and a distancing from popular cults, especially those who were suspected of opposition to the imperial mandate and heterodox morality.[31] At the same time, as we see below, ideas of transcendence, millenarian change and renewal of the moral order in popular culture came to be informed by Buddhist, Daoist and even Confucian ideas transmitted by literati and religious entrepreneurs at the margins of those religions.

[29] *The Travels of Marco Polo*, Ed. Peter Harris (London: Everyman's Library Classics & Contemporary Classics).

[30] Quoted in Eugenio Menegon, *Ancestors, Virgins and Friars: Christianity as a Local Religion in Late Imperial China*. Harvard Yenching Institute (Cambridge, MA: Harvard University Press, 2009), pp. 119, 134.

[31] Hubert Seiwert in collaboraton with Ma Xisha, *Popular Religious Movements and Heterodox Sects in Chinese History* (Leiden and Boston: Brill, 2003), pp. 3–5.

The imperial state's relationship with Confucianism was more complex.[32] From one perspective, the political history of China may be seen as a contest between imperial authority and Confucian or Confucianized elites seeking to claim the authority of Heaven. We are familiar with the drastic measures taken by the imperial unifier, the first emperor of the Qin, to destroy Confucianism by burning the books and burying scholars alive. The subsequent Han dynasty sought to incorporate the Confucians, and, indeed, it developed Confucianism into a state ideology. Less known, however, is that it was during the Han that Confucius was 'made' into a lineal descendant of the Shang. Thus, he was converted into an imperial ancestor who gave the emperor the greater right of ancestral access to his worship.[33]

From the Confucian perspective, the elite had to fight both the incorporation by imperial power and the challenge posed by the Buddhists (and to a lesser extent, the Daoists). Indeed, it is possible that by fighting the stronger notion of transcendence of the Buddhists they were forced into an alliance with the state. The importance of the non-Axial Age practice of ancestor worship among Confucians was a principal cosmological doctrine that brought them within the embrace of the imperial state, particularly since, in principle, the Buddhists rejected the very concept. Indeed, according to Kai-wing Chow, the orthodox Confucian reaction against the heart–mind school of neo-Confucianism emphasized not simply ritualism but also ancestral ritualism and the lineage system to counter the moral autonomy of the Taizhou neo-Confucianists and syncretists. Indeed, some among the orthodox Zheng Zhu neo-Confucianists attacked their rivals' views of Di as a supreme deity and insisted on regarding the Di rite as the rite to the king's first ancestor. They thus associated this imperial rite with the ideology of the descent-line of the emperor rather than with the worship of Heaven.[34]

Early Chinese religiosity did not seem to associate death with the transcendent principle of Heaven. Rather, ancestor worship was the non-Axial Age mode of responding to the problem of death. Ancestor-making involved elaborate, regular and continuing ritual performances and sacrifices. Ancestors did not disappear into a transcendent or entirely different world; they continued to have effects in the world of humans. Only those ancestors who were not cared for with proper sacrifices and rituals

---

[32] C. K. Yang, *Religion in Chinese Society* (Berkeley, CA: University of California Press, 1967).

[33] *Ibid.*, pp. 45–7.

[34] Kai-wing Chow, *The Rise of Confucian Ritualism in Late Imperial China: Ethics, Classics, and Lineage Discourse* (Stanford University Press, 1994), p. 145.

became restless spirits and ghosts, while those who were cared for properly conveyed good fortune to their filial descendants. Such an anthropomorphic conception of the deceased applied not only to ancestors but also to heroes or virtuous men whose spirits protected communities by occupying the title of a tutelary deity such as the City God.

A second mode of co-optation of the Confucian literati was none other than the famed bureaucracy and the examination system. Indeed, the latter was more important than the former because, while the bureaucracy absorbed a small number of officials, the examination system churned out hundreds of thousands of lower degree holders ineligible for office or still larger numbers who aspired to join the degree-holding elite but failed to qualify. These were nonetheless people who had been trained often from childhood in the Confucian classics and orthodox ideology.

Because of the various difficulties of surveillance over a large modern-sized bureaucracy, the imperial bureaucracy was relatively small in relation to the society it governed. Thus, it had to rely on an ingenious model of local government without requiring too much of the imperial government. By the nineteenth century, there was one representative of the bureaucracy governing from 300,000 to 400,000 people. The imperial state was able to govern by delegating the symbolic power of the government while at the same time keeping public funds – ideally – out of the reach of those to whom it delegated this power. The literati or degree-holding gentry (*shenshi*) recruited through the examination system possessed the 'accreditation' and symbolic power to distinguish themselves as an elite by their formal access to officialdom. Thus, they were designated as community representatives who had the sanction of the imperial state to manage their own problems (perhaps the *fengjian* model of imperial times did have an influence). The gentry society model involved the entrustment of an ideologically state-oriented elite with the imprimatur of state power without expending fiscal and political power on social maintenance.

By the Qing dynasty (1644–1911), an orthodoxy had thus been built around the imperial state, which included the lineage ideology, a state-oriented literati and an elaborate state cult. The last named included reverence to Confucius and Confucian doctrines, but it was by no means exhausted by them. The sacrifices and reverences (*jisi*) performed by the emperor, as the supreme priestly figure, to Heaven and deities such as Guandi, the god of war and loyalty, were reproduced through the state cult of sacrifices by bureaucrats and village leaders all the way down to the tutelary deity (*tudi*) of the village. This was the territorial-ascriptive and bureaucratic model of religion (it combined *jisi* and *jiao* as teaching). This territorial and bureaucratic organization allowed the rituals to be synchronized across the empire in what we may call the *ritual synchronization of the polity* as the performance of power.

This elaborate and capacious apparatus of ideological orthodoxy, which included cosmological and institutional modes of securing elite loyalties, was thus made possible in large part by the existence of a relatively open meritocratic system which fostered aspirations of upward and state-ward mobility among the elites. The genius of this imperial system may be seen in comparison to the European states, which were radically transformed by the commercial and cosmological (Protestant) revolutions. The Chinese state was able to forestall the destabilization caused by the pervasive commercialization which burgeoned from the Tang Song transition. In Europe this destabilization ultimately led to the rise of new commercial classes that overthrew the imperial orders, but in China the rural and urban commercial elites were often co-opted into the imperial system.

Although the imperial orthodox order was able to secure the collaboration of significant segments of society, particularly the elites, I do not want to overemphasize the co-optation of these intermediate groups. Ironically, the longevity of the imperial institution in China was due not only to their partial co-optation but also to the role and continuing participation of local literati and even lineages in a counterculture that the state could have opposed but tolerated as long as there was a superficial acknowledgement of the orthodox order. It is to the strategies and tactics in the repertoire of dialogical transcendence to which we now turn.

Dialogical transcendence and popular religion

Although the emperor claimed exclusive access to Heaven, the Chinese imperial model was not a theocracy. Local communities were permitted to worship a panoply of gods and religions, and the court itself was filled with a variety of jockeying religious representatives. But the imperial state remained suspicious of popular cults and spirit mediums for harboring heterodox views, not only because they might seek to usurp the mandate of Heaven, but also because they engaged in ideologically 'destabilizing' activities, such as the unauthorized mixing of men and women. Periodically, both state and elites conducted campaigns to sweep out popular religions that were not state-oriented or part of the state cult, such as those led by Chen Hongmou in the eighteenth century. Thus, many of the ideas and practices related to alternative conceptions and popular access to Heaven were driven deeper into popular culture, where they mingled and often camouflaged themselves in the thicket of popular religiosity. Here it would be difficult to do what a minister of the state of Chu had counseled: "to cut the communications between Heaven and

Earth" so as to prevent "each household indiscriminately performing for itself the religious observances."

Early observers of community religion in village society were deeply impressed by the pervasive presence of the state cult, particularly as expressed in the tutelary gods and the celestial bureaucracy modeled on the imperial bureaucracy.[35] More recently, Stephan Feuchtwang and others have argued that the differences between the state cult and popular religion were both organizationally and cosmologically significant. Popular religion conceived the cosmos as more personalized and violent, with threatening and rewarding forces operating through mythic efficacy.[36] Licensed institutionalized versions of Buddhism and Daoism seem to have had a relatively marginal role in the lives of ordinary people by the late Qing period.

But what I have earlier identified as the cultural nexus of power in rural society – networks of communities, beliefs and practices through which local leaders exercised their normative leadership and mediated the relationships of the community with the outside within a cultural framework – also served as a series of overlapping, camouflaging and translucent canopies from the viewpoint of higher authorities and orthodoxy. These canopies mediated between the higher and lower levels and often camouflaged alternative claims to and of transcendence, temporalities, and social statuses. Thus, Buddhist monks were mainly called on only to perform funerary rites and Daoists as experts in exorcism and prophesy, but communal religion frequently absorbed non-orthodox rites and ideas from these religions. This absorption was relatively unsupervised because many of these monks and priests were themselves not ordained or socialized by institutionalized Buddhism and Daoism.

Under the canopies, popular religiosity turned out to be a vibrant field of communication and negotiation, accommodation and adaptation, and camouflage and resistance between state orthodoxy and popular cultural nexus, enabled in part because different groups of elites participated in several different spheres between the top and the bottom. In an earlier study of the Guandi cult, I tried to show how the imperial state sought to appropriate the popular and apotheosized hero from the Three Kingdoms as an orthodox figure elevated to the highest of gods and carrying the classics in one hand, even as popular lore told martial stories of his bandit-like exploits and vows of sworn brotherhood and loyalty. The figure and

---

[35] Arthur Wolf, "Gods, Ghosts and Ancestors," in Arthur Wolf, Ed., *Studies in Chinese Society* (Stanford University Press, 1978), pp. 131–82.

[36] Stephan Feuchtwang, *Popular Religion in China: The Imperial Metaphor* (London: Routledge Curzon, 2001), pp. 74–84.

myth of Guandi was superscribed by various groups and communities at all levels of society, drawing on older and contemporary interpretations, each marked by a distinctive interpretation to serve its own charter. At the same time, the imperial version of the Guandi myth was acknowledged and mobilized for other purposes. Villagers in north China would duly worship him on his imperially sanctioned birthday at the moment of ritual synchronization, but also on his locally celebrated birthday. As such, the myth of Guandi not only preserved the diversity within a capacious culture, but also served as a medium of communication and negotiation among different groups.[37]

Since popular religiosity was often embedded in community religion, local elites, particularly the non-literati elites, participated actively in them at multiple levels. Thus, on the one hand, they took part in the state-mandated territorial cults, but also undertook the leadership of local ceremonies and communal festivals, including the all-pervasive practice of spirit mediumship. In parts of south and southeast China, the notion of locality was stretched out over considerable territory by the very acts of ritual and ceremonial commemoration interlinking temple commun-ities.[38] Such activities were important expressions of community leader-ship, networking and sources of authority for the local elite. This cultural nexus also accommodated alternative if not always subversive forms such as the growing number of syncretic and redemptive societies at the end of the Qing period.

Buddhist and Buddhistic sectarian groups often utilized the tropes of popular culture to accommodate orthodoxy and negotiate the salvationist aspects of the religion, which was sometimes viewed as heterodox. In particular, renunciation was regarded as antifilial. The popular story of Mu Lian, in which children who had taken the vow of celibacy nonetheless perform the greatest and most valorous deeds of filial piety, rescuing their immoral parents from evil forces, represents this kind of accommodation. The sectarian, sutra-reading societies' ideal of salvation was particularly attractive to women, who also found in them an alternative form of sociability outside the home. The story of Miao Shan – an incarnation or stand-in for the Boddhisattva Guan Yin – speaks particularly to a kind of sectarian, feminist filiality. In this story a young woman who refused to marry the man of her father's choice is thrown out of the family and joins a nunnery. However, when her family subsequently suffers great troubles,

---

[37] Prasenjit Duara, "Superscribing Symbols: The Myth of Guandi, Chinese God of War," *Journal of Asian Studies*, 47(4) (1988): 778–95.
[38] Kenneth Dean, "Local Communal Religion in Contemporary Southeast China," *China Quarterly*, *173* (2003): 336–58.

she returns with the powers of the Boddhisattva to rescue them. The story of the Daoist immortal, Han Xiangzi, tells a similar tale of defying his intolerant Confucian uncle, but ultimately saving him in an act of deliverance. Such were the types of negotiation between mundane orthodoxy and suspect transcendence in the dialogical model.[39]

Of course, at the other extreme, there were groups and societies that were much harder to camouflage even under these multiform and fluid cultural canopies. Several sectarian movements – inflected by Daoism and Buddhism – also harbored millenarianism and the coming of a sage to herald a new world. The messianism contained in their notion of transcendence more closely resembled the Abrahamic traditions, including the imperative to convert others in order to be saved during the apocalypse. The sources of popular millenarianism in China were several, including the Buddhist conception of time as *kalpas* (ages), but also the role of the spirit medium able to access the will of Heaven. By the nineteenth century, such millenarianism could be found among sectarian Daoist or Buddhist societies and also among a few redemptive societies who appealed to Confucian notions of Heaven and sought to access the will of Heaven through spirit writing. This is, of course, precisely what had alarmed the minister from Chu.

Indeed, as many scholars have pointed out, popular rebellions throughout imperial Chinese history were often inspired by religious and particularly prophetic movements. These included the Daoistic Yellow Turbans (184–205 CE), the Way of the Five Pecks of Rice (also second century CE) and, later, Buddhistic or syncretic movements such as those associated with the White Lotus (a term for different rebel groups which combined different ideals of transcendence in the middle centuries of the second millennium), as well as, later still, Taiping Christianity. Perhaps most interesting in this regard, from the point of view of dialogical transcendence, are the Christian Taipings, who ruled vast territories in south China from 1850 to 1864. While, as Christians, the transcendent God was the central feature of their religiosity, it was through the older Chinese tradition of spirit possession that the Taipings sought to establish their authority. They represented a creative intertwining of the transcendent authority of God (*shangdi*) and the popular authority of spirit mediumship. However, their severe iconoclasm directed against popular images and idols alienated them from vast segments of society. Note how even the

---

[39] Daniel Overmyer, "Values in Chinese Sectarian Literature," in David Johnson, Andrew Nathan and Evelyn Rawski, Eds., *Popular Culture in Late Imperial China* (Berkeley, CA: University of California Press, 1985), pp. 219–54. For Han Xiangzi, see Yang Erzeng, *The Story of Han Xiangzi: The Alchemical Adventures of a Daoist Immortal*, Trans. and Introduced Philip Clart (Seattle, WA and London: University of Washington Press, 2007).

Boxers at the turn of the century cultivated exercises to draw upon the superior power of Heaven to repulse the barbarian violation of the sacred lands. It is important to view these movements within the framework of tension between transcendent and practical order. While they rebelled because of historical conditions and opportunities, they were authorized and legitimated by transcendent ideals.

Even orthodox religious groups in popular society could and did invoke the gap between transcendent ideals and the present order. They were, as David Ownby has put it, "both *against* and *from within* the mainstream." For example, some of them condemned the Buddhist church "for having abandoned its own mission of self-abnegation and transcendence."[40] Ownby's study of the apocalyptic Way of the Temple of the Heavenly Immortals exemplifies how these societies merged deeply orthodox or 'fundamental' values from Confucianism or Daoism with popular cultural traditions to reconstruct community along traditional and even utopian prescriptions.[41] These societies called on the ideals of transcendent authority to change the established order; as such, they evoked the momentum of Axial Age civilization tension to propel society to change towards the transcendent ideal.

From the middle of the Ming dynasty in the sixteenth century, a new type of popular religion begins to emerge and spread rapidly across China. The groups of this type were frequently based on a literary scripture known as the *baojuan* composed by religious leaders who were drawn from the disillusioned, disgruntled or marginal elites in the orthodox order. They often drew mass followings among men and women from various classes including the elites. Some among these, such as the sutra-reciting Luojiao, had a principally Buddhist orientation, whereas the Sanyijiao sect (Three in One Teaching) of Lin Zhaoen derived from a more Confucian background, and still others derived from the Daoist tradition. Yet, because of the relative absence of institutionalized controls within and over them, these new religions operated within a common 'sectarian milieu' sharing many beliefs and symbols taken from each other as well as from local, popular practices – such as spirit writing and other forms of spirit mediation. While competition certainly prevailed among them, the trend was expansive and accommodating of different religious ideas.[42]

---

[40] David Ownby, "Chinese Millenarian Traditions: The Formative Age," *American Historical Review*, *104*(5) (1999): 1513–30, at p. 1528.

[41] David Ownby, "Imperial Fantasies: The Chinese Communists and Peasant Rebellions," *Comparative Studies in Society and History*, *43*(1) (2001): 65–91, at pp. 15–20.

[42] For *baojuan*-reciting groups, see Overmyer, "Values in Chinese Sectarian Literature"; for Sanyijiao, see Kenneth Dean, *Lord of the Three in One: The Spread of a Cult in Southeast China* (Princeton University Press, 1998). See also Seiwert, *Popular Religious Movements*, pp. 358–65.

Redemptive societies: social renewal and self-formation

One of the most important contributions to Axial Age theory in recent years is the work of Armando Salvatore on the social history of transcendence in the Abrahamic traditions. Salvatore identifies the historically recurrent role of transcendence in the effort to renew society and mediate social tensions in the public realm. He is thus able to revise Habermas' notion of the public sphere from a long, Axial Age historical perspective. He shows how, particularly in Christianity and Islam, the transcendent *telos* provided not only an opportunity and stimulus for renewal/change through the Axial Age renaissance of the thirteenth century and the modern Enlightenment but also the sacred authority to build the social bond and 'connective justice' in the community.

One of Salvatore's most important claims is that in the Abrahamic traditions of the Euro-Mediterranean area, including west Asia, an archaic public sphere was *warranted* by the relationship of *ego* to *alter* through God. He goes on to demonstrate the role of Christian monastic movements and Sufi mystic brotherhoods in shaping the syntheses of the Axial renaissance by mediating *telos* and *phronesis* or linking transcendent goals with public reasoning in everyday society. Thus, by integrating the authority of God with communicative reason, the new messiahs created modalities of intersubjective understandings in the public sphere.

However, Salvatore rarely clarifies or identifies *alter*: does it represent differentiated segments within the community of the faithful or those outside it? He indicates that in the later Abrahamic traditions proselytizing is a central feature that goes beyond the community paradigm of the first Axial breakthrough associated with Jewish and Greek models. It was no longer enough to accomplish canonically prescribed duties and rituals to attain salvation. It became imperative to win over others to the faith and to lead a virtuous life. In other words, converts had to embrace a type of "social bond based on a fellowship of faith and on the idea of a God-willed connective justice."[43] What was the relation between conversion and *phronesis* or practical reasoning?

What I have identified as redemptive societies in late imperial, and particularly twentieth-century, China may be seen to play a role similar to Christian or Sufi sects in the public sphere. But there are also very significant differences particularly in their accommodative, non-exclusive orientation. In 1993, when I was researching associational life in the local archives of the former Manchukuo, the Japanese puppet state in northeast

---

[43] Armando Salvatore, *The Public Sphere: Liberal Modernity, Catholicism and Islam* (New York: Palgrave Macmillan, 2007), p. 101.

China (1932–45), I stumbled upon these redemptive societies. Manchukuo was a state four times the size of Japan with a population that had reached 40 million by the early 1940s. The most popular type of civic association to be found there was the redemptive societies, the largest of them boasting a membership of 8 million people. Subsequent research – now conducted by a consortium of research universities in eight countries in North America, Europe and Asia – has found that these societies existed in equally large numbers all over China, and, although they remained basically under the radar of Westerners and Westernized elites in China and Chinese studies, they were clearly the largest socioreligious groups in both urban and rural republican China with followings many times the size of groups affiliated with the May 4th movement. The Falun Gong, which surfaced at the end of the last millennium, represents the briefest effort of the redemptive societies to re-establish themselves formally in the PRC.

I have called these societies redemptive because salvation was vital to their agenda. The salvationist element was typified by the declaration of their goal to "save the self, to save humanity, and to save the world through self-abnegation."[44] Such redemption often included faith in a deity, such as Laozi, or a sanctified figure, but this figure was not all-powerful and their religious practices typically called on deities from other religions and even the spirits of recently deceased spiritual leaders. Such groups developed out of the 'new religions' of the late Ming period – described above and studied by Hubert Seiwert, Kenneth Dean and others – in the 'sectarian milieu' of Ming-Qing China. Some of these movements developed remarkable syntheses drawing from the variety of transcendent ideals and cultivation practices that had become widely available by Ming-Qing times.

Late imperial syncretism, which urged the extinguishing of worldly desires and engagement in moral action, gained popularity among the Confucian gentry and the Buddhist and Daoist laity in the sixteenth and seventeenth centuries.[45] Timothy Brook, who does not much care for application of the term 'syncretism' to the Chinese phenomenon in the Ming period, prefers to describe it as the 'condominium of the three teachings'. He believes that these gentry and laity echoed the preceding Mongol period attitude of ecumenical openness where each religion was

---

[44] As Xiong Shiling, a prime minister in the republican period, observed, "All the ancient religions take self-abnegation (*wusi, wuyü, wuwo*) to be the principle whereby to redeem the self, humanity, and the world (*jiuji, jiuren, jiushi*). This is also the truth of Datong." Quoted in Duara, *Sovereignty and Authenticity*, p. 110.

[45] Kai-wing Chow, *The Rise of Confucian Ritualism in Late Imperial China: Ethics, Classics, and Lineage Discourse* (Stanford University Press, 1994), pp. 21–5.

seen to furnish access to the truth not easily seen by the others. The Three Teachings tradition was also encouraged by Wang Yangming and the Taizhou school of neo-Confucianism. They saw the importance of the truths contained in Buddhism and Daoism, although they accorded their philosophy of *xinxue* (learning of the heart-mind) the highest place. Wang and his school believed that ultimately the Three Teachings would have to be transcended to realize the Dao.[46]

To this day, most Chinese popular temples sponsor the joint worship of Buddhist, Daoist, and local and official deities, a practice datable to at least the Ming period. While the ideal of combining the three in one was almost universal in popular religion, different figures or founders performed different syntheses among these redemptive societies. In other words, accommodation was accompanied by a hierarchicization or at least a functional differentiation of the three religions: Confucian morality for ethics, Buddhism for death and the afterlife, and Daoism for appreciation of nature. Nontheless, the pursuit of the Way that is common to the Three Teachings is, according to Brook, "the great ecumenical vision of Chinese religion."[47]

The end of the Qing empire and the collapse of imperial orthodoxy in 1911 opened up a new era in the expansion and transformation of these redemptive societies. The political fragmentation of the republican period and the interest of various warlords and politicians in these societies allowed these groups to participate and play a major role in the emergent modern public sphere, as they often could not do openly in the imperial – and later the Guomindang (KMT) and Communist (PRC) – periods. For example, the New Religion to Save the World (*Jiushi Xinjiao*) sought to save the world – as did many of the others – not only through philanthropic activities, such as hospitals, orphanages and refugee centers, but also through dissemination and publicity (schools, newspapers, libraries and lectures), through charitable enterprises – such as factories and farms employing the poor – through savings and loan associations; and even through engineering projects such as road and bridge repair.[48] As for the Red Swastika of the society with that name, while this can, of course, be

---

[46] Timothy Brook, "Rethinking Syncretism: The Unity of the Three Teachings and Their Joint Worship in Late-Imperial China," *Journal of Chinese Religions*, 21 (1993): 13–44. Note that the term 'syncretism' is often rejected because of its association with the missionary colonialism which referred to local mixings of Christianity with popular practices as impure and inferior. My goal in the concept of dialogical transcendence is precisely to reverse the status of such a valuation.

[47] *Ibid.*, p. 22.

[48] Xingya zongjiao xiehui (Revive Asian Religions Association), Ed. *Huabei zongjiao nianjian* (*HZN*) (*Yearbook of the Religions of North China*) (Beiping: Xingyayuan Huabei lianlobu, 1941), pp. 485–6, at pp. 491–3.

understood in Buddhist terms, it was also modeled upon – was an Eastern equivalent of – the Red Cross Society. The Red Swastika Society was at the forefront of relief work after the Nanjing massacre in 1937 and became the largest welfare and social relief organization in Shanghai during the civil war of 1946–9.

Many of these societies were formally established or saw their rapid expansion during the period from World War I through the 1920s, when the discourse of Western civilization as being overly materialist and violent began to emerge globally.[49] These societies sought to correct the material civilization of the West with the transcendent ideals of the East. The resultant synthesis they envisaged took the shape of a religious universalism that included not only Confucianism, Daoism and Buddhism but also Islam and Christianity. In other words, they expanded their ecumenical vision and adopted a more self-consciously accommodative stance.

Some of the most famous of the redemptive societies were the Daodehui (Morality Society), the Daoyuan (Society of the Way) – and its philanthropic wing, the Hongwanzihui (Red Swastika Society) – the Tongshanshe (Fellowship of Goodness), the Zailijiao (The Teaching of the Abiding Principle) the Shijie Zongjiao Datonghui (Society for the Great Unity of World Religions, first organized in Sichuan in 1915 as the Wushanshe), and the Yiguandao (Way of Pervading Unity). A principal source for the spread of these societies in the early twentieth century comes from Japanese surveys of religious and charitable societies in China conducted in the 1930s and 1940s.

According to Japanese researchers and officials of the puppet administrations in north China, these societies claimed to command enormous followings. Thus, the Fellowship of Goodness claimed a following of 30 million in 1929[50] and the Red Swastika Society, a following of 7–10 million in 1937.[51] There are also some notable Chinese works on individual societies such as the famous study of the Yiguandao by Li Shiyu of Shandong University, who joined the society on several occasions in

[49] Wanguo Daodehui Manzhouguo zonghui bianjike, Ed., *Manzhouguo Daodehui nianjian* (*MDNJ*) (*Yearbook of the Manzhouguo Morality Society*) (Xinjing: Wanguo Daodehui Manzhouguo zonghui bianjike, 1934), 4:1; Toshihiro Takizawa, *Shyukyo chōsa shiryō* (*Materials from the Survey of Religions*), vol. III: *Minkan shinyō chōsa hōkokushō* (*Report on the Survey of Popular Beliefs*) (Shinkyō (Xinjing): Minseibu (Minshengbu), 1937), pp. 67ff; and Xingya zongjiao xiehui (Revive Asian Religions Association), Ed., *HZN*, pp. 505–7f.

[50] Takayoshi Suemitsu, *Shina no mimi kaisha to jishan kaisha* (*China's Secret Societies and Charitable Societies*) (Dalian: Manshu hyoronsha, 1932), p. 252.

[51] Toshihiro Takizawa, *Manshū no kaison shinyō* (*Beliefs of Manchuria's Towns and Villages*) (Shinkyō: Manshū jijo annaijo, 1940), p. 67.

order to study them. Wing-tsit Chan's study of Chinese religion tends to dismiss them. He regards these societies as "negative in outlook, utilitarian in purpose, and superstitious in belief"[52] and cites the figure of a mere 30,000 adherents for the Red Swastika Society in 1927, as opposed to Takayoshi Suemitsu's figure of 3 million followers in 1932.[53] However, Chan notes that the Fellowship of Goodness (Tongshanshe) claimed more than a thousand branches in all parts of China proper and Manchuria in 1923.[54] However, a more recent study by Shao Yong, while perhaps even more critical of these societies than Chan, cites figures that are closer to the Japanese estimates.[55]

While the modern redemptive societies inherited the mission of universalism and moral self-transformation from this syncretism, these societies also retained the association of the older syncretic societies with sectarian traditions, popular gods and spirit-mediumistic practices such as divination, use of the planchette, and spirit writing.[56] In this way, they continued to remain organically connected to Chinese popular society. Redemptive societies were important agents of both cosmological syntheses and social integration, or what we might term 'connective ethics', between different communities, cultures, temporalities, classes and genders.

On the one hand, these societies had connections to elite Axial traditions of transcendence; on the other hand, they remained committed to popular practices concerned with 'human flourishing'. An Yiguandao text composed during the republic, declares that its purpose is to enable recovery of one's true nature – the good mind (*liangxin*) of Confucianism and Buddha nature (*foxing*) – by drawing the truth of the universe into one's personal life. Even the Yiguandao – among the most esoteric of these societies – had, by the early republic, adjusted its cosmology and conception of transmission of the Way to the requirements of

---

[52] Wing-tsit Chan, *Religious Trends in Modern China* (New York: Columbia University Press, 1953), p. 167.

[53] *Ibid.*, p. 164; Suemitsu, *Shina no himitsu kessha to jizen kaisha*, p. 302.

[54] *Ibid.*, p. 165.

[55] Shao Yong, *Zhongguo huidaomen* (*China's Religious Societies*) (Shanghai: Renmin chubanse, 1997). Shao Yong does not furnish a systematic estimate of the membership of these societies, which he calls "huidaomen." He supplies scattered figures of membership in different localities drawn from various sources, including the societies' own statements. Thus, for instance, in one place, he suggests that the Tongshanshe membership in Hunan province alone exceeded 20,000 in 1918 (p. 174). Again, for 1938, he suggests that the societies had a combined membership of 1 million in the provinces of Henan, Shandong, and Anhui (p. 325). Most astonishing is his revelation that membership of the Morality Society was as high as 8 million in 1936–7 in Manchukuo alone (p. 321).

[56] *Ibid.*, pp. 22–7.

modern history and progress.[57] Note also the following interview with a
Daoyuan leader during the 1920s:

Q: What is the Daoyuan about?
A: To simultaneously cultivate the inner and outer; the inner through meditation
    and the outer through philanthropy.
Q: What is the Dao of Daoyuan?
A: It is the source of all things (*wanyou genyuan*). It is not a single religion; it has
    the power to clarify the good... Actually the *Dao* has no name, but we in the
    human world have to give it a name to show our reverence. So we revere the
    founders of the five religions... We also respect nature, morality, and
    cultivate the self through charity.[58]

To be sure, we cannot read modern theories of communicative rationality and democracy into these groups, but, judging from their archives in
the twentieth century, their older traditions of accommodation and tolerance fit rather well with their novel modern practices and procedures that,
for instance, gave 'rights' to women in their organization.[59] Organized
with charters and bylaws, armed with a strong this-worldly orientation and
rhetoric of worldly redemption, these societies resembled other modern
religious and morality societies all over the world. The Morality Society
declared that it sought to synthesize the scientific view of the world with
the religious and moral visions of Asian thought. The society which had
Kang Youwei, the great reformer and constitutional monarchist, as its
president from 1920 until his death in 1927, argued that without moral
and spiritual regeneration, human evolution (*jinhua*) would stall and turn
even more destructive because of the present trend towards hedonistic
materialism.[60]

The Red Swastika society, like several others, not only pursued traditional and modern charities, but its activities also included international
activities, such as contributions to international relief efforts and the
establishment of professors of Esperanto in Paris, London and Tokyo.[61]
The Zailijiao, which emerged in the very late Qing period and had established twenty-eight centers in Beijing and Tianjin by 1913,[62] appeared to

[57] Fu Zhong, Ed., *Yiguandao Lishi* (*History of the Yiguandao*). Taipei: Zhengyi shanshu,
      1997, pp. 278–80, 308–9. See also Li Shiyu, *Xianzai Huabei mimi zongjiao* (*Secret Religions
      in North China Today*) (city and publisher unknown, 1948), pp. 50–5.
[58] For the Daoyuan interview, see Suemitsu, *Shina no mimi kaisha to jishan kaisha*, pp. 266,
      326–8. See also Takizawa, *Manshū no kaison shinyō*, pp. 76–8; and Chan, *Religious Trends*,
      pp. 164–7.
[59] Duara, *Sovereignty and Authenticity*, pp. 139–40.
[60] *MDNJ*, *1*, 3–6; 4:1, and Takizawa, *Shyukyo chōsa shiryō*, p. 67.
[61] Suemitsu, *Shina no mimi kaisha to jishan kaisha*, pp. 292–305, 354.
[62] *HZN*, pp. 507–27.

have forty-eight centers in Tianjin alone by the late 1920s. It was a strictly disciplinarian movement and developed drug rehabilitation centers using herbal medicines and self-cultivation techniques (*zhengshen*), which were said to cure over 200 opium addicts a year.[63] This outer or worldly dimension was matched by a strong inner dimension relating to moral and religious cultivation of the individual spirit and body, as discussed below.[64]

Some Japanese researchers tried to grasp the social nature of these societies through loosely Marxist categories. Takizawa saw them as new religions characteristic of an early capitalist society through which incipient capitalist groups sought to bring the rich and poor together in a traditional idiom. For the rich, it was a means of gaining popular support, while the poor welcomed both the philanthropy and the religious ideas. At the same time, these scholars were insistent on recognizing the religious passion and devotion of the adherents to their mission.[65] They suggested that those who sought to use these societies could not always appropriate this passion for their own purposes. However, while they may have had the effect of muting class tensions, the religiosity of these societies continued to predispose them to universalism. Let us look a little more closely at one such society, the Morality Society (Daodehui).

Founded in 1919 by the high literati of Shandong around a child prodigy who had once been a companion of the Xuantong emperor, the Morality Society flourished until the establishment of KMT power and the antireligious movements in 1928.[66] It had developed a mass following within China and extensive networks around the world. Kang Youwei, its president, believed that the ultimate significance of the nation arose from its self-transcendence in the universalist utopia of *Datong* ('Great Unity').

In northeast China, the Morality Society suddenly expanded in the mid 1920s, when the legendary Wang Fengyi (1864–1937) joined it, bringing with him his massive following and extensive network of schools in Liaoning and Rehe.[67] Wang was a self-educated, rural intellectual who came from a modest, rural background in the Chaoyang county, Rehe. His adoring followers referred to him as the righteous sage (*yisheng*), and

---

[63] Suemitsu, *Shina no mimi kaisha to jishan kaisha*, pp. 262–3.
[64] For the fullest details on the social welfare activities of these societies, especially for the Red Swastika Society, see the Shanghai city social bureau's reports, *Shanghaishi shehuiju yewu baogao* (*SSJYB*) (*Reports of the Shanghai Municipality Social Bureau on Enterprises and Activities*), Jan.–Dec. 1930; Jan.–Dec. 1931, Jan.–June 1932, Jan. 1946 (Shanghai: 1930–2, 1946).
[65] Takizawa, *Manshū no kaison shinyō*, pp. 282–4, and Suemitsu, *Shina no mimi kaisha to jishan kaisha*, pp. 337–40.
[66] Shao, *Zhongguo huidaomen*, p. 321.   [67] *Ibid.*, pp. 306–7.

he was popularly known as *shanren* ('man who does good'). His activities have been characterized as being in the tradition of *jiaohua*, or advocating ethical transformation. Upon enlightenment of the *Dao*, he threw himself into lecturing and doing good, urging filiality and the study of the sages, and curing various ills with his theory of nature.[68] He developed a doctrine and practice of self-knowledge, self-realization and self-reliance based upon a complex theory synthesizing the doctrine of the Five Conducts (based on the five natural elements) and *yinyang* cosmology, with the teachings of the three religions.

In brief, the technical aspect of his theory sought to show how the five elements (*wuxing*) – wood, fire, earth, metal and water – shape the five behavioral characteristics of a person (*wuxing*) not in a determinative way, but in combination with how the person cultivates (*xiudao*) these elements in the different circumstances of life. At one level, his theory prescribed inner cultivation, but the self was ultimately realized in outward actions within a framework of changing circumstances. Self-exploration *and* self-reliance were the keynotes in Wang's philosophy.[69]

While Wang's philosophy was strongly rooted in the Taizhou school of Wang Yangming, the technology of the self he developed was elaborated in the wider religion of the 'three-in-one' (*sanjiao heyi*). According to Lin Anwu, a contemporary follower who called himself a 'post-new Confucian',[70] Wang affirmed the basic goodness of nature or natural dispositions (*tianxing*) and the three bonds (*gang*) of Confucianism (father–son, ruler–subject and husband–wife). He found them compatible with the three treasures of Buddhism, and the three transformations (the *hua* of *xing*, *xin* and *shen*) of Daoism, all of which could be understood within the Buddhist realms of the three worlds.[71] Yet, the goal of the philosophy, Lin wrote, "is neither theoretical nor technical, but practically related to experiences in one's life; one can in this way find the roots of one's life. A person may thus return to the *principles* underlying the bonds between the world, heaven and humans."[72] Through his cosmological synthesis invoking transcendent ideals, Wang Fengyi developed an entire theory of self and social transformation that won him a wide following.

---

[68] Lin Anwu, "Yin dao yi li jiao – yi Wang Fengyi 'shierzi xinchuan' wei gaixin zhankai" ("Establishing the 'Way' as Religion – Explorations of Wang Fengyi's 'Twelve Character Teachings'"), in *Zhonghua minzu zongjiao xueshu huiyi lunwen fabiao* (Publication of the Conference on the Study of Chinese Religion) (Taipei: 1989), p. 12.

[69] *Ibid.*, pp. 15–17.

[70] John Makeham, Ed., *New Confucianism: A Critical Examination* (New York: Palgrave Macmillan, 2003), p. 43.

[71] Lin Anwu, "Yin dao yi li jiao – yi Wang Fengyi 'shierzi xinchuan' wei gaixin zhankai," pp. 13–15.

[72] *Ibid.*, p. 19.

Recently, Wang Fengyi's writings have drawn considerable attention among the various Confucian circles in contemporary China and the West.[73]

Wang's commitment to 'transform the world' (*huashi*) had been noted locally even before his association with the Morality Society. The Chaoyang county gazetteer observed that his efforts had led to improvement of customs and the spread of education. Over a hundred segregated schools initiated by his son were eponymously called Wang Guohua schools.[74] He was praised as having "enlightened (*kaiming*) our women's world that had been steeped in darkness for thousands of years."[75] Wang was extremely energetic, traveling widely and establishing schools and branches of the society all over Manchukuo and north China. He received the patronage of important politicians, such as the Manchu literatus, Bai Yongzhen, whose calligraphy adorns Wang's little book of teachings.[76]

Women were particularly important in his mission to restore Chinese civilizational values and 'transform the world'. The new society that Wang conceived would combine modern ideas with enduring Chinese ideals of selfhood and the world. Wang had been at the forefront of the development of virtuous girls' schools, having established 270 of them by 1925, all of which became part of the Morality Society when he joined it around that time. While the importance of gender segregation doubtless derived from his commitment to classical morality, he was also clearly committed to a conception of woman that linked the past to the future. He reported a conversation with a Christian pastor in which Wang exposes the insufficiency of historical religions. All religions certainly pointed to the same 'Way' (*Dao*), but they neglected or demeaned women in the education of it. He insisted that women be educated and independent (*liye*) so that they could understand the 'Way'.[77]

In my book on Manchukuo, I discuss in some detail the autobiographical narratives of women of the Morality Society compiled at a summit

---

[73] Makeham, *New Confucianism*. Indeed, Wang's five-element style of emotional healing is championed both in China and the West. See Heiner Fruehauf, "All Disease Comes from the Heart: The Pivotal Role of the Emotions in Classical Chinese Medicine," Classical Chinese Medicine.org, 2006 (www.jadeinstitute.com/jade/assets/files/Fruehauf-AllDiseaseComesFromTheHeart.pdf). See also (http://classicalchinesemedicine.org/dev/wang-fengyis-five-element-style-of-emotional-healing6-parts/) and (www.swarthmore.edu/healing-through-the-emotions-the-confucian-therapy-system-of-wang-fengyi.xml).

[74] Chaoyang xianzhi, 1930: juan 19: 14–16; juan 35: 45–6; *MDNJ*, 8(23).

[75] *Ibid.*, juan 35: 46–7.   [76] Minguo Renwuzhuan, 166; Dongebi fangzhi, 10, 521.

[77] Manzhouguo Daodehui bianjike (Manzhouguo Morality Society editorial department), Ed., *Disanjie Manzhouguo Daodehui daode jiangxi yulu (DMDY)* (*Oral Records of Morality Seminars of the Third Manzhouguo Morality Society*) (Xinjing (Shinkyō): Manzhouguo Daodehui huijike, 1936), 4: 207.

meeting of the society in the mid 1930s. In the passages below, I will try to indicate how their recounting of the modes of self-formation in relation to a greater ideal, both in and not of this world – *wuxingde wuqi* (literally, 'formless weapon for moral good') – represents the method of these societies in reaching out on different scales in their universe. By this time, their ideals included several modern, Enlightenment notions, including the service of women in the public sphere. In particular, I want to indicate the ways in which the women negotiated the contradictory dimensions of their philosophy in order to attain their goals.

The narrative was typically grounded in a self-analysis based on Wang's philosophy of the five natural elements as they were present in the individual's personality. The balancing of these elements – such as the contrary qualities of fire and water – could be achieved by self-reflection and changing behavior. An entire vocabulary drawn from the Confucian tradition – such as *lishen, liye, lizhi* (to establish self, livelihood and resolve) *zhiming, zhixing, zhizhi* (to know one's destiny, nature and limits) – furnishes the categories of reflection and action. From an outsider's perspective, however, the most interesting aspect of these autobiographies may be the tension they record between the dimensions of the philosophy that hold women in subjection and those elements which energize and motivate them to attain the heights of their commitment.

Despite Wang Fengyi's progressive approach to women, he still sanctioned the 'Three Followings' (*sancong*) of Confucianism that obliged women to follow their fathers, their husbands and their sons in their life course. Yet, urban society in Manchukuo was relatively modern – compared to much of the rest of Asia – and these women were distinctly aware of the freedoms of the working and Westernized women in their society. Among the most celebrated aspects of the Morality Society for these women was the existence of the society itself, which allowed them to perform their roles and discharge their moral duties in the public sphere, referred to by the neologism *shehui* (society).

A Mrs. Chen recounts the significance of public service, which includes the independence it can bring to women. Mrs. Bai echoes this view, saying that women over forty remember how in their youth they could hardly venture outside the home; this confinement often created a grasping and nasty attitude within the women's quarters. Now that the society had been set up, they could exchange knowledge, listen to lectures about their public role and be able to discharge their moral commitments. In this day and age, the women urge that the Confucian category of *lishen* – to establish the self – should not be interpreted as it might have been in an earlier age as bodily comportment, but more as the means to set up a livelihood or *liye*. Mrs. Chen observes that once they have set up a living, they can devote themselves to the task of purifying the world (*huozhe neng sheshen shijie*). In this way, because one would not be working for money or fame, one could rid oneself of greed. Was this not the best way to *lishen*?[78]

Listen to Grandmother Cai, who declares that, at age thirty-three, she had defied the elders and gone off to educate herself. Although she was unfilial, she has now fulfilled her responsibility to devote herself (*jinxin*) to the education of her children and grandchildren. In concluding, she comments that she is a vegetarian, is deeply religious, and has tried to rid herself of vain desires. Grandmother Cai engages a common strategy in these narratives that may be seen as part of what Michel Foucault once called 'games of truth', the means whereby experience is converted into truth. They detach themselves from one kind of value in the philosophy and attach themselves to another of its values. Thus, universal education, personal spirituality and sacrifice, and, most of all, public service tend to trump unfiliality and service to a distrustful or abusive husband.

Mrs. Liu recounts the pain of her mother being ordered back to her natal home and how she and her brother were forbidden to visit her. Now, as adults, the children have established a source of livelihood (*liye*) for their mother and have devoted themselves to rebuilding the family. She declares:

The sages ask us to follow the three male figures (*sancong*) and learn from our husbands. We listen to our husbands, but they do not hear us. My husband eats meat and is not very virtuous, whereas I have only eaten meat once and I am a filial daughter-in-law. Should I not be the one from whom he should learn the Way?

The narratives are replete with this theme of the personal search for autonomy, which is, however, deeply grounded in the quest for the moral and universal goals of the redemptive society. Mrs. Chen observes that the ways in which her parents were 'good people' were different from the way she can be a morally pure person. Her parents were good people of a village or county; she is a good citizen of the entire nation and the world. Another society member I interviewed in Taipei in 1993, whom I shall call Mrs. Gu, recalls that as a young girl in Manchukuo she had rejected the patriarchal family system and determined that women should be independent. As she grew older, she realized that the 'formless weapon of moral power' cultivates the public heart (*gongxin*) to give up the private and serve the people. Political regimes, whether the Japanese or the KMT, could not stop her and her co-workers from pursuing the Way for salvation of the world.

---

[78] *Ibid.*, 4: 181.

These narratives reveal dialogical transcendence at work in the modern era. A transcendent, invisible force of good is discerned and cultivated through the particular circumstances and experiences of life. Of course, changing societal norms, structures and power shape the content of these experiences. But the moral authority to defy, resist and, as we have seen, *negotiate* with these often deeply oppressive norms derives from an autonomous and transcendent force. The conversion of a deeply felt experience into truth may well be the epistemic locus of transcendence I have described. But, if so, following Nagarjuna, that locus requires skepticism and tolerance and cannot be the mandate of certitude and absolutism. At the same time, we note that dialogical transcendence does not only authorize personal and experiential transformation but also, reciprocally, motivates commitment to the universal.

Redemptive societies and the modern state in East Asia

Many of the redemptive societies sought to work with the state as long as they were given the space to fulfill their spiritual obligations in relative peace. In other words, their conception of transcendence made it possible for them to attain salvation through this-worldly activity. However, neither the KMT nor the communist state had a place for them. Although in the northeast, many, including the Morality Society, worked with the Japanese puppet regime in Manchukuo, in Japan the state was highly intolerant of similar Japanese societies – as we shall see below.[79]

The opposition between imperial orthodoxy and sectarian and redemptive societies over the course of Chinese history developed a certain cultural logic: orthodoxy and the state repeatedly make the claim that

[79] For a more detailed account, see Duara, *Sovereignty and Authenticity*. When Manchukuo was established, the Morality Society responded to the Japanese formulation of *wangdao*, and it and the Swastika Society became the most influential groups. Wang sought government permission to organize a major summit in Xinjing and rapidly created branches all across the new state. By 1934, the 312 branches of the Manchukuo society operated 235 "righteous" or "virtuous" schools, 226 lecture halls, and 124 clinics. By 1936, a year before Wang's death, it boasted 13 head offices, 208 city and county branch offices and 529 *zhen*-level branches. Its membership and office-holders boasted top officials, merchants, and landowners at all levels of society from the major cities to the subcounty townships. Many of the leading Chinese figures in the Manchukuo government, such as Yuan Jinkai and Zhang Jinghui, were associated with it. The message of peace, morality and spiritual salvation of the world by the East befitted these successors of the old gentry elite. As a *jiaohua* (moral education) agency, it revealed a strong propagandist urge. It put great stock by its cadres or activists (*shi*), who were characterized as benevolent and resolute. Through their activities in schools, in lectures, in spreading *baihua* commentaries of classical morality, and in establishing popular enlightenment societies to "reform popular customs and rectify the people's minds and hearts," the society propounded a strong rhetoric of reaching out to all – rich and poor, men and women.

this kind of popular religion represented a cover for politics. But at its core is the logic of access to transcendent power. The cosmology of religious believers tends to empower those inspired by transcendent authority, but the empowerment is not for that reason political. By banning religious groups, the state extends the logic that politicizes them.

Despite its hostility, the imperial state had to tolerate a great many of these societies as long as they superficially acknowledged the orthodox order and as long as a fair segment of the elites were involved in them. The modern, nationalist and homogenizing states of the KMT and the PRC were much less tolerant of these groups and banned them. The imperial logic these states inherited was reinforced by the certitude of scientism as the condition for nation-building and national competitiveness. The KMT regime (1927–49) classified them as superstitious cults and launched attacks on them. During the 1930s, they relented somewhat by separating and legalizing the charitable functions from the religious ones. But, particularly after the Japanese invasion of China, they were unable to enforce the proscription. The PRC regime, on the other hand, pursued a brutal campaign of elimination of these groups throughout the 1950s. Although since the cultural liberalization of the 1990s there has been a cautious re-emergence, they continue to be stamped out with considerable ferocity.[80]

When we turn to the history of modern secularization in China, the conception, for most Sinologists, has a distinct air of irrelevance. As we have seen, secularism in Europe developed to contain the religious warfare between Protestants and Catholics and the warfare among other faith-based communities that were susceptible to politicization partly because of the nature of the vertically integrated, proto-national formations I have identified above. The institution of secularism was designed to contain this competition by bringing religions under an enlarged state order and giving them limited protection from their enemies, and, gradually, the state itself. Thus, religion became privatized or otherwise subordinated in the modern nation-state.[81]

The Chinese historical condition was such that it did not develop an environment in which confessional faiths could openly thrive – except perhaps for the brief but massive Taiping Christian movement in the

---

[80] Prasenjit Duara, "Knowledge and Power in the Discourse of Modernity: The Campaigns against Popular Religion in Early 20th Century China," *Journal of Asian Studies*, 50(1) (1991): 67–83.

[81] Reinhart Koselleck, *Critique and Crisis: Enlightenment and the Pathogenesis of Modern Society* (Cambridge, MA: MIT Press, 1988), pp. 80–5.

mid-nineteenth century – thus limiting their ability to mobilize the population. Yet, despite the absence of a historical legacy of faith-based communities, the republican state in early twentieth-century China quickly adopted the Western concept of secularism. Unsurprisingly perhaps, when it adopted this conception, the state was suddenly required to develop church-like organizations in order to deal with a legitimate religious counterpart. Vincent Goossaert has demonstrated that the republican state sought to actually create or foster church-like organizations, thus calling into existence national-level Buddhist and Daoist organizations. It came to understand that the modern state could secure the advantages of the secular system only by mobilizing such organizations and resources within a new framework of state regulation. This was not a successful strategy, in part because, as we have seen, the licensed forms of institutional Buddhism and Daoism did not command their flocks, as such. The sources of religious loyalty among the ordinary folk continued to lie elsewhere.[82]

At the same time, the republican successor to the imperial state in China was able to reconfigure the problem of religiosity in a novel way. Since the bulk of popular religiosity was organized neither as faith-based religions nor as institutionalized churches, it was easy for the state simply to deny their status as religion. Popular religion, including sectarian and redemptive societies, was variously classified as superstitious or heterodoxies. Religious groups were not only denied the limited protection that a secular state was obliged to furnish but were also proscribed and severely attacked throughout the twentieth century. In many ways, the state was much less tolerant of popular religiosity than the imperial orthodoxy had been.

Although at considerable cost, the modern Chinese state in the Han heartland has avoided the communalization and politicization of religion that has taken place through the global spread of identity politics. As we have seen, this is an intertwined processes of the nationalization of religion and the sacralization of the nation. Neither India nor Japan has escaped this fate. The spread of communal politics in British India since the late nineteenth century, and the effort to confessionalize and nationalize Hinduism, (Hindutva) in the last quarter of the twentieth century will be taken up in the next chapter. The comparison of China and Japan is more instructive in this context.

---

[82] Vincent Goossaert, "Republican Church Engineering: The National Religious Associations in 1912 China," in Mayfair Yang, Ed., *Chinese Religiosities: Afflictions of Modernity and State Formation* (Berkeley and Los Angeles, CA: University of California Press, 2008), pp. 209–32.

China and Japan

It is fruitful to study the Chinese case together with the Japanese one, because there was considerable interaction between the two both before and after the turn of the twentieth century. Both societies were also frequently responding to similar problems and drawing from circulating ideas and common cultural resources.

Tokugawa Japan apparently had a similar mold of a state cult based on Confucian ideas of Heaven, Shinto rites and control of Buddhist temple structures that shored up the authority of the shogunate. The Tokugawa sought to make local temples the organs of state control of religion. Households were ordered to register at a Buddhist temple, and thus, while in a sense, Buddhist sects were favored, they were also kept under strict control. Similarly, the control of licensed Buddhism often led to formalized ritualism and the emergence of redemptive and syncretic religions (for instance, those based on the Lotus Sutra), and, especially from the early nineteenth century, religions that were often persecuted but also accommodated if they operated within certain limits.[83]

The traditional sociological view of the question of Japanese civilization is that it is decidedly non-transcendent. Even while there may have been transcendent strains brought in with Chinese conceptions of Heaven and Buddhist notions of Nirvana – or Dao and *dharma*, according to Kitagawa – the dominant power was an 'immanent theocracy' which ruled over a 'national' community that was also a soteriological community. "In short, both Shinto and Buddhism were transmuted, thanks to newly created (eighth century CE) myths which sanctioned their amalgamation, and served the cause of immanental theocracy, which permeated every aspect of national community."[84] In Robert Bellah's view, the Japanese polity knew early and well the implications of the transcendental position. The rulers sought to "use the axial to overcome the axial," and he calls Japanese civilization a tradition of 'submerged transcendence'.[85]

While I agree that the political system was able to overcome the sources of Axial transcendence in the last millennium in Japan, doctrines and ideals of transcendence were never fully submerged. Of course, few conceptions of transcendence remain untouched by desires of fulfillment in

---

[83] Susumu Shimazono, *From Salvation to Spirituality: Popular Religious Movements in Modern Japan* (Melbourne: Trans-Pacific Press, 2004), p. 77.

[84] Joseph M. Kitagawa, "The Japanese 'Kokutai' (National Community): History and Myth," *History of Religions*, *13*(3) (1974): 209–26, at pp. 221, 223. See also S. N. Eisenstadt, *Japanese Civilization; A Comparative Review* (University of Chicago Press, 1996); Robert N. Bellah, *Imagining Japan: The Japanese Tradition and Its Modern Transformation* (Berkeley and Los Angeles, CA: University of California Press, 2003).

[85] Bellah, *Imagining Japan*, pp. 7–9, 13.

the here and now. Conversely, one might argue that the Japanese state tradition of 'submerged transcendence' also had to come to terms with ideals of transcendence in society. As Bellah has argued, the transcendent vision of Nichiren and Pure Land Buddhist followers and others could be accommodated in the pre-Meiji period as long as they did not constitute a political challenge.[86]

As in China, Japan witnessed the flourishing of large numbers of something very like the redemptive societies – described as 'new religions' by Shimazono Susumu – during the nineteenth and twentieth centuries. These groups, such as the Tenrikyō, Ōmotokyō, Hitonomichi, Reiyukai and others – constituting 15–20 percent of the population – were deeply salavationist, syncretic and, rhetorically at least, universalist.[87] A strong relationship developed between the Daoyuan (parent of the Red Swastika Society) and the Ōmotokyō after the former sent a delegation to aid the 1924 Tokyo earthquake victims. The mission of the Ōmotokyō states, "From the perspective of world history, it is clear that no single nation has the power to control other nations, that no one culture can have universal relevance, or that any one religion can assimilate all the people of the world. So we must strive to bring peace by love and faith in the Great Source (Ōmoto)."[88]

In Japan, as in China a few decades later, there was a breakout from this older mold in the transition to a nation-state. In the first place, while they rejected historical Confucian or Buddhist rituals, the idea of a national religion or state rites was seen by both states at the turn of the century as a necessary desideratum of a nation-state. After all, while the idea of freedom of religious belief and the separation of state and church had emerged even before the American and French revolutions, most European states continued to have state or national churches consistent with the confessional model. It was not until 1905 that the French National Assembly passed the law separating church and state (which, according to some authorities, still did not entail a full separation).[89]

Moreover, both East Asian states were threatened by Christian conversions, and although the Meiji state declared the freedom of religious worship, state Shinto was developed as a response to Christian and Buddhist conversion. Moreover, Chinese reformers at the turn of the century were convinced by powerful missionaries, such as Robert

[86] *Ibid.*, pp. 20–1.   [87] Shimazono, *From Salvation to Spirituality*, pp. 71–5 and *passim*.
[88] Takayoshi Suemitsu, *Shina no mimi kaisha to jishan kaisha*, p. 317.
[89] C. T. McIntire, "The Shift from Church and State to Religions as Public Life in Modern Europe," *Church History*, *71*(1) (2002): 152–77, at p. 153.

Morrison and Timothy Richards, that the secret to modernity lay in science and the church.[90]

It is clear that the Meiji model of state religion merged modern nation-state paradigms with an East Asian historical model of the state with monopoly access to Heaven through rites and sacrifices (*jisi*). Indeed, one might suggest that these rites and sacrifices cannot be seen as 'religion', and Shinto priests and bureaucrats certainly opposed the classification of state Shinto as religion.[91] Rather, the state sought to represent these rites as the ritual authority underpinning state power that was part of the inherited cosmology of the East Asian state, which came, however, to be resignified less in cosmological than symbolic terms. What exactly they sought to achieve – in terms of citizenship – is worthy of understanding. Here I want to suggest, in a most preliminary way, that the *jisi* model adapted the imperial Chinese conception of the *ritual synchronization of the polity* as the performance of power. The bureaucratization, standardization and synchronization of Shinto shrine worship throughout the nation (and empire) were accompanied by the pedagogy of the Three Teachings: conscription, national taxation and compulsory education.[92]

Whether or not state Shinto could be considered religion represented a highly contested issue in the Japan of the time. Without delving too deeply into the issue, we may let it suffice to say that in late nineteenth-century Japan, the ambiguity of state religion reflected a changing global discourse of religion and a geopolitical situation that the Meiji state confronted and came to address in its own way. In Europe at the time, the status of state religions became less and less tenable as nationalism required stronger territorial-political than religious identity. Geopolitically, Japan was simultaneously faced with pressure to conform to contemporary Western standards while also recognizing that it would have to build its national power to compete with them. In this context, by formally separating state Shinto from shrine Shinto (religion), the Meiji state was able to declare that Shinto represented public rituals while also demanding a kind of confessional patriotism and obligations from its citizens.[93]

Over the forty years of its evolution from a feudal polity to a powerful nation-state and contender for hegemony in the Pacific, the Meiji state

---

[90] Jerome Ch'en, *China and the West: Society and Culture, 1815–1937* (London: Hutchinson, 1979), pp. 100, 108, 272.

[91] Helen Hardacre, *Shinto and the State, 1868–1988* (Princeton University Press, 1989), p. 49.

[92] *Ibid.*, pp. 32, 70–6.

[93] Yijiang Zhong, "Gods Without Names: The Genesis of Modern Shinto in Nineteenth-Century Japan," Ph.D. dissertation, University of Chicago, 2011. See, in particular, ch. 5, "Gods Without Names, 1876–1884."

was transformed into a Leviathan that not only determined religious issues but also managed the sacred power of the nation in the emperor, who was allegedly a direct descendant of the founding goddess of the nation, Amaterasu. Imperial divinity was transformed into the embodiment of national authenticity, a symbol of timelessness that gave ultimate coherence to the evolution of the historical nation. It is this particular figuration of coherence that animates the politics of the Yasukuni priests and right-wing politicians today. In other words, the 'immanent theocracy' was transformed into an extraordinarily powerful 'regime of authenticity', able to impose enormous burdens on its people. As Rabindranath Tagore observed about his much beloved Japan in 1916, "The people accept this all-pervading mental slavery with cheerfulness and pride because of their nervous desire to turn themselves into a machine of power, called the Nation, and emulate other machines in their collective worldliness."[94]

Indeed, such was the hegemonic power of the post-restoration nation-state that even where the Buddhists and redemptive societies might have had an ambivalent relationship to the state, they were often pre-reflexively co-opted by the nationalist and imperialist discourses which depicted the Japanese as champions of progressive history and Enlightenment civilization in Asia. Hence, it was not surprising to find that many Buddhists and new religions adapted their universalism to the cause of civilizing their Asian neighbors by way of imperialism. To be sure, the minor-key status of pacific, transcendent and universalist movements in Japan was never wiped out, and it returned to play a significantly more important role in postwar Japanese society.

Conclusion

This chapter has sought to view the social history of Chinese religions from the perspective of dialogical transcendence, revealing several features that distinguish this historical matrix from other historical societies. The ways in which the institutional and civilizational imperatives in imperial China absorbed processes circulating both inside and from outside the Sinosphere reveal a highly durable configuration since at least the Mongol period. How this state–popular religion configuration fared in the latest and most powerful circulatory historical force – the national modernization process – is a complex story.

---

[94] Rabindranath Tagore, "Nationalism in the West," in Ramachandra Guha, Ed., *Nationalism* (New Delhi: Penguin Books, 2009), p. 49.

At one level, modern China was able to escape the confessional-communalism that deeply affected most other societies in Asia and per-haps the world. Many of these societies struggled and still struggle to overcome the confessionalization of religion and its transmutation into ethnic or national regimes of authenticity. The relocation of moral author-ity from the confessional or 'authentic' regimes to the regulatory ideal of an impartial secular truth – embodied, for instance, in the rule of law or humanitarianism – remains a struggle, even in the European heartland, where the possibility of regression to religio-nationalism is ever-present.

It would appear that one of the principal differences between China and Japan was the latter's ability to approximate the confessional model of nationalism in the late nineteenth century while the former did not; however, we will follow the effort to produce a Confucian religion in the next chapter. As Isomae Junichi has observed, the Protestantization of the field of Japanese religion was to introduce two tendencies: the claim of Buddhists, Shinto thinkers and others to derive their authority from a transcendent source but also to submit to the Meiji regime of national authenticity embodied in the emperor.[95] Various traditions of dialogical transcendence existed both before and after the 1868 restoration, but the Meiji state revealed a greater capacity to 'submerge' these movements or subordinate them to its own newly crafted confessional nationalism of the imperial cult.

In light of the fact that an important factor behind this submergence was the Sinosphere tradition of state ritualism, which the Meiji government, arguably, reshaped into the imperial cult, why was the Chinese state unable to do the same? At least two factors are involved:

(1) The Chinese emperor was not treated as a god; others could gain the mandate of Heaven. The Japanese emperor represented an alleged line of continuity from the mists of time. In this sense, the tran-scendent tradition was much stronger in China.

(2) Historically, the final overthrow of the imperial system in China in 1911 also produced a weak state which allowed not only the flourish-ing of the various redemptive societies but also secessionist and seceding parts of the old empire, especially in the Buddhist west and northwest of Mt. Wutai. The costs of establishing a confessional state built on Confucian religion or ritualism – notwithstanding the efforts to do so – by a weak state were too high.

The modern Chinese states of the Guomindang and the Chinese Communist Party preferred to found their moral authority and

---

[95] Isomae Jun'ichi, "Deconstructing 'Japanese Religion': A Historical Survey," *Japanese Journal of Religious Studies*, 32(2) (2005): 235–48.

sovereignty claims on a mixture of scientific socialism, or Sun Yat-sen's 'people's livelihood', and nationalism. While nationalism was often formally pronounced along the lines of the civic territorial nation or brotherhood of nationalities, a strong sense of ethnic Han nationalism lies close to the surface. This nationalism was built in the early twentieth century around lineage ideology, which, as we have seen, represented the more immanent dimensions of Chinese religiosity. Song Shenqiao, Frank Dikötter and others have demonstrated the powerful role of the myth of the Yellow Emperor (Huangdi) as the apical ancestor of the Chinese people, whose unity, whether in the territory or abroad, is confirmed by the common biological tie.[96] Small wonder then that metaphors of filial obligations also pervade the state–citizen relationship.

Yet, the Chinese state has still to tackle the transcendent aspirations of its people, who are seeking faith-based religions, be it Christianity, Buddhism or the redemptive traditions of dialogical transcendence. The cases of Hong Kong, Taiwan and elsewhere clarify that when the state does not deny religions their right to express their aspiration for transcendence, they tend to be engaged but happily non-political. In Taiwan, after 1987, when the democratizing state permitted the once-banned Yiguando and other religions to practice in the open, piety and engagement followed a civic religion model. Without providing adequate space for these historical traditions of dialogical transcendence, the PRC will find it difficult to achieve a just and ultimately sustainable society.

[96] Frank Dikötter, *The Discourse of Race in Modern China* (Stanford University Press, 1992); Song Shenqiao, "Wo yi wo xue jian Xuanyuan – Huangdi shenhua yu wan Qing de guozu Jiangou" ("The Myth of the Yellow Emperor and the Construction of National Lineage in the Late Qing"), *Taiwan shehui yanjiu jikan*, 28 (1997): 1–77.

6 The traffic between secularism and transcendence

The chapter explores the fate of religious practices and ideas in the realms of dialogical transcendence in nineteenth- and twentieth-century Asia when these traditions sought to adapt to the new models of religion emanating from the powerful West. They responded in two ways – sometimes combining both. The first was the confessionalization of religion built around the self–Other distinction, which was sensed as critical to survival and advancement of nations in the new world. The second was the development of the modern realm of spirituality as a source of self- and collective formation that often accompanied the demarcation of the secular from the religious spheres.

In the last chapter we saw that the binary of religion and secularism developed from modern Western histories cannot quite capture the distinctiveness of Chinese religious and political experiences. Here by developing the idea of 'traffic' between the religious and secular spheres, I hope to grasp the impact of secularization more meaningfully. Accordingly, I will discuss the recent debates about secularism and then proceed to analyze several episodes, practices and figures in modern Asian history to illustrate how the transcendent and other religious ideas often do not disappear but, rather, migrate into different spaces and institutions with sometimes remarkably generative and equally constraining effects in the moral, social, political and even, environmental spheres (explored in the last chapter). The static binary upon which much social theory of the modern has been constructed has to be rendered mobile in order to grasp new possibilities for a sustainable world.

Following the discussion of 'traffic' in East Asia, I shift my attention to the Peranakan Chinese in the European colonies of Southeast Asia in the first half of the twentieth century. The circumstances of living in a colonial society generated some divergence among the Peranakans from the path of religious traffic in China and located them at the intersection of trends in the Indosphere and the Sinosphere. Their historical circumstances, however, fostered a unique expression of interiority and identity, albeit in the new circulatory grammar of religion. The Peranakan case and the colonial connection will allow us to transition to the study of the traffic in South Asia in the second half of the chapter.

The notion of traffic refers to the movement between the sphere of religious ideas and practices and the sphere of the 'secular'. As such, it belongs to the family of circulation but attends more to the inhabitation – and sometimes colonization – by an old idea or practice in a new or unfamiliar setting in the *same* society. Like forms of circulation we have noted earlier, it, too, is often camouflaged or justified in terms of a different, often superior principle of organization – usually secular principles that deny a transcendent sanction. We may think of instances such as Max Weber's idea of the Protestant ethic mutating into capitalist accumulation and Carl Schmitt's concept of confessional principles shaping the nation, as traffic, although its implications as a methodological concept remain unexplored. Traffic also includes a reverse flow whereby secular practices penetrate the organization of religious activities, many instances of which we will observe in Asia.

A zone often associated with traffic is the *modern* realm of 'spirituality', which in Euro-American modernity is seen as arising simultaneously with the secular. Peter van der Veer has ably discussed modern spirituality as being distinct from – though also produced in mutual interaction with – both secular and institutional religion.[1] Spirituality may be a vague concept, but it is not at all marginal to modernity. Indeed, it allows for the kind of individuated religious choices that Charles Taylor suggests is the hallmark of modern religiosity, especially in the West. At the same time, spirituality can become tied to both the nation and more universal communities.

The great variety of adjectives that attach to 'spirit', such as 'revolutionary', 'cultural revolutionary', 'scientific', 'team', 'national', and 'cosmopolitan', with powerful consequences obliquely suggests a poorly understood concept of transcendence that, however, still has the capacity to mobilize collective formations. Indeed, we might speculate on the spiritual realm as a kind of a 'parking zone' of the 'supplement' – a Derridean idea referring to concepts or terms that are external to, but lie between, conceptual systems (here secular and religious) – and may be opportunistically deployed to make claims that are not entirely consistent with their basic principles.

---

[1] Peter van der Veer, "Spirituality in Modern Society," *Social Research*, 76(4) (2009): 1097–1120.

Secularism debates

In the last chapter, I touched upon the origins of secularism in Europe, which was traced, however complexly, to the end of the religious wars in the seventeenth century. The relative stability of the Westphalian order was maintained by the absolutist state, which arose in part by relegating the conscience or the inner moral person to a private sphere of the mind rather than to the public *actions* of citizens. As citizens, individuals were subject to the political authority of the state. Thus, according to Reinhard Koselleck, was produced the difference between inner devotion (spirituality) and morality and outer politicality. The history of secularism in Europe is the process whereby the absolutist state and its successor, the nation-state, institutionalized this separation through a 300-year period of state building and identity formation. Some version of this idea of secularism began to circulate throughout the world from the beginning of the twentieth century.[2]

Jose Casanova has presented a careful argument about the viability of the idea of the secular in contemporary global society. He reveals that, according to its original theory, secularism should have led to (1) decline of religious beliefs and practices, (2) marginalization of religion in the private sphere, and (3) differentiation of the secular sphere from religious institutions and norms. However, he notes that only the third – differentiation of religion from its more universal and diffuse role in historical societies – remains the historically verifiable process. Indeed, he argues that unless religions differentiate and separate from the political or theocratic ambitions and adapt to societal needs, they will tend to fail in the modern world.[3]

Charles Taylor's narrative of the emergence of secularism in modern Europe, while compatible with Casanova's analysis, reveals secularism to be an outcome of historical developments within European religions, particularly Protestantism. In Taylor's view, the self in premodern Christianity was a porous self, open to be shaped and determined by natural and supernatural phenomena. With the disenchantment of the external world and the interiorization of belief accompanying the Protestant Reformation, there emerged a 'buffered' self which looked to the relationship with the transcendent not in the outside world but within the self.

---

[2] Reinhart Koselleck, *Critique and Crisis: Enlightenment and the Pathogenesis of Modern Society* (Cambridge, MA: MIT Press, 1988) pp. 80–5.
[3] Jose Casanova, *Public Religions in the Modern World* (University of Chicago Press, 1994), pp. 211–12.

To be sure, various other historical factors such as the civilizing and disciplining process of early modern Europe also conditioned the individual to ideas of a sufficient self. But, gradually, this limitation of the role of God proceeded to the degree that the buffered self lost the need for God Himself. Taylor urges that the buffered self may be viewed as the generalization or downward extension of the Axial logic which demanded a renunciatory faith only for the elect or virtuosos in earlier periods. In this sense, secularism represents what I like to call a 'transcendence of transcendence'.

In his voluminous work, Taylor details different periods in which religious belief comes to be tied to various forms of modern identity such as nationalism or ethnicity and providential political missions; but, in the contemporary age, he finds faith and belief in the West to have become a voluntary phenomenon unmoored from its institutional underpinnings. As such, it is now part of personal or collective self-expression and a source of personal authenticity. People no longer need to find faith in the religions into which they were born; they may and do seek religious expression in a variety of world religious ideas, be it Buddhism or Mayan spirituality.[4]

Taylor's perceptive analysis appears, however, to be restricted to the contemporary West. Indeed, it works with a concept of religion that is more or less equated with faith and belief. This definition is an Abrahamic or even Protestant one that cannot be sustained for many other parts of the world. Belief and faith play a more central role in the Abrahamic faiths than in many others where ritual, cultivation practices, reciprocities, vows, divination, sacrifice and a host of other modes of human–superhuman intercourse play an equally important, if not more important, role. Indeed, in the popular religion of multicultural Singapore, people often wander from deity to deity in pursuit of the most efficacious ones. Thus, while a measure of belief is necessary, belief can be fickle, and cultivation of moral behavior or duty may play a supreme role.

Talal Asad has been among the most trenchant critics of the universalization of the idea of religion in the West. According to Asad, the idea of religion is a recent invention and represents a back-projection of the Reformation ideal of faith to all forms of faith and spirituality. Whether or not we can accept Asad's theory in totality, his formulations have been deeply illuminating and allow the scholar, particularly of the non-West, to cast the net of what may be legitimately considered religious much more widely. Additionally, he writes, "The space that religion may properly

---

[4] Charles Taylor, *A Secular Age* (Cambridge, MA: the Belknap Press of Harvard University Press, 2007).

occupy in society has to be continually redefined by the law because the reproduction of secular life within and beyond the nation-state continually affects the discursive clarity of that space."[5] Thus, by viewing secularism as a *project* of modernity, we may observe the inherent fluidity and fungibility – or traffic – of the categories of religion.

However, Asad is in danger of overgeneralizing his deconstructive proposition when he argues that there was no such thing as religion before the modern effort to contain and define it. For him, what remains in its place are multifarious practices, rituals and ideas whose role and charge vary in relation to the power structures that control them. To be sure, all our analytical categories have become suspect as a result of deconstruction. Concepts like 'class', 'society', 'culture', 'history', 'nation' and countless others that emerged as conceptual distillations of human activities no longer possess the stability they possessed in a more positivistic age. Such categories are now seen to bear the definitional profile of a historical and political moment, and since we live in an accelerating historical time, these definitions are increasingly seen as having passed their moment and unable to capture many aspects of how 'classes' and 'religions' behave. Yet, even if the deconstructive effort cannot be simply wished away, we continue to require conceptual categories and need to find a way to build the *definitional effect* into our understanding of the field.

Martin Riesebrodt has contested Asad's denial of the concept of religion by generating a perspectivist approach to religion that he calls 'referential legitimation'. Through competition, borrowings, identifications and syncretisms, those elements referred to as 'religious' tend to recognize each other and be recognized by third parties as belonging to the same or comparable frameworks of classification. Among his various examples is the case of the Mughal emperor Akbar's syncretic religion Din-i-ilahi, created in 1582, in which he sought to reconcile the religious differences among his subjects by creating a forum for dialog between representatives of Islam, Hinduism, Christianity, Jainism and Zoroastrianism.[6]

In other words, it is precisely through circulatory history that a common or, at least, compatible frame of reference and intelligibility is established. Let me draw on the Chinese case. Confucianism is notoriously difficult to define as a religion if we use metaphysical criteria, and, as we know, some even consider Confucius to be an agnostic. But Riesebrodt's method of referential legitimation works well here to show that Confucians did

---

[5] Talal Asad, *Formations of the Secular: Christianity, Islam, Modernity* (Stanford University Press, 2003), p. 201 and ch. 1.
[6] Martin Riesebrodt, *The Promise of Salvation: A Theory of Religion*, Trans. Steven Rendall (University of Chicago Press, 2010), pp. 21–37.

recognize a class of activities and ideas from Buddhism, Daoism, Christianity, Islam, etc., that indicated that they were working with an idea of religion that they called 'teachings' *(jiao)*. Recall Kublai Khan's response to Marco Polo and the Yongzheng emperor's warnings to the Jesuits to remain within the limits of 'teachings'. But what were the limits of this notion of religion?

Even until the late nineteenth century, Western scientific knowledge, first brought in by the Jesuits, was seen to have its origins in classical China. In Chinese historiography, this tendency is known as the 'Chinese origins of Western science'. Jesuit scientific cosmography was absorbed by neo-Confucians by framing it within Chinese cosmology. This was not simply a way of nationalizing science but, rather, bringing it within the Chinese moral and religious purview and utilizing it often for ritual purposes (e.g., modern astronomical knowledge to understand the will of Heaven). While many Confucians were engaged in this way of appropriating science, others, such as antireformist Wo Ren, warned that the spread of mathematical knowledge among Chinese literati youth in the latter part of the nineteenth century would drive them into the arms of Christianity!

The point I am trying to make here is that actors such as Wo Ren 'misreferenced' science as religion. We could, of course, make the argument that the assumptions of science do occupy the same categorical realms as religion; that science does indeed make cosmological claims. But, if so, the categorical separation of science from religion is not merely arbitrary but also tremendously consequential as the way religion will come to be understood by hiving off certain kinds of cosmological assumptions that it would once have regarded as a part of its own domain. As we know, this redefinition of the referential logic of religion was circulated and had to be learnt – with mixed success – around the world. Thus, while a working notion of religion can be gained through 'referential legitimation', the *definitional effect* of secularism on modern religion still had to be learnt by practitioners and accounted for by scholars.

Learning a new definitional effect does not, however, automatically remove the sacred power embedded in a transcendent or other religious practice even if it is now seen to be secular. As Asad perceptively noted, the secular has to be continually redefined – and secured – by law. Let us turn to the sacred and its transmigration.

The traffic of the sacred

With the idea of religion coming under attack, what can we possibly do about concepts like the sacred, which has an even longer history of critique? I have clarified my position on transcendence in earlier chapters and will not revisit the issue. Among critics of the Durkheimean notion of the sacred, the latest is Riesebrodt, who, while agreeing with Durkheim's view of religion as a response to crisis, contingency and the limits of human capacities, believes that the sacrality of society is of limited generalizability.[7] There is no doubt that the degree and effects of sacrality vary greatly in time and space, but the sacred remains an important resource that different types of authority continue to deploy in different contexts and institutions. Witness the sacred at the heart of what I have described as the nationalist regime of authenticity.

In older religions, the sacred typically surrounds the worldly expressions of transcendence endowing them – their spaces and times – with reverence and inviolability. But, as we have seen, it can also envelop the non-transcendent such as the nation or the lineage. How can we understand the relations between the sacred and the social and political operations of power that shape its role in different societies? The most important debates on this question are represented by the Durkheimean versus the Marxist or materialist positions. For Durkheim, religion is a 'social fact' and the source of moral authority of a society or an ethical collectivity. For the Marxists, religion is not a social fact but a class fact: sacred authority is a function not of societal needs as a whole but of elite structures to enable domination.

I do not doubt that sacred authority is manipulated or dominated by power-holders (but not by all power-holders, since one of the historical roles of transcendent power has been precisely to split authority); but it is less easy to grasp whether that is the only *raison d'être* of sacred authority. In some ways, our contemporary consumerist society, which has perhaps the least space for sacred and transcendent regimes of any society, may be the best material we possess to test the hypothesis that sacrality is *solely* a function of class domination. While the rigorous test of such a hypothesis will require an entirely separate agenda of research, suffice it to say that class and capitalist domination continues to be rampant. But social integration and moral values are in decline, and the revival of religion appears in many cases to be directed against the decline of values and to some extent against domination. Sacred authority is autonomous and capable of being mobilized by the counter-establishment.

In Chapter 2, I have discussed the difference between the *regime of eternity* and the *regime of authenticity*, reflecting the difference between historical religions, where the transcendent trumped or fashioned the

---

[7] *Ibid.*, pp. 64–5. See also Tomoko Masuzawa, *In Search of Dreamtime: The Quest for the Origin of Religion* (University of Chicago Press, 1993).

202	The traffic between secularism and transcendence

course of history, and nationalisms and identity movements, where the stillness of the true or the 'unchanging authentic' underlay the course of an ever-changing history, bounding and channeling the river of time. In both regimes, what secured their authority was none other than the *sacred* attaching to the universal transcendent (religions) and the partial transcendent (nation). The migration or the traffic of the sacred into the secular has been observed by many turn-of-the-century thinkers such as Weber, Durkheim and Carl Schmitt. Indeed, the idea of traffic I develop here seeks to capture and elaborate as an analytical concept the particular contributions of these social theorists, each of whom saw this migration as part of his philosophy.

Carl Schmitt, the German philosopher who joined the Nazi Party, is perhaps the most provocative.

All significant concepts of modern theory of the state are secularized theological concepts not only because of their historical development – in which they were transferred to the theory of the state, whereby, for example, the omnipotent God became the omnipotent lawgiver – but also because of their systematic structure, the recognition of which is necessary for a sociological consideration of these concepts. The exception in jurisprudence is analogous to the miracle in theology.[8]

By the analogy of the 'miracle', Schmitt suggests that the power of the modern state to define the 'exception' is the revelation of the true nature of the sovereign, which is necessarily modeled on an omnipotent God. The true sovereign in modern society has to be 'underived', ultimately indivisible and resolute in making decisions during times of emergency. But this sovereign for Schmitt was also necessarily a limited sovereign, a limited transcendence, limited to protecting 'us' from the 'Other', friend from enemy. Regarding the relationship between theology and jurisprudence, he notes, "Both have a double principle, reason (hence there is a natural theology and a natural jurisprudence) and scripture, which means a book with positive revelations and directives."[9] The confrontation of friend and enemy is ultimately at a metaphysical level – one between faiths.[10] Note that Schmitt's religious model for the modern state came not from Christian universalism but from the confessional faiths of the seventeenth and eighteenth centuries.

Despite his public allegiance to secularism, Durkheim sought to replace the disappearing moral ethos of religion with the idea of society itself, through what he called civil religion. When Durkheim revealed religion to be none other than society worshipping itself, he also circulated the idea

---

[8] Carl Schmitt, *Political Theology: Four Chapters on the Concept of Sovereignty*, Trans. George Schwab (University of Chicago Press, 2005/1985), p. 36.
[9] *Ibid.*, p. 37.   [10] Tracy Strong, "Foreword," in Schmitt, *Political Theology*, p. xxx.

that society itself is sacred – a notion that the women of the Daodehui would have readily understood. For Durkheim, this sacrality was necessary for the moral order in any society – whether it was the tribe or the modern nation-state. According to Vincent Pecora, the undisguised sacralization of the social urged by this kind of proposal also influenced Nazi thinkers like Carl Schmitt in developing a corporatist order of society subject to the state.[11]

Sacrality is closely associated with, and is frequently the condition for, sacrifice. Ivan Strenski suggests that the modern theory of sacrifice – a French theory derived from the 'intransigent Roman Catholics' in the post-Reformation era – developed by Durkheim and the Durkheimeans at the end of the nineteenth century, was very much a kind of bourgeois version of religious sacrifice. In contrast to the Catholics, the Durkheimean theory emphasized not 'giving up' the self, but 'giving of' the self. The former, as we will see in our discussion of Gandhi, was giving up the self *in toto*, whereas, in the latter, something belonging to the self is sacrificed, but, "prudently, he sets himself aside."[12] Indeed, sacrifice comes to require a mediating victim such as the nation's soldier. Civil religion would require a new kind of altruism whereby sacrifice would have to be adapted to balance humanism with the ideology of self-interest. Durkheimeans, of course, did not "invoke theistic sanctions to support sacrifice, but their devotion to 'humanity' and 'society' (at least as embodied in the French nation) surely counts as a fundamental value as operationally transcendent as traditional beliefs in God."[13]

Although Western social theorists were keen to demonstrate the systemic novelty of the modern, they were also deeply concerned about the loss of the inviolable. Thus, while most of them may not have created a generalized notion such as 'traffic', they were keenly aware of how the sacred was or could be transferred in particular areas of inquiry.

Traffic in East Asia

The global institutionalization of the bifurcation of 'religion' and the secular is inseparable from the circulation of the nation-state form across the world in the twentieth century. Given that nation-states were founded

---

[11] Vincent Pecora, *Secularization and Cultural Criticism: Religion, Nation, and Modernity* (University of Chicago Press, 2006), pp. 124–6; see also George Schwab, "Introduction" to Schmitt, *Political Theology*, pp. l, li.
[12] Ivan Strenski, *Contesting Sacrifice: Religion, Nationalism and Social Thought in France* (University of Chicago Press, 1997), p. 166.
[13] *Ibid.*, p. 179.

on ideals of science, progress, popular sovereignty and freedom, these states became cosmologically and practically committed to the creation of religion as a distinct and contained sphere. Whereas, in most prenational states, religion was often fused with the polity, modern nation-states seek to keep them apart. For instance, Article 36 of the 1982 constitution of the PRC states that the state may not compel or discriminate against people's religious *beliefs*; it also specifies that "no one may make use of religion to engage in activities that disrupt public order, impair the health of citizens or interfere with the educational system of the state." Although there are, of course, significant differences, the US constitution institutes a similar separation: The First Amendment declares that "Congress shall make no law respecting an establishment of religion, or prohibiting the free exercise thereof."

At the same time, both the state, by means of its legal, classificatory and coercive powers, and social groups are constantly breaching this separation and remaking religion and the secular sphere. One of the factors enabling this breach is actually the lack of definition of religion itself in most national constitutions or international law.[14] This underspecification enables the changing content of the meaning of religion.

Reacting to the perceived or alleged claims of Christianity (itself undergoing reformulation) as the spiritual ideology of the modern era, Chinese and Japanese groups began to create their own new distinctions among ritual, religion, superstition and secularism, which also circulated in the East Asian region as a whole. I consider several instances of this reconstitution and circulation, such as state ritualism, the Confucian religion movement and the New Life movement of the Kuomintang (KMT), among others.[15]

We have seen that in Japan the state cult (a modified *jisi* model) was adapted to attain the goals of the nation-state while claiming that it was not

---

[14] T. Jeremey Gunn, "The Complexity of Religion and the Definition of 'Religion' in International Law," *Harvard Human Rights Journal, 16* (2003): 189–215, at pp. 190–1.

[15] Specifically, I want to explore the different ways in which the new religion has been adapted – particularly by elites – to serve or articulate with modern projects of subject formation, such as in citizenship, nationalism, ethnicity and civil society. What explains the different modes of absorption? Next, I want to show that however the new conception of religion is absorbed by the elites – especially modernizing elites – it has to deal with the older reality of popular society in which cosmological ideas permeate many different practices in everyday life, such as trade, agriculture, gender, sexuality, food, community life, etc. As we know, these practices are often characterized as superstitious, backward and irrational. One of the most complex historical issues of twentieth-century Asian history is the manner in which modernizing forces in these societies have sought to incorporate popular life-forms. I will argue that the new understandings of religion also represent modes – different modes – of transforming and overhauling an entire society.

religion. From the beginning of the twentieth century, the imperial Qing state also sought in some ways to adapt the state cult to modern goals, but for various reasons this did not take hold in the same way as in Japan. During its last decade (1900–11), the Qing made efforts to elevate the state cult with national rites for Confucius and introduce sacrifices to Confucius in the new schools.[16] The republic of 1912, however, abandoned the education of the Confucian classics in primary schools. The president of the republic, Yuan Shikai, was not averse to the reverence for Confucius, but he was ultimately opposed to the effort to establish it as a national religion. The reasons for his opposition relate to the dangers of alienating the Christian missionaries and imperialist powers and further alienating the Buddhists and Muslims.[17]

The state cult around Confucius could not win over the territorially vast ethnic regions which had adhered to the Qing notions of intercultural and interreligious demonstrations of imperial sovereignty. Most of Mongolia had already seceded, and neither Tibet nor Xinjiang (known by ethnic nationalists as Eastern Turkestan) remained securely within the new imperial-national formation. In 1914, however, Yuan revived the synchronized sacrifices and reverences to Heaven and Confucius (and the consolidation of the Yue Fei/Guandi temples). But he was careful to declare that reverence for the sages was not a religious act.[18] Like the Meiji state, he, too, was making a distinction between state rituals drawn from history (*jisi*) and 'religion' which citizens were free to choose. But his writ did not reach far during the republic and he died soon after.

During the same first decade of the century, there was also an effort to transform Confucianism into a national religion (Kongjiaohui, or Confucian Religion Association) by a group of literati, led most notably by Kang Youwei, who came to believe that religion (in the modern sense) was a necessary condition of the modern transformation. Much is being written about this movement, so I will not go into its details. In his youth, Kang became convinced that monotheism and a devotion to a single God were the key to Western success. He admired Martin Luther deeply, devoted himself to the elevation of Confucius as God and expressed considerable intolerance of other Chinese deities or even the

---

[16] Ya-pei Kuo, "Redeploying Confucius: The Imperial State Dreams of the Nation, 1902–1911," in Mayfair Yang, Ed., *Chinese Religiosities: Afflictions of Modernity and State Formation* (Berkeley and Los Angeles, CA: University of California Press, 2008), pp. 65–86.

[17] Mori Noriko, "Riben he Zhongguo jindaihua guochengzhongde guojiaowenti" ("The Problem of National Religion in the Transition to Modernity in China and Japan"), paper presented at the International Symposium on "Constructing Modern Knowledge in China, 1600–1949," Academia Sinica, Taiwan, October 25–6, 2004, p. 6.

[18] *Ibid.*, p. 6.

other sages of the Confucian tradition.[19] Whether or not Kang 'believed' in Confucius as God, we can think of his effort as one which sought to produce a civic religion for the new nation-state. It sought to attain a certain model of citizen that drew upon current understandings of monotheism and Protestantism. In other words, Kang sought to create a new idea of a religion that was infused with ideals of modern citizenship – a reverse traffic based upon new circulations.

In response to those who urged that a national religion was incompatible with religious freedom, Kang Youwei drew attention to the many European countries, including England, Germany and Denmark, which supported national churches. Kang sought to model Kongjiao explicitly along the current practices and organization of Christianity. He proposed sacrifices to Confucius and Heaven by officials, and by establishing Confucius associations all over the country, he sought to institutionalize Confucian preachings and Sunday worship, a Confucian calendar (like the Christian system of dating) and the celebration of Confucius' birthday. In these ways, the Kongjiao movement sought to absorb what they conceived to be the power of Christianity while rejecting the content of Christian beliefs. At the same time, by establishing it as a 'national religion', they clearly sought to create a tradition that was suitable for the creation of a national citizenry.[20]

As the second decade of the century came to a close, the growth of radicalism within China, which dovetailed with secularizing international developments such as the Russian Revolution and the disestablishment of national churches, made the movement for a national religion increasingly unviable among the intellectual circles in Chinese society. Indeed, the May 4th Movement was premised not merely upon anti-Confucianism but also upon an unremitting hostility to religion. The Confucian religion movement became increasingly obscured, and many of its advocates, such as Zheng Xiaoxu, now began to declare it a Confucius *studies* movement. At the same time, the religious interpretation of Confucianism or the effort to see it as a part of a redemptive faith became more developed in the new syncretic redemptive societies, such as the Daodehui, which flourished during this period (see Chapter 5) and of which Kang became the president in the 1920s. Dialogical transcendence appears to have prevailed over Kang's early commitment to radical monotheism.[21]

---

[19] Wei Leong Tay, "Saving the Chinese Nation and the World: Religion and Confucian Reformation, 1880s–1937," MA dissertation submitted to the National University of Singapore, 2012, pp. 25–35.

[20] *Ibid.*; see also Mori Noriko, "Riben he Zhongguo jindaihua," p. 5.

[21] See Duara, *Sovereignty and Authenticity*, ch. 4.

Let us also look at another Confucian moral campaign, the New Life movement, initiated in 1934 by Jiang Jieshi (Chiang Kai-shek). Modeled significantly upon the YMCA movement, it sought to infuse notions of modern citizenship with Confucian ethics and spirituality.[22] As Madame Jiang Jieshi, or Song Meiling, the daughter of a Christian entrepreneur adopted by missionaries, described it, the movement sought to draw upon Confucian ideals as the inner counterpart of spiritual and moral renovation (*gexin*) in relation to outer political and economic reform. The campaign was originally launched after the elimination of communists from the Jiangxi soviet and was designed to create an ethic of citizenship drawn from national traditions. In this case, Confucianism was being reconstructed along the model of contemporary Christian practices, but perceived as appealing to an authentic national tradition.

It is instructive that neither the New Life movement nor the Confucian religion movement emphasized the cosmological dimension – the unity of Heaven, Earth and man – or the ethic of filiality which had been central to historical Confucianism. Moreover, Jiang is known to have emphasized the *chi*, or shame – national shame – of China's humiliation, which he interpreted as something he and the Chinese people needed to endure until the time was ripe to avenge the nation. Indeed, according to Grace Huang, Jiang, who began to systematically read the Bible in 1934, admired Jesus especially for being able to endure great humiliation through the spirit of forbearance, sacrifice and struggle.[23] Adapting a universalist doctrine to a regime of authenticity involved commitment to the honor of nation and state.

There is also a growing literature on the Chinese communist production of new rituals that were crucial to the formation of revolutionary citizens. Writers have recorded the ritual performances and theatricalized politics of the 'speak bitterness' and '*fanshen*' (to 'turn over the body') practices of revolutionary rebirth, a process similar to conversion. These revolutionary rituals, which were increasingly performed around the savior figure of Mao Zedong, peaked during the Cultural Revolution. They

---

[22] It is worth exploring to what extent the New Life movement also represented an extension – or development – of the state cult. Between Yuan Shikai and the New Life, there were various efforts to modernize the state cult by eliminating sacrifices to nature gods and memorializing semideified heroes (see C. K. Yang, *Religion in Chinese Society* (Berkeley and Los Angeles, CA: University of California Press, 1967), p. 365). Certainly, the fact that the New Life was a statist top-down movement of mobilization caused it to resemble the state cult or the Shinto state rather more than a movement of interiorized moral reconstruction. Indeed, perhaps this dissonance made it appear so ridiculous to modern Chinese and outsiders.

[23] Grace Huang, "The Politics of Knowing Shame: Agency in Jiang Jieshi's Leadership (1927–1936)," Ph.D. dissertation submitted to the University of Chicago, 2003.

were particularly important for the emotional investment of the people in the redemptive role of the Chinese Communist Party during the first twenty years of its rule. To be sure, the contradictions and tensions between the iconoclastic secularism of communist ideology and the practice of sacred rituals contributed to the volatile conditions of the Maoist period. It is thus not surprising that the subsequent decades opted for a gentler and more stable ideology of the spirit, such as the campaign for 'socialist spiritual civilization' and the movement against the 'spiritual pollution' of bourgeois and foreign values.[24] The idea of traffic permits us to see not only the somewhat arbitrary divisions of the secular from the religious but also how political or other actors seek to endow new, secular ideas and institutions of citizenship with the moral authority of older cosmological systems – Confucian, Christian and other – even when the latter are renounced.

Korea and Vietnam

Finally, I want to mention two important redemptive movements in the Sinosphere: the Chondogyo in Korea and the Caodai religion in Vietnam. Both movements deserve much fuller attention than my expertise will permit, but they are particularly important when we observe how dialogical transcendence was adapted to create an autonomous sovereign space under – and to resist – colonial domination. Emerging at the end of the nineteenth and early twentieth centuries, they represented religiosity in the mold of Chinese redemptive societies. At the same time, they developed new purposes and goals in the public sphere under the Japanese and French empires, respectively. Both had very large, national followings, and they combined inclusion, condominium, syncretism, spirit mediumship and a redemptive mission. Both societies aspired to replace the colonial government with a more universalistic state based on their ideals.

The Chondogyo (Teachings of the Heavenly Way) grew out of the Donghak peasant rebellion in late nineteenth-century Korea that advocated resistance to Western imperialism and the restoration of 'Eastern Learning' (Donghak). The Chondogyo combined Confucian ideals with

---

[24] See Ann Anagnost, *National Past-Times: Narrative, Representation, and Power in Modern China* (Durham, NC: Duke University Press, 1997); David E. Apter and Tony Saich, *Revolutionary Discourse in Mao's Republic* (Cambridge, MA: Harvard University Press, 1994); Stephan Feuchtwang, *Popular Religion in China: The Imperial Metaphor* (London: Routledge Curzon, 2001), pp. 220–50; Prasenjit Duara, "History and Globalization in China's Long Twentieth Century," *Modern China*, *34*(1) (2008): 152–64.

Buddhism, Daoism and Korean shamanism, and subsequently incorporated the Christian idea of God. Even today the Chondogyo claims over 1 million adherents in South Korea and allegedly over 2 million in North Korea. A recent statement of Chondogyo thought declares that its truth is both transcendent and within each self and every space; thus, "we must live in conformity to the cosmic order and realize the infinite within the self."[25]

In 2007, I was surprised to see the extent to which the principal Chondogyo church and headquarters was indeed modeled on the congregational principle of the Protestant church, including a pulpit, stained-glass windows and a simple symbol of worship: a silver bowl of clear water. At the same time, a Confucian style altar contains the memorial of the founder. The basic prayer developed in the nineteenth century by its founder goes thus:

Infinite energy being now within me, I yearn that it
may pour into all living beings and created things.
Since this energy abides in me, I am identified with God
and of one nature with all existence. Should I ever forget
these things, all existing things will know of it.[26]

Although the Chondogyo periodically split into factions, including those committed to a reformist program under Japanese rule, the society was known to have led the resistance to the Japanese occupation particularly in the early stages and during the landmark March 1919 independence movement against colonial rule. While it remained highly nationalistic during most of its history, it is committed to remain constructively but essentially 'antigovernment' in spirit. Moreover, its nationalism is phrased as the liberation of each and every nation from alien domination, which it views as not at all contradictory to a cooperative world society.

In the prewar era, Chondogyo members undertook meditation and self-cultivation in order to "transform one's nature through bodily practices" (以身 換性) and produce solidarity of spiritual will and organizational strength. The second generation of intellectuals in the organization, particularly those associated with its journal, *Kaebyŏk*, became more engaged with radical social issues, and, while many of

[25] Yook Suk-san, *Chondogyo: The Religion of the Cosmos That Blossomed in Korea*, Trans. Young Hee Lee (Seoul: Central Headquarters of Chondogyo, 2002). For North Korean adherents, (http://en.wikipedia.org/wiki/Cheondoism).

[26] R. Pierce Beaver, "Chondogyo and Korea," *Journal of Bible and Religion, 30*(2) (1962): 115–22, at p. 120.

them became affiliated with Marxist or socialist movements, they continued to represent the prophetic voice which sought to socialize their religious ideal that "People are Heaven."[27] The transcendent has migrated from Heaven to the people.

With respect to its goals of discipline, sacrifice and spiritual preparation of the self, Chondogyo resembles other movements in Asia under colonial rule or occupation. For instance, Confucian groups that were ejected from the Chinese mainland with the communist victory also developed ideals of spiritual preparation for recovery of the mainland. But several of those, such as the founders of the New Asia College in Hong Kong, did not necessarily see themselves as engaging in religious activities. Rather, they viewed their activities as secular efforts to recover and maintain the *spirit* of Chinese civilization.

Caodai, or more fully, the Great Way of the Third Age of Universal Redemption (*Đài Đạo Tam Kỳ Phổ Độ*), was founded by educated Vietnamese in 1926. It represented a classic redemptive society that sought to fuse spirit-mediumship, or, more specifically, spirit writing of the literati, with Daoism, Confucianism, Buddhism, Hinduism and Christianity. Caodaists not only boasted that they were the largest religion in Vietnam but also claimed to attract more followers in a single decade than did Christianity during its 300-year history in Vietnam. According to Janet Hoskins, Caodai currently has 3–6 million followers within Vietnam and around 50,000 overseas. It was also able to bridge the gap between rural society and the urban elite more successfully than other organizations.[28]

The narrative of Caodai foregrounded the spiritual destiny of the Vietnamese nation to realize the great religious truths and traditions of Asia. The Vietnamese were a chosen people because they, having *suffered* more than any other people under the most repressive colonial regime in Asia, were charged with the mission of "uniting all these religions into One to bring them back to the primordial unity." Through séances and spirit writing, Caodaists engaged in reverential conversations with the great sages, including not only their founding sage, but also Laozi, Confucius, Buddha and Jesus as well as a host of more recent figures

[27] Jae-yon Lee, "Magazines and the Collaborative Emergence of Literary Writers in Korea, 1919–1927," Ph.D. dissertation submitted to the University of Chicago, May 31, 2012, pp. 84–124.

[28] Janet A. Hoskins, "God's Chosen People: Race, Religion and Anti-Colonial Resistance in French Indochina," Asia Research Institute Working Paper Series no. 189, September 2012. National University of Singapore. See also Janet A. Hoskins, *The Divine Eye and the Diaspora: Vietnamese Syncretism Becomes Transpacific Caodaism* (Honolulu, HI: University of Hawaii Press, in press).

such as Shakespeare, Rousseau, Sun Yat-sen, Gandhi, Tagore and the most celebrated, Victor Hugo.[29]

Western observers, such as Norman Lewis and Graham Greene, who were flabbergasted by such a spectacle, mocked the religion. Lewis described their "palace in candy form from a coloured fantasy by Disney, an example of funfair architecture in extreme form: Over the doorway was a grotesquely undignified piece of statuary showing Jesus Christ borne upon the shoulders of Lao Tse and in his turn carrying Confucius and Buddha. They are made to look like Japanese acrobats about to begin their Act." Hoskins responds to such a view by interpreting Caodai as a "'religion of reversal,' one that imagined a world in which Asian spiritual masters would come to replace Western colonial masters."[30] Moreover, the inclusion of great Western humanist figures like Hugo, who was the great enemy of the conqueror of Indochina, Napoleon III, does not represent fawning awe of Westerners but honors the spirit of those who can speak truth to power.

Like many other expressions of dialogical transcendence, there is a politics of hierarchical encompassment in Caodai. Christianity is given a distinctly lower place – as are popular spirits – in the hierarchy of sages and gods, at the top of which is the Buddha (also represented by his 'predecessors', Brahma, Vishnu and Shiva). In terms of worldly engagement, Caodai was involved in the rural reconstruction projects so popular among reformers and spiritual leaders across Asia during the first half of the twentieth century, whether it was Liang Shuming, Gandhi or the Chondogyo. An American observer noted that there "is a Gandhiesque flavor about creating a community which is economically self-sufficient," remarking that the Great Temple in Tay Ninh had a village, school, printing press and weaver's looms.[31]

At the same time, although Caodai foreswore armed violence, unlike most other redemptive societies, it willy-nilly became involved in resistance. By virtue of the fact that it was the closest thing to a mass movement, the French came down hard on it in 1940. Caodaists first resisted the French by allying with the Japanese, and then with the French against the

---

[29] Hoskins, "God's Chosen People," p. 15: quotation from a spirit message from the Jade Emperor.

[30] Lewis cited in Janet Hoskins, "Seeing Syncretism as Visual Blasphemy: Critical Eyes on Caodai Religious Architecture," *Material Religion*, 6(1) (2010): 30–59, at p. 40; for quotation from Hoskins, see p. 44.

[31] Virginia Thompson, quoted in Hoskins, "God's Chosen People," p. 23. The most important Caodai leader, Phạm Công Tắc, described himself as following the path of Gandhi, although he may have been prepared to use force more readily. See Janet Hoskins, "A Posthumous Return from Exile: The Legacy of an Anticolonial Religious Leader in Today's Vietnam," *Southeast Asian Studies*, 1(2) (2012): 213–46.

Vietminh, who attacked Caodai communities and killed many Caodai leaders.[32] By and large, the accommodationist and absorptive stance of Caodai was open to circulatory global phenomena, while its strong sense of autonomy founded upon transcendent universalism empowered it to overcome the worldly hegemony of colonialism.

Circulation and traffic among Peranakans

In the story so far, we have discussed the traffic between religion and secular expressions of self and citizen in East Asia. The story of the Chinese Peranakan of the Dutch East Indies during the first part of the twentieth century introduces the traffic between religion and ethnic-national identity formation. Lying, as it were, at the intersection of two different regional systems – the independent, if politically subordinate, East Asian region and the dependent European colonial region – the Peranakan community allows us to observe the imbrication of different sets of circulatory ideas and practices. Thus, it may also allow us to identify the particularity of the secular–religious differentiation in modern China.

The Indies Peranakans traced their origin back five centuries to Chinese trader immigrants to the Indies, who created what G. W. Skinner has called "Creole cultures" (or a third culture) in Southeast Asian societies. At the upper levels, these merchant communities interacted – often as bureaucrats and advisers – with the royal court and aristocracies in local society. At the lower level, too, the traders frequently intermarried with local women and spoke the local languages or the lingua franca.

While, in the non-colonial parts of Southeast Asia, such as Thailand or Cambodia, the Chinese tended over several generations to assimilate with the local populations, in the colonial societies of British Malaya, the Dutch East Indies and the Spanish Philippines, colonial policies of segregation among both Europeans and indigenous people tended to stabilize the Creole culture among these earlier immigrants. These Creole communities became important economic and managerial intermediaries between the colonial power and native population, on the one hand, and, on the other hand, as new Chinese immigration grew in the later part of the nineteenth century, between them and the colonial power. In many cases, they were blamed for the ills of the colonial system by serving as its most proximate instrument of exploitation.[33]

---

[32] Hoskins, "God's Chosen People," pp. 25–9.
[33] G. W. Skinner, "Creolized Chinese Societies in Southeast Asia," in Anthony Reid, Ed., *Sojourners and Settlers: Histories of Southeast Asia and the Chinese* (Sydney: Allen and Unwin, 1995), pp. 50–93, at pp. 50–63.

The wave of new immigrants from China, known as the *sinkeh* in Malaya and *totok* in the Dutch East Indies, transformed the status of the Creole communities in the colonies. In the Philippines, the *mestizos*, who had earlier sided with the indigenous population against the Spanish, were largely assimilated into that population. In Malaya, the Baba Peranakans tended to assimilate with the *sinkeh*; only the Dutch East Indies Peranakans, for a host of historical reasons, remained distinctive. Today they still make up about 3 percent of the population of Indonesia. They spoke bazaar Malay, the lingua franca of urban Dutch East Indies, and wrote their literature in this language, as opposed to the Chinese written by *totoks* and the court Malay favored by the Indonesian elites.[34] In 1920, less than a third of all Chinese in Indonesia used Chinese as their main language or everyday speech. Even in the 1930s, about 80% of Indonesian Chinese were born there, and 80% of those born there had fathers born in Indonesia.[35]

The survival and evolution of Peranakan identity had to do with their particular relationship to the Dutch colonial state and to China and the new Chinese. But the identity itself was significantly expressed in the language and practices of religion, which marked them off not only from their local neighbors but also, in interesting ways, from the other Chinese. Initially, at the turn of the century, it was the Peranakans who sought to take the lead in the re-Sinicization (or perhaps simply Sinicization) project. As the Chinese nationalist organizer Hu Hanmin commented, in 1908, there were few Peranakans who knew their Chinese names or had anything Chinese about them save for the queue, ironically a symbol, particularly for the revolutionary nationalist, of the subordination of Chinese to the Manchus. Kwee Tek Hoay (郭德怀) added they knew their homeland not by its name of *Zhonghua* but by the pejorative Western appellation, *Tjina*.[36]

The early Peranakan Sinicizers were responding in part to the efforts of Chinese nationalists seeking to mobilize their wealth and identities, but the initiative also came simultaneously from local and regional efforts at mobilization. The connections between Peranakans in various parts of

[34] Leo Suryadinata, "From Peranakan Chinese Literature to Indonesian Literature: A Preliminary Study," in Suryadinata, Ed., *Chinese Adaptation and Diversity* (Singapore University Press, 1993), pp. 101–3.

[35] J. A. Mackie and Charles A. Coppell, *A Preliminary Survey: The Chinese in Indonesia* (Deakin: Australian Institute of International Affairs, 1976), pp. 1–18, at pp. 6–7.

[36] Hu Hanmin, "Nanyang yu Zhongguo geming" ("Nanyang and the Chinese Revolution"), in *Zhonghua minguo kaiguo wushinian wenxian*. 1.11 Gemingzhi changdao yu fazhan (Taipei: Zhonghua minguo kaiguo wushinian wenxian bianzhuan weiyuanhui, 1964), pp. 457–84.

Southeast Asia facilitated by the new media of newspapers and magazines, as well as the wave of arrivals from China, led to a new consciousness of China and Chineseness. For instance, the Confucian texts, *The Great Learning* and *Doctrine of the Mean*, were translated into Malay in 1900. In the Dutch East Indies, this consciousness among the Peranakan elite became institutionalized in the Tiong Hoa Hwe Koan (Zhonghua Huiguan, THHK). This was formed in 1900 by "awakened" Peranakan leaders to propagate the Confucian religion, support Chinese education and reform the customs of the Chinese.[37]

During this early period, the most influential Chinese nationalist group in Southeast Asia was the reform party led by Kang Youwei and Liang Qichao. The emergence of national consciousness among Peranakan leaders coincided with the failure of the 100 Days Reform and the subsequent Boxer Rebellion, which was regarded as disastrous. Consequently, reform of Chinese customs and the introduction of modern education in Chinese, English or Dutch were high among the agenda of the THHK. But of equal, if not greater, significance for them was the propagation of the 'Confucian religion'. The goal of the reformers was "to create a religion or a moral system that was pure for use as a guide and a source of improvement in their social lives ... [reforms were to be undertaken] insofar as possible in keeping with *those principles of the prophet Confucius* so necessary to civilized conduct" (emphasis added).[38] Indeed, as D. E. Willmott observed in his 1960 study, interest in religion among the Chinese in Indonesia had grown steadily until then.[39] The urge to reform customs among the Chinese elites led not to the decline of religion, as it did in among Chinese intellectuals, but, rather, to new articulations of faith and practice as well as to the spread of Christianity.

The reasons that religion became more rather than less influential in the Dutch East Indies compared to the situation in China seem to be rather clear. In the Dutch East Indies, religion not only represented a desideratum of a modern community (as part of a rational and deistic civilization), but it also became even more closely tied to the problem of national and civilizational identity. Compare this Confucian movement to Kang

---

[37] See Kwee Tek Hoay, *The Origins of the Modern Chinese Movement in Indonesia (Atsal Moelahnja Timboel Pergerakan Tionghua jang Modern di Indonesia)*, from *Moestika Romans*, 73–84 (1936–9), Trans. and Ed. Lea E. Williams, Translation Series, Modern Indonesia Project, Southeast Asia Program (Ithaca, NY: Cornell University Press, 1969), p. 17. See also Kwee's writings in *Moestika Dharma*; e.g., "God and Wars," *Moestika Dharma: Mandblad tentang Agama, Kabatinan dan Philosofie* [monthly magazine about religion, spirituality and philosophy], 92 (1939/Year VIII): 405–8.

[38] Kwee, *The Origins of the Modern Chinese Movement*, p. 6.

[39] Donald E. Willmott, *The Chinese of Semarang: A Changing Minority Community in Indonesia* (Ithaca, NY: Cornell University Press, 1960), p. 188.

Youwei's in China. Indeed, the two movements were closely related. The founders of the THHK were profoundly influenced by Kang's ideas and programs. The Confucian school was expected to meet twice a month on the first and fifteenth day to hear sermons and explanations of Confucian texts in the manner of their Chinese counterpart, although they were also self-consciously following the example of the missionary schools.[40] In 1903, Kang Youwei gave several lectures to throngs of listeners at the THHK center in Batavia. He served as their adviser, and the leaders even asked him to adjudicate a dispute over religious protocol, which I will discuss below.

Yet, as noted above, Kang's Confucian religion movement disappeared into the Confucian studies association and into the suppressed redemptive societies. The reasons for this were connected to the rise of the antireligious May 4th Movement and Kang's inability to secure state support. I suggested that the KMT's New Life movement may be seen as its secular successor, but while the latter participated in the traffic by fashioning itself as the traditional conscience of the new citizen, it did not see itself as a religion, nor did it represent a source of moral authority separate from or transcending the state. Moreover, the social and political environment in which Kang sought to cultivate the Confucian religion movement did not necessitate a strong identitarian movement to distinguish the self from powerful rejecting or assimilating Other(s) *in religious terms.*

It is true that Kang responded to the pressure of Christianity and the imperialist discourse of civilization. But if, for the moment, we can distinguish analytically the effort to create a religion perceived as a requirement of moral citizenship from that which was primarily an identitarian movement – a movement, if you will, for recognition – then I believe the balance for Kang lay in the former. Certainly, the powerful anti-Christian and antireligious movement launched by the intelligentsia in the 1920s reveals that they did not seek their alternative source of identity in the recognized religions.

In the colonial environment of the Dutch East Indies, the balance was reversed in the Confucian movement, as religion was perceived to be essential to the challenge of identity. This challenge came not only from Christianity's hegemonic presence in the colonial environment, where the rulers identified it with civilized religion, but also from Islam, which claimed to represent the majority of the population and was identified with the religions of the book. Islam had competitive claims to civilization

---

[40] Kwee, *The Origins of the Modern Chinese Movement*, p. 15.

particularly when monotheism and anti-idolatry were assumed to be the norms or, perhaps, the rules of the game of civilized religion. In these ways, the Confucian Association and the Sam Kauw Hwee among Peranakans resembled other non-Islamic colonial religious renewal or reform movements such as modern Buddhism in Sri Lanka or Burma, and Vedanta Hinduism in British India.

Confucian religion in the Dutch East Indies tended to become a kind of confessional nationalism and had to play a larger role than either as civic conscience or as privatized religion. This ideology had to both sanction reform and create an authentic foundation for Chinese identity. But if reform and change eroded the authentic, they threatened identity. This is, of course, a classic aporia of nationalist ideology, and haunted the Peranakans no less than everyone else.

Like Kang Youwei and the reformers in China, THHK also identified Confucianism with education and reform. Modern educational opportunities were a key demand of the Peranakan community as the best means to improve their situation. Denied Dutch education, the THHK launched Chinese schools to improve their educational opportunities. This was initially quite successful and had the effect of pressuring the Dutch to introduce Dutch education for Chinese as early as 1905. Ironically, if not entirely unpredictably, this had the further effect of reducing enrollments in the THHK Chinese schools, and the educational enterprise of the THHK was widely regarded as a failure. But, of course, since it was designed to pressure the Dutch, its failure was also its success. At the same time, it reinforced the Dutch or non-Chinese orientation of the Peranakans.[41]

The reform of "superstitious and burdensome customs," especially in the area of funerals and marriages, was an area of great concern among the THHK. The Peranakan writer, dramatist and reformer Kwee Tek Hoay (1886–1952) wrote a history of the THHK entitled *The Origins of the Modern Chinese Movement in Indonesia*. He spent a good third of the book documenting the efforts of the awakened leaders to battle against everything 'false' and reform the impure customs, superstitious beliefs and offerings to idols and shrines among the Dutch East Indies Chinese that were far "from the ancestral rites, temple ceremonies and other customs of the Chinese tradition." His

---

[41] In 1910, the Dutch also responded to the Chinese nationality law of 1909 by establishing the category of Dutch 'subjects', which included persons born in the colony of parents who were domiciled there. In practice, Chinese governments did not give up the claim of Chinese citizenship among Peranakans until the Sino-Indonesian Treaty abolishing dual nationality in 1960. Mackie and Coppel, *A Preliminary Study*, p. 9.

story of the THHK is an exciting and heroic tale about the reformers who battled victoriously against the forces of the official cultural authority of the Peranakan community located in the *gongguan*. This was the office of the Chinese major in Batavia which managed ceremonies and festivities and ran a traditional school (*yixue*) that taught Chinese characters, although rather lackadaisically.[42]

After gaining control of the community leadership in the early 1900s, the THHK reformers went about reforming the festivities. During the ceremony of the rites for the wandering ghosts in the seventh lunar month (Keng Hoo Peng, or *jing heping*), a contest had developed where contestants raced to grab ritual objects at the top of raised platforms. This appeared to be somewhat violent and turbulent, but it was a festive occasion. The reformers simply stopped the flow of money to sponsor the event. They also used the power of the purse to limit the activities of the priest who prayed for the community at the altars of many gods. They paid the priest a small bribe and asked him to ignore the gods not provided for in his fees! They prohibited gambling and other competitions at the festivities.[43]

Kwee's heroic narrative turns somewhat tragic at this point because, as he admits, the reform of customs was not popular. A good part of the blame is assigned to uneducated and conservative women of Muslim background. This led to the adulteration of pure Chinese traditions with indigenous elements. Thus, prayers were offered not only on lunar holidays of the Chinese calendar but also on Mohammed's birthday. Wedding and funeral customs were burdensome and full of superstitions involving offerings at shrines and temples. Moreover, lack of education contributed to a blind conservatism. The women and traditionalists insisted on practices such as ritual mourning and wailing as a necessary expression of filial piety. Yet, Kwee finds evidence in the Xiaojing that Confucius was opposed to ritual mourning: "Children who are truly filial do not pretend to weep at a parent's funeral." THHK provided an alternative marriage ceremony similar to a civil ceremony. However, it did not have many takers and performed only about six ceremonies over many years. It appears true, as he claims, that many of the marriage custom reforms penetrated the community anyway, but it is not clear that they were seen as redounding to Confucian or even Chinese ideas.[44]

The limited success of Confucianism as a reformist religion among Peranakans caused many of the Confucianists to move away from their religious radicalism. In the early stages, the THHK had been both

---

[42] Kwee, *The Origins of the Modern Chinese Movement*, pp. 17–18, 62–3.
[43] *Ibid.*, p. 312.   [44] *Ibid.*, pp. 33–52.

monotheistic and iconoclastic, even more so than Kang Youwei during the Kongjiao phase. For instance, the THHK objected to having a portrait of Confucius at the altar in the THHK building – Kang found this unproblematic – because it would make it difficult to prevent people from coming to pray for favors. Its adherents said it would become just another temple in Batavia.[45]

Reformers like Kwee began to turn away from their radical iconoclasm in the early 1930s to a more syncretic faith and a dialogical approach that was simultaneously more tolerant and interiorized. Sam Kauw Hwee (or Sanjiaohui, 三教会), also called Tridharma, was the Peranakan version of the Chinese three-in-one redemptive society that combined elements of Confucianism, Buddhism and Daoism. Sam Kauw Hwee was established by Kwee in 1934 and soon became more popular than the Confucian Association, establishing thirty branches all over Indonesia in 1955. Tridharma accepted popular religiosity and gods, or Toapekong, in the Chinese pantheon and emphasized the common goals of all religions. "Taoism showed mankind the path leading to the solitary state beside the First Source called Tao (Dao); Buddhism taught how a person might come to be alone with Wet (Law), truth or Dharma, and in this way reach Nirvana; and Confucianism showed how to live in accordance with the True Way and, in this way, become Seng Djen (Sheng Ren, a superior man)."[46] Although the methods of these groups differed, their aims were the same: to reach perfect happiness. Indeed, Kwee was also influenced by Hinduism (and, as we shall see, by Islam); themes of spirituality and reincarnation recur in his literary works.

Like the modern Vedantist thinkers – Vivekananda and Ramakrishna – in colonial India, Kwee created a bi-level religiosity. One may entertain many different religious practices and even the worship of gods. But these are only means to achieve the same one God. In this way, Sam Kauw Hwee permitted the reformists to accept icons and popular practices but retain or, rather, reconstitute the transcendent. This transcendence responded both to the emerging power of Islam and to the modern interiorization of faith.[47] Tridharma posited the existence of an ultimate

[45] *Ibid.*, pp. 24–6.
[46] Leo Suryadinata, "Kwee Tek Hoay: A Peranakan Writer and Proponent of Tridharma," in *Peranakan's Search for National Identity: Biographical Studies of Seven Indonesian Chinese* (Singapore: Times Academic Press, 1993), p. 50.
[47] Denys Lombard and Claudine Salmon have shown that there was historically a strong mixing of Chinese and local Muslim communities at both the elite and popular levels for hundreds of years. Although Dutch colonial policies segregating the communities tended to stabilize the Creole culture discussed by Skinner, Lombard and Salmon detect a distinct movement towards integration with Indonesian culture, particularly in response

God who was often called *Tian* (Heaven) and was sometimes identified with Allah. On the ninth day of the seventh month, the Chinese always prayed to the God, Allah. They worshipped the wide and endless sky (*Tian*), "because only the sky itself can portray or represent the greatness of God." According to an observer of Tridharma in the 1950s, the society emphasized "ceremonial devotion to the ancestors and to the Supreme God, Tuhan Allah. The idea is not to ask for special favors but to purify oneself and offer honor and praise. Magic is considered superstition for the spiritually illiterate."[48] Kwee attempted to show that, despite the plentitude of gods and practices, the focus of Tridharma is a single goal and a single god beyond all manifestations: *Tian* (Allah and Jesus). For him, the Toapekong were like angels or helpers of God, who could assist people to find their way to God.

Kwee's religious journey from radical Confucian religiosity to the abstraction that equated Allah and Heaven may be read as a code to the layered complexities of Peranakan history in the twentieth century. Turning away from the alienating moralism of the modernizing Confucian elite, Kwee created the syncretic Sam Kauw Hwee, which seems to be an effort to encompass and systematize what already existed in the culture. This cultural base was and is necessary for the identity of the Chinese community – mainly the Peranakans – who will make their home in Indonesia but not lose their Chinese self. Indeed, the turn to Tridharma also coincides with the turn away from the China orientation of the THHK that became more and more marginal to the Peranakans in the mid-twentieth century.

But if Tridharma was the organizational means of retaining the lines of communication with the popular base – a role for religion which came to be seen as unnecessary in republican China – it also came to represent a form of religiosity that could address the perceived requirements of a global religion. The emphasis on the supreme deity was accompanied by the advocacy of personal righteousness and public service. Organizationally, the Sam Kauw Hwee units, too, were modeled on the Christian church with Sunday activities, pastors, charities, counseling and the like. Sermons were held on topics such as Mencius and the idea of democracy, Atma and Atman, and karma and reincarnation. Its leaders, like the charismatic Bhikhu Jinarakhita (trained originally as an engineer in the Netherlands), espoused Eastern spirituality and decried Western

---

to the *dakwah* or Muslim proselytizing movements right up to World War II. Denys Lombard and Claudine Salmon, "Islam and Chineseness," *Indonesia*, 57 (1994): 115–32.
[48] Willmott, *The Chinese of Semarang*, p. 250.

materialism. According to some accounts, Kwee Tek Hoay and the Sam Kauw Hwee never succeeded in synthesizing the duality between popular religion and the interiorized God.[49] Needless to say, we are not unduly concerned with the consistency of his position but seek to understand the impulse behind this modern dialogical transcendence. The Sam Kauw Hwee allowed the Peranakans to have their gods and God; it encompassed popular Chinese culture and represented a true religion – the source of both identity and reform.

From the mid 1930s until the 1950s, Kwee published copiously in his own journal *Moestika Dharma* and produced many short monographs on the subject of religion and culture. He came to believe that Confucianism was a highly tolerant religion offering a model of harmony and attentive to nature through rituals and ceremonies devoted to it. He compared the Confucian saying that "all within the four seas are brothers" favorably with the theosophical idea that "there is no religion higher than truth." On the matter of whether Tridharma was expansive enough to accommodate the Abrahamic religions, his view was that there was no bar to these faiths as long as their followers treated the followers of Buddhism, Confucianism and Daoism with respect and equality. He feared that such an attitude would not prevail, so he was reluctant to bring them into the fold.[50]

But what of interiorization? How does a differentiation of church and state devised in a remote place come to mean something for Kwee? After the establishment of KMT power in China under Jiang Jieshi, Kwee wrote an essay sharply denouncing the nationalist clamor and urging Chinese to return to China and fully embrace the national project in the motherland. After outlining the hardships that returning Chinese and, particularly Peranakans who did not read Chinese, had experienced, he pressed for self-reliance. He argued that the Chinese overseas could best help China by going out into the world and becoming successful. The territory of China had no mystique for him. "If his heart remains Chinese his thoughts and sympathies will remain with the fatherland. Remember, a Peranakan Chinese of Trinidad who cannot read Chinese like Eugene Chen is worth

---

[49] *Ibid.*, pp. 250–3.
[50] Kwee was also prone to rather bald generalizations such as the following: "China has no record of bloodshed caused by religious conflicts." Kwee Tek Hoay, *The Nature of San Jiao: The Three Religions Embraced by the Chinese and Sam Kauw Hwe.* Association to Foster the Teaching (Tjitjoeroeg: Drukkerij "Moestika," 1942) . See also *The Religion of the Chinese: Related to Feasts, Offerings, Rituals, Traditions or Old Customs and Beliefs for Generations Since Ancient Time*, collected and discussed by Kwee Tek Hoaij (Tjitjoeroeg: "Moestika" Printing House,1937). My thanks to Evi Sutrisano for translating some of this text.

more than a million indigenous inhabitants of China of the caliber of a Chang Tso Lin."[51]

Kwee reinforced his case for an interior – or non-territorial – sense of Chineseness by comparing it with religion. Many people, he said, believe that salvation or benefit will come from devotion to Buddha, Christ or Mohammed, or by building and repairing temples to Toapekung. "In truth the salvation or damnation of a man depends upon his own deeds... The gods only point the way. This is because the destiny of every man is in his own hands... The blessing of eternal salvation can only be gained by striving for it within oneself." Similarly, Kwee urged, the Chinese in Indonesia ought to look within themselves, depend on their own abilities, improve their position in this country, and accommodate themselves "in a group of various races."[52] In the end, his Chineseness itself became modeled upon the principle of interiorized spirituality. Did this traffic contribute to the confessionalization of Chineseness? To the extent that the transcendence he advocated was dialogically related to the variety of faiths and practices, Kwee's Tridharma could not homogenize Chineseness. But it could prepare them for a nationalist society by delineating the inner self that could adapt to it.

India

In May 2007, the BSP (Bahujan Samaj Party), the party of the Dalits (previously known as Untouchables) led by a woman, Mayawati, astounded observers in India by winning the elections in India's most populous state, Uttar Pradesh (UP). The BSP secured 206 seats in the 403-member state assembly. Soon after the buzz appeared that the populist Mayawati may one day even become the prime minister of India.

Some months earlier, in October 2006, Mayawati, who practices Buddhism in everyday life, had made the intriguing comment that she and her followers would formally embrace Buddhism after the BSP gained an absolute majority in the Centre, or Union Government of India – a curious declaration of traffic.[53] Indeed, Mayawati had declared this on the 50th anniversary of the date of the conversion of B. R. Ambedkar to Buddhism on October 14, 1956. Dr Ambedkar was one of the great leaders of modern India and hailed from the Untouchable community.

---

[51] Suryadinata, "Kwee Tek Hoay," p. 39; Kwee Tek Hoay, "Misleading Clamour," in Leo Suryadinata, Ed., *Political Thinking of Indonesian Chinese 1900–1995: A Sourcebook* (Singapore University Press, 1997), p. 26.

[52] Kwee, "Misleading Clamour," pp. 46–7.

[53] "Mayawati to Embrace Buddhism," *The Hindu*, October 16, 2006.

With twin doctoral degrees in political science from Columbia University and the London School of Economics, as well as a legal degree, he was the first law minister of independent India and the principal architect of the constitution of India.[54] We will return to the story of Ambedkar, Dalit conversion to Buddhism and Mayawati's curious comment about the political fulfillment of a religious vow. Let me first identify the main streams of the traffic between religion and the secular politics in twentieth-century India.

Modern Indian social and intellectual currents are typically said to begin with Raja Ram Mohun Roy (1772–1833), the father of the Bengal Renaissance, who advocated reform of Hinduism, abolition of the practice of sati, monotheism, deism and rational religion. He also became a Unitarian in search of a universal and natural religion, and was influential among Unitarians and Transcendentalists in the UK and the United States. It has been argued that Ram Mohun was responding to both Orientalist and Protestant conceptions, but he also came to his positions through a deistic tradition in the Hindu-Persian learning (with an emphasis on Advaita Vedantism) of his time, which was doubtless reinforced by the British attack on Brahmans (he was himself a Brahman).[55] Although he also sought to defend Hinduism from such attacks, what has been relatively understudied is the extent of his transnational connections and influence.

Ram Mohun was a product of a cosmopolitan culture in Calcutta. He knew Persian, Arabic, Sanskrit, Bengali and English. In his case, the attacks on Brahminism and Hinduism by the missionaries led not to a nationalistic defense but a defense of ethical deism, which, in fact, invited attacks from the Brahman orthodoxy. He created the Brahmo Samaj to propagate his alternative vision. Roy is said to have traveled to Tibet in 1791, and in 1830 sailed to England to represent India on judicial and revenue matters. While there, he was lionized by the Unitarians but died just as he was planning to leave for America in 1833. As we have seen, American Transcendentalists such as Thoreau were inspired by his ideas of a deep spiritual unity of humankind.[56]

The case of Ram Mohun Roy and his circle of friends and admirers reveals a kind of religious-intellectual universalism that may have

---

[54] For the main developments in Ambedkar's life, see Francis Pritchett's website (www.columbia.edu/itc/mealac/pritchett/00ambedkar/timeline/1910s.html).

[55] Peter van der Veer, *Imperial Encounters: Religion and Modernity in India and Britain* (Delhi: Permanent Black, 2006), pp. 44–5.

[56] H. D. Sharma, *Raja Rammohan Roy: The Renaissance Man* (Rupa & Co, 2002); see also Marilyn Richards and Peter Hughes, "Rammohun Roy," Unitarian Universalist Historical Society (UUHS) 1999–2007(http://uudb.org/articles/rajarammohunroy.html).

represented a perception of the collective heritage generated by early modern circulations. His search for a new society was inseparable from his search for a new cosmological and cosmopolitan fusion. This was a period before the hardening of national boundaries and also before the strict separation of the religious from the secular and explains why, in India, the new fusion did not serve exclusivist Hindu or Muslim nationalism.

Matters took a different course by the last third of the nineteenth century, which witnessed the spawning of social reform movements across South Asia and the wider region. These were generated in the public sphere and in the context of debates with missionaries, as well as under the reigning ideas of rationality and progress. It has been argued that, by this time, the bulk of ideas developed about community and reform were tied to regional elite formation, especially in the Punjab, Bombay Presidency and Bengal, which had developed a distinctly Hindu orientation to their anticolonial nationalism. Even successors of Roy's Brahmo Samaj, including such liberals as Rabindranath Tagore, cultivated the love of a spiritually conceived motherland (at least until 1917).

Confessionalizing Hinduism: the Arya Samaj

Hindu political nationalism, or Hindutva, is often traced to the Arya Samaj of Dayananda Sarwasati, which was dominant in the Punjab and western India in the last decades of the nineteenth century. Like the Brahmo Samaj of Bengal, the Arya Samaj advocated a rational religion, monotheism, deism and social reform. The great nineteenth-century Bengali reformer Vivekananda, who developed the Ramakrishna mission, developed a "practical Vedantism," arguing for the Vedanta as embodying the *universal* truths of all religions and resembling the dual gesture of Kwee's Tridharma. The Arya Samajists were more religiously radical and nationalistic and emphasized the infallibility of the Vedas. Their missionary zeal is also widely believed to have sharpened the communal tensions with Christians and Muslims. The two movements fed into the two currents of the twentieth-century mainstream of Gandhian and anti-Gandhian nationalism. Brahmo and Vedantist ideas of a reformed and universalist Hindu spirituality informed Gandhi's ideas of an ascetic citizenship, or *satyagrahi*, whereas the Arya Samaj was closely associated with the Hindu Mahasabha and its fundamentalist progeny, although in multiply crossed ways.[57]

---

[57] Peter van der Veer and Hartmut Lehmann, Eds., *Nation and Religion: Perspectives on Europe and Asia* (Princeton University Press, 1999), pp. 33–7.

Chetan Bhatt has clarified some of the problems with this kind of linear identification between the Arya Samaj and Hindutva movements. Bhatt argues that, while it is possible to argue for the rise of a separate Hindu *political* nationalism only in the 1920s, ideologically speaking, there was a convergence of Hindu nationalist ideas among many Hindus of varying stripes from the late nineteenth century.[58] This cultural nationalism represented ideologies of "primordialism" that emerged in negotiation with European primordialist ideologies of social Darwinism, Orientalist ideas of Aryanism[59] and Christian superiority. It was also formed in opposition to Muslim nationalism, which, as is well known, became entrenched once the British began to create separate electorates for Muslims and other minorities.

Yet, while the Arya Samaj cannot be understood in a linear mode, it represented perhaps the most radical confessionalization of Hinduism. Dayananda's critique and reform of Hindu society was more thoroughgoing than those of the Brahmo Samaj, which frequently reverted to traditional, caste-bound practices during the nineteenth century. He opposed idolatry, priesthood, multiplicity of rituals, caste restriction, untouchability, child marriage, restrictions on the education of women, etc. While in some ways, this resembles Kang's early and failed formulation of the Confucian religion (Kongjiao), it is also not difficult to imagine the step towards Veer Savarkar's Hindutva – an ethnic or communal body inhabiting a religious shell emptied of its dialogical tendencies. But Dayananda's new organization was not emptied of faith: the Arya Samaj held up the infallibility of the sacred Vedas, a singular, already written and *revealed* truth, and one organizational structure (the Vedic church).

The radical reformism of the Arya Samaj split precisely on this question of infallibility, which is a fundamental dilemma in the modern conception of religion. When religion becomes unified, rationalized, interiorized, and increasingly temporalized and historicized, what happens to its classic, unchanging truths, the revelation and the charisma at the heart of religion? Does it lead to the transcendence of transcendence? Within the Arya Samaj of the 1920s, this split opened between the College faction and the Gurukul faction over whether or not the Dayanand Anglo-Vedic

---

[58] Chetan Bhatt, *Hindu Nationalism: Origins, Ideologies and Modern Myths* (Oxford: Berg, 2001), pp. 26, 34.

[59] Note the close friendship between Max Müller and James Legge; both of these translators and interpreters of the classics were to play an important role in the self-conception of modern Indians and Chinese within a similar framework of identitarian intelligibility. See Norman J. Girardot, *The Victorian Translation of China: James Legge's Oriental Pilgrimage* (Berkeley, CA: University of California Press, 2002).

College curriculum should be focused on Dayananda's ideas of Vedic science and whether Vedic science and Sanskrit education should be given priority over Western scientific education. Finally, the College faction, which opposed the radical or even fundamentalist Vedic position, quit the Arya Samaj.[60]

Let me touch on just one aspect of the well-known Hindutva, or Hindu nationalist, lines of evolution from the Arya Samaj. Once the British developed the strategy of representative self-governance, Hindu and Muslim communal interests, as well as other identity groups such as the outcaste communities, developed a logic of expansion through the electoral system. Thus, while the Indian National Congress under Gandhi and Nehru advocated a territorial concept of nationhood, including Hindus, Muslims and Untouchables, among others, both the Hindu Mahasabha and the Muslim League demanded representation of communal interests within the British colonial framework.

From 1925, the Hindu Mahasabha allowed its provincial bodies to contest provincial elections and take up government posts. This was directly related to opposing Muslim and non-Brahmin parties in legislatures. It also penetrated the National Congress.[61] When combined with the growing role of Hindu and Islamic symbolism in the public sphere (under Tilak, for instance), this sphere became a lethal arena of competitive politics. By erasing particular differences among groups now lumped together as Hindus, not only did Hindutva become a newly constructed political identity capable of mobilizing religious sentiment, but also this reification of different religious communities subsequently found its way into the constitutional and judicial vocabulary of India.

To return to the problem of temporality. How do modern religions conserve the authoritative transcendent not in the face of routinization as such, but in the face of temporalization? How do they reconcile with the temporality and sociology of linear time upon which ideas of reform and change are based? Let me comment on a contemporary Arya Samaji reformer in India called Swami Agnivesh.

Born in a Brahmin family in south India steeped in Brahmin ritualism, Agnivesh often recounts his conversion to the Arya Samaj at the age of 17 in Calcutta during the 1950s. Agnivesh was deeply impressed by the questioning attitude of the Arya leaders he met and adopted the saffron robes of the Samajis. His critical questionings, however, led beyond the Aryas to Marxism, and when he sought to integrate the two in his thought and work, he was expelled from the society's primary group. Subsequently,

---

[60] Bhatt, *Hindu Nationalism*, p. 22.   [61] *Ibid.*, p. 61.

he came to see Marxism itself as a religion in its dogmatism and authoritarianism. He now sees himself as committed to human rights (and animal and environmental rights), but still perceives himself as an Arya Samaji.[62]

Swami Agnivesh has been one of the most energetic activist spiritual leaders in north India. He runs a major organization to combat the practice of bonded labor, particularly among children. His Bandhua Mukti Morcha conducted campaigns across the Gangetic plain in north India, pressuring local politicians to pledge their written allegiance to the cause of opposing child labor. Their efforts yielded success in the passage of the Child Labor (Prohibition and Regulation) Act in 1986.[63] He was also initially involved in the popular anticorruption movement led by Anna Hazare in the summer of 2011.

Agnivesh makes a crucial distinction between spirituality and religion. Religion is ossified and dominating whereas spirituality is liberating and transformative. "The prophetic task of our times," he says, "is to highlight the contradiction between religion and spirituality." According to him, the source of spirituality does not lie in a holy book or revelation, as in the Western religions, but in inner process or yoga. The scriptures lead beyond the scriptures, declare the Upanishads. Agnivesh may have transcended the transcendence of the Arya Samaj, but he conserves his personal ideals in the concept of spirituality.[64]

Further, spirituality is not abstract but needs to be embodied and realized in practice, although certainly not in the kind of escapist practice of the priestly class. He follows Tolstoy in identifying spirituality as addressing our "vertical and horizontal relations": to love God and one another. "The rise of religious fundamentalism is made possible only by the dilution of our commitment to social justice." Thus, social responsibility, an awareness of our total context and responsiveness to that dynamic historical context, is what distinguishes spirituality from religion.[65]

Thus, we see Swami Agnivesh opting for the progressive, temporal dimension of modern religion. Commitment to social reform and change is his keyword. This leads us to question whether he needs a timeless God or a transcendent truth, and, if not, can he qualify as religious? Agnivesh believes in God. He thinks that the secular human-rights advocates cannot have a deep knowledge of their commitment without understanding their

---

[62] Swami Agnivesh, *Religion, Spirituality and Social Action: New Agenda for Humanity* (Gurgaon: Hope India Publications, 2003).
[63] *Ibid.*, pp. 22, 80–3.   [64] *Ibid.*, p. 163.   [65] *Ibid.*, pp. 8, 39–42.

relationship with God. But his God – or what he often calls his spirituality – is a profoundly individual phenomenon. "We believe that God, the self within us, seeks itself, in the classical Vedantic parlance. The self seeks itself through the self."[66]

The parallels between Kwee and Agnivesh are striking. Neither can find transcendence in the confessionalization of their religious tradition and turn to interior spirituality. While, for Kwee, spiritual reform is to strengthen the self of a threatened minority, for Agnivesh, who advocates social activism, the latter can only be based on a radical interiorization of faith. This is modern religion *par excellence* and not because the state has mandated the interiorization of religion. It is the society in which he lives that mandates constant change, reform and progress so that any objective locus of transcendent faith must in time become irrelevant, if not dogmatic and fossilized.

Yet, of course, the interiorization of faith is hardly an easy business. Agnivesh speaks of the daily battles within himself, his struggles with aversion and attachment, and the fight to transcend his body. While deeply opposed to the clergy and institutionalization of religion, he reserves a special ire against the materialism and consumerism spawned by globalization. Not only does this kind of materialism draw us to feed unnecessary desires, but it also leads to the loss of a God-centered view, which, for him, is to be blind to the group and the interdependence within which our existence takes place.[67]

It would seem that Agnivesh wants to realize and materialize God through the process of collective actions of social responsibility. He is a Gandhian who believes in a limited role for the state and a strong role for civil society – in particular, NGOs and individuals who are active in defending justice in society. He is concerned that the pervasiveness of the profit motive will eat into their commitment, and he is active in seeking to bring them together, to create a forum for learning and sharing, and to collectively make a difference in society. He has warned religious leaders at global conferences that NGOs, including his own little Mukti Morcha, will become the more authentic custodians of true spiritual values.[68] Agnivesh's non-denominational spiritual engagement in civil society may be an interesting index of the para-spiritual dimensions of voluntary service in contemporary society. In Agnivesh's personal story, we may see how his ideal of transcendent truth is relocated from organized religion to the spiritual realm, where it is secured to enable his commitment to society.

---

[66] *Ibid.*, p. 25.   [67] *Ibid.*, pp. 100–23.   [68] *Ibid.*, pp. 50–1, 73.

Engaged transcendence: Gandhi's political experiments

It would be hard to find a more apt instance of 'transcendence in the secular world' than Mahatma Gandhi. Even though the intellectual industry on Gandhi continues to burgeon, I find his example very important to further my arguments in two ways. First, unlike, say, Agnivesh, Gandhi is relatively unconcerned about history; history certainly does not trump the truth to which humans should aspire, live by and even die for. Second, Gandhi defied the modern division of politics and ethics. Ethics was fundamental for political action, not just a limit to it (though it is said that Gandhi could sometimes be un-Gandhian). Thus, he was against (modern) forms of political mobilization which imposed – if not forced – an idealized representation of the good life upon people who may have been ignorant, suspicious or opposed to this ideal. In other words, I will argue that Gandhi drew upon older Asian modes of ethical self-formation and adapted them to modern politics. While such a politics can hardly survive the imperative for competitive mobilization in the modern political realm, the legacy of Gandhian ethical engagement in the public space is a powerful force in India and the world.

What is Gandhi's truth that transcends history? Gandhi's truth was not scientific, but moral. It is only our moral experience in society and the world, whether in the midst of war, such as in the *Mahabharata*, or in everyday social activities, that we experience what it is to be truthful.[69] But while firmly located in society, the core of being human for Gandhi was to embrace 'truth' beyond the world of society and politics. As such, it was a dialogical, but engaged, transcendence. Akeel Bilgrami has argued that Gandhi's critique of abstract – rather than moral – truth as the basis of the scientific, instrumental procedure paralleled the critique of the same by Heidegger in his 'world picture' idea which opposed the human subject to nature and the world.[70] The sole emphasis on cognitive truths could only lead to domination of the world around us and enables instrumental rationality to replace our ethical choices for the good life.

While Gandhi drew his ideas from both local Hindu and Jain traditions of his Saurashtra homeland in Gujarat, he also imbibed the Vendantist thought of Vivekananda and nineteenth-century reformers. But, even more, Gandhi drew on a global spirituality which had already circulated through India several times. The ideas of the American

---

[69] Uday S. Mehta, "Gandhi and the Burden of Civility," *Raritan: A Quarterly Review, 33*(1) (2014): 37–49.

[70] Akeel Bilgrami, "Gandhi, the Philosopher," *Economic and Political Weekly*, September 7, 2003, reprinted in *Ahimsa Online – International Day of Non-Violence, on January 30*, pp. 1–19.

Transcendentalists, which had flowed from India to the West, returned to Gandhi via the theosophists and others. He was also deeply influenced by Christian ethics and the anarchist ideals of Tolstoy, among others. Gandhi's experiments with ethical politics in the modern era focus on how the individual can express her humanity through ethical transformation in everyday, social life, whether in the midst of war or resistance to unjust rule.

Politics could never be associated with violence or instrumentalism. Gandhi decried most forms of competitive politics and mobilization that utilized individuals as instruments of some other purpose, such as the majority of nationalisms. Gandhi may be said to have formulated the ethical method of dialogical transcendence in which no truth – however universal its advocates may deem it – can be forcibly imposed upon another. Non-violence did not simply mean avoiding physical harm to others; it also meant refraining from criticizing or judging others who did not agree with you. Such a judgment, according to Bilgrami's interpretation of Gandhi, could only descend into a cycle of negativity of the self–Other dynamics of politics.[71]

Since Gandhi opposed the external imposition of one's will upon another even when based on a principle, the ethical activist – the *satyagrahi* – for Gandhi, could only serve as the example for the people to follow. Civil resistance by the ethical activist demanded extraordinary sacrifices and devotion, which Gandhi sought to demonstrate as an exemplar. For the activist, the demands entailed devotion to the truth of one's conscience, suffering, steadfastness in solitude and, above all, non-violence. For Gandhi, the demands he made on himself also included celibacy, dietary restrictions, silence, spinning and other personal vows of discipline.

Gandhi arrived at this understanding through his synthesis of historical religious thought and contemporary reflection, but the exemplary leader bears an uncanny resemblance to a most important ethical ideal of Chinese thought – namely, the sage-king who ruled by example. Not by intervention, but through the sheer radiance of his moral example was the sage-king able to rule his people. To be sure, Gandhi is unlikely to have known about the Confucian ideal. But Gandhi's contribution to and innovation in the modern world lay in developing an ethical politics which linked the personal and the local to transcendent goals. In this way he drew upon older philosophies and practices of cultivation – including asceticism, sacrifice, meditation and exemplariness – to generate

---

[71] Bilgrami, "Gandhi, the Philosopher."

resistance and action for modern goals, such as the independence of India from unjust British rule.

The extent to which Gandhi was a defender of Hinduism is a debate I will not enter here. Gandhi's reformed Hinduism certainly repudiated the crime of untouchability, and he called the Dalits the 'people of God'. But at the same time, he was opposed by many outcaste leaders like Ambedkar for opposing separate electorates for their communities. It is therefore relevant at this point to explore how the outcaste communities turned the religious and spiritual resources at hand to advance their lot in the modern world. Before turning to Ambedkar, I will discuss another community, the Namasudras of Bengal.

Untouchability and the limits of transcendence

Sekhar Bandyopadhyay's study of the upwardly mobile Namasudra community of East Bengal since the nineteenth century presents us with an illuminating tale of how the religious life presented both opportunities and traps for the lower castes in gaining respectability and self-determination at the cusp of Indian modernity. Originally an outcaste community of several millions in the deltaic regions of East Bengal (now Bangladesh), the Namasudras made a living as boatmen and fisherfolk on the edges of settled society. During the course of the nineteenth century, they brought the marshlands under cultivation and launched their successful transformation into peasants. In the process of the upward mobility of the caste – or Sanskritization – the Namasudras faced, not surprisingly, the obstructions of caste society, which continued to refer to them by the hated appellation of *Chandal*. In response, the Namasudras developed their own religion, Matua, which provided them with the self-confidence and collective solidarity to negotiate their way right into modern society. Indeed, the solidarity of Namasudras through the vehicle of Matua has brought them political success as recently as 2011.[72]

The religious and intellectual environment in which Matua arose is worth describing in some depth because it speaks vividly to the themes of syncretism and transcendence that we have engaged. Together with the entrenched caste society of India, there had always flourished various heterodox, anticaste movements and groups that drew from a vast variety

---

[72] Sekhar Bandyopadhyay, "Popular Religion and Social Mobility in Colonial Bengal: The Matua Sect and the Namasudras," in Rajat Kanta Ray, Ed., *Mind, Body and Society: Life and Mentality in Colonial Bengal* (Calcutta: Oxford University Press, 1995), pp. 153–92. For events in 2011, see Postscript in Sekhar Bandyopadhyay, *Caste Protest and Identity in Colonial India: The Namasudras of Bengal, 1872–1947* (New Delhi: Oxford University Press, 2011).

of religious and popular ideas, which, as in imperial China, were not always sharply demarcated from orthodox or elite formulations. Presumably, the camouflage of outward conformity was not as necessary in India because these groups were not faced with state prohibition. But as we shall see, the hegemonic force of social co-optation was very powerful.

Anti-Brahmanical and even materialist movements are perhaps as old as Vedic orthodoxy in India, Buddhism (and Jainism) being among the most long-lived and influential globally, if not in India. Just as in China the redemptive and egalitarian message of Buddhism was in part absorbed into neo-Confucianism and the Unity of the Three Teachings, Buddhist ideas were also drawn into various pietistic Hindu movements before Buddhism largely disappeared from the subcontinent after the eleventh century. In my view, however, the mysterious disappearance of Buddhism in India represented an unparalleled tragedy because no counter movements ever arose that could match the consistency and doggedness with which Buddhism remained committed to refuting the naturalization of caste by Brahminical thought.[73]

Nonetheless, the Bhakti tradition did foster a variety of sectarian and syncretic movements that were either oppositional or sought to remain at a distance from Hindu orthodoxy. Bhakti syncretism also reflected the monumental power of Islam, which swept across north India from the early second millennium and in Bengal from the sixteenth century. By the nineteenth century, almost half of the lower castes in Bengal had converted to Islam; and Christianity began to play an increasingly important role in the later half of the century.

Syncretic Bhakti, from which the Namasudras drew, included the Vaishnavism of Sri Caitanya (1486–1534), the most important Vaisnavite saint in eastern India, and the Sahajiya tradition of lower orders (see Chapter 4). By the nineteenth century, however, the early radicalism of Caitanya Vaishnavism had begun to rigidify into the orthodoxy of the Gaudiya Vaishnavities, but several heterodox strains developed new syntheses, drawing into their fold the seekers and the oppressed from both Hindu and Muslim groups preaching devotion, divine love and simple rites of initiation as the condition for discipleship. Indeed, the name *Matua* represents a transvaluation of the word for the madcap or intoxicated, drunk with the love of god (the Harekrishnas represent one line of succession of Caitanya Vaishnavism in the world today).[74]

---

[73] Vincent Eltschinger, *Caste and Buddhist Philosophy*, Trans. from French by Raynald Prevereau (Delhi: Motilal Banarsidass, 2012), p. 159 and *passim*.
[74] Bandyopadhyay, "Popular Religion and Social Mobility," pp. 158–69.

The early leaders of Matua, father and son, Harichand and Guruchand, repudiated distinctions of society including, of course, caste, but also gender discrimination. They saw no need for mediation by Brahmin or any other clergy – the simple devotion to and love of God was enough to draw one into the fold. Even more significantly, they rejected the dominant theology of unitary Vedantism, in which the world was illusory and true salvation lay in the yoking of the soul with the formless God. For them, this other-worldly view served to condition the masses into servility and turned them away from seeking a proper livelihood and worldly betterment. Harichand coined the catchy phrase *hate kam, mukhe nam* (perform worldly duties while chanting the name of God). Matua emphasized education and a work ethic proper to an upwardly mobile community.[75]

But for all their subversiveness, Matua leaders succumbed to the lures of Hindu caste society, which was entwined with the aspiration of upward mobility. Hierarchies within the family returned, and women were no longer to be independent seekers of salvation, but attain it through devotion to the husband. Even caste taboos began to penetrate their social practices. Not least, the guru was declared to be the deity and notions of the world as illusion began to surface.[76]

Yet, what might have ended up as yet another story of Sanskritization was thrown in another direction by the appearance of a new institution in twentieth-century India – the democratic politics of numbers. Matua leaders gained recognition from the colonial authorities and even had the appellation of *Chandal* dropped from government decennial classifications in 1911. Right until the late 1930s, when they saw an opportunity to shape the emergent state power of independent India, they refused to cooperate with Gandhi and the nationalist Congress Party, arguing, "The day we feel this is our country, we will lay down our lives to remove the miseries of our motherland."[77]

The Matua case references South Asian history at a crossroads. The logic of politics and society had begun to bifurcate; where would the energies of transcendence flow? Would the spirit of transcendence migrate to the defense of political autonomy (as it did ultimately in the West) while the new religion continued to be associated with the principles of caste society? Would it require a truly radical transcendence to break with older patterns, as Dayananda sought, subordinating politics and society to its vision? And, if so, would it necessarily become confessionalized and communal? We might think of Mayawati's curious vow to

---

[75] *Ibid.*, p. 178.   [76] *Ibid.*, pp. 172–3.   [77] *Ibid.*, p. 180.

convert *en masse* to Buddhism after securing power at the center as a conviction that the promise of transcendence can only be guaranteed after the capture of power. But, of course, transcendence secured by political power is often corrupted by the latter. How did Ambedkar grapple with this fraught landscape?

Ambedkar, Buddhism and secular transcendence

Even if Ambedkar did not know the story of Matua, the sectarian history of India readily told the tale of how an upwardly mobile, anticaste and antiestablishment religion could be absorbed by the power of upper-caste orthodoxy and the system of economic dependency it controlled. Although he was among the principal architects of the modern Indian constitution, it was perhaps too early for Ambedkar to be sure that the political logic of numbers would be able to resist the reassimilation of Dalits into caste society. It would require the independent moral authority of Buddhism to anchor such a powerful resistance. Indeed, Buddhism possessed a double transcendence. It was rooted in an alternative Indian cosmology; and perhaps, in view of its absence in present-day India, it was saturated by the sustaining figure of hope.

Despite his larger-than-life stature, Ambedkar was often vilified for opposing Gandhi and his upper-caste model of Hindu reform. From 1932, Ambedkar came to believe that the Dalits would have to be represented through institutions of their own and could not rely on Hindu reformers' goodwill to advance their status in society. Following the example of the Muslims and the Hindu Mahasabha, he started to call for separate Dalit electorates. Gandhi was deeply committed to the uplift of those he called Harijan but only as part of Hindu society; he thus launched a fast to pressure Ambedkar to give up his demand and ultimately succeeded.[78] However, for over twenty years, Ambedkar reserved the option of converting himself and the community to Buddhism. Some Hindus in the Congress Party saw this also as an ultimate trump card held by Ambedkar, but most Hindus did not see it as a great threat.

Ambedkar only converted to Buddhism a few weeks before he passed away in 1956. Since then, the number of Buddhist converts among the Dalits has increased very rapidly. But I wish to explore here how Ambedkar

---

[78] Christopher Queen, "Dr. Ambedkar and the Hermeneutics of Buddhist Liberation," in Christopher S. Queen and Sallie B. King, Eds., *Engaged Buddhism: Buddhist Liberation Movements in Asia* (Albany, NY: State University of New York Press, 1996), pp. 45–73. See also Gauri Vishwanathan, *Outside the Fold: Conversion, Modernity and Belief* (Princeton University Press, 1998), p. 212.

perceived Buddhism in modern life. Was it simply a proxy for Dalit identity? If so, why did he not advocate conversion to Islam, Christianity, Sikhism or some other available and relatively egalitarian identity such as Marxism (which Ambedkar took very seriously)?

At one level, Ambedkar's preference for Buddhism clearly had to do with the necessity of creating a distinct identity for Dalits that Marxism could not do because, for him, it lacked the ethics and symbols of identity. Many of the other faiths carried the danger that they, too, might reduce the Dalits to the status they carried within the Hindu system; certainly, Indian Christianity, Islam and Sikhism did not lack casteist or caste-like prejudices. Gauri Vishwanathan has argued that Ambedkar was deeply concerned to forge and guard the right of Dalits to represent themselves. If separate electorates could not be secured, then Buddhism would have to do it.[79] Ambedkar was fighting on several fronts simultaneously.

But Buddhism was intended to achieve much more than a secure, separate identity. For Ambedkar, Buddhism was ultimately, as we will see below, about a universal ethics. He chose his symbols carefully. Ambedkar converted to Buddhism on October 16 (1955), on the day of Emperor Asoka's conversion over 2,000 years before. He also pressed for the Asoka Chakra (or the wheel of *dharma*) at the center of the Indian flag and the Sarnath lions from the Asokan pillar as the national emblem. In his narrative, the Untouchables were those (Hindu) 'broken men' who converted to Buddhism in 400 CE and were ostracized by caste society following the triumph of Brahmanism.[80] In other words, Ambedkar was adapting Buddhism as a redemptive ethic not only for Dalits but also for the nation and the world.

So far, we still have a functional understanding of Ambedkar's Buddhism. He studied Buddhism closely, and a good portion of his writings represents commentaries on it. In much of these writings, he emphasized a distinctly rational, ethical and universally redemptive version of Buddhism that was quite compatible with a form of ethical socialism. In other words, in these writings, it was a more or less radical, though not monotheistic, transcendence. Although the Bhakti of Kabir (*Kabirpanth*) and several regional saints were very important during his childhood and for his father and the Untouchable community at large,[81] Ambedkar and his core supporters rejected Bhakti as a tame register of protest that could not prevent reproduction of abject subordination.

---

[79] Vishwanathan, *Outside the Fold*, pp. 213–14.   [80] *Ibid.*, pp. 230–1.
[81] B. R. Ambedkar, "Author's Unpublished Preface," in *The Buddha and His Dhamma*, April 6, 1956 (www.columbia.edu/itc/mealac/pritchett/00ambedkar/ambedkar_bud dha/04_01.html).

Nor, however, could Ambedkar entirely control the Buddhism that he launched. He could not sustain the vision of the modern prophet, shorn of magic and charisma. Dalit Buddhists are deeply serious about Buddhism, but they also continue to participate in Hindu festivals and rituals, albeit often with a defiant ebullience. They also defy Ambedkar by deifying both him and the Buddha as personal God and Supreme Deity.[82]

For my study, Ambedkar anticipated a key struggle to distinguish not only morality, but also the sacred from religion. In *The Buddha and His Dhamma*, a work written as a sequence of logical propositions, he wrote:

7. Religion, it is said, is personal, and one must keep it to oneself. One must not let it play its part in public life.
8. Contrary to this, Dhamma is social. It is fundamentally and essentially so.
9. Dhamma is righteousness, which means right relations between man and man in all spheres of life...
14. Society may choose not to have any Dhamma as an instrument of Government. For Dhamma is nothing if it is not an instrument of Government.
15. This means Society chooses the road to anarchy.[83]

At the same time, Ambedkar was well aware of the necessity of embedding the morality of Dhamma in the sacred. He employed evolutionism to develop the argument that the inviolability of the sacred arose from its importance for 'society' as a kind of counter-logic to protect the weak. However, the strong seek to utilize it for their sectional purposes, and it was to oppose such use that the Buddha preached the Dhamma as the sacred morality of the universal.

It is in his practical quest to realize the message of the Buddha that Debjani Ganguly finds another Ambedkar – not only the prophet of a rational ethic but also of a universal ethic – the Ambedkar who wrote a mythographic narrative about the Buddha. She quotes Ambedkar, "It must make the language in which it is produced live. It must become an *incantation*, instead of being read as an ethical exposition. Its style must be lucid, *moving* and must produce a *hypnotic* effect."[84] Ganguly, who identifies as a post-secularist, chooses to view this Ambedkar not as an instrumental tactician but as cognizant of the "heterogeneous, non-commensurable ways of being in the world."[85] The force of dialogical

---

[82] Debjani Ganguly, "Buddha, Bhakti and Superstition: A Post–Secular Reading of Dalit Conversion," *Postcolonial Studies*, 7(1) (2004): 49–62; see pp. 58–9 for ethnographic material.
[83] Ambedkar, *The Buddha*, pp. 323–5.
[84] Ganguly, "Buddha, Bhakti and Superstition," p. 55.   [85] *Ibid.*, p. 57.

transcendence, the awe of the sacred and the figures of hope, continues to condition the demands of the transcendent spirit in the secular world.

Conclusion

This chapter explored the impact upon traditions of dialogical transcendence in Asia of global circulations of a set of ideas and practices: the Protestantization of religions, secularization, spiritualization and nation-building. In the traffic embedded within a circulatory process, ideals, energies and requirements from the older religious systems are rechanneled in the new; but, equally, contemporary religion is also reconstituted by secular or hybrid forces especially insofar as the traffic is conditioned by a circulatory process that has already undergone the one-way traffic in the West. To what extent has it led to the loss of dialogics and gain in confessionalism and national homogenization? Have older traditions of dialogical transcendence found pathways of expression with new global ideals of spirituality in new domains?

In East Asia, where relatively autonomous modern states dominated during the first half of the twentieth century, and given a strong state tradition in the region, there were efforts – whether historically aware or not – to channel religious resources to build the *ideal citizen* for the nation-state. As state or national projects, neither the transcendent nor the dialogical element was particularly welcomed by these agents. We have seen this in the realm of state ritual synchronization of the modern polity; the moral campaigns of the state to instill a depoliticizing and civilizing process drawing from both Confucianism and Christianity; the literati effort to transform Confucianism into a national religion modeled on the contemporary Christianity; and, not least, the communist determination to interiorize its sacred goals among the populace. *National identity* was built – among other ways – around the state-dominated cult of the ancestor, Amaterasu or the Yellow Emperor.

In East Asia, it was the redemptive societies – discussed in Chapter 5 – which continued to absorb the newly available globally circulating resources – such as humanitarianism, Christianity or Islam – that also endowed them with new visions of transcendent autonomy and social responsibility, as we saw in Korea and Vietnam. But neither in China nor in prewar Japan were they allowed to develop their potential. More recently, in greater China we have seen the flourishing of many religious movements that can be viewed through the lens of dialogical and engaged transcendence. We will explore some of these in Chapter 7.

Throughout the twentieth century in China, the hold of a scientistic and nationalist ideology tended to trump the traditions of dialogical transcendence that pervaded mass society. As we have seen, this tended to magnify the cosmological divergence between elites and states, on the one hand, and popular culture, on the other hand, and this divergence emerged as one of the most pervasive fault lines in society. The radically secularist elite strata have consistently attacked the view of popular religion, but they have not succeeded in preventing its re-emergence until very recently in the ethnic margins of western China. During the present century, it appears that different modes of religious expression are being cautiously permitted in the Chinese heartland under the label of folk religion (*minjian zongjiao*).

In the colonial societies of East, Southeast and South Asia, traditions of dialogical transcendence were espoused by social groups rather than the state, which had more opportunities to express and develop their historical potential in the face of opportunities and challenges from globalization. Here I sum up the various directions in which they developed based upon the circulations and traffic we have studied.

First, we have considered how the traffic of religious ideas sought to create an equivalence with Western, Christian ideologies of civilization and the self. This is most evident in Korea, Vietnam and India (but also in China and Japan). Among the Peranakans, we saw also the creation of equivalence with Islamic perceptions of truth and self.

Second, we noted the role of this traffic in the creation of the ethics of citizenship not only from a narrowly nationalist perspective but also for a wider and more incorporative cosmopolitan society. To be sure, whether for Kang Youwei, Chondogyo, the Caodai, Gandhi or Ambedkar, the path to a cosmopolitan world would have to pass through the stage of independent nationhood, but in all these cases the motivating and legitimating argument for the nation was a universalism that combined historical ideals with contemporary ones. In other words, many of these had to negotiate between the nationalizing trend and their dialogically transcendent backgrounds.

Third, I have tried to grasp the ways in which religious restructuring in the colonies (and in the Japanese nation-state in Chapter 5) led to efforts to confessionalize the non-Abrahamic religions; that is, to depluralize the religious community and demand conformity and loyalty to a single truth. In the twentieth century, the goal was to build the national community and identity on the exclusivism of confessional faiths. In significant part because of the weak historical power of confessionalism in the non-Abrahamic societies, most of these efforts, such as Kang's or Kwee's Confucian religion movement, could not succeed. In India, however, Dayananda Saraswati's Arya Samaj and the Hindu Mahasabha did have more success, in part because of the competitive politics in which it became involved with Muslim and Dalit communities. The contemporary Hindutva ideology – like state Shinto before World War II – represents a classic instance of an exclusivist political community based not upon substantive religious ideas, but upon the ideal of a homogenized Hindu culture.

Finally, while religion has been important for communal formation in India, it has also provided a vocabulary for oppositional and radical ideologies across Asia. I have focused on Gandhi, Agnivesh and Ambedkar, who, like their colonized counterparts in Korea and Vietnam, maximized the autonomy afforded by their affiliation to the transcendent. Dialogical transcendence, which emphasizes the plurality and openness of these faiths, has often been translated as well into engaged transcendence. To be sure, this worldly engagement has to deal with the modern cosmology of history in which the truth of change tends to trump the truth of transcendence. Yet, I believe we are in an era where the quest for transcendence is not confined to the yearning for an absolute and substantive truth that has been foreign to most traditions in the region. Transcendence today clusters around spirituality, ideals, reverence, justice and hope – human aspirations that do – dialogically – transcend history.

7   Regions of circulation and networks of sustainability in Asia

The globalization of the last few decades has brought forth some unexpected developments that in turn have recast our perspectives on modern history. Regions such as the European Union, Mercosur, NAFTA and ASEAN have emerged as intermediate zones between the deterritorializing impulses of capitalism and the territorial limits of nationalism. The search for markets and resources drives corporations. Not-for-profit organizations are also seeking out and creating new transnational spheres of activity, and their numbers have expanded dramatically over the last twenty years.[1] At the same time, still other considerations tend to limit the transnational drive to more geographically and historically familiar regions.

Let us recall that the cartographic representation of Asia does not represent any natural or cultural unity. Indeed, Asia was merely the name of the area east of the Greek ecumene in ancient times. But that does not mean that there were no empires and networks of activity spanning and linking different parts of the region. Today, Asia, centered on ASEAN, is one of the more important – though by no means the only – core areas around which Asian societies and nations are coalescing. These coalescing networks evoke historical patterns of circulation whose salience evaporated or was marginalized by the centrality of national histories during much of the twentieth century.

In this chapter, I discuss the role of some of the networks that generated the circulatory history of maritime Asia; I go on to assess the significance of the current resurgence of activities around ASEAN among the major economies and societies of Asia, chiefly, China, Japan and India. These

---

[1] According to IMF chief, Christine Lagarde, in just 20 years, "the number of these groups associated with the United Nations rose from 700 to nearly 4000." "A New Multilateralism for the 21st Century: The Richard Dimbleby Lecture," London, February 3, 2014 (www.imf.org/external/np/speeches/2014/020314.htm). See also Karen T. Litfin, "Sovereignty in World Ecopolitics," *Mershon International Studies Review*, 41(2) (1997): 167–204, at p. 177; "Non-Governmental Organization," in *Wikipedia* (http://en.wikipedia.org/wiki/Non-governmental_organization).

activities have created important interdependencies in the economic realm and renewed exchanges and flows in the social and cultural realms. But they have also revealed problems regarding resource control and migrant labor, and this is exacerbated by political tensions between the nation-states of the region. The region is thus faced by great opportunities and equally powerful challenges.

Not only can transnational activities enhance development and overcome national parochialism through interdependencies, but transnational collaboration is also required to address the problems of regional commons – water, air and forests – and environmental sustainability. In the final section, I consider how emergent networks are trying to deal with these issues even as nationalist exclusivism and the quest for hegemony continue to present major obstacles to a new, cosmopolitan world order.

Space, territory, network and region

This chapter focuses on the processes of region-formation and its importance for transnational activism and cooperation. I distinguish here between region-formation and regional*ism*. Region-formation is the activity of networks, groups and organizations in both modern and premodern times around trade, labor, religion or other activities following established geographical, geopolitical or geotechnological routes. Regionalism is the self-conscious creation of a modern transnational politicized entity – such as the EU, the Greater East Asia Co-Prosperity Sphere or ASEAN – possessing varying degrees of sovereign power with regard to the constituent nation-states. Although I am more interested in region-formation, regionalism is often intertwined with it.

We can adapt the famous theory of space developed by Henri Lefebvre to grasp the notion of 'region'. His classic study shows how powerful systems like capitalism produce the kinds of space they require.[2] These spaces are constituted by relationships which can be abstracted, standardized, exchanged and secured by property rights. In capitalist space, physical factors of production, such as land and water, become commodities. Regionalism and even region-formation to a great extent tend to follow the dominant or hegemonic modes of *spatial production* during a period. During the twentieth century, the paradigm of large-scale production of social space was the territorial nation-state under conditions of global capitalist production and exchange.

---

[2] Henri Lefebvre, *The Production of Space*, trans. Donald Nicholson-Smith (Oxford: Blackwell, 1992).

National spaces are often continuous with this kind of space, which the nation-state authorizes not only by guaranteeing property rights but also by seeking to homogenize the population as citizens with overarching loyalty not to their substantive communities or life-worlds but to the national community via the nation-state. This homogenizing tendency of the nation-state may, of course, be reproduced within nested formations where the horizontal identity is expressed in associations, provinces, language groups, etc., theoretically under the sovereign nation-state. *In the national model of space, there is an effort to make culture and political authority congruent.*

Of course, this also produces tensions between national and capitalist space. Most significantly, the territorial sovereignty of the nation-state can limit the deterritorializing imperative of capitalism. To briefly recapitulate the history of the 'nation form' here, the nation-state system itself represented a prior globalization – a cognitive globalization – of the norms and methods of institutionalizing power in nation-states to compete for global resources. But the globalism of the nation-state system was pre-reflexive; the institutions of the nation-state systematically misrecognize its global provenance and embeddedness in order to claim sovereignty and agency in a competitive world.

In the post-Cold War era, the growing collusion between transnational capital and nation-states means that the latter are not as capable of protecting the interests of the community and the natural world in their territories. Not only are many national institutions diverted from promoting public services and protecting the commons, but also profit-driven economic globalization has caused environmental degradation across the world that can hardly be addressed only by national policies. The growing economic interdependence of the world requires new sources of political and cultural authority to be able to manage and regulate it.

Thus, on the one hand, the loosening of the relationship between territorial nationalism and the community – or non-congruence between political authority and culture – can have disastrous consequences, especially if non-territorial nationalism also invokes and enrolls culture – such as Indianness or Chineseness among the diaspora – to pursue neo-liberal capitalism. At the same time, other networks of culture-politics, relatively distanced from nationalism and opposed to unsustainable capitalism, are also being generated in the present era. Their capacities are easy to underestimate especially because, as networks of civil society, they are bereft of strong institutional and territorial power. For every success, they may encounter several failures. But they claim the moral high ground, mobilizing the intangible forces of commitment and sacrifice, knowledge and transparency, and representing perhaps the most interesting instance of traffic of the transcendent that we have known.

Contemporary network theory, in particular Bruno Latour's actor-network-theory (ANT), provides important support for ideas of circulatory histories that not only are relevant to the current era of accelerated change and mobilities – in opposition to social scientific theories of stable structures and systems – but also clarify how earlier networks of circulation – for example, those which spread the major religions of Hinduism, Buddhism, Confucianism and Islam (especially in Southeast Asia) – may have worked. Let me briefly suggest the usefulness of these ideas for our purposes.

According to ANT, developments in the world depend upon a web of connections between humans and non-humans, including things that are recruited, enrolled and assembled for the achievement of certain goals (bringing food to the table or launching a rocket). Human actors are both agents and objects, just as things – or ideas and histories – can be agentive: ideas can turn against one, animals can be recalcitrant and technologies can have agentive side effects (one is reminded of counter-finalities). Latour argues that these networks are made invisible or obscured by ideologies (of what he calls the 'Modern Constitution') because they are transgressive of the legitimating principles underlying the production of the institutional order.[3]

Philosophically, the argument is consistent with the view taken in this work against a strong subject–object binary whether the subject is the sovereign God, man or the nation. The focus on network activities, whether or not they are transgressive, spotlights the ways in which small 'cultural' transformations do their work and are often obscured or misrecognized by Culture and institutional processes. Networks in this sense are effective carriers of circulatory histories not only because they can cross various boundaries of territories, institutions and ideologies but also because their effects can be multiscalar and their webbed form can produce unexpected coalitional results.

Historically, in maritime Asia, region-making was undertaken by networks which circulated a variety of materials, technologies, species and ideas and enrolled other networks in foreign lands. When the modern production of space became hegemonic, these networks were in many ways themselves recruited by capitalist and territorial organizational systems. But some of these networks continued to maintain their transborder

---

[3] Bruno Latour, *We Have Never Been Modern*, Trans. Catherine Porter (Cambridge, MA: Harvard University Press, 1993). See also Bruno Latour, *Reassembling the Social: An Introduction to Actor-Network-Theory* (Oxford University Press, 2007).

and multiscalar character, and in the current era of hyperconnectivity, networks have become a new force to be reckoned with.

Imperial regionalism

During the nineteenth and twentieth centuries, the relationship between global capitalism, regional formations and the nation-state was mediated by imperialism. Much of nineteenth-century Asia was dominated by the 'free trade' imperialism of the British Empire when several historical networks of the Asian maritime trade were able to adapt and expand their operations. By the late nineteenth century and during the first half of the twentieth century, imperialism came to be driven by nationalism to compete effectively in a capitalist system whether this was to secure the resources, markets or military needs of the capitalist nation. This yielded a complex relationship between imperialist nations and their colonial or dependent territories, which they sought to develop as imperial regions.[4]

To turn first to the nineteenth century, colonial empires, most notably the British Empire, created significant regional interdependencies in Asia. This had the effect of intensifying some of the old relationships and generating new linkages between the cities (and hinterlands) of Aden, Bombay, Calcutta, Singapore, Hong Kong and Shanghai as entrepôts and financial centers for Asian trade. For a long time, the study of Asian trade in the colonial period was conducted apart from the rich and high-quality scholarship of the precolonial maritime Asian or Indian Ocean trade, thus yielding a skewed picture of the former. It was perhaps taken for granted that the financial, technological and political-military superiority of the colonial powers in the nineteenth century had completely subordinated, even if not eliminated, these networks. Such seems to have been the assumption which lay behind the dual-economy model of Boeke and others. More recent work on the Indian Ocean – along the Persian Gulf and the Arabian Sea as well as the South China Sea – has shown how faulty was this picture.

Since at least the thirteenth century, the maritime region from the Red Sea to the South China Sea represented an interlinked system of trade routes. From the 1400s, the routes were held together most importantly at the cosmopolitan port city of Malacca, to which the monsoon winds

---

[4] See Eric Hobsbawm, *Nations and Nationalism Since 1780: Program, Myth, Reality* (Cambridge University Press, 1990), p. 102; Hannah Arendt, *The Origins of Totalitarianism* (New York: Harcourt Brace Jovanovich, 1973), pp. 152–3. Arguably, even after World War II, during the Cold War, the political mechanism developed to compete for global resources was national imperialism or the means whereby a national superpower exercised its hegemony over subordinated nation-states.

brought Indian, Persian and Arab traders. There they waited for the reversal of the monsoon winds to carry in the trade from the Chinese empire and eastern regions before returning. The networks of Chinese, Indian, Jewish, and Arab merchants, among others, with their sophisticated credit-transfer mechanisms and trading techniques had enabled the wholesale and forward carrying trade across the Indian Ocean littoral from Zanzibar to China.[5]

According to Rajat K. Ray, while Asian networks from the nineteenth century were doubtless subordinated to colonial trade and power, the older networks of Chinese, Indian and Baghdadi Jewish communities, which possessed long-distance credit networks and negotiable financial instruments operable in several countries, adapted and expanded their operations within certain spheres. Their business practices enabled them to occupy a realm between the European world of banks and corporations and the small Asian peddler and retail markets. Indeed, without the financial and marketing services provided by these mobile merchant communities of Asia, European capital would not have been able to penetrate the hinterlands. During the course of the twentieth century, not only did these networks expand to the lower latitudes of Africa and Southeast Asia, but they also emerged as the modern Asian business and industrial classes that were able to integrate the three-tiered colonial economies into the national and post-national economies.[6]

On the East Asian side, the multiple connections and shifts between the precolonial maritime networks and modern Asian networks have been studied masterfully by Hamashita Takeshi. By the Qing period, the Chinese imperial tribute system had become the framework for commercial transactions based upon the price structure in China. The entire tribute-trade zone became loosely integrated by the use of silver as a medium of trade settlement. It became the axis around which wider trading networks in the region were organized. Thus, for instance, the private trade between Siam and south China was fueled by profits from the tribute mission, and when trade in this region declined, traders in

---

[5] Rajat K. Ray, "Asian Capital in the Age of European Expansion: The Rise of the Bazaar, 1800–1914," *Modern Asian Studies*, 29(3) (1995): 449–554, at pp. 464, 472; Janet Lippman Abu-Lughod, "The World System in the Thirteenth Century: Dead-End or Precursor?," in Michael Adas, Ed., *Essays on Global and Comparative History* (Washington, DC: American Historical Association, 1993), pp. 9–11. For the precolonial Asian networks, see also the magisterial study of K. N. Chaudhuri, *Asia Before Europe: Economy and Civilisation of the Indian Ocean from the Rise of Islam to 1750* (Cambridge University Press, 1990).

[6] Ray, "Asian Capital in the Age of European Expansion," p. 553. See also Sugata Bose, *A Hundred Horizons: The Indian Ocean in the Age of Global Empire* (Cambridge, MA: Harvard University Press, 2006).

south China were able to switch to trading alongside other tribute missions, from, say, Ryukyu to Nagasaki. Tribute trade also linked the European trade with the East Asian one. While it may have appeared as an exclusively political relationship, in reality the tribute system also expressed trading opportunities under a loose regulatory system of several different states within an imperial Chinese tribute zone.[7] Hamashita has not only shown how European-dominated patterns rode on older networks of Asian trade, but he has also recently revealed what he calls the "crossed networks" (*kōsa nettowaku*) of Chinese and Indian overseas financial groups in East, South and Southeast Asia.[8] The Japanese conquests and the partial overtaking of control of this trade opened new opportunities for regional integration, but it turned out to be more destructive than enabling during the short period it existed.

To move on to imperial regionalism in the interwar years of the twentieth century, national imperialisms sought to develop a regional or (geographically dispersed) bloc formation promoting economic autarky as a means for the imperial power to gain global supremacy or advantage. Here they sought to establish common standards, measures, currency and laws facilitating integration – if uneven development – across the bloc. After World War I, the indebtedness of Britain to the United States and its weakening competitiveness vis-à-vis other imperialist powers caused Britain to impose the doctrine of imperial preference and the sterling zone in its colonies and dependencies. This was, however, also a time when the anti-imperialist movement in the colonies began to make increasing demands for economic and political parity. Thus, imperialists sought to create economic blocs in which colonies or subordinate territories were promised self-governing status and other concessions and sometimes even constituted as nominally sovereign nation-states, although they remained militarily in thrall to the metropole. The imperialism of nation-states reflected a strategic reorientation of the periphery to be part of an organic formation designed to attain global supremacy for the imperial power. As Albert Lebrun declared after World War I, the goal was now to "unite France to all those distant Frances in order to permit

[7] Hamashita Takeshi, "The Tribute Trade System and Modern Asia," in A. Latham and H. Kawasatsu, Eds., *Japanese Industrialization and the Asian Economy* (London: Routledge, 1994), pp. 91–107.
[8] Hamashita Takeshi, "Kōsa suru Indokei nettowaku to Kajinkei nettowaku: Honkoku sōkin shisutemu no hikaku kentō" ("Intersecting Networks of Indians and Chinese: A Comparative Investigation of the Remittance System"), in Akita Shigeru and Mizushima Tsukasa, Eds., *Gendai Minami Ajia 6: Sekai Sisutemu To Nettowâku (Contemporary South Asia 6: World System and Network)* (Tokyo University Press, 2003), pp. 239–74.

them to combine their efforts to draw from one another reciprocal advantages."[9]

But it was less the older imperialist powers than the new ones, such as Japan, the United States and the Soviet Union, that proved able to switch to this mode of the regional imperialism of nation-states. With the increased need for resource and social mobilization within colonies or dependencies, it was more efficient for the imperialists to foster *modern* and *indirectly* controlled institutions in them. The goal was to control these areas by dominating their institutions of mobilization, such as banks, the transportation infrastructure and political institutions, which were created to resemble those of the metropole (such as legislative councils, institutions of political tutelage, and political parties like the communist parties or the Concordia in Manchukuo). In short, unlike colonialism or British free-trade imperialism, the interwar imperialists attended to the modernization of institutions and identities. They often espoused cultural or ideological similarities – including sometimes anticolonial ideologies – even while racism and nationalism accompanied the reality of military-political domination.

To compete with Britain and France, Germany had sought to develop a regional bloc in central and eastern Europe since the end of the nineteenth century.[10] This trend accelerated during the interwar years, and German commercial influence before the war peaked in 1938, when Austria was incorporated into the Reich and Hitler annexed the Sudeten region of Czechoslovakia. Hannah Arendt regarded the pan-German (and Russian pan-Slav) movements as an expression of 'continental imperialism' whereby late-comer nationalists sought to develop their empires through the nationalistic pan-German movement.[11] The German economic New Order in Europe, built upon states that were essentially German puppets or had German military governors, was designed to supply the German war effort. However, there were also plans to build an economic region around a prosperous Germany linked to new industrial complexes in central Europe and captured areas of the western Soviet Union. This unitary European market, however, remained a nationalistic German

---

[9] As quoted in D. Bruce Marshall, *The French Colonial Myth and Constitution-Making in the Fourth Republic* (New Haven, CT: Yale University Press, 1973), p. 44.

[10] Barry Eichengreen and Jeffrey A. Frankel, "Economic Regionalism: Evidence from Two Twentieth-Century Episodes," *North American Journal of Economics and Finance*, 6(2) (1995): 89–106, at p. 97.

[11] Arendt, *The Origins of Totalitarianism*, pp. 222–3. This racist ideology seemingly authorized the Germans to annex or dominate territories belonging to other states. At the same time, Nazi racism excluded such large numbers of people that even the rhetoric of anti-imperialism or solidarity of cultures was made impossible.

vision – and we should be wary of seeing it as a predecessor of the EU. The German plan represented in several ways no more than an abortive version of the new imperialism.[12]

Beginning with the formation of the puppet state of Manchukuo (1932–45), the Japanese economic bloc idea grew by the mid 1930s into the East Asian League (*Tōa renmei*) and the East Asian Community (*Tōa kyōdōtai*), and still later into the idea of the Greater East Asian Co-Prosperity Sphere (*Dai-Tōa Kyōeiken*). Manchukuo signals fundamental changes in the nature of the Japanese empire. The most intensive phase of industrialization and development in Korea and Taiwan came after 1931 and emerged as part of the plan for strategic autarky centered upon Manchukuo. The rapid growth in industrialization, education, and other aspects of development in Korea and Taiwan took off in the early 1930s, and accelerated with the invasion of China in 1937. The Japanese wartime empire resembled the German New Order in that the entire occupied zone became subordinated to Japanese war needs, and Japan's defeat represented a failure of the new imperialism.

This form of imperial regionalism, then, was characterized by an unsustainable tension: a commitment to creating a common space akin to the nation that extended the benefits and pains of creating a globally competitive region, but extended them *unevenly* over the whole. By the same token, the imperial-national region was often ripped apart by enduring nationalist prejudices fostered in earlier times and simultaneous processes of nation-building, especially within the imperial metropole. In other words, while it sought to create a region of interdependence and cooperation, the national interests of the imperial power made this an unsustainable region.

What was the spatial composition of this imperialist region? While most of the subordinate nations or colonies within the region were by no means fully integrated with capitalist urban centers, the infrastructure of capitalist market relations – including standardizing of weights and measures, currency unification, and the physical and educational infrastructure – were being laid across many of these societies both within each colony or country and across them. The integration was a dual and interactive process undertaken by the colonial states and metropolitan capitalists as well as by Asian merchants, who, as shown above, dominated the indigenous financial markets through bills of exchange, promissory notes and other negotiable instruments (such as the Chinese *gu* or the South

---

[12] See Richard Overy, "World Trade and World Economy," in Ian C. B. Dear and M. R. D. Foot, Eds., *The Oxford Companion to World War II* (Oxford University Press, 2001) (2003 DOI: 10.1093/acref/9780198604464.001.0001 eISBN: 9780191727603).

Asian *hundis*). As Hamashita has shown, Singapore and Hong Kong were colonial cities in which the Chinese and Indian money-transfer and remittance networks intersected, and their resources became part of a vast regional financial market interfluent with the Western-dominated banking sector.[13] But if the material lives and economic practices of Asians were becoming interlinked on an everyday basis, how was this reflected in the representation of the region?

The anti-imperialist regional project in Asia

While the British and the Japanese empires were trying to create autarkic, interdependent regions to sustain their imperial power in Asia, anti-imperialist thought linked to rising Asian nationalism was seeking to build an alternative conception of the region. These intellectual proponents of an Other Asia evoked earlier linkages between their societies, but it should be noted that their conceptualization of Asia was itself premised and enabled by contemporary imperialist technologies and modes of regional integration.

The idea of Asia among these Asians was expressed largely through a cultural movement that is instructive for us to explore. I will review here the efforts of three intellectuals, Okakura, Tagore and Zhang Taiyan, because in this early period, Asianism was principally an intellectual and cultural effort until it was overtaken by the Japanese military for imperialist purposes. Okakura Tenshin, or Kakuzo, is perhaps most famous for his opening line, "Asia is one," in his book, *The Ideals of the East with Special Reference to the Arts of Japan*, written in 1901 (published in 1903).[14] Okakura, who was deeply knowledgeable about Chinese art and culture and closely connected with South Asian Asianists, such as Tagore and Ananda Coomaraswamy, as well as American art entrepreneurs, such as Ernest Fenellosa, probably did more than anyone else, to establish Asian art as a legitimate and viable domain of high art, fit for museums and the art market.

It was through his conception of the great civilizational arts of China and India, and not least the aesthetic values of Buddhism, that Okakura saw the unity of the Asian ideals that reigned before what he regarded as the marauding of the Mongols and their successors. But even as Okakura was articulating the ideal of Asia, at the same moment he was also carving out a place for Japan in the civilized world of the West as the inheritor and leader of this present fallen Asia. Okakura saw Japan as a survivor and a leader. "Thus Japan is a museum of Asiatic civilization and yet more than a museum, because the singular genius of the race leads it to dwell on all phases of the ideals of the past, in that spirit of living Advaitism which welcomes the new without losing the old."[15] The temples of Nara reveal the great art of the Tang, and the much older influence of Shang workmanship can also be found in Japan.

Rabindranath Tagore and Okakura had a close friendship, and Okakura spent considerable time in India, acquiring a deep respect for its arts and culture even while introducing the utterly fascinated circle in the Tagore house, Jorasankho, to Chinese and Japanese culture. Both men also sought to live their lives according to their ideals, even donning the clothing of their historical cultures while most Western-educated gentlemen were opting for the prestige of the West. Thus, Okakura dressed in a dhoti when he visited the Ajanta Caves, and Tagore often wore the Daoist hat given him during his first China visit. Yet, of course, let it not be forgotten that they possessed self-confidence in advocating Asian culture because they were so knowledgeable and polished in the arts of the West. Moreover, theirs was also sometimes a troubled relationship, in part because Okakura could not quite overcome the social Darwinist presuppositions and imagery of Indian backwardness, and partly because he was an object of exotic curiosity, if not ridicule, among many Indians who had never seen East Asians, particularly in their traditional dress.[16]

Some have seen – in what I believe is an ahistorical impulse – a form of Japanese Orientalism in Okakura's paternalistic attitude towards the older Asian societies. Japanese pan-Asianism at the turn of the century had several different strains, including imperialistic ones but also egalitarian and compassionate feelings towards fellow Asians exploited and devastated by more aggressive cultures. At the same time, pan-Asianism also cultivated a deep claim of Japanese leadership in Asia and a self-imputed responsibility to raise Asians from their fallen state. Okakura saw Japan as the hall or museum – the enabler – that would display all the different civilizations of Asia. This enabling role could, of course, easily be transformed into a superiority to and instrumentalization of what it enabled. It was this tendency – or what we might call a 'structure of feeling' – that grew into the ideological foundations of Japanese imperialism, endowing

---

[15] *Ibid.*, pp. 7–8.
[16] Rustom Bharucha, *Another Asia: Rabindranath Tagore and Okakura Tenshin* (Delhi: Oxford University Press, 2006). See also Mark Ravinder Frost, *'That Great Ocean of Idealism': Calcutta, the Tagore Circle and the Idea of Asia, 1900–1920.* Nalanda-Sriwijaya Centre Working Paper Series no. 3 (June 2011), pp. 8, 22 (http://nsc.iseas.edu.sg/docu ments/working_papers/nscwps003.pdf).

it with the mission to lead Asians. Indeed, as is well known, it was the subservience of pan-Asianism to Japanese militarist imperialism that doomed its future in the twentieth century.

Zhang Taiyan, or Zhang Binglin, is widely considered to be one of the most powerful intellectuals of late Qing and early republican China. The great writer Lu Xun certainly regarded him as such and saw himself as a lifelong student of Zhang. Many see Zhang as a maverick thinker who was both narrowly racist in his violent anti-Manchu revolutionary views and deeply humanist and learned – being not only the foremost scholar of ancient Chinese learning but also widely read in Buddhist philosophy, especially the Yogacārā, or Consciousness-Only (*weishi* or *vijnapati matra*), school of Buddhism, of which he was a practitioner.[17]

Zhang became committed to Buddhism during his years in jail (1903–6) as a result of his revolutionary activities. He suffered greatly in jail and watched his younger colleague Zou Rong die under terrible privation. He claims that he was saved only by his voracious readings of Buddhist philosophy. We do not have the time here to discuss the allegation of this maverick's inconsistency except to indicate that *alaya* (storehouse) think-ing permits different levels of consciousness and commitment depending on the needs of the time. This philosophy disposes one to think very differently from the principle of commitment to ethical consistency.

Zhang espoused the cause of freedom from imperialism in Asia while in Japan after his release from prison. There he attended the meetings of the Indian freedom fighters commemorating the birthday of the Maratha warrior Shivaji, who fought against the Moguls. He is said to have auth-ored the manifesto of the Asian Solidarity Society, created in Tokyo around 1907. It begins thus:

Among the various Asian countries, India has Buddhism and Hinduism; China has the theories of Confucius, Mencius, Lao Zi, Zhuang Zi and Yang Zi; then moving to Persia, they also have enlightened religions, such as Zoroastrianism. The various races in this region had self-respect and did not invade one another... They rarely invaded one another and treated each other respectfully with the Confucian virtue of benevolence. About one hundred years ago, the Europeans moved east and Asia's power diminished day by day. Not only was their political and military power totally lacking, but people also felt inferior. Their scholarship deteriorated and people only strove after mate-rial interests.[18]

[17] Viren Murthy, *The Political Philosophy of Zhang Taiyan: The Resistance of Consciousness* (Leiden: Brill, 2011), pp. 112–15.

[18] Zhang Taiyan, "Yazhou heqinhui yuezhang" ("The Charter of the Asia Solidarity Society"), in Zhu Weizheng and Jiang Yihua, Eds., *Zhang Taiyan xuanji: zhushiben*, (Shanghai renmin chubanshe, 1982/1907), pp. 428–30.

Zhang's Asianism emerged from his commitment to the values of Buddhism but also from an anti-imperialist position. He saw the threat as one from warlike cultures to the peaceful, agrarian societies. But while committed to the ultimate values of peace, like Okakura, he acknowledged the necessity of creating a modern nation-state along the Western model to combat the imperialist powers. Nationalism was a necessary moment in the conception of pan-Asianism.

Only Tagore opposed this position. Tagore was deeply repulsed by nationalism. Writing about nationalism in Japan, he observed, "I have seen in Japan the voluntary submission of the whole people to the trimming of their minds and clipping of their freedoms by their governments... The people accept this all-pervading mental slavery with cheerfulness and pride because of their nervous desire to turn themselves into a machine of power, called the Nation, and emulate other machines in their collective worldliness."[19] Tagore's pan-Asianism was deeply affected by his personal friendships in China, but even here, during his last visit to China in 1929, he was severely attacked by leftist intellectuals and the KMT because of his views.[20] Most of all, he was bitterly disappointed by the growing nationalism of his own homeland in India where revolutionary nationalists overtook the Swadeshi movement he had once supported. Their growing narrowness – revealed, for instance, in their goal to burn every piece of foreign cloth – had also begun to affect the relations between Hindus and Muslims.

Tagore was committed to an alternative cosmopolitanism drawn from Asian traditions, which he sought to realize in Santiniketan. According to Saranindranath Tagore, Tagore's philosophy of education rose above both abstract and lifeless rationalism and violent nationalism and particularism. He was persuaded that reason would emerge only after a primary identification with an inherited tradition. Education would have to nurture the attitude of seeking reason to bridge radical differences by recognizing the consciousness of humanity's latent oneness.[21] One of the great hopes of Santinekatan was realized with the institution of Cheena Bhavan (China Hall) initiated by the scholar Tan Yunshan,

---

[19] Rabindranath Tagore, "Nationalism in the West," in Tagore, *Nationalism*, Introduction by Ramachandra Guha (New Delhi: Penguin, 2009), pp. 33–63, at p. 49.

[20] Stephen N. Hay, *Asian Ideas of East and West: Tagore and His Critics in Japan, China and India* (Cambridge, MA: Harvard University Press, 1970), pp. 323–4.

[21] Saranindranath Tagore, "Postmodernism and Education: A Tagorean Intervention," paper presented at "Tagore's Philosophy of Education," conference dedicated to the memory of Amita Sen, Kolkata, March 29–30, 2006. See also Saranindranath Tagore, "Tagore's Conception of Cosmopolitanism: A Reconstruction," *University of Toronto Quarterly*, 77(4) (2008): 1071–84.

whose children, notably Tan Chung, remain cultural ambassadors between China and India. Among others, Tagore's own relatives were pioneers in introducing Chinese arts and scholarship to Indians.

Tagore's cosmopolitanism, which he derived from the Advaita or the monistic philosophical tradition, has some unexpected parallels with contemporary thinkers from different traditions such as Jurgen Habermas. Tagore's commitment to the universality of reason, as made possible by working through difference, resembles Habermas' idea of communicative rationality as emerging from the negotiation of various value claims of different groups and communities. But, as with Habermas' theory of communicative rationality, Tagore's educational philosophy could not withstand power; this was expressed in Tagore's case in the historical force of nationalism and allied ideologies. The logic of communicative acts and education is not the only or dominant logic of society – the logic of power often frames this discussion through reified expressions of community (as in nationalism or communal religion). For most of the century, while Tagore was celebrated, his cosmopolitan educational project in Santiniketan was ignored and marginalized by the imperatives of a competitive nationalism.

Through this brief survey, we have seen how three major Asian thinkers were able to conceive of the unity of Asia founded on various different principles. Their idea of a common historical and religious culture, conceived sometimes as a utopian golden age of peaceful coexistence and dynamic exchange before the arrival of foreign invaders, may have prompted Asianists to think of original Asian value. Note also how in each case, their notion of Asia excluded societies from the Middle East and central Asia, which each regarded as foreign invaders of their societies. Nonetheless, pan-Asianism, as several scholars have shown, was also an important trend in the Middle East as they reached out, especially to Japan, for allies against Western imperialism. Indeed, Tagore's four-week visit to Iran in 1932, when he and his hosts sought to highlight the Indo-Iranian civilizational nexus, was perhaps one of his most successful Asian visits.[22] By and large, the three thinkers we have considered were looking for new beginnings in the search for values alternative to the dominant civilizational narratives of the West. In this sense, they were the founders of a cultural anti-imperialism and articulators of an Asian cosmopolitanism.

However, their thought was in advance of their time in that it could not be sustained by the political societies in which they lived. Ideas of race,

---

[22] Sugata Bose, *A Hundred Horizons: The Indian Ocean in the Age of Global Empire* (Cambridge, MA: Harvard University Press, 2006), pp. 260–5.

culture, anti-imperialism and imperialism to be found in pan-Asianism all spelt a lethally close relationship with the dominant trend of nationalism. In the case of Okakura, pan-Asianism became easily absorbed by Japanese imperialism; in the case of Zhang, nationalism took priority because of the circumstances. In the case of Tagore, the nationalism of his time made his ideas and institutions irrelevant for a long period.

The spatial vision of Asia that these thinkers possessed was based not on the actual interactions of people from the different countries – of which there was a great deal – but on an abstract and essentialized notion of culture and civilization formed in the mirror image of the Western concept of civilization. Just as that celebration of the superior achievements of a race and religion – apart from specific classes and areas – worked to further a program of domination of the Other, so, too, the idea of Asian civilization was hijacked by Japanese militarism.

Asia after World War II

The Cold War division of the world into two camps controlled militarily by nuclear superpowers seeking to dominate the rest of the developing and decolonizing nations may be seen as a kind of supraregionalism. While, in fact, the two camps or blocs represented transterritorial spaces including non-contiguous nations, the contiguity of core Eastern and Western Europeans nations within each camp served as a stepping-stone for subsequent regionalism to develop within Europe. We see this tendency in Asia as well where regional interactions were promoted between the countries of CENTO (1955–79), SEATO (1955–77) and ASEAN (1967) that were basically security alliances. The Japanese efforts to cultivate Asian markets during and after the Vietnam War also created some economic and cultural grounds for later integration. After the Cold War, ASEAN, which was designed, unlike the European community, to serve the nation, not only expanded to include the ex-communist nations of Southeast Asia but also became more oriented to serve the economic needs of the region.[23] Moreover, places like Hong Kong, which played an indispensable role as a conduit for exchange between the two camps, were able to reinforce and benefit handsomely from older regional links especially between Southeast Asia and China.[24]

---

[23] Muthiah Alagappa, *Asian Security Practice: Material and Ideational Influences* (Stanford University Press, 1998).
[24] Prasenjit Duara, "Hong Kong and the New Imperialism in East Asia 1941–1966," in David Goodman and Bryna Goodman, Eds., *Twentieth Century Colonialism and China: Localities, the Everyday, and the World* (London: Routledge, 2012), pp. 197–211.

Another effort to create a regional entity during the early Cold War was the movement of non-aligned nations principally in Asia, although it also included the African nations. The culmination of this movement was the Bandung Conference, a meeting of the representatives of twenty-nine new nations of Asia and Africa, held in Bandung, Indonesia, in 1955, fifty years after the Russo-Japanese War signaled the beginnings of pan-Asianism. The conference aimed to express solidarity against imperialism and racism and promote economic and cultural cooperation among these nations. China, India and Indonesia were key players in the meeting. The conference finally led to the Non-Aligned Movement in 1961, a wider Third World force in which participants avowed their distance from the two superpowers – aligning themselves with neither the United States nor the Soviet Union – during the Cold War. However, conflicts developed among these non-aligned nations, as, for instance, between India and China in 1962, which eroded the solidarity of the Bandung spirit. At any rate, the non-aligned nations also tended to be nationally autarkic in their economic strategies – moving further away from regional linkages.

Thus, all in all, although there were significant foundations for the post-Cold War regionalism to be found in the Cold War itself, the economic energies of Asian countries in the two camps were directed more towards the nation and the supraregion than the region itself. The congruence between political and cultural realms also came to be directed towards the two loci.

The post-Cold War scene is usually characterized as one of globalization. To be sure, the nation-state and nationalism have by no means disappeared; they have developed a new relationship to transnational capitalism. In this reconfiguration, regionalism has clearly strengthened, emerging as an intermediate zone between the deterritorializing impulses of capitalism and the territorial limits of nationalism. Unlike in the Cold War, contemporary Europe, NAFTA, MERCOSUR in South America, APEC, ASEAN (+3; +6; that is, the East Asian Summit) are largely economic rather than security-based regionalisms. Moreover, most of these regions are not overwhelmingly dominated by one imperial power or hegemon.

Within East Asia and Southeast Asia – and, more recently, India – Asian economic integration has increased significantly, principally after the end of the Asian financial crisis of the late 1990s. The economic integration of East, South and Southeast Asia, which had grown steadily under imperialist-dominated trade, declined precipitously at the end of World War II.[25] Intraregional trade began to pick up in the 1980s, but it was the

---

[25] Peter A. Petri, "Is East Asia Becoming More Interdependent?," *Journal of Asian Economics, 17*(3) (2006): 381–94.

Asian financial crisis – the shock of the common crisis – that seems to have awakened the states to the reality of regional networks and focused their attention on cooperation. Today, what the Asian Development Bank (ADB) calls 'integrating Asia' including ASEAN, China, Japan, Korea, India, Hong Kong and Taiwan, conducts over 50% of its trade with itself in comparison to trade with the outside world, compared with only 33% in 1980s. Six major indicators of interdependence tracked for the sixteen Asian economies have increased markedly in the ten years since the financial crisis.[26]

A significant factor behind the increased trade is the participation of these economies in a regional supply-chain production network. Production is divided into smaller steps, and each part is assigned to the most cost-efficient producer. Thus, for instance, an electronic product may be produced or assembled in China with hardware from Taiwan and software from India. Indeed, much of this type of vertical integration of production has been enabled by new information and communication technologies and open markets. At the same time, the bulk of these goods has been produced for consumption in Europe and North America. The present crisis in consumption may well be leading to deepening markets for these goods within Asia. In recent years, ASEAN is developing free-trade agreements (FTAs) with each of the East Asian nations and India. The Chinese-ASEAN FTA of 2010 created the third largest common market by trade volume. The significantly lower-volume trade between ASEAN and India has also, however, been growing at a compounded annual rate of 27% and has accelerated with the signing of the ASEAN-Indian FTA in 2009.[27]

Financial integration has been relatively weaker within Asia than between individual Asian countries and Western economies. This is particularly noticeable because of the enormous savings generated within Asia that are not productively invested in projects within the region. However, after the 1997–8 financial crisis, the Chiangmai Initiative was undertaken to provide emergency liquidity of US$80 billion in case of a foreign exchange crisis in the ASEAN +3 countries. In 2009, the fund was increased to US$120 billion, Japan and China agreeing to contribute a

---

[26] *Emerging Asian Regionalism: A Partnership for Shared Prosperity* (Manila: Asian Development Bank, 2008), pp. 70, 97–8.
[27] "Cabinet Nod for Asean FTA," *Times of India*, July 25, 2009 (http://economictimes.india times.com/News/Economy/Foreign-Trade/Cabinet-nod-for-Asean-FTA/articleshow/4818 081.cms). For China-ASEAN FTA, see Collin Spears, "SINO + ASEAN = East Asian Unification? Not Quite: Part I," *Brooks Foreign Policy Review*, posted May 15, 2009 (http://brooksreview.wordpress.com/2009/05/20/sino-asean-east-asian-unification-not-quite-part-i/).

third each, South Korea to put up 16% and ASEAN, the balance of 20%.[28] In the past few years, several other countries have entered into bilateral swap agreements. Such agreements have been reached, for instance, between India and Japan, and in response to the precipitous decline of the South Korean *won*, South Korea entered separately into bilateral swap agreements with China and Japan.

Macroeconomic interdependence in the region is also indicated by the co-movement of macroeconomic variables. For instance, the correlation of GDP among many of these states over 3-year moving averages is very strong. The GDP correlation coefficient has gone up from .07 before the crisis to .54 after the crisis. Price movements are similarly correlated, and price shocks in one area are being transmitted to other areas with greater intensity. With the growth of macroeconomic interdependence, a growing need to manage it has appeared. For instance, exchange rates require monitoring and coordination so that central banks do not shoot each other in the foot.[29] In this context, it is heartening to learn that economic interdependence within Asia is the major – perhaps the only – factor reducing conflict among these Asian nation-states.[30]

There is some indication of greater cultural interest of Asians in Asia. We see this in the increase in the number of tourists circulating in the region to above precrisis levels. Not only has the market demand for Asian art rocketed, but also there are plenty of exhibitions and showings of Asian art in which artists and curators experiment with new ideas of Asia as well as art. These shows often deliberately distance themselves from the culturally unified notion of Asia or reified versions of national civilizations prevalent among the works of predecessors like Okakura and Nand Lal Bose. They often seek to showcase the contemporary, urban, multicultural experience of Asia, emphasizing heterogeneity and cultural encounters.[31] At a popular level, the circulation of East Asian cinema, manga, anime, TV shows, food, design and allied areas in East and Southeast Asia has been the most conspicuous cultural development in Asia since the 1990s.

Asian connections and challenges

To be sure, greater interactivity is hardly without its problems. Perhaps most revealing of the emergent space and complex nature of network

---

[28] *The Straits Times*, "Review and Forum," May 5, 2009. The fund was doubled in 2012.
[29] *Emerging Asian Regionalism*, pp. 153–5.
[30] See Benjamin E. Goldsmith, "A Liberal Peace in Asia?," *Journal of Peace Research*, 44(1) (2007): 5–27.
[31] C. J. Wan-Ling Wee, "'We Asians'? Modernity, Visual Art Exhibitions, and East Asia," *Boundary 2*, 37(1) (2010): 91–126.

Asia is the subject of migration and sojourning within the region. Through this optic, we can observe the extent of the move away from the national production space and explore the possibilities and dangers of the new type of spatial production. As globalization has proceeded over the last two and a half decades, nation-states have adopted, albeit to different degrees, strategies of neo-liberal privatization and opening to world markets and circulations. The movement of people across the globe and region for purposes of work and livelihood has expanded considerably. The PRC has 35 million migrants across the world, India 20 million and the Philippines 8 million. Remittances, cultural values and styles, and technical and professional knowledge from their host societies have a major impact on domestic economy and society. As of 2001, more than 6 million migrants from Asia work in the more advanced economies of Japan, Singapore, Taiwan, South Korea, Hong Kong and Malaysia.[32]

Elite migrants and transmigrants circulating within Asia are a novel phenomenon of these last few decades, and they have ushered in a new culture of professional Asians in the major cities. They are embedded in both knowledge and business networks and have often been trained in Western academic establishments, where they developed their professional cultural ethos and connections. These professionals are a significant element in the cultural profile of the new global and metropolitan cities in Asia, whether in Shanghai, Bangalore, Dubai, Singapore or Hong Kong. As the workshop on "Inter-Referencing Asia," held in Dubai in 2008, pointed out, there is "an intensification of traffic in people, urban models, and cultural forms between Asian cities, big and small." In many ways, these cities are increasingly linked by corridors of exchange with other Asian cities, as they are with their own national or regional hinterlands. The workshop identifies these Asian or, indeed, intra-Asian cities as 'extra-territorial' metropolises that are produced not only by national resources but also through a set of global and intra-Asian flows of labor, capital and knowledge.[33] The complex known as Biopolis and its sister establishment Fusionopolis in Singapore represent classic instances of such extraterritoriality. The scientists, technicians and professionals who work here day and often night for Asian and global biotech companies hail from every part of Asia (often with Western academic degrees). These gigantic, mall-like complexes feature every kind of Asian eatery and

---

[32] *Emerging Asian Regionalism*, p. 225.
[33] Aihwa Ong and Ananya Roy, Workshop Directors, "Inter-Referencing Asia: Urban Experiments and the Art of Being Global," International Conference on "Inter-Asian Connections," Dubai, UAE: February 21–3, 2008.

omniplexes featuring anime festivals, while construction and maintenance is performed by gangs of other Asian migrant labor.

It is this new relationship between elite and working-class migration
that I wish to comment upon. As is well known, many Asian nations are
succeeding in wooing back their talented émigrés to invest their knowledge and capital in their original homelands. Historically, this kind of
migration and courtship has been exceptional. Migration over the last
century and a half has largely been labor migration, mostly in plantation,
mining and infrastructure construction, but migration of people who have
ended up in different niches in the host societies. The matrix in which this
migration took place has been constituted by networks and institutions of
global capitalism and the modern nation-state whether in its *imperialist*
manifestation or its nationalist one. While, as we have seen, the relationship between the nation-state and capitalism has largely been a collusive
one, there has also been a tension in that relationship. To put it simply,
while global capitalism has encouraged the flows of labor, nationalist
states have *sought to both regulate and curb this flow, responding to a set of
other interests* including affected domestic working classes and constitu-
encies based on racial and nationalist ideologies. Decolonizing nation-
states turned out to be as limiting of immigrant populations as older
imperialist nation-states.

The laboring population that has both benefited and suffered most
greatly from this tension between global capitalism and the nation-state
has been the Chinese communities, first in the Americas and then in
Southeast Asia. The exclusion laws against Asians in the United States
until 1942 imposed strict quotas and controls on labor migrants from
China. Indeed, the matrix of law and control had made much immigrant
labor the *exception* in the sense of Giorgio Agamben's *Homo Sacer: Sovereign
Power and Bare Life* and Mae Ngai's *The Impossible Subject*[34] – such immigrants were necessary to labor on undesirable tasks for a pittance, but they
were without rights, suspended between capital and the state, and often
between nation-state jurisdictions. To be sure, many of these laborers were
also able to creatively manipulate their suspension between powers, as
shown by the 'paper sons' of Chinese migrants, who entered the United
States in large numbers during the early twentieth century.[35]

---

[34] Giorgio Agamben, *Homo Sacer: Sovereign Power and Bare Life* (Stanford University Press,
1998); Mae M. Ngai, *Impossible Subjects: Illegal Aliens and the Making of Modern America*
(Princeton University Press, 2004).

[35] 'Paper sons' were Chinese immigrants who claimed, using false papers, to be sons of
American citizens. See Prasenjit Duara, "Between Sovereignty and Capitalism: The
Historical Experiences of Migrant Chinese," in Duara, *The Global and Regional in
China's Nation Formation* (London: Routledge, 2009), ch. 7.

What has changed in the relationship between global capitalism and the nation-state? How has the globalization of recent decades changed this institutional matrix affecting migrants? One new element, as I have tried to show, is the substantially new flow of high-value workers – or professionals. To speak impressionistically, it would seem that this is informed by the growth of what is called the knowledge economy or knowledge-based service and production in the global economy. The fact that so much of it is Asian and circulating in the Asian region is a still more complex and interesting question. The return and transmigration of a professional and managerial stratum does signify a shift in the institutional matrix. Whereas the nation-state worked to regulate the deterritorialized flows of the labor, capital and culture of capitalism even when collaborating with it, now the nationalist opposition to these flows is significantly smaller, especially from the institutions of the nation-state. As large states like India and the PRC reach out to global professionals among overseas and global Chinese (*huaren* and *haigui*) and non-resident Indians (NRIs), they create a non-territorial, ethnic identity – as children of the Yellow Emperor, Hindutva or Hindus – that fits with a neo-liberal model of globalization and competitiveness. Until recently, this has also coincided with state withdrawal in many areas of provisioning public goods, such as education and healthcare.

On the other hand, labor migration, especially in seasonal and construction work, has expanded to many more societies. These labor migrants are more typically sojourners who have short-term labor contracts and are prevented from assimilation into the host society. Many, such as the recent case of the Rohingas in Southeast Asia, are regularly abused and exploited by local authorities and labor contractors. Moreover, unlike the situation during globalization in the pre-World War I period, there is increased sojourning by women employed as domestic workers, nurses, entertainers and prostitutes, which in turn is also reshaping families across Asia. We need to focus more on the continuing power and role of the nation-state to regulate and expel immigrants. The nation-state continues to control the prerogative of return for them. It controls their tenure and bodies,[36] and can satisfy the constituent interests of domestic workers and nationalist interests. They can serve as an important safety valve or whipping boy.

---

[36] For instance, female domestic workers are required to undergo pregnancy and HIV tests every 6 months in Singapore. Those who are pregnant often face dismissal and deportation. "Maid to Order: Ending Abuses Against Migrant Domestic Workers in Singapore," Human Rights Watch, December 7, 2005, pp. 5, 90 (www.hrw.org/en/reports/2005/12/06/maid-order).

Thus, the new order in Asia must be seen in its totality. The figure of
the professional global transmigrants, their flexible citizenship and self-
improvement projects, and the state's interest in utilizing them must be
seen against the ground of the continuing power of the restructured
nation-state to control and expel at the lower levels of the social hierarchy.
While these Asian nations must be able to draw in and deploy migrants at
the higher levels, they must be able to push out migrants at the lower
levels. Thus, the new Asia does not by any means suggest the weakening of
nationalism, but rather a refiguration or restructuring of the nation-state
to adapt to global capitalism.

The challenge of regional commons

Perhaps the most important challenge for the emerging region is the imperative to coordinate and manage the interdependence arising from the
common and linked set of problems in the realm of climate change,
environmental degradation, water scarcity, and public health, among
others. The provisioning of these commons, which the ADB dubs 'regional
public goods', is evidently urgent. Consider a colossal and dire public-
goods problem – or crisis of the commons – that cannot be managed
without a concerted regional effort. The Tibetan plateau is the source and
watershed of ten major rivers that provide fresh water to many different
countries in South and Southeast Asia in addition to China. Climate
change and environmental degradation have depleted the water resources
available in all these countries, and the problem is particularly severe in
north and northwest China, which is suffering the most severe drought in
the last half-century, with precipitation levels 70–90% below normal and
water tables depleted from excessive well drilling.[37] Recently, there has
been a proposal to divert the waters of several Tibetan rivers, including the
Yarlong Tsangpo (known as the Brahmaputra in India and Bangladesh),
northwards to irrigate the north China plains. This proposal, known as the
Great South–North Water Transfer Project, appears to have the backing of
the highest authorities. Needless to say, the effects of this diversion on
South Asia could lead to unprecedented water-wars.[38]

The two rivers flowing from the Tibetan plateau across southwest
China and Southeast Asia that are of greatest concern are the Nu, or

[37] Mark Selden, "China's Way Forward? Historical and Contemporary Perspectives on
Hegemony and the World Economy in Crisis," *Asia-Pacific Journal*, posted March 24,
2009.
[38] Brahma Chellaney, "China–India Clash over Chinese Claims to Tibetan Water," posted
at *Japan Focus* on July 3, 2007.

Salween (discussed further below), and the Lancang, or Mekong (Maps 7.1a and 7.1b). China has already built or is in the process of creating nine dams upstream on the Lancang/Mekong in its territory, while Laos has sixteen dams on the tributaries with many more in the building and planning stages, five of which are on the Mekong.[39] The most controversial of these is the Xayaburi dam. More than 60 million people and a hundred different ethnic groups live along the Mekong, and several researchers have warned that the furious dam building undertaken by the PRC government and that of Laos may result in a colossal disaster of food shortage, destruction of livelihood and irregular movement of people, and this, in turn, could eventuate – or has already eventuated – in violence and civil war.[40]

Both the PRC and Laos view these water resources as the source of essential and highly profitable hydropower necessary for the development of their nations. Viewed from the river bank, the Mekong waters are the source of invaluable livelihood supplies such as food, water and firewood. Hydropower alters, perhaps irreversibly, the hydrology of the ecosystem by decimating fish stocks, preventing natural fertilization of the flood plains, inundating agricultural and forest lands, and promoting saline intrusion into the Mekong delta. Reportedly, China's Manwan dam on the upper reaches is silting up twice as fast as expected (Map 7.1b). A study that changed some key, but questionable, assumptions of the forecasted benefits of planned dam development showed that the potential profits of up to US$33 billion could become a net loss of up to US$274 billion for the economy.[41]

Dams have also been built on the Brahmaputra in Tibet, a seismically volatile area like the neighboring Salween watershed, and this could lead to catastrophes downstream in the event of an earthquake. Although the PRC authorities assert that the impact of dam building has not affected downstream waters significantly, the PRC government has not been very

[39] There are about forty Chinese state-owned enterprises and private firms involved in damming and ancilliary development in the region. Cristelle Maurin and Pichamon Yeophantong, "Going Global Responsibly? China's Strategies Towards 'Sustainable' Overseas Investments," *Pacific Affairs*, 86(2) (2013): 281–303, at p. 296.

[40] Christopher G. Baker, *Dams, Power and Security in the Mekong: A Non-Traditional Security Assessment of Hydro-Development in the Mekong River Basin*. NTS Research Paper no. 8 (Singapore: RSIS Centre for Non-Traditional Security (NTS) Studies for NTS-Asia, 2012), pp. 1–3, 26. See also *Power and Responsibility: The Mekong River Commission and Lower Mekong Mainstream Dams*. A joint report of the Australian Mekong Resource Centre (University of Sydney and Oxfam Australia, 2009).

[41] Scott W. D. Pearse-Smith, "Lower Mekong Basin Hydropower Development and the Trade-off Between the 'Traditional' and 'Modern' Sectors: 'Out with the Old, in with the New,'" *Asia-Pacific Journal, 10*(23) (2012).

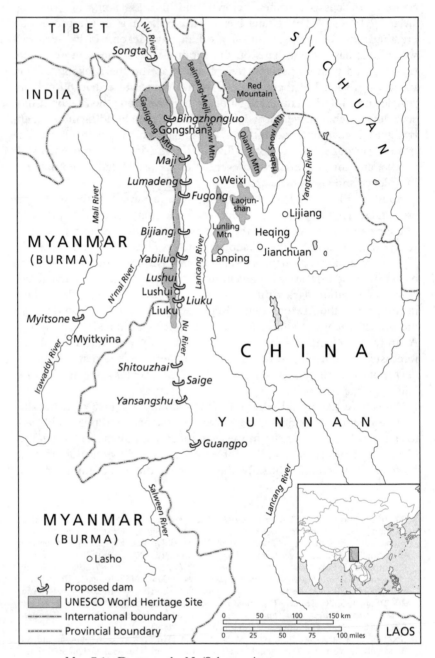

Map 7.1a Dams on the Nu/Salween river.

Map 7.1b Dams on the Lancang/Mekong river.

forthcoming with the necessary data and has not permitted independent scientific studies of the dams. Greater regional efforts must begin with pooling all the necessary data.[42]

To be sure, the environmental degradation and social uproar that has been caused by dam building and other projects of unsustainable development are hardly limited to cross-border regions. Both India and China have witnessed, although in different ways, critical protests against these gargantuan projects within their heartlands. We have seen how the civic organization created by NGOs and communities opposed to the Narmada dam, the NBA (Narmada Bachao Andolan, or Save the Narmada Agitation), networked and pressured global and national agencies to discontinue the building of large-scale dams across much of the world. During the late 1990s, the NBA coordinated their protest activities with those of NGOs and experts in India as well as with antidam and environmental organizations across the world in Brazil, Spain, the United States, and elsewhere. They ultimately brought considerable pressure upon the World Bank and other international donor agencies, which responded by forming an independent agency empowered to review the environmental and social impact of building large dams in 1998, the World Commission of Dams (WCD), under the leadership of Nelson Mandela. The commission has created a set of globally applicable priorities and procedures regarding the environment, livelihood, transparency and community empowerment in the creation of dams. This kind of social activism and the global attention it brought have certainly contributed to the discouragement of the further building of large dams in India.[43]

While they cannot consistently express themselves as actively as in other parts of Asia, the role of domestic and transnational NGOs in shaping China's responses to environmental problems has been under-appreciated. For instance, with regard to the Three Gorges project on the Yangtze river, transnational environmental activism affected not only governmental action but also the actions of investment companies such as Morgan Stanley. Deploying both environmental and human-rights arguments, international NGOs responded to local NGOs and prominent Chinese activists such as Dai Qing, whose book *Yangtze, Yangtze* (1994)

---

[42] Geoffrey Gunn and Brian McCartan, "Chinese Dams and the Great Mekong Floods of 2008," *Japan Focus*, March 21, 2009.

[43] Shripad Dharmadhikary, "Implementing the Report of the World Commission on Dams: A Case Study of the Narmada Valley in India," *American University International Law Review*, 16(6) (2001): 1591–1630, at pp. 1601, 1608, 1630. See also Patrick McCully, "The Use of a Trilateral Network: An Activist's Perspective on the Formation of the World Commission on Dams," *American University International Law Review*, 16(6) (2001): 1453–75.

brought considerable international attention to the dam. The international activists succeed in getting Western governments to rescind their financial and technical support for the project and also engineered shareholder opposition to the plans of Wall Street financiers for the second tranche of loans to be made to the PRC government in 2000. As such, they not only brought global scrutiny of the project, but also forced the Chinese government on the backfoot and to seek costly sources of domestic financing. Bellette Lee makes the interesting point that the human-rights angle gave moral authority and inspiration to sustain the local environmental movement at a time when environmentalism in China did not have the same kind of institutionalized global authority that the former possessed.[44]

The next significant encounter in the environmental history of Chinese dam construction revealed some important differences. In 2003, the Yunnan provincial government decided to construct thirteen dams on the upper reaches of the Nu river (Map 7.1a). Since the central government encourages the sale of excess power, the provincial government saw hydropower not only as a means to satisfy the energy demands of the province but also as a source of revenue. The Nu river (together with the Yarlong Tsangpo) happened to be one of the last undammed major rivers in China. When the news report of the dam project was released, NGOs and governments of the neighboring Southeast Asian countries protested to the Chinese authorities, citing the destruction of the natural habitat and the anticipated environmental, social and economic impact of the project on their countries. From 2004 until the present, not only did civil protest against the dam (and other dams; e.g., on the Jinsha) become a major public event, but transnational NGOs and UNESCO also played a crucial role in supporting and enabling the civic activists.[45]

Fearful of the impact downstream, several NGOs from Southeast Asia, including the Salween Watch Coalition comprising eighty NGOs from Myanmar and Thailand, together with several international NGOs, including International Rivers and Conservation International, cooperated with their Chinese counterparts, such as Friends of Nature, Green Volunteers and Yunnan Green Watershed, to put pressure on the Chinese government. A media campaign was begun to raise national and

---

[44] Yuen-ching Bellette Lee, "Global Capital, National Development and Transnational Environmental Activism: Conflict and the Three Gorges Dam," *Journal of Contemporary Asia, 43* (2013): 102–26.

[45] Ralph Litzinger, "In Search of the Grassroots: Hydroelectric Politics in Northwest Yunnan," in Elizabeth Perry and Merle Goldman, Eds., *Grassroots Political Reform in Contemporary China*, pp. 282–99, at pp. 285–8; see also Andrew Jacobs, "Chinese River's Fate May Reshape a Region," *New York Times*, May 4, 2013.

international awareness of the issue, and the activists successfully appealed to Premier Wen Jiabao, a geologist by training, who halted the project in April 2004. By one count, 159 newspaper articles were written on the project from 2003 to 2006. The movement began again in 2009 when permission was granted to the Huadian and Huaneng corporations to construct a scaled-back project of four dams on the river. Once again, Premier Wen intervened and work was once again suspended.[46] The plan was resuscitated in March 2013, just ahead of Premier Wen's retirement, and though the new version seeks to build only five of the thirteen original dams, the political circumstances leading to its revival are unclear.

The new phase in environmental activism in China – despite the setback – is significant for several reasons. First, compared to the Three Gorges case, the voice and agitation of the concerned public, though still conducted largely within official boundaries, was far more open and widespread. Second, the participation of regional and international NGOs and the PRC government's desire to adhere – in some respects – to international norms of transparency on environmental issues (although it rejects the standards of the WCD) enabled domestic NGOs to pressure the government more successfully than in the previous decade. Finally, UNESCO, international environmental networks (such as Conservation International) and, above all, local NGOs frequently invoked the sanctity of the UN-mandated World Heritage Site called the Three Parallel Rivers of Yunnan Protected Areas (Map 7.1a), drawing upon new sources of inviolable authority around culture and biodiversity. The engagement of secular activists and NGOs with ideas of inviolability, heritage, native place, indigeneity and sacred forests, waters and land is a topic we will return to in the conclusion to this book.[47]

Although 2013 has seen a setback, it is worthwhile to explore Yunnan further from the perspective of political ecology. Yunnan is a province favored by biological and cultural diversity, with long and powerful transnational linkages forged by its physical and cultural connections. As we have seen, Yunnan is also 'the cradle of NGOs' and especially environmental civil society. I return to it here to discuss in particular the ways in which the emergent and intertwined networks at various scales are

---

[46] Heejin Han, "China's Policymaking in Transition: A Hydropower Development Case," *Journal of Environment & Development*, 22(3) (2013): 313–36, at pp. 323–4 and *passim*.

[47] "Goldman Environmental Prize Winner Yu Xiaogang on Hydropower and Community in China," Alex Pasternak's interview with Yu Xiaogang, posted April 12, 2008 (www.treehugger.com/about-treehugger/goldman-environmental-prize-winner-yu-xiaogang-on-hydropower-and-community-in-china.html).

reshaping society, identity and nature as they recruit local, national, regional and global resources, often across boundaries.

The involvement of Western transnational environmental agencies in Yunnan began with the entry of the World Wildlife Fund (WWF) in the late 1980s – heralded and warranted by the visit to the region by Prince Philip of the UK – which is committed to preserving biodiversity and, in particular, the remaining wild elephants in China. Michael Hathaway has traced the subsequent history of this involvement in what he calls the 'environmental winds' that have swept the region since. By using the word 'winds', Hathaway chose a popular Chinese expression to convey something close to what I have been calling the circulatory processes of encounter, engagement and propulsion. Developing the Latourian idea of networks, he showed how activist networks make their ideas travel by working with localities, intellectuals, professionals and government agencies, among others. Hathaway showed that this is hardly a one-way flow because Chinese intellectuals and scientists were also connected with regional networks spreading from Thailand to the Philippines and across to Himalayan South Asia. The involvement of global civil society organizations also offered new opportunities to extend and develop their ideas and projects.[48]

Although Hathaway is not unsympathetic to the critique made, for example, by Vandana Shiva of Western transnational environmental NGOs and their 'global speak', the story he tells is revealing. When the consultants and experts of the WWF first arrived in 1987, their view of the problem of threatened biodiversity dovetailed quite nicely with the Chinese party-state view of the problem: that backward peasants and indigenous people were causing the problems by their unscientific methods of slash-and-burn, or swidden, agriculture and other wasteful practices. Together, the authorities and consultants applied what has come to be known globally as 'coercive conservation', with draconian punishments for shooting marauding elephants and for farming or foraging in the Xishuang Banna Nature Reserve near the Myanmar–Laos border. By the time Hathaway arrived to do his research around the Reserve in 2000, attitudes had changed considerably. Certainly, the failure of several of the conservation projects contributed to a change of attitude, especially among the foreign experts, but peasants and the minority communities also often saw opportunities to cooperate in a common cause. Unquestionably, though, there were shifting directions of global environmental winds that contributed to the changes in Yunnan.[49]

---

[48] Michael J. Hathaway, *Environmental Winds: Making the Global in Southwest China* (Berkeley, CA: University of California Press, 2013).
[49] *Ibid.*, pp. 82–3, 113.

Changing attitudes towards 'local' and 'indigenous' knowledge and rights had emerged seemingly rhizomatically within a few decades in several parts of the world. Doubtless the critique from the south also contributed to this emergence, as it converged with the discourse of indigenous rights. This new wind was seized by Yunnanese scientists and activists like Pei Shengji, Yu Xiaogang and others. Because indigeneity still has a negative connotation in China, these intellectuals reworked the discourse of 'sacred lands and forests' and expanded their arguments to foster the idea of environmental justice for all rural peoples.

The botanist Pei Shengji was already regionally influential. He had published his first English language essay on sacred forests entitled *Cultural Values and Human Ecology in Southeast Asia* as early as in 1985; he also headed the International Center for Integrated Mountain Development in Kathmandu, a think tank centered on the Himalayas, drawing the Yunnan intellectual community closer to debates and issues around the Himalayas.[50] These scientists promoted the notion that ethnic and cultural diversity is closely tied to biodiversity, and during the International Society for Ethnobiology (ISE) World Congress held in Kunming in 1990, delegates from fifty-two countries initiated the Global Coalition of Biological and Cultural Diversity to promote dialog between indigenous people, scientists and environmentalists.[51]

Thus, in 2002, when the Critical Ecosystem Partnership Fund (CEPF), declared the mountains of Southwest China a biodiversity hotspot – a zone of abundant but threatened biodiversity – networks within Yunnan province were well positioned to respond to the initiative. CEPF is a 2001 initiative of Conservation International partnered by the World Bank, the MacArthur Foundation, the Global Environmental Facility, L'Agence Française de Développement and the government of Japan. The goals of CEPF are to restore 200 threatened global biodiversity hotspots by "focusing [its] attention on nurturing key organizations and individuals who would be capable of seizing opportunities for conservation . . . and encouraging alliances within a growing civil society sector and between government and civil society to design and implement programs."[52]

---

[50] *Ibid.*, pp. 127–32.
[51] Darrell Posey and Graham Dutfield, *Beyond Intellectual Property: Toward Traditional Resource Rights for Indigenous Peoples and Local Communities* (Ottawa: IDRC Books, 1996), pp. 2–3 (http://web.idrc.ca/en/ev-9327-201-1-DO_TOPIC.html); J. Baird Callicott, *Earth's Insights: A Survey of Ecological Ethics from the Mediterranean Basin to the Australian Outback* (Berkeley and Los Angeles, CA: University of California Press, 1994) p. 12.
[52] "Assessing Five Years of CEPF Investment in the Mountains of Southwest China Biodiversity Hotspot: A Special Report," Critical Ecosystem Partnership Fund, August 2008, pp. 5–7, 17 (www.cepf.net/Documents/final_mswchina_assessment_aug08.pdf).

The 5-year report of CEPF investment in Southwest China (2008) claims that it has increased the capacity of nearly 150 organizations to participate in conservation efforts and supported the extension of government and community reserves to 194,228 hectares, upgraded 500,000 hectares of nature reserves and created a World Heritage Site of nature reserves (2003) of almost 1 million hectares (in the upper reaches of the Yangtzi, Mekong and Salween (see UNESCO Heritage Site on Map 7.1a)).[53] CEPF also underscores the importance of poverty reduction in its goal of sustaining biodiversity by promoting and aiding community conservation efforts, providing jobs and training in various projects, and strengthening civil society.[54]

Ralph Litzinger has warned that these transborder agencies, which are forms of deterritorialized sovereignty (allied with capital, but alert to its destructiveness), cannot operate seamlessly in what remains an entrenched system of national sovereignties. In China they are producing anxiety among state agencies that are afraid not only of losing control of the biological resources of the country but also of the new types of citizen subjectivities that they may have to confront.[55] Indeed, CEPF has had to tread cautiously in the politics of dam building in Yunnan. It reports,

In 2003, however, dams on the Nu (Salween) River or tributaries of the Yangtze River, as well as other hydropower projects on pristine alpine lakes *sacred* to local populations in Sichuan emerged as urgent concerns [emphasis added]. It was then followed by a major water diversion scheme from the South to the North, and last but not least, mining in the western provinces also became an issue. CEPF resources enabled local organizations to participate in public dialogue on the merits of these projects; analyzing Environmental Impact Assessments and conducting relevant scientific investigations; and producing and disseminating publications that provided a broad perspective on costs and benefits.[56]

Arguably the most famous environmental activist in China, Yu Xiaogang, has been at the heart of the region's struggle for social and environmental justice in the face of the colossus of state-backed corporate power bent on dam building. He was educated in Thailand's Asian Institute of Technology and worked in the Yunnan Academy of Social Science. He has been awarded the Magsaysay and the Goldman Award (regarded as the Asian and Environmental Nobel, respectively). For much

---

[53] *Ibid.*, p. 17.
[54] *Ibid.*, pp. 13–14. See also Ralph A. Litzinger, "Contested Sovereignties and the Critical Ecosystem Partnership Fund," *PoLAR: Political and Legal Anthropological Review*, 29(1) (2006): 66–87.
[55] Litzinger, "Contested Sovereignties and the Critical Ecosystem Partnership Fund," 66–87.
[56] "Assessing Five Years of CEPF," pp. 8–9.

of the last decade Yu and his Kunming-based NGO, Green Watershed – buoyed by the global environmental winds (he reads deeply in the records of the WCD) and the declaration of the region as a UNESCO World Heritage Site – were fairly successful. His 2002 report on the social impact of the Manwan dam on the Mekong apparently influenced Wen Jiabao to reconsider how evicted communities were dealt with. Yu Xiaogang even brought a delegation of affected residents to an international hydropower conference in Beijing in 2004, an action that contributed to the suspension of the Nu river project.[57]

Sovereignty and the river

The Mekong River Commission, an intergovernmental organization, was originally established (as the Mekong River Committee) under the aegis of the United Nations Development Program (UNDP) to promote large dams in Southeast Asia during the 1950s. It has recently been subject to considerable soul-searching, as it has had to respond to the great surge in community and civil activism across borders. A report published by the Australian Mekong Resource Centre demonstrates the ways in which this intergovernmental commission has become the object of much critical ire and protest. For instance, a letter signed in 2007 by over 200 civil society groups and others from the Mekong and other countries launched a scathing critique of "extraordinary abdication of responsibility" on the part of the Mekong River Commission. In 2008, the international conference on "Mekong Mainstream Dams: People's Voices Across Borders," held in Bangkok, presented a report that effectively articulated the normative role and responsibilities of the commission. These civil-society groups have since been increasingly pressing the Mekong River Commission to adhere to the more inclusive and sustainable priorities and procedures of the WCD. Of course, behind the demands and hand-wringing by the Mekong River Commission looms the role of Chinese corporates and state power as the principal issue for all parties in inland Southeast Asia.[58]

> I live upstream
> And you live downstream.
> Our eternal friendship flows
> With the river waters we share.

---

[57] "Goldman Environmental Prize Winner Yu Xiaogang." See also Hathaway, *Environmental Winds*, pp. 140–7. According to Hathaway, Yu was negatively affected by the 2004 visit to Beijing. His NGO was shut down.

[58] *Power and Responsibility: The Mekong River Commission*, pp. 9, 49.

So quoted an ASEAN official recently, seeking to remind contemporary Chinese leaders of these lines of goodwill penned by erstwhile
Foreign Minister Chen Yi when he visited Burma in 1957. ASEAN has
been particularly active with regard to the role of China in the Mekong
subregion since 1996. Alarmed by the destabilizing effects of the ambitious development plans for the Lancang/Mekong river basin, ASEAN
has brought together these countries and China within its framework of
dialog and cooperation with China, including a China-ASEAN Strategy
on Environmental Protection (2009–15) and several more agreements
and working groups to promote sustainable and inclusive management
of water resources.[59]

Indeed, ASEAN has over the last two decades enacted a raft of
environmental legislation and programs for the region as a whole.[60] Its
concern with the environment went through various phases: from an
early phase before the 1990s when the emphasis was on 'continuous
availability of natural resources' to one of 'responsibility and stewardship' particularly in the face of transnational challenges in the region,
and, most recently in the last decade, to institutionalizing a set of
ambitious environmental goals for the 'community of states and people'
as a whole.[61] Yet, even according to the ASEAN's own 'state of the
environment' evaluation, the region's environment remains extremely
fragile. Hydropower dams, land grabs, expansion of plantations and
destruction of biodiversity, forest fires, and industrial pollution by
locals and multinationals are rampant. Growth is predicated on the
exploitation of the environment and government enforcement, particularly in the less developed member nations, has left much to be
desired. Beyond the multilateral global and regional agreements seeking to prevent such exploitation, ASEAN has even developed norms to
serve as the foundation for cooperation between the states, such as
polluter pays, common but differentiated responsibility, the precau-
tionary principle, etc.[62]

---

[59] Apichai Sunchindah, "The Lancang–Mekong River Basin: Reflections on Cooperation
Mechanisms Pertaining to a Shared Watercourse," RSIS Centre for Non-Traditional
Security Studies, No. PO13–01, February 2013, pp. 6–7. The Chinese translation is
my own.
[60] For a comprehensive view of agreements and treaties as well as the institutional structure
of ASEAN environmental governance, see Overview of ASEAN Cooperation on
Environment (http://environment.asean.org/about-us-2/).
[61] Lorraine Elliott, "ASEAN and Environmental Governance: Rethinking Networked
Regionalism in Southeast Asia," *Procedia Social and Behavioral Sciences*, 14 (2011): 61–4
(www.sciencedirect.com/science/article/pii/S1877042811001935).
[62] Carl Middleton, "ASEAN, Economic Integration and Regional Environmental
Governance: Emerging Norms and Transboundary Environmental Justice," paper

Interestingly, however, the various initiatives undertaken by government-level institutions have had perhaps a greater effect on societal agencies than on the agencies for their implementation. Civil society groups in Thailand, Cambodia, Indonesia and the Philippines are becoming increasingly vigilant in holding the state and private sectors accountable to these laws and procedures. In fact, Lorraine Elliot has shown that ASEAN has actually been the instigator of the web of "trans-governmental networks, knowledge networks, consultation and coordination networks and compliance networks. ASEAN policy-makers have made explicit strategic and political claims for the advantages of network arrangements in this institutional context."[63]

In turn, these semiformal networks have been tasked to cooperate with institutions of international and local civil society, who have become increasingly important in supporting ASEAN programs and facilitating dialog and cross-border cooperation and oversight. Moreover, the activities of these networks may have had an effect on Chinese investors and builders in the region as well. To be sure, such social developments may still seem weak in comparison to the powerful states and multinational corporations that dominate the development agenda of the region, but it is a significant emergence that cannot be ignored by them. For several years, the nascent transnational advocacy network in the region, according to the recent work of Pichamon Yeophantong, has had significant influence in shaping policy and even upon Chinese state-owned enterprise and corporate behavior in the region.

In some places, like Myanmar and Cambodia, local civil society groups have not only come together to protest dam building, but, in the case of the Myitsone dam project in Myanmar, in 2011, they also even forced the termination of the Chinese project (Map 7.1a). Several other factors were also at work behind this termination, including the opposition of the Kachin Independence Army, which waged a local war, and Aung Sang Suu Kyi's support for the civil movement, leading to its cancelation by the Myanmar government. Resistance to dam building in the Cambodian Cardamom Forest (Map 7.1b) involved the use of international agencies to publicize the builder's non-conformance with Chinese Corporate Social Responsibility (CSR) regulations in the Chinese media and abroad. This kind of civil activism, which demands and makes accessible credible information while staking a higher moral ground, has, according to

presented at ICIRD 2012 International Conference Towards an ASEAN Economic Community (AEC): Prospects, Challenges and Paradoxes in Development, Governance and Human Security, July 26–7, 2012, Chiang Mai, Thailand.

[63] Elliott, "ASEAN and Environmental Governance," p. 63.

Pichamon, actually transformed both Chinese state and corporate behavior in responding to local needs.[64]

The ASEAN model, as we have seen, is based on an open and inclusive regionalism that creates commitments to regional sustainability and peace. As opposed to institutionalized regionalism, it is a 'networked regionalism' which is claimed to be more effective in enhancing intra-regional engagement. It certainly has a much looser architecture than the EU, which occasionally resembles a federated-nation-state. New kinds of networks – regarding environmental issues, for example – have emerged around issues and projects that have not been effectively implemented by the responsible institutional structures. Indeed, the quickening pace of ASEAN integration has spawned a vast and vibrant space of civil society including those sponsored by ASEAN administration and those committed to an 'alternative' or 'people-centered ASEAN'.[65] At any rate, the development of the region not only furnishes a wider framework to observe and manage the problem of the commons, but it also provides opportunities for alliances and networking with a variety of informational and organizational resources across and beyond sovereign nations.

ASEAN and Asia

Regional integration in Asia has been centered on ASEAN, which has both increased the scope of interconnections within and become a magnet for drawing other Asian and Pacific powers into its ambit. ASEAN has thus emerged as an important center for a variety of larger though looser regional formations, such as ASEAN +3, the East Asian Summit, APEC, the recent Trans-Pacific Partnership (TPP) mooted by the United States and the Regional Comprehensive Economic Partnership (RCEP) favored by China.[66] In this context, ASEAN's goal is to achieve long-term peace

---

[64] Pichamon Yeophantong, "China, Corporate Responsibility and the Contentious Politics of Hydropower Development: Transnational Activism in the Mekong Region?," Global Economic Governance Programme, University of Oxford, July 2013; GEG WP 2013/82, pp. 4–9, 11–13. See also Cristelle Maurin and Pichamon Yeophantong, "Going Global Responsibly? China's Strategies Towards 'Sustainable' Overseas Investments," *Pacific Affairs*, 86(2) (2013): 281–303.

[65] Alexander C. Chandra, *Civil Society in Search of an Alternative Regionalism in ASEAN* (Winnipeg: International Institute for Sustainable Development, 2009).

[66] The Regional Comprehensive Economic Partnership combines these two ASEAN-centered trade pacts and rivals the TPP. The sixteen participating countries entered negotiations in 2013, with an eye to forging an agreement by the end of 2015. The negotiations for both the RCEP and the TPP also are paving the way for the Free Trade Area of the Asia Pacific that the APEC member states are aiming to introduce around 2020. See Shiraishi Takashi, "Evolving a New Order for the Asia-Pacific," *Topics of the Times*, December 9, 2011 (www.nippon.com/en/editor/f00003/).

by creating responsibilities and obligations among powers to act within its normative scheme, or core principles, called the Treaty of Amity and Cooperation (TAC). ASEAN has worked to enmesh the larger powers by means of commercial diplomacy that is expected to bring material benefits to both sides but also to tie these powers to the region. Free-Trade Agreements (FTAs) and a complex web of bilateral and multilateral security and cooperative agreements and forums that sustain exchanges and create interdependencies have drawn in all the major powers to sign the TAC.

Among the first signatories were China and India, which were integrated into the regional order in 2003. By 2009, sixteen countries outside ASEAN had signed including the United States. ASEAN has also undertaken FTAs with seven other countries in the region including Australia and New Zealand. From a balance of power perspective, ASEAN could possibly have created – or retained – a strong alliance with the United States alone, but it has pursued a more subtle strategy of balancing its influence with powers that could shape the destiny of the region. To be sure, there is a pecking order in what Evelyn Goh calls the 'strategy of diversified dependence', with the United States as a global superpower, China as the second power and regional powers such as India and Japan located in the next tier. In other words, certain geopolitical circumstances are necessary for the flourishing of network activism. In recent years, China's role has become more complicated as territorial disputes have developed or been exacerbated in the South China Sea between China and the Philippines and Vietnam and between China and Japan over the Diaoyutai, or Senkaku, islands. As we have seen, cooperative relations between China and ASEAN are crucial for the environmental security of the Southeast Asian mainland, and the future of this relationship may well shape the future of regional interdependence.[67]

Be that as it may, it is just as important to note how a larger regional formation has emerged based on circulations and networks, which in many ways work through, across and around the present system of nation-states. There are significant continuities and novelties in this multipolar

---

[67] Evelyn Goh, "Great Powers and Hierarchical Order in Southeast Asia: Analyzing Regional Security Strategies," *International Security*, *32*(3) (2007/8): 113–57, at p. 140 (for quotation). See also Julie Gilson, "Strategic Regionalism in East Asia," *Review of International Studies*, *33* (2007): 145–63; Ellen Frost, "China's Commercial Diplomacy in Asia: Promise or Threat?," in William Keller and Thomas G. Rawski, Eds., *China's Rise and the Balance of Influence in Asia* (University of Pittsburgh Press, 2007, pp. 95–120). To be sure, there is much more to be said regarding the international relations of the region, particularly regarding the policy of the US 'pivot towards Asia' and the notion of containing China, but I would rather focus on the long-term meaning of the emergent regional formation.

space traversed by capital, labor, intergovernmental organizations, transnational and civil society networks, local communities and shared commons. Region formation in Asia is a multipath, uneven and pluralistic development that is significantly different from European regionalism. Furthermore, the region itself has no external limits or territorial boundaries and does not seek to homogenize itself within. Individual nations, economic, regulatory, cultural entities and NGOs have multiple links beyond the core, and when a country beyond the core arrives at the threshold of a sufficiently dense set of interactions and dependencies with it, it may be brought within the region's frameworks of governance. Conceivably, this could include even regions outside the cartographic scope of Asia – say, for instance, South Africa. At least, this has been the pattern in recent years.

While the nation-state continues to exercise deeply rooted powers, there is, regionally, no congruence or sustained effort at producing congruence between politics and culture by any state. The absence of a single dominant nation-state that still prevails in the region contributes significantly to this, but it is also the case that the individual nation-state finds it difficult to make a coherent case for a nationalism congruent with its territorial conception. In part, this has to do with state withdrawal and growing identification with transterritorial ethnic groups such as the overseas Chinese or Indians (often at the expense of peripheries and non-dominant ethnics or marginal co-nationals).

Moreover, both capitalism and the nation-state have been transformed to the point where they celebrate heterogeneity and multiculturalism even as these sociocultural factors are themselves commoditized. As the authors of the popular management book *Globality* suggest, for multinationals the very idea of domestic markets has been replaced by niche markets.[68] Finally, since the nation-state is much more invested and aware of regional and global interdependence, a split has appeared in the interests and rhetoric of popular nationalism and the nation-state, most evidently in the PRC, but also in India, Thailand and elsewhere. All of these factors make the political homogenization of culture or its essentialization an unnecessary and difficult process. The weakness and failure of the effort to create the ideology of Asian values in the late 1990s is a case in point.

Culturally, this plurality indicates a move away from an essentialist identity formation even when different Asians consume common cultural goods. Thus, consuming South Korean TV serials with the voracious appetite that has been revealed in the rest of Asia does not end up

[68] Harold Sirkin, James Hemerling and Arindam Bhattacharya, *Globality: Competing with Everyone from Everywhere for Everything* (New York: Business Plus, 2008).

transforming an identity from, say, Vietnamese or Taiwanese to South Korean. Rather as Chua Beng Huat has pointed out, it requires the consumer to "transcend his or her grounded nationality to forge abstract identification with the foreign characters on screen, a foreignness that is, in turn, potentially reabsorbed into an idea of [East] 'Asia'."[69] Indeed, I am not sure that this foreignness even need be reabsorbed. The reception of the Asian cultural product can remain a site of circulation and interaction, one that implicitly questions pure identity in the recognition of multiple connections and interdependence. It can remain without the potential of absorption into another political project of nationalism or another grand Othering process.

Identities are designed to emphasize exclusivity; presumably, that is their nature. Historically, efforts to bridge differences have often been the loser in the era of identitarian politics heralded by the nation-state and nationalism. In an earlier work, I argued that in prenationalist societies, political forces such as imperial or feudal states did not seek to dominate every aspect of a person's identity. These societies were characterized by soft boundaries where individual community difference (say, in diet or belief in deities) would not prevent large-scale and un-self-conscious borrowing in other respects. Modern nationalisms sought precisely to create hard boundaries between communities by privileging a defining characteristic of community (say, language) as constitutive of the self in a self-conscious way that often developed intolerance for the non-national Other.[70]

The Asian maritime networks of the precolonial era exemplified such a framework. This long-distance trade involved a wide variety of merchant communities at different points who did not speak the same languages or trade in the same currencies. Yet, as Abu-Lughod says, goods were transferred, prices set, exchange rates agreed upon, contracts contracted, credit extended, partnerships formed, records kept and agreements honored. Trade was contained "within the interstices of a larger collaboration in which goods and merchants from many places were intermingled on each other's ships and where unwritten rules of reciprocity assured general compliance. This system was not decisively challenged until the sixteenth century, when the Portuguese men-of-war violated all the rules of the game."[71]

[69] Beng-huat Chua, "Conceptualizing an East Asian Popular Culture," *Inter-Asia Cultural Studies*, 5(2) (2004): 200–21, at p. 217.

[70] Prasenjit Duara, *Rescuing History from the Nation: Questioning Narratives of Modern China* (University of Chicago Press, 1995), ch. 2.

[71] Abu-Lughod, "The World System in the Thirteenth Century," p. 11.

In several ways, contemporary Asian regional interdependence resembles the maritime Asian networks, because of the separation of political, economic and military levels and power. To be sure, I am by no means arguing that we return – or can return – to prenational modes of identities; rather, I want to see whether the nationalist congruence between state and culture exemplified by the hard boundary may have represented a long twentieth-century moment. Certainly, the present regional nexus resembles the earlier Asian maritime networks in terms of this non-congruence. Although the actual products flowing through the Asian maritime networks were minuscule compared to today's figures, the cultural flows they enabled – packaged in Hinduism, Buddhism, Confucianism, Daoism and Islam – were nothing short of world-transforming. They created multiscale, interlinked cultural universes, which, however, were rarely accompanied by the kind of political domination that became hegemonic from the nineteenth century. To be sure, today's cultural identities are shaped by circulations of culture, knowledge, technology, goods, services and finance that are dizzying in their velocity while also becoming deeply commodified or consumerist. Nonetheless, the older Asian models of cultural circulation without state domination of identity present us with a historical resource to explore new possibilities.

But if history affords us a glimpse of old possibilities for the new, the challenges of the present are much more sobering. Regional formation is taking place under capitalist liberalization and state restructuring. While this favors the emergence of a professional and capitalist Asian community with its cultural openness and abilities to forge multiple linkages and new cultures from their encounter, the power of the nation-state remains entrenched in relation to the movement, especially the transnational movement of labor. The neo-liberal circumstances under which regional formation is taking place can easily develop the concept of Asia for the rich and their representatives who attend to financial flows, knowledge economies and corporatization, while containing or displacing the poor and privatizing public goods. It is well established that while globalization produces wealth, it also creates stratification and a deeper gulf between the rich and the poor. There is no a priori reason why regionalization will not do the same.

The other problem is, of course, that of the privatization and nationalization of the commons, environmental degradation and unsustainable development. While the challenges are enormous, we have also identified some initial moves that have emerged to respond to them. ASEAN in particular, with all of its deficiencies and weaknesses, has outlined ways and means to deal with these challenges. But perhaps just as important are the civil society networks that these activities have spawned and that can serve as watchdogs for inclusivity and transparency. We can hope and work towards the goal that this same logic of social inclusion will extend to goals that can transcend localities and communities to include strangers who have come to serve and build their societies.

Regions in the modern world are linked by geophysical, communication and material networks that extend beyond nations and territorial boundaries, and, sometimes, form a common identity. Wherever identity formation has been attempted in the history of twentieth-century regionalisms, however, it has frequently represented the efforts of imperialists who seek to create a larger collective that the imperial nation-state can dominate. Region-formation by networks is, however, accelerating and condensing the space of interactivity. Of course, there is the consideration that the region will no longer be recognizable as it becomes folded into wider global networks. Yet, if regions are to be built upon virtual technologies linking them to many spaces and times, the geophysical features that once supplied the means of region-formation now supply its imperative. If, in the future, they should vanish, we, too, will vanish with them.

Reprise and Epilogue: of reason and hope

As I thought about hope, I suddenly became fearful. When Runtu had wanted the incense burner and candle stand, I had secretly laughed at him: he could never forget his idols. But is the hope that I now cherish also not an idol? Only his was within easy reach, mine was remote and harder to reach.

In the twilight, a stretch of jade green sand opened up beyond the sea in front of my eyes. Above in the deep blue sky there hung a golden moon. I thought hope is not something that can be said to exist or not. It is just like a road on the ground. On the ground itself there is no road, it is made only when many people walk on it.

Lu Xun, "Guxiang" ("My Old Home")[1]

This study has developed several interrelated arguments and I present them in their bald form, throwing caution to the winds, for the reader to assess them and their relationships to each other.

The model of modernity and modernization based on conquest of nature and driven by increasing production is no longer sustainable. The crisis it has created cannot be adequately addressed by the existing system of competing nation-states and heroic histories of national progress, but only by recognition that our histories are shared and our destiny, planetary. Archaic histories tended to merge their linear representations of community with cosmological and universal ideals, while contemporary histories have yet to join theirs with the cosmic imperatives of our times. These histories need to be guided by circulatory realities that index our common belonging in a battered and ever more fragile planet.

One set of arguments in the book sought to understand the historical emergence of this model of modernity which was generated not only by

---

[1] Lu Xun, "Guxiang" ("My Old Home"), in *Nahan, Lu Xun Quanji* [reprint] (Taipei: Tangshan, 1989/1921), vol. II, pp. 80–94. The translation is my own.

economic and political factors but also by the activation of certain cultural and religious dispositions over other currents to create the competitive nation-state. In particular, I referred to the confessionalization of the religious community that contributed in various ways to creating communities of identity (of self versus Other) that were prototypes of the nation form. The sovereign nation became the preferred collective form to enhance efficiency and appropriate global resources for continuously increasing production. Once the logic of cultural autonomy became largely subordinated to the political and economic goals of the community – the nation in this case – the checks on the idea that we are entitled to untrammeled resource expansion regardless of future generations and the rest of the world were severely weakened.

Following another set of arguments, I turned to older models of religious and cultural expression that focused on alternative models of the self in relation to the transcendent beyond the exclusive community. Self and collective were engaged – through bodily practices, self-cultivation exercises, rational and mystical processes, and community activities at various scales and orders of belonging, natural and social – in dialogical exchange with transcendent goals that may have been contentious and hierarchical, but rarely systemically exclusive. To be sure, these traditions also coexisted together with more exclusionary ones in Abrahamic societies. Furthermore, as seen within the larger framework of circulatory histories, when the imperative to compete for survival in the modern world spread to other societies, several Asian societies with dominant traditions of dialogical transcendence sought to confessionalize their religious traditions for national mobilization and exclusivity. However, the continued survival of dialogical traditions in the less modernized societies of the world may well be seen as an opportunity to engage them in the task of creating different paths of self-formation.

Much of Asia is also becoming a networked region which could – and has already – produced unanticipated emergences joining, for instance, forest communities with global NGOs, non-literate tribal women with Bangalore-based voice-messaging NGOs, and Daoist priests with British royalty. Local ideas of sacred place and nature continue to abound across Asia and many other parts of the global south; and while they are susceptible to denial and abuse, as we have noted, they remain an important source for regenerating nature. Indigenous and local knowledge are in dialog with scientific techniques of agroforestry and disaster recovery; cultural and biological diversity are being found to be intimately connected. Not least, it is the networked region operating in awareness of the evaporating commons that offers some lessons in experimenting with new models of dialogical transnationality even while facing immense challenges.

I also referred to the phenomenon of traffic to explore how the yearnings and uses of transcendence migrate to ostensibly secular spaces. The recognition of this traffic is significant because it allows us to reimagine the secular as a space for aspiration, hope and justice beyond the sphere of economic and political ideas, which may be more constrained by institutions, procedures, path dependencies and vested interests. Globally, today, the urge to moral idealism and a new ethos of responsibility in civil – that is non-violent – society may well represent the migration of the transcendent regarding which Weber's colleague, Georg Simmel, was so persuaded. What Václav Havel dubbed the 'politics of the anti-political' has become an enormous though amorphous, weakly institutionalized but networked, moral force spreading across much of the world.[2]

It is beyond my capacity to speculate about the extent and ways in which the networks of global and regional civil society, their coalitions and allies – among intergovernmental agencies, universities, motivated bureaucratic and corporate actors, and, most of all, local communities – may be able to reconfigure the absolute sovereignty of nations; still less what congeries of players might populate a diffuse and cosmopolitan sovereignty were such a condition to appear. To reconstitute sovereignty in its nineteenth- to twentieth-century form at a global level would amount to reproducing the Leviathan of all Leviathans, almost certainly a disaster of unimaginable proportions. But if one of the tasks is to excavate ways of writing a history of the future that can pull together the resources of transcendent will for a sustainable world, I believe that this will require a degree of inviolable sanctity and some kind of sovereign power. The following Epilogue makes some suggestions about what kind of inviolability that might be and ways of thinking about transcendence as a dialogical project.

I have sought to establish the necessity of a universal perspective for a sustainable world. For it to be realized, we identified two requirements: (1) a dialogical universalism; and (2) the capacity not only to transcend the here and the now but also to muster the resolve for its realization.

---

[2] Havel defines the expression as follows: "politics not as the technology of power and manipulation ... but politics as one of the ways of seeking and achieving meaningful lives, of protecting them and serving them." Václav Havel, "Politics and Conscience," in Jan Bažant, Nina Bažantová and Frances Starn, Eds., *The Czech Reader: History, Culture, Politics* (Durham, NC: Duke University Press, 2010), pp. 440–56, at p. 455. For the phenomenal expansion of civil society and non-state actors across the globe in recent decades, see Karen T. Litfin, "Sovereignty in World Ecopolitics," *Mershon International Studies Review, 41*(2) (1997): 167–204.

Much of this book has dealt with the descriptions and expressions of dialogical transcendence – a reaching beyond the self that is not committed to a single all-powerful God, truth or eschaton. Dialogue involves incrementalism and negotiation between local needs and universal requirements and is intertwined with ideals from the living historical repertoire that can engage the changing requirements of the present. Its value today will lie in the capacity to create a sustainable ideal which much of the world can endorse. The second requirement is the capacity of culture to create personal and collective commitment, a problem of hope and sacrality.

In my short analysis of Kant's ideal of universalism in Chapter 1, I identified the gap between theories, science, planned projects and their realization. This gap is the space of accidents – often productive – contingencies, failures, counter-finalities, and the wreckage of hubris. On the other hand, it is also the space of faith, belief and hope. Beyond the scrutable and the certain, this space has anchored human constructions of the transcendent through which we have historically come to know and authorize the universal good. Whether we call it eternal objects, God, gods, Gaia or merely chance, the inscrutable in emergence has historically been secured through the framework of transcendence and the sacred. However reified it may have been, its reverence secured the source of life that our brave new world has endangered. Modern universalisms have tended to lack confidence in investing the transcendent or utopian truths they propose with symbols and rituals of sacred authority. Their hesitation doubtless has good reasons that we may see from the rampaging power of extreme nationalisms, such as Nazism, or blinding faith in utopian science triumphant over reason. But no movement of major social change has succeeded without a compelling symbology and affective power.

I have discussed transcendence as a meta-epistemic concept affiliated with several historical roles and functions. We have referred to it as a revolution in knowledge producing a reflexive and synoptic capacity to abstract from the here and now. In this work, it has appeared more frequently in its role as regenerating a non-worldly moral authority that typically has universal applicability. Additionally, I have elaborated the differences between radical and dialogical transcendence particularly in the modes of self-cultivation and collective belonging. There is another attribute of the transcendent that I have only occasionally touched upon. It is personally and vividly illustrated by the great revolutionary writer and ironist, Lu Xun, in the epigraph of this chapter. Hope, like its ally, justice (beyond particular laws), belongs to the class of what Derrida calls un-deconstructible elements. It is a summons, a call that was not constructed and cannot be taken apart; it arises even when it has been destroyed. The golden moon that guides the travelers on the jade-green Earth lights the path between what exists and what does not, the space between and beyond the subjective and the objective.[3]

In *Religion Within the Limits of Reason Alone*, Kant argues that the worldly representation of religion involves not only belief and institutions but also the figure of the good, which is prior to our propensity to evil that grows when free will is bound by desire. Kant thought of religious belief and institutions as having become infected by the 'bounded will', or the propensity to evil.[4] In Paul Ricoeur's reading of this text, just at the point when evil reaches its extreme (in the medieval Church), the figure of faith for Kant produces hope and regeneration (in the Reformation). Thus, Ricoeur calls Kant's view of religion a philosophical hermeneutics of hope. Ricoeur's own work on the Bible shows how symbolism and activities 'figure' this primordial good through symbols and narratives of hope that are anterior to – and excavated from – their scriptural interpretation by different powers, clerical or secular.[5]

Working with the Abrahamic religions, Ricoeur identifies faith, hope and the sacred as a primordial complex identified with 'manifest communities' founded on numinous and preverbal experiences of the sacred in nature before they become book-centered, interpretive, intratribal and iconoclastic 'proclamation communities'. At the same time, he does not believe that interpretive reason or kerygmatic logic can negate the primordial sacred. Rational exposition and logical interpretation derive from and are dependent upon the symbolism of the sacred, say, the figure of Christ; but, just as much, they are necessary for the sacred. From this he argues that the task of contemporary interpreters and philosophers of religion is to rationally explicate such figures of hope in a contemporary world of injustice and suffering.

---

[3] See John D. Caputo, "Without Sovereignty, Without Being: Unconditionality, the Coming God and Derrida's Democracy to Come," *Journal for Cultural and Religious Theory*, 4(3) (2003): 9–26. Kant, too, appeals to the "call to citizenship in a divine state." He, of course, sees this recognition of God only in moral terms, while for speculative philosophy this calling remains an impenetrable mystery. Immanuel Kant, *Religion with the Limits of Reason Alone*, Trans. with Introduction and Notes by Theodore M. Greene and Hoyt H. Hudson (New York: Harper and Brothers, 1960), pp. 133–4. For Derrida, if there is a God, he only exists in or as this *call*, as the unconditioned, but without power and especially sovereign power.

[4] Kant, *Religion with the Limits of Reason Alone*, pp. 21–7.

[5] Paul Ricoeur, *Figuring the Sacred: Religion, Narrative and the Imagination*, Trans. David Pellauer, Ed. Mark I. Wallace (Minneapolis, MN: Fortress Press, 1995), p. 77 (for Kant); see also "Part III, The Bible and Genre: The Polyphony of Biblical Discourses," pp. 129–80.

Ricoeur gives us a useful way to imagine new modes of relating the sacred to rationality. Indeed, from a more contemporary perspective, Habermas also urges that the persuasive force of communicative reason can be brought to mediate the binding norms of ritual or sacred obligation that we may owe to the national constitution, the national flag or our customs.[6] In the course of writing this book, I began to wonder if the thorny task of mediating the sacred with reason could be eased if we can recognize that the gap between ideal, project, and effort and its realization may be occupied not principally by faith or belief, but by hope. Consider some of the cases I discussed in the book where reverence and reason were inseparably entwined with hope.

Whether by the Confucian sage or the laywomen of the Morality Society, *Tian* and *Dao* were viewed as the source and highest judge of the ethical mission for humans. Yet, neither Heaven nor the Way is anthropomorphic like an all-powerful God with a clear and singular message, and failure to follow its path – by this time in Chinese history – does not result in punishment either immediately or in the afterlife. The sacrality of Heaven was intertwined with reason and hope; indeed, the ambiguities of Heaven's message ironically subjected it to rational deliberation and empirical persuasion. By the time of the republic of 1912, even the three sacred followings (*sangang*) for women could be interpreted with relative flexibility. Indeed, one might say that the flexibility for self-empowerment undergirded its symbolic power. The transcendent was tapped as a figure of hope for a variety of ethical and empowering personal projects that validated this very transcendence. The recent revival of *yangsheng* practices in everyday life, where classical ideas intersect with contemporary needs and new ideals, to achieve a better integration of individual life with family, community and nature, reveals that dialogical transcendence is alive and well in China and being tapped in similar ways.[7]

Similarly, the environmental, rural reconstructionist and moral (anti-corruption) movements inspired by Gandhianism draw on a complex matrix of goals and methods. Their moral authority derives significantly from Gandhi – his message, goals, methods, life and the movement he spawned – as a figure of hope, who himself reworked circulatory

[6] Jurgen Habermas *et al.*, *An Awareness of What Is Missing: Faith and Reason in a Post-Secular Age*, Trans. Ciaran Cronin (Cambridge: Polity Press, 2010).
[7] Judith Farquhar and Zhang Qicheng, *Ten Thousand Things: Nurturing Life in Contemporary Beijing* (New York: Zone Books, 2012). One of the two authors of this recent ethnography, Zhang Qicheng, has written the following: "If you know the Dao you will embody this understanding and reach a plane of 'unity with the Dao,' and you can then return to the originary state of life, and you can completely achieve transcendence," p. 273.

knowledge and practices into a transcendent ideal. They have engaged this authority to address contemporary issues and problems of local communities while also being simultaneously influenced by popular protest movements across the world, especially with regard to environmental problems. Indeed, as we have seen in Chapter 7, they have built effective alliances with these movements to change global policies, such as that of the World Bank. Of course, even the sacrality of hope may be appropriated by political forces, as in the saffronization of the Green movement. The way ahead for such movements will require reliance on the value of critical rationality even as they need to trump another ideal of unceasing material progress in order to achieve a sustainable modernity.

Can hope be *seen to be* the kernel of the sacred? In this crisis where humanity becomes more desperate, the salience of hope in the sacred or the sacredness of hope does not appear too far-fetched. The conclusion is hardly the place to launch a new investigation into this enormous and admittedly complex topic.[8] But I cannot help noting that the structure of hope is not dissimilar to dialogical transcendence. Hope by itself is based on reasonable expectations and efforts made to realize them. In its pragmatic character, it is more open to reason than faith and belief. At the same time, when hope rises beyond reasonable hope it points to something beyond – and beyond faith – to an impetus to live and seek that is greater than we and without which life is meaningless. If it is no more than the instinct for survival, the connectedness with this greater force itself inspires awe and reverence. Can we link the sacrality of figures of hope to this connectedness?

I am reminded of the Jewel Net of Indra, particularly as it is interpreted in the Huayan school of Chinese Buddhism, which developed in the sixth century CE. The basic idea is of a net of infinite dimensions hanging over the Vedic god Indra's palace in the mythic Mount Meru. The net is held together by multifaceted gems, each of which reflects all the others.

---

[8] The realm of hope has also been theorized by leftist thinkers who have recognized the inadequacy of materialist and scientific vision of historical activity, especially when it comes to revolutionary transformations. We think in particular of Ernst Bloch's mammoth *The Principle of Hope* and the figure of messianism invoked by Walter Benjamin. Bloch's great achievement is the recognition that secularism is necessary for humans to walk on their own feet; but, at the same time, to realize that religions also embed their utopian hope so necessary for humans. His task was to secularize hope; to insert its themes and symbols into a dialectical secular practice where they retain their interpretive potentials. At the same time, the radical recognition of the necessity and positivity of hope remains bound up with the eschatological or totalizing utopianism so central to the Abrahamic faiths. See Gerard Raulet, "Critique of Religion and Religion as Critique: The Secularized Hope of Ernst Bloch," Trans. David J. Parent; Ed. Tim Luke. *New German Critique*, 9 (1976): 71–85.

According to J. Baird Callicott, while the Vedanta interpretation of this is static, with each gem merely reflecting the singular truth in the center, in Huayan Buddhism's version there is no single center. "Rather the mirror-like facet of each gem reflects all the others in the net referring to mutual identity and mutual causality." The figure of Indra's net reflects not identity but a network in which mutuality represents the essence of interdependence and hence compassion for all beings in nature.[9] Might it be too fanciful to suggest that, while there is no center, the light which shines and reflects from each gem in our time, radiates from the golden moon of hope which can be said neither to exist nor not to exist?

Armed with this metaphor of networks of hope, let me return to the object of hope pursued by the networks of civil society that we discussed above. In *Friction: An Ethnography of Global Connections*, Anna Tsing explores a revealing predicament. She notes that whenever a local out-come favorable to a universal or globally desirable ideal is achieved – say, a successful effort to save a forest in Borneo – the strategic, coalitional and politically messy process that led to the outcome is erased, and the project is envisioned as an expression of interests-free, depoliticized, desocietalized, and delocalized universalism.[10] In his study of the human-rights movement, Samuel Moyn refers to a similar problem as the movement turned from a minimalist politics-transcending-moral ideal to a maximalist agenda. In the face of the decline of political utopias in the 1970s, the human-rights movement was obliged to absorb all manner of social and economic rights into a highly contested political program. He writes, "Signs of trouble came when the contingency of their emergence ... was quickly forgotten. It was convenient almost immediately to represent human rights as a matter of longstanding tradition."[11] Human rights was elevated to a status with the capacity to correct all wrongs.

It is worth reflecting on why this is the case. Would the efforts of scholars and activists to highlight the difficulties of the achievement show up the process as compromised and unheroic and diminish the aura of the sacred – and indeed of the rational as sacred – that envelops them? Why do we need so radically to transcend our own collective, albeit

---

[9] Callicott explains: X is caused by Y and Z, so in it all others are present. Thus, if X is not X, there would be no Y, Z, etc. Hence, X is also the cause of all things. J. Baird Callicott, *Earth's Insights: A Survey of Ecological Ethics from the Mediterranean Basin to the Australian Outback* (Berkeley and Los Angeles, CA: University of California Press, 1994), pp. 88–90.

[10] Anna Tsing, *Friction: An Ethnography of Global Connections* (Princeton University Press, 2005), pp. 95–100.

[11] Samuel Moyn, *The Last Utopia: Human Rights in History* (Cambridge, MA: Harvard University Press, 2010), p. 214.

messy, efforts to show that we abide by a single, pure truth or norm? Surely, the heroism lies in the achievement itself which is co-produced by the actors together with something beyond them.

Hope as an essential ingredient of a transcendent force may allow for more dialogical and honest engagement with messy realities. Achievements, to be sure, are liable to be politically appropriated for some other sacred purpose such as the nation, but this may be a fight worth fighting. Indeed, the decentered, multiply ordered networks are already beginning to create new objects, spaces and flows of sacrality and inviolability founded on their hopes of a sustainable world. These spaces furnish them with the autonomy required to launch resistance and regeneration. I refer not only to the commons of local communities protected – however weakly – by pan-Asian ideas of sacred forests, lands and waters, or newer ideas of indigeneity and conservation, but also to the more authoritatively declared heritage zones to preserve natural and cultural diversity which we have encountered in several of the chapters.

The depredations of accelerating globalization have also spawned new spaces and forms of authoritative knowledge to address them. There are over 100,000 'protected areas' in the world, including almost 1,000 World Heritage Sites (cultural and natural), which cover 12 percent of the land area of the world. Some studies have shown that they have reduced rates of deforestation, protected species and conserved land and water. To be sure, these zones are not without their own problems, especially with regard to the livelihoods of the poor and introduction of market mechanisms that tend to promote norms of economic efficiency over the ethics of community participation and the rights of the marginalized. Nonetheless, they are a hopeful beginning.[12]

It has been not just environmental law but also international law in many other areas that has had to make judgments on rights and jurisdictions across boundaries of territory, spaces and species; these areas include human rights, global finance, the seabed, outer space, Antarctica, migratory birds, and myriad others. Over the last few decades, this has led to the emergence and, indeed, expansion of the idea of the

---

[12] Sharachchandra Lele, Peter Wilshusen, Dan Brockington, Reinmar Seidler and Kamaljit Bawa, "Beyond Exclusion: Alternative Approaches to Biodiversity Conservation in the Developing Tropics," *Current Opinion in Environmental Sustainability*, 2 (2010): 94–100, at pp. 94–5, 98; Ashish Kothari, "Protected Areas and People: The Future of the Past," *PARKS: International Journal of Protected Areas and Conservation*, 17(2) (2008): 23–4; Michael R. Dove, "A Political-Ecological Heritage of Resource Contest and Conflict," in P. Daly and T. Winter, Eds., *Routledge Handbook of Heritage in Asia* (London: Routledge), 2011, pp. 182–97. For list of World Heritage Sites, see website (http://whc.unesco.org/en/list/).

commons, or the 'common heritage of humankind', which applies even within national jurisdictions. By holding humans and nations to higher standards beyond existing arrangements and national jurisdictions, international law possesses, in William P. George's words, "a transformative, and in that sense a transcendental" dimension.[13] Just as importantly, this is a force that posits inviolability without significant military backing and pursues its case through rational and responsible argumentation.

The custodians of this sacred space, as we have seen, are turning out to be the networks of hope constituted by the coalitions of civil society, local communities and their allies. Their vibrant and jostling character causes them to resemble the traditions of dialogical transcendence rather than the institutionalized custodians – churches, priests or mandarins – who seek purification in the name of the transcendent. In many respects they represent a weak force but can be sufficiently resilient to outlast the strong. One of their great strengths as a moral force is their ability to mediate the sacred with the rational. Armed with scientific, legal, technical and, not least, local knowledge, these coalitions represent our principal hope.

---

[13] William P. George, "Looking for a Global Ethic? Try International Law," *Journal of Religion*, 76(3) (1996): 359–82, at p. 369.

Bibliography

Abu-Lughod, Janet L. *Before European Hegemony: The World System AD 1250–1350*. Oxford University Press, 1989.

"The World System in the Thirteenth Century: Dead-End or Precursor?," in Michael Adas, Ed., *Essays on Global and Comparative History*. American Historical Association Series. Washington, DC: American Historical Association, 1993, pp. 9–11.

Aburrow, Yvonne. "The Day-Star of Approaching Morn: The Relationship Between the Unitarians and the Brahmo Samaj" (http://bristolunitarians. blogspot.sg/2013/08/the-rammohun-roy-connection.html).

Acton, John E. E. D. *Essays in the Liberal Interpretation of History by Lord Acton*, Ed. with introduction by William H. McNeill. University of Chicago Press, 1967.

Adams, Charles. "Reflections on the Work of John Wansbrough," *Method and Theory in the Study of Religion*, 9 (1997): 75–90.

Agnivesh, Swami. *Religion, Spirituality and Social Action: New Agenda for Humanity*. Gurgaon, India: Hope India Publications, 2003.

Aguiar, Carolina M. "Cosmopolitanism," in *Globalization and Autonomy*, CAPES Foundation (www.globalautonomy.ca/global1/glossary_pop.jsp? id=CO.0074).

Alagappa, Muthiah. *Asian Security Practice: Material and Ideational Influences*. Stanford University Press, 1998.

Alam, Muzaffar. "The Debate Within: A Sufi Critique of Religious Law, Tasawwuf and Politics in Mughal India," *South Asian History and Culture*, 2(2) (2011): 138–59.

Ambedkar, B. R. "Author's Unpublished Preface," *The Buddha and His Dhamma*, April 6, 1956 (www.columbia.edu/itc/mealac/pritchett/00ambedkar/ambed kar_buddha/04_01.html).

The Buddha and His Dhamma. Nagpur: Buddhabhumi Publications, 1997.

Timeline in Francis Pritchett's website (2014) (www.columbia.edu/itc/mealac/ pritchett/00ambedkar/timeline/1910s.html).

Ames, Roger. *Confucian Role Ethics: A Vocabulary*. Ch'ien Mu Lecture Series. Hong Kong: Chinese University Press, and Honolulu, HI: University of Hawaii Press, 2011.

An, Yanming. "Liang Shuming: Eastern and Western Cultures and Confucianism," in Chun-Ying Cheng and Nicholas Bunnin, Eds., *Contemporary Chinese Philosophy*. Oxford: Blackwell Publishers, 2002, pp. 147–63.

Anagnost, Ann. *National Past-Times: Narrative, Representation, and Power in Modern China*. Durham, NC: Duke University Press, 1997.

Andaya, Barbara W. "Connecting Oceans and Multicultural Navies: A Historian's View on Challenges and Potential for Indian Ocean-Western Pacific Interaction," in N. Lenze and C. Schriwer, Eds., *Converging Regions: Global Perspectives on Asia and the Middle East* (Farnham: Ashgate, in press).

Anderson, Benedict. *Imagined Communities: Reflections on the Origins and Spread of Nationalism.* London: Verso, 1991.

Andrade, Tonio. "Beyond Guns, Germs, and Steel: European Expansion and Maritime Asia, 1400–1750," *Journal of Early Modern History*, *14* (2010): 165–86.

Anghie, Antony. "Francisco De Vitoria and the Colonial Origins of International Law," *Social Legal Studies*, 5 (1996): 321–36.

Apter, David E., and Tony Saich. *Revolutionary Discourse in Mao's Republic.* Cambridge, MA: Harvard University Press, 1994.

Arendt, Hannah. *The Origins of Totalitarianism.* New York: Harcourt Brace Jovanovich, 1973.

Armstrong-Buck, S. "Whitehead's Metaphysical System as a Foundation for Environmental Ethics," *Environmental Ethics*, 8 (1986): 241–59.

Arnason, Johann P. "The Axial Age and Its Interpreters: Re-Opening a Debate," in Johann P. Arnason, S. N. Eisenstadt and Björn Wittrock, Eds., *Axial Civilizations and World History.* Leiden: Brill, 2005, pp. 19–50.

Arrighi, Giovanni. *The Long Twentieth Century: Money, Power, and the Origins of Our Times.* New York: Verso, 1994, pp. 32–3.

Asad, Talal. *Formations of the Secular: Christianity, Islam, Modernity.* Stanford University Press, 2003.

Assmann, Jan. "Monotheism and Polytheism," in Sarah Iles Johnston, Ed., *Religions of the Ancient World: A Guide.* Cambridge, MA: The Belknap Press of Harvard University Press, 2004, pp. 17–31.

Atwell, William. "Another Look at Silver Imports into China, *ca.* 1635–1644," *Journal of World History*, *16*(4) (2005): 467–89.

Bahrawi, Nazry. "The Andalusi Secular," in *Critical Muslim 6: Reclaiming Al-Andalus.* London: Hurst, 2013, pp. 47–56.

Baker, Christopher G. *Dams, Power and Security in the Mekong: A Non-Traditional Security Assessment of Hydro-Development in the Mekong River Basin.* NTS Research Paper no. 8. Singapore: RSIS Centre for Non-Traditional Security (NTS) Studies for NTS-Asia, 2012.

Bala, Arun. *The Dialogue of Civilizations in the Birth of Modern Science.* New York: Palgrave Macmillan, 2006.

Bandyopadhyay, Sekhar. "Popular Religion and Social Mobility in Colonial Bengal: The Matua Sect and the Namasudras," in Rajat Kanta Ray, Ed., *Mind, Body and Society: Life and Mentality in Colonial Bengal.* Calcutta: Oxford University Press, 1995, pp. 153–92.

 Caste Protest and Identity in Colonial India: The Namasudras of Bengal, 1872–1947. New Delhi: Oxford University Press, 2011.

Bao, Maohong. "Environmental NGOs in Transforming China," *Nature and Culture*, 4(1) (2009): 1–16.

Bartelsen, Jens. *A Genealogy of Sovereignty.* Cambridge University Press, 1995.

Bayly, C. A. *The Birth of the Modern World, 1780–1914.* Oxford: Blackwell Publishing, 2004.

Bean, Susan. *Yankee India: American Commercial and Cultural Encounters with India in the Age of Sail 1784–1860.* Salem, MA: Peabody Museum Press, 2001.

Beaver, R. Pierce. "Chondogyo and Korea," *Journal of Bible and Religion, 30*(2) (1962): 115–22.

Beck, Ulrich, and Edgar Grande. "Varieties of Second Modernity: The Cosmopolitan Turn in Social and Political Theory and Research," *British Journal of Sociology, 61*(3) (2010): 409–43.

Bellah, Robert N. *Imagining Japan: The Japanese Tradition and Its Modern Transformation.* Berkeley and Los Angeles, CA: University of California Press, 2003.

———. *Religion in Human Evolution: From the Paleolithic to the Axial Age.* Cambridge, MA: The Belknap Press of Harvard University Press, 2011.

Bendix, Reinhard, and Guenther Roth. *Scholarship and Partisanship: Essays on Max Weber.* Berkeley and Los Angeles, CA: University of California Press, 1971.

Benjamin, Walter. "Theses on the Philosophy of History," in *Illuminations.* New York: Schocken Books, 1969, pp. 253–64.

Bentley, Jerry H. "Early Mode Europe and the Early Modern World," in Charles H. Parker and Jerry H. Bentley, Eds., *Between the Middle Ages and Modernity: Individual and Community in the Early Modern World.* Lanham, MD: Rowman & Littlefield, 2007, pp. 13–31.

Benton, Lauren. *A Search for Sovereignty: Law and Geography in European Empire, 1400–1900.* Cambridge University Press, 2010.

Berger, Douglas. "Nagarjuna (*c.*150–*c.*250)," in *Internet Encyclopedia of Philosophy* (www.iep.utm.edu/nagarjun/).

Bethencourt, Francisco. "European Expansion and the New Order of Knowledge," in John Jeffries Martin and Albert Russell Ascoli, Eds., *The Renaissance World.* London and New York: Routledge, Taylor & Francis Group, 2007, pp. 118–39.

Bharucha, Rustom. *Another Asia: Rabindranath Tagore and Okakura Tenshin.* Delhi: Oxford University Press, 2006.

Bhatt, Chetan. *Hindu Nationalism: Origins, Ideologies and Modern Myths.* Oxford and New York: Berg, 2001.

Bilgrami, Akeel. "Gandhi, the Philosopher," *Economic and Political Weekly, 38*(39) (2003): 1–19.

Bilimoria, Purushottama. "Environmental Ethics of Indian Religious Traditions," *paper presented at symposium "Religion and Ecology" at American Academy of Religion Annual Conference,* San Francisco, November 1997 (http://home.cogeco.ca/~drheault/ee_readings/East/Suggested/Bilimoria.pdf).

Black, Antony. "The 'Axial Period': What Was It and What Does It Signify?," *Review of Politics, 70*(1) (2008): 23–39.

Bokenkamp, Stephen R. "Time After Time: Taoist Apocalyptic History and the Founding of the T'ang Dynasty," *Asia Major,* 3rd Series, *7*(1) (1994): 59–88.

Boli-Bennet, John, and John W. Meyer. "The Ideology of Childhood and the State: Rules Distinguishing Children in National Constitutions, 1870–1970," *American Sociological Review, 43* (1978): 797–812.

Borschberg, Peter. "From Self-Defence to an Instrument of War: Dutch Privateering Around the Malay Peninsula in the Early 17th Century," *Journal of Early Modern History, 17* (2013): 35–52.

Bose, Sugata. *A Hundred Horizons: The Indian Ocean in the Age of Global Empire*. Cambridge, MA: Harvard University Press, 2006.

Bradbury, Roger. "A World Without Coral Reefs," *New York Times*, July 13, 2012 (www.nytimes.com/2012/07/14/opinion/a-world-without-coral-reefs. html?src=recg&_r=0).

Braudel, Fernand. *The Mediterranean and the Mediterranean World in the Age of Philip II*, vol. I. Berkeley and Los Angeles, CA: University of California Press, 1995.

Brook, Timothy. "Rethinking Syncretism: The Unity of the Three Teachings and Their Joint Worship in Late-Imperial China," *Journal of Chinese Religions, 21* (1993): 13–44.

Callahan, William A. "Chinese Visions of World Order: Post-Hegemonic or a New Hegemony?," *International Studies Review, 10* (2008): 749–61.

Callicott, J. B. *Earth's Insights: A Survey of Ecological Ethics from the Mediterranean Basin to the Australian Outback*. Berkeley and Los Angeles, CA: University of California Press, 1994.

Caputo, John D. "Without Sovereignty, Without Being: Unconditionality, the Coming God and Derrida's Democracy to Come," *Journal for Cultural and Religious Theory, 4*(3) (2003): 9–26.

Casale, Giancarlo. *The Ottoman Age of Exploration*. Oxford University Press, 2010.

Casanova, Jose. *Public Religions in the Modern World*. University of Chicago Press, 1994.

Chan, Wing-tsit. *Religious Trends in Modern China*. New York: Columbia University Press, 1953.

Chandra, Alexander C. *Civil Society in Search of an Alternative Regionalism in ASEAN*. Winnipeg: International Institute for Sustainable Development, 2009.

Chang, Hao. "Neo-Confucian Moral Thought and Its Modern Legacy," *Journal of Asian Studies, 39*(2) (1980): 259–72.

Chang, K. C. "Shamanism and Politics," in Chang, *Art, Myth and Ritual: The Path to Political Authority in Ancient China*. Cambridge, MA: Harvard University Press, 1983, pp. 44–55.

Chau, Adam Y. *Miraculous Response: Doing Popular Religion in Contemporary China*. Stanford University Press, 2006.

Chaudhuri, K. N. *Asia Before Europe: Economy and Civilisation of the Indian Ocean from the Rise of Islam to 1750*. Cambridge University Press, 1990.

Chellaney, Brahma. "China–India Clash over Chinese Claims to Tibetan Water," *Asia-Pacific Journal: Japan Focus*, posted on July 3, 2007 (www.japanfocus. org/site/view/2458).

Ch'en, Jerome. *China and the West: Society and Culture, 1815–1937*. London: Hutchinson, 1979.

"Chendoism," *Wikipedia*, 2014 (http://en.wikipedia.org/wiki/Cheondoism).

Chernilo, Daniel. "Cosmopolitanism and the Question of Universalism," in G. Delanty, Ed., *Handbook of Cosmopolitan Studies*. New York: Routledge, 2012, pp. 47–59.

Ching, Julia. "The Problem of God in Confucianism," *International Philosophical Quarterly*, *17*(1) (1977): 3–32.

Chow, Kai-wing. *The Rise of Confucian Ritualism in Late Imperial China: Ethics, Classics, and Lineage Discourse*. Stanford University Press, 1994.

Christian, David. *Maps of Time: An Introduction to Big History*. Berkeley, CA: University of California Press, 2005.

Chua, Beng-huat. "Conceptualizing an East Asian Popular Culture," *Inter-Asia Cultural Studies*, *5*(2) (2004): 200–21.

Cobb, John B."Deep Ecology and Process Thought," *Process Studies*, *30*(1) (2001): 112–31.

Cohen, Paul A. *History in Three Keys: The Boxers as Event, Experience, and Myth*. New York: Columbia University Press, 1998.

Coll, Steve. *Ghost Wars: The Secret History of the CIA, Afghanistan, and Bin Laden, from the Soviet Invasion to September 10, 2001*. New York: Penguin Press, 2004.

Collins, Steve. *Nirvana and Other Buddhist Felicities: Utopias of the Pali Imaginaire*. Cambridge University Press, 2003.

Costas, Douzinas. "Identity, Recognition, Rights, or What Can Hegel Teach Us About Human Rights?," *Journal of Law and Society*, *29*(3) (2002): 379–405.

Creppell, Ingrid. "Secularization: Religion and the Roots of Innovation in the Political Sphere," in Ira Katznelson and Gareth Steadman Jones, Eds., *Religion and the Political Imagination*. Cambridge University Press, 2010, pp. 23–45.

Day, Alexander. "The End of the Peasant? New Rural Reconstruction in China," *Boundary 2*, *35*(2) (2008): 49–73.

Dean, Kenneth. *Lord of the Three in One: The Spread of a Cult in Southeast China*. Princeton University Press, 1998.

"Local Communal Religion in Contemporary Southeast China," *China Quarterly*, *173* (2003): 336–58.

"The Daoist Difference: Alternatives to Imperial Power and Visions of a Unified Civilisation," *Asia Pacific Journal of Anthropology*, *13*(2) (2012): 128–41.

de Bruijn, Thomas. "Many Roads Lead to Lanka: The Intercultural Semantics of Rama's Quest," *Contemporary South Asia*, *14*(1) (2005): 39–53.

de Certeau, Michel. *The Writing of History*, Trans. Tom Conley. New York: Columbia University Press, 1988.

Deleuze, Gilles. *Pure Immanence: Essays on a Life*, with introduction by John Rajchman, Trans. Anne Boyman. New York: Zone Books, 2001.

Deng Xiaoping. "Uphold the Four Cardinal Principles," *Selected Works (1975–82)*. Beijing Foreign Languages Press, 1984.

Derrida, Jacques. *Of Grammatology*, Trans. Gayatri Chakravorty Spivak. Baltimore, MD: Johns Hopkins University Press, 1974.

"Ousia and Grammè: Note on a Note from *Being and Time*," in Derrida, *Margins of Philosophy*, Trans. Alan Bass. University of Chicago Press, 1982, pp. 29–67.

Desmond, Clarke M., and Charles Jones, Eds. *The Right of Nations: Nations and Nationalism in a Changing World*. New York: St. Martin's Press, 1999.

Dharmadhikary, Shripad. "Implementing the Report of the World Commission on Dams: A Case Study of the Narmada Valley in India," *American University International Law Review*, *16*(6) (2001): 1591–1630.

Dikötter, Frank. *The Discourse of Race in Modern China*. Stanford University Press, 1992.

Dimberg, Ronald, G. *The Sage and Society: The Life and Thought of Ho Hsin- yin*. Monographs of the Society for Asian and Comparative Philosophy, no. 1. Honolulu, HI: University of Hawaii Press, 1974.

Dixin, Xu, and Wu Chengming. *Chinese Capitalism, 1522–1840*. London: Palgrave Macmillan, 1999.

Dove, Michael R. "A Political-Ecological Heritage of Resource Contest and Conflict," in P. Daly and T. Winter, Eds., *Routledge Handbook of Heritage in Asia*. London: Routledge, pp. 182–97.

Dreyer, Edward L. *Zheng He: China and the Oceans in the Early Ming, 1405–1433*. Library of World Biography Series. London: Longman, 2006.

Duara, Prasenjit. "Superscribing Symbols: The Myth of Guandi, Chinese God of War," *Journal of Asian Studies, 47*(4) (1988): 778–95.

"Knowledge and Power in the Discourse of Modernity: The Campaigns Against Popular Religion in Early Twentieth-Century China," *Journal of Asian Studies, 50*(1) (1991): 67–83.

Rescuing History from the Nation: Questioning Narratives of Modern China. University of Chicago Press, 1995.

Sovereignty and Authenticity: Manchukuo and the East Asian Modern. Lanham, MD: Rowman & Littlefield, 2003.

"Historical Consciousness and National Identity," in Kam Louie, Ed., *The Cambridge Companion to Modern Chinese Culture*. Cambridge University Press, 2008, pp. 46–67.

"History and Globalization in China's Long Twentieth Century," *Modern China, 34*(1) (2008): 152–64.

"Between Sovereignty and Capitalism: The Historical Experiences of Migrant Chinese," in Duara, *The Global and Regional in China's Nation Formation*. London: Routledge, : 2009, ch. 7.

The Global and Regional in China's Nation Formation. London: Routledge, 2009

"The Cold War as a Historical Period: An Interpretive Essay," *Journal of Global History, 6*(3) (2011): 457–80.

"Hong Kong and the New Imperialism in East Asia 1941–1966," in David Goodman and Bryna Goodman, Eds., *Twentieth-Century Colonialism and China: Localities, the Everyday, and the World*. London: Routledge, 2012, pp. 197–211.

Dumont, Louis. *Homo Hierarchicus: The Caste System and Its Implications*. University of Chicago Press, 1980.

Efird, Rob. "Learning by Heart: An Anthropological Perspective on Environmental Learning in Lijiang," in Helen Kopnina and Eleanor Shoreman-Oiumet, Eds., *Environmental Anthropology Today*. New York: Routledge, 2011, pp. 254–66.

"Learning the Land Beneath Our Feet: The Place of NGO-Led Environmental Education in Yunnan Province," *Journal of Contemporary China, 21*(76) (2012): 569–83.

Eichengreen, Barry, and Jeffrey A. Frankel. "Economic Regionalism: Evidence from Two Twentieth-Century Episodes," *North American Journal of Economics and Finance, 6*(2) (1995): 89–106.

Eisenstadt, Shmuel N., Ed. *The Origins and Diversity of Axial Age Civilizations.*
    Albany, NY: State University of New York Press, 1986.
Japanese Civilization: A Comparative Review. University of Chicago Press, 1996.
    "The Axial Conundrum Between Transcendental Visions and Vicissitudes of
    Their Institutionalizations: Constructive and Destructive Possibilities,"
    Análise Social, 46(199) (2011): 201–17.
Eliade, Mircea. *The Myth of Eternal Return,* with introduction by Jonathan
    Z. Smith. Princeton University Press, 2005/1954.
Elliott, Lorraine. "ASEAN and Environmental Governance: Rethinking
    Networked Regionalism in Southeast Asia," *Procedia – Social and
    Behavioral Sciences,* 14 (2011): 61–4 (www.sciencedirect.com/science/
    article/pii/S1877042811001935).
Eltschinger, Vincent. *Caste and Buddhist Philosophy,* Trans. Raynald Prevereau.
    Delhi: Motilal Banarsidass, 2012.
Elvin, Mark. *The Retreat of the Elephants: An Environmental History of China.* New
    Haven, CT: Yale University Press, 2004.
Esbjörn-Hargens, Sean, and Ken Wilber. "Toward a Comprehensive Integration
    of Science and Religion: A Post-Metaphysical Approach," in Philip Clayton
    and Zachary Simpson, Eds., *The Oxford Handbook of Religion and Science*
    (Oxford University Press, 2006), pp. 523–46.
Esherick, Joseph. *The Boxer Uprising.* Berkeley and Los Angeles, CA: University of
    California Press, 1988.
Farquhar, Judith, and Zhang Qicheng. *Ten Thousand Things: Nurturing Life in
    Contemporary Beijing.* New York: Zone Books, 2012.
Fei, Xiaotong. "Xiangtu bense," in *Xiangtu Zhongguo.* Shanghai: Guanchashe,
    1947, pp. 1–7.
Feuchtwang, Stephan. *Popular Religion in China: The Imperial Metaphor.* London:
    Routledge Curzon, 2001.
Flood, Gavin. *The Secret Tradition of Hindu Religion.* London and New York:
    I. B. Taurus, 2006.
Foucault, Michel. "Nietzsche, Genealogy, History," in Donald F. Bouchard, Ed.,
    Language, Counter-Memory, Practice, Trans. Donald F. Bouchard and
    Sherry Simon. Ithaca, NY: Cornell University Press, 1977.
The History of Sexuality, vol. III: *The Care of the Self,* Trans. Robert Hurley. New
    York: Vintage Books, 1988.
Frederick, Michael J. *Transcendental Ethos: A Study of Thoreau's Social Philosophy
    and Its Consistency in Relation to Antebellum Reform.* Cambridge, MA: Harvard
    University Press, 1998 (http://thoreau.eserver.org/mjf/MJF3.html).
Freeman, Michael. "The Right to National Self-Determination," in Clarke
    M. Desmond and Charles Jones, Eds., *The Rights of Nations: Nations and
    Nationalism in a Changing World.* New York: St. Martin's Press, 1999,
    pp. 47–50.
Frost, Ellen L. "China's Commercial Diplomacy in Asia: Promise or Threat?," in
    William Keller and Thomas G. Rawski, Eds., *China's Rise and the Balance of
    Influence in Asia.* University of Pittsburgh Press, 2007, pp. 95–120.
Frost, Mark Ravinder. *'That Great Ocean of Idealism': Calcutta, the Tagore Circle
    and the Idea of Asia, 1900–1920.* Nalanda-Sriwijaya Centre Working Paper,

Series no. 3, June 2011 (http://nsc.iseas.edu.sg/documents/working_papers / nscwps003.pdf).

Fruehauf, Heiner. "All Disease Comes from the Heart: The Pivotal Role of the Emotions in Classical Chinese Medicine," *Classical Chinese Medicine.org* *15*, 2006 (www.jadeinstitute.com/jade/assets/files/Fruehauf-AllDisease ComesFromTheHeart.pdf).

Fu Zhong, Ed. *Yiguandao Lishi* (*History of the Yiguandao*). Taipei: Zhengyi shan-shu, 1997.

Ganguly, Debjani. "Buddha, Bhakti and Superstition: A Post-secular Reading of Dalit Conversion," *Postcolonial Studies*, *7*(1) (2004): 49–62.

George, William P. "Looking for a Global Ethic? Try International Law," *Journal of Religion*, *76*(3) (1996): 359–82.

Geyer, Michael, and Charles Bright. "World History in a Global Age," *American Historical Review*, *100*(4) (1995): 1034–60.

Ghosh, Amitav. "The *Ibis* Chrestomathy" [the glossary of the cosmopolitan seafarer language], in Ghosh, *Sea of Poppies*. New York: Picador, 2008.

Gilson, Julie. "Strategic Regionalism in East Asia," *Review of International Studies*, *33*(1) (2007): 145–63.

Girardot, Norman J. *The Victorian Translation of China: James Legge's Oriental Pilgrimage*. Berkeley, CA: University of California Press, 2002.

Glahn, Richard V. *Fountain of Fortune: Money and Monetary Policy in China, 1000–1700*. Berkeley, CA: University of California Press, 1996.

Goh, Evelyn. "Great Powers and Hierarchical Order in Southeast Asia: Analyzing Regional Security Strategies," *International Security*, *32*(3) (2007/8): 113–57.

Goldsmith, Benjamin E. "A Liberal Peace in Asia?," *Journal of Peace Research*, *44*(1) (2007): 5–27.

Gong, Gerrit W. *The Standard of "Civilization" in International Society*. Oxford: Clarendon Press, 1984.

Goodenough, Ursula, and Terrence W. Deacon. "The Sacred Emergence of Nature," in Philip Clayton and Zachary Simpson, Eds., *The Oxford Handbook of Religion and Science*. Oxford University Press, 2006, pp. 853–71.

Goody, Jack. *The Theft of History*. New York: Cambridge University Press, 2006.

Goossaert, Vincent. "Republican Church Engineering: The National Religious Associations in 1912 China," in Mayfair Yang, Ed., *Chinese Religiosities: Afflictions of Modernity and State Formation*. Berkeley and Los Angeles, CA: University of California, 2008, pp. 209–32.

Goossaert, Vincent, and David A. Palmer. *The Religion Question in Modern China*. University of Chicago Press, 2011.

Gorski, Philip S. "The Mosaic Moment: An Early Modernist Critique of Modernist Theories of Nationalism," *American Journal of Sociology*, *105*(5) (2000): 1428–68.

The Disciplinary Revolution: Calvinism and the Rise of the State in Early Modern Europe. University of Chicago Press, 2003.

Gottlieb, Roger S. "The Transcendence of Justice and the Justice of Transcendence: Mysticism, Deep Ecology, and Political Life," *Journal of the American Academy of Religion*, *67*(1) (1999): 149–66.

Green, Nile. "Breathing in India, *c.* 1890," *Modern Asian Studies*, *42* (2008): 283–315.
Guardian, The. "World Carbon Emissions: The League Table of Every Country," *The Guardian*, June 21, 2012 (www.guardian.co.uk/environment/datablog/2012/jun/21/world-carbon-emissions-league-table-country).
Guha, Ramachandra. "Toward a Cross-Cultural Environmental Ethic," *Alternatives: Global, Local, Political*, *15*(4) (1990): 431–47.
How Much Should a Person Consume? Environmentalism in India and the US. Berkeley and Los Angeles, CA: University of California Press, 2006.
Gupta, Uma D., Ed. *Tagore: Selected Writings on Education and Nationalism.* Delhi: Oxford University Press, 2009.
Gunn, Geoffrey, and Brian McCartan. "Chinese Dams and the Great Mekong Floods of 2008," *Asia-Pacific Journal: Japan Focus*, March 21, 2009.
Gunn, T. Jeremy. "The Complexity of Religion and the Definition of 'Religion' in International Law," *Harvard Human Rights Journal*, *16* (2003): 189–215.
Habermas, Jurgen. *Time of Transitions*, Ed. and Trans. Ciaran Cronin and Max Pensky. Cambridge: Polity Press, 2006.
Habermas, Jurgen, *et al.* *An Awareness of What Is Missing: Faith and Reason in a Post-Secular Age*, Trans. Ciaran Cronin. Cambridge: Polity Press, 2010.
Haider, Najaf. "Precious Metal Flows and Currency Circulation in the Mughal Empire," *Journal of Economic and Social History of the Orient*, *39* (Special Issue, Money in the Orient) (1996): 298–364.
Hall, Everett W. "Of What Use Are Whitehead's Eternal Objects?," *Journal of Philosophy*, *27*(2) (1930): 29–44.
Hamilton, Clive. "Geoengineering: Our Last Hope, or a False Promise?," *New York Times*, May 26, 2013.
Han Heejin. "China's Policymaking in Transition: A Hydropower Development Case," *Journal of Environment & Development*, *22*(3) (2013): 313–36.
Hanhimaki, Jussi M., and Odde Arne Westad. *The Cold War: A History in Documents and Eyewitness Accounts.* Oxford University Press, 2004.
Harbsmeier, Cristoph. "Some Notions of Time and of History in China and in the West, with a Digression on the Anthropology of Writing," in Chun-chieh Huang and Erik Zücher, Eds., *Time and Space in Chinese Culture.* Leiden: Brill, 1995, pp. 49–71.
Hardacre, Helen. *Shinto and the State, 1868–1988.* Princeton University Press, 1989.
Hargens, Sean Esborn, and Ken Wilber. "Towards a Comprehensive Integration of Science and Religion: A Post-Metaphysical Approach," in Philip Clayton and Zachary Simpson, Eds., *The Oxford Handbook of Religion and Science.* Oxford University Press, 2006, pp. 523–46.
Harris, Peter, Ed. *The Travels of Marco Polo.* London: Everyman's Library, 2008.
Hathaway, Michael J. *Environmental Winds: Making the Global in Southwest China.* Berkeley, CA: University of California Press, 2013.
Havel, Vaclav. "Politics and Conscience," in Jan Bažant, Nina Bažantová and Frances Starn, Eds., *The Czech Reader: History, Culture, Politics*, Durham, NC: Duke University Press, 2010, pp. 440–56.
Hay, Stephen N. *Asian Ideas of East and West: Tagore and His Critics in Japan, China and India.* Cambridge, MA: Harvard University Press, 1970.

Hegel, Georg Wilhelm Friedrich. *Philosophy of History*: III. Philosophic History (Thesis 17) (www.marxists.org/reference/archive/hegel/works/hi/history3.htm).

Hellenthal, Garrett, George B.J. Busby, Gavin Band, James F. Wilson, Cristian Capelli, Daniel Falush, and Simon Myers. "Supplementary Materials for *A Genetic Atlas of Human Admixture History*," *Science, 343* (2014): 747–51(http://admixturemap.paintmychromosomes.com/).

Hobsbawm, Eric. *Nations and Nationalism Since 1780: Program, Myth, Reality*. Cambridge University Press, 1990.

Hoskins, Janet. "God's Chosen People: Race, Religion and Anti-Colonial Resistance in French Indochina," Asia Research Institute Working Paper Series no. 189, September 2012, National University of Singapore, 2009.

"Seeing Syncretism as Visual Blasphemy: Critical Eyes on Caodai Religious Architecture," *Material Religion*, 6(1) (2010): 30–59.

"A Posthumous Return from Exile: The Legacy of an Anticolonial Religious Leader in Today's Vietnam," *Southeast Asian Studies*, 1(2) (2012): 213–46.

Hu Hanmin. "Nanyang Yu Zhongguo Geming" ("Nanyang and the Chinese Revolution"), in *Zhonghua Minguo Kaiguo Wushinian Wenxian*. 1.11 Gemingzhi Changdao Yu Fazhan. Taipei: Zhonghua Minguo Kaiguo Wushinian Wenxian Bianzhuan Weiyuanhui, 1964, pp. 457–84.

Huang, Grace. "The Politics of Knowing Shame: Agency in Jiang Jieshi's Leadership (1927–1936)." Ph.D. dissertation, University of Chicago, 2003.

Human Development Report. 2013 Summary, *The Rise of the South: Human Progress in a Diverse World*. New York: United Nations Development Programme, 2013.

Ileto, Ray. "Religion and Anti-Colonial Movements," in Nicholas Tarling, Ed., *Cambridge History of Southeast Asia*, vol. II: *The Nineteenth and Twentieth Centuries*. Cambridge University Press, 1992, pp. 197–248.

Iqtidar, Humeira. *Secularizing Islamists? Jama'at-e-Islami and Jama'at-ud-Dawa in Urban Pakistan*. University of Chicago Press, 2011.

Isomae Jun'ichi. "Deconstructing 'Japanese Religion': A Historical Survey," *Japanese Journal of Religious Studies*, 32(2) (2005): 235–48.

Ivanhoe, P.J. *Ethics in the Confucian Tradition: The Thought of Mengzi and Wang Yangming*. Indianapolis, IN: Hackett, 2002, 96–8.

Jackson, Carl T. *Vedanta for the West: The Ramakrishna Movement in the United States*. Bloomington, IN: Indiana University Press, 1994.

Jacobs, Andrew. "Chinese River's Fate May Reshape a Region," *New York Times*, May 4, 2013.

Jaspers, Karl. *The Origin and Goal of History*. New Haven, CT and London: Yale University Press, 1953.

Jensen, Robert. "Damn the Dams: An Interview with Medha Patkar," posted on *Alternet*, February 26, 2004 (http://uts.cc.utexas.edu/~rjensen/freelance/patkar.htm).

Jianli, Huang. "Umbilical Ties: The Framing of the Overseas Chinese as the Mother of the Revolution," *Frontiers of History in China*, 6(2) (2011): 183–228.

Jun, Jing. "Environmental Protests in Rural China," in Elizabeth J. Perry and Mark Selden, Eds., *Chinese Society: Change, Conflict and Resistance*, 3rd edn. New York: Taylor and Francis, 2010, pp. 197–214.

Kabir. *Songs of Kabir*, Trans. Rabindranath Tagore, Introduction by Evelyn Underhill. New York: Macmillan [1915].

Kalland, Arne, and Gerard Persoon, Eds. *Environmental Movements in Asia*, Richmond: Curzon Press, 1998.

Kalupahana, David J., Trans. *Mulamadhyamakakarika of Nagarjuna: The Philosophy of the Middle Way*. Delhi: Motilal Banarsidass, 1991.

Kan, Shirley. *U.S.–China Military Contacts: Issues for Congress*. Updated May 10, 2005, CRS Report for Congress, Congressional Research Service. Library of Congress, Washington, DC. Order Code RL32496 (http://fpc.state.gov/documents/organization/48835.pdf).

Kant, Immanuel. *Religion with the Limits of Reason Alone*, Trans. with introduction and notes by Theodore M. Greene and Hoyt H. Hudson. New York: Harper and Brothers, 1960.

"Idea for a Universal History from a Cosmopolitan Point of View," in Kant, *On History*, Ed. with introduction by Lewis White Beck. Indianapolis, IN: Library of Liberal Arts, 1963.

Kauffman, Stuart A. *Reinventing the Sacred: A New View of Science, Reason and Religion*. New York: Basic Books, 2008.

Kaviraj, Sudipta. "An Outline of a Revisionist Theory of Modernity," *Archives européennes de sociologie, 46* (2005): 497–526.

Khagram, Sanjeev. *Dam and Development: Transnational Struggle for Water and Power*. Ithaca, NY and London: Cornell University Press, 2004, pp. 51–5.

Kim, Youngmin. "Political Unity in Neo-Confucianism: The Debate Between Wang Yangming and Zhan Ruoshui," *Philosophy East and West, 62(2)* (2012): 246–63.

Kitagawa, Joseph M. "The Japanese 'Kokutai' (National Community): History and Myth," *History of Religions, 13(3)* (1974): 209–26.

Koselleck, Reinhart. *Futures Past: On the Semantics of Historical Time*, Trans. Keith Tribe. Cambridge, MA: MIT Press, 1985.

Critique and Crisis: Enlightenment and the Pathogenesis of Modern Society. Cambridge, MA: MIT Press, 1988.

Kothari, Ashish. "Protected Areas and People: The Future of the Past," *PARKS: International Journal of Protected Areas and Conservation, 17(2)* (2008): 23–34.

Krishna, Daya. "Three Conceptions of Indian Philosophy," in Daya Krishna, Ed., *Indian Philosophy: A Counter-Perspective*. Delhi: Oxford University Press, 1991, pp. 5–12.

Kuo, Ya-pei. "Redeploying Confucius: The Imperial State Dreams of the Nation, 1902–1911," in Mayfair Yang, Ed., *Chinese Religiosities: Afflictions of Modernity and State Formation*. Berkeley and Los Angeles, CA: University of California Press, 2008, pp. 65–86).

Kwee, Tek Hoay. "God and Wars," *Moestika Dharma: Mandblad tentang Agama, Kabatinan dan Philosofie* [monthly magazine about religion, spirituality and philosophy], *92* (1939): 405–8.

Ed. *The Religion of the Chinese: Related to Feasts, Offerings, Rituals, Traditions or Old Customs and Beliefs for Generations Since Ancient Time*. Tjitjoeroeg: "Moestika" Printing House, 1937.

The Nature of San Jiao: The Three Religions Embraced by the Chinese and Sam Kauw Hwe. Tjitjoeroeg: "Moestika" Printing House, 1942.

The Origins of the Modern Chinese Movement in Indonesia (Atsal Moelahnja Timboel Pergerakan Tionghua jang Modern di Indonesia), from Moestika Romans, *73–84*, 1936–9, Trans. and Ed. Lea E. Williams. Translation Series, Modern Indonesia Project, Southeast Asia Program. Ithaca, NY: Cornell University, 1969.

"Misleading Clamour," in Leo Suryadinata, Ed., *Political Thinking of Indonesian Chinese 1900–1995: A Sourcebook*. Singapore University Press, 1997.

Lagerway, John. *China: A Religious State*. Hong Kong University Press, 2010.

Latour, Bruno. *We Have Never Been Modern*, Trans. Catherine Porter. Cambridge, MA: Harvard University Press, 1993.

Reassembling the Social: An Introduction to Actor-Network-Theory. Oxford University Press, 2007.

Lawrenz, Jürgen. "Hegel, Recognition and Rights: 'Anerkennung' as a Gridline of the Philosophy of Rights," *Cosmos and History: The Journal of Natural and Social Philosophy*, 3(2–3) (2007): 153–69.

Lee, Jae-yon. "Magazines and the Collaborative Emergence of Literary Writers in Korea, 1919–1927," Ph.D. dissertation, University of Chicago, May 31, 2012.

Lee, Y.-S. F., and Alvin Y. So, Eds. *Asia's Environmental Movements: Comparative Perspectives*. New York and London: M. E. Sharpe, 1999.

Lee, Yuen-ching Bellette. "Development as Governing Tactics – the Three Gorges Dam and the Reproduction and Transformation of State Power in Dengist China," Ph.D. dissertation, University of Chicago, 2013.

"Global Capital, National Development and Transnational Environmental Activism: Conflict and the Three Gorges Dam," *Journal of Contemporary Asia*, 43(1) (2013): 102–26.

Lefebvre, Henri. *The Production of Space*, Trans. Donald Nicholson-Smith. Oxford: Blackwell, 1992.

Lele, Sharachchandra, Peter Wilshusen, Dan Brockington, Reinmar Seidler and Kamaljit Bawa. "Beyond Exclusion: Alternative Approaches to Biodiversity Conservation in the Developing Tropics," *Current Opinion in Environmental Sustainability*, 2 (2010): 94–100.

Lemche, Jennifer. "The Greening of Chinese Daoism: Modernity, Bureaucracy and Ecology in Contemporary Chinese Religion," *Master's thesis, Department of Religious Studies*, Queen's University, Canada, 2010.

Li Shiyu. *Xianzai Huabei mimi zongjiao (Secret Religions in North China today)*. City and publisher unknown, 1948.

Liang, Yongjia. "Shehui Yishi zhong de Yin" ("Renunciation as Ideology"). *Shehuixue Yanjiu (Sociological Studies)*, 23(5) (2008): 43–56.

Lieberman, Victor. *'Strange Parallels'. Southeast Asia in Global Context*, c. *800–1830*, vol. II. Cambridge University Press, 2009.

Lin Anwu. "Yin dao yi li jiao – yi Wang Fengyi 'shierzi xinchuan' wei gaixin zhankai" ("Establishing 'the Way' as Religion – Explorations of Wang Fengyi's 'Twelve Character Teachings'), in *Zhonghua minzu zongjiao xueshu huiyi lunwen fabiao*. Taipei: Conference on the Study of Chinese Religion, 1989.

Litfin, Karen T. "Sovereignty in World Ecopolitics," *Mershon International Studies Review*, *41*(2) (1997): 167–204.

Litzinger, Ralph. "In Search of the Grassroots: Hydroelectric Politics in Northwest Yunnan," in Elizabeth Perry and Merle Goldman, Eds., *Grassroots Political Reform in Contemporary China*. Cambridge, MA: Harvard University Press, 2007, pp. 282–99.

"Contested Sovereignties and the Critical Ecosystem Partnership Fund," *PoLAR: Political and Legal Anthropological Review*, *29*(1) 2006: 66–87.

Liu Lihong. "Wang Fengyi's Five Element Style of Emotional Healing (6 Parts)," 2012 (http://classicalchinesemedicine.org/dev/wang-fengyis-five-element-style-of-emotional-healing6-parts/).

Lowe, Victor. *Understanding Whitehead*. Baltimore, MD: Johns Hopkins University Press, 1962.

Luhmann, Niklas. *Ecological Communication*, Trans. John Bednarz, Jr. University of Chicago Press, 1989.

Lu Xun. "Guxiang" ("My Old Home"), in *Nahan, Lu Xun Quanji* [reprint]. Taipei: Tangshan, 1989/1921, vol. II, pp. 80–94.

Mackie, J. A. C., and Charles A. Coppell. "A Preliminary Survey," in *The Chinese in Indonesia*. Melbourne: Nelson in association with Australian Institute of International Affairs, 1976, pp. 1–18.

Madan, T. N. "Religions of India: Plurality and Pluralism," in Jamal Malik and Helmut Reifeld, Eds., *Religious Pluralism in South Asia and Europe*. Oxford University Press, 2005, pp. 42–76.

Makeham, John, Ed. *New Confucianism: A Critical Examination*. New York: Palgrave Macmillan, 2003.

Makin, Al. *Representing the Enemy: Musaylima in Muslim Literature*. Frankfurt am Main and New York: Peter Lang, 2010.

Marin-Guzman, Roberto. "Crusade in Al-Andalus: The Eleventh-Century Formation of *Reconquista* as an Ideology," *Islamic Studies*, *31*(3) (1992): 287–318.

Markovits, Claude, Jacques Pouchepadass and Sanjay Subrahmanyam. "Introduction: Circulation and Society Under Colonial Rule," in Markovits *et al.*, Eds., *Society and Circulation: Mobile People and Itinerant Cultures in South Asia, 1750 – 1950*. Delhi: Permanent Black, 2003, pp. 1–22.

Marshall, D. Bruce. *The French Colonial Myth and Constitution-Making in the Fourth Republic*. New Haven, CT: Yale University Press, 1973.

Marx, Anthony W. *Faith in Nation: Exclusionary Origins of Nationalism*. Oxford University Press, 2003.

Masuzawa, Tomoko. *In Search of Dreamtime: The Quest for the Origin of Religion*. University of Chicago Press, 1993.

Maurin, Cristelle, and Pichamon Yeophantong. "Going Global Responsibly? China's Strategies Towards 'Sustainable' Overseas Investments," *Pacific Affairs*, *8*(2) (2013): 281–303.

McBride, Richard D. *Domesticating the Dharma: Buddhist Cults and the Hwaŏm Synthesis in Silla Korea*. Honolulu, HI: University of Hawaii Press, 2008.

McCully, Patrick. "The Use of a Trilateral Network: An Activist's Perspective on the Formation of the World Commission on Dams," *American University International Law Review*, *16*(6) (2001): 1453–75.

McIntire, C. T. "The Shift from Church and State to Religions as Public Life in Modern Europe," *Church History*, *71*(1) (2002): 152–77.

McNeill, William H. *The Pursuit of Power*. University of Chicago Press, 1982.

Mehta, Uday S. "Gandhi and the Burden of Civility," *Raritan: A Quarterly Review*, *33*(1) (2014): 37–49.

Menegon, Eugenio. *Ancestors, Virgins and Friars: Christianity as a Local Religion in Late Imperial China*. Harvard Yenching Institute. Cambridge, MA: Harvard University Press, 2009.

Metzger, Thomas A. *Escape from Predicament: Neo-Confucianism and China's Evolving Political Culture*. New York: Columbia University Press, 1977.

Meyendorff, John. *Byzantine Theology: Historical Trends and Doctrinal Themes*, rev. 2nd edn. New York: Fordham University Press, 1983.

Middleton, Carl. "ASEAN, Economic Integration and Regional Environmental Governance: Emerging Norms and Transboundary Environmental Justice," paper presented at International Conference on International Relations and Development (ICIRD): Towards an ASEAN Economic Community (AEC): Prospects, Challenges and Paradoxes in Development, Governance and Human Security, Chiang Mai, Thailand, July 26–7, 2012.

Miller, James. "Daoism and Nature," notes for a lecture delivered to the Royal Asiatic Society, Shanghai, on January 8, 2008 (personal communication).

Minkowski, Christopher. "Advaita Vedānta in Early Modern History," *South Asian History and Culture*, *2*(2) (2011): 205–31.

Mittag, Achim. "Historical Consciousness in China: Some Notes on Six Theses on Chinese Historiography and Historical Thought," in Paul Van Der Velde and Alex McKay, Eds., *New Developments in Asian Studies: An Introduction*. London: Kegan Paul, 1998, pp. 47–76.

Mitter, Partha. "Mutual Perceptions in the Contact Zone: India and America," paper presented at the Smithsonian American Art Museum, Washington, DC, conference, "A Long and Tumultuous Relationship: East–West Interchanges in American Art," October 1–2, 2009.

Mohanty, J. N. "Some Thoughts on Daya Krishna's 'Three Myths'," in Daya Krishna, Ed., *Indian Philosophy: A Counter-Perspective*. Delhi: Oxford University Press, 1991, 52–3.

Mollier, Christine. *Buddhism and Taoism Face to Face: Scripture, Ritual, and Iconographic Exchange in Medieval China*. Honolulu, HI: University of Hawaii Press, 2009.

Momigliano, Arnaldo. "The Disadvantages of Monotheism for a Universal State," in Momigliano, *On Pagans, Jews, and Christians*. Middletown, CT: Wesleyan University Press, 1987.

Mori Noriko, "Riben he Zhongguo Jindaihua Guochengzhongde Guojiaowenti" ("The Problem of National Religion in the Transition to Modernity in China and Japan"), paper presented at International Symposium, "Constructing Modern Knowledge in China, 1600–1949," Academia Sinica, Taiwan, October 25–6, 2004.

Moyn, Samuel. *The Last Utopia: Human Rights in History*. Cambridge, MA: Harvard University Press, 2010.

Murray, Warwick E. "Neo-liberalism Is Dead, Long Live Neo-Liberalism? Neo-Structuralism and the International Aid Regime of the 2000s," *Progress in Development Studies*, *11*(4) (2011): 307–19.

Murthy, Viren. *The Political Philosophy of Zhang Taiyan: The Resistance of Consciousness.* Leiden: Brill, 2011.

Myerson, Joel, Sandra H. Petrulionis and Laura D. Walls, Eds., *The Oxford Handbook of Transcendentalism.* Oxford University Press, 2010.

Nagel, Thomas. *Mind and Cosmos: Why the Materialist Neo-Darwinian Conception of Nature Is Almost Certainly False.* Oxford University Press, 2012.

Naquin, Susan, and Evelyn S. Rawski. *Chinese Society in the Eighteenth Century.* New Haven, CT: Yale University Press, 1987.

Needham, Joseph. *Science and Civilization in China.* Cambridge University Press, 1971, vol. IV.

Nishimura, Mutsuyoshi. "Climate Change and Asia," IISS-JIIA Conference, 2–4 June 2008, Hotel Okura, Tokyo, Japan: Second Session – Asian Environmental Nightmares (www.iiss.org/conferences/global-strategic-chal lenges-as-played-out-in-asia/asias-strategic-challenges-in-search-of-a-com mon-agenda/conference-papers/second-session-asian-environmental-night mares/climate-change-and-asia-mutsuyoshi-nishimura/).

O'Hanlon, Rosalind, and David Washbrook. "Religious Cultures in an Imperial Landscape," *South Asian History and Culture*, *2*(2) (2011): 133–7.

Okakura, Tenshin, *The Ideals of the East with Special Reference to the Arts of Japan.* Tokyo: ICG Muse, 2002.

O'Neill, Onora. *Constructions of Reason: Explorations of Kant's Practical Philosophy.* Cambridge University Press, 1989.

Ong, Aihwa. "Graduated Sovereignty in South-East Asia," *Theory, Culture & Society*, *17*(4) (2000): 55–75.

Orzech, Charles D. "Puns on the Humane King: Analogy and Application in an East Asian Apocryphon," *Journal of the American Oriental Society*, *109*(1) (1989): 17–24.

Politics and Transcendent Wisdom: The Scripture for Humane Kings in the Creation of Chinese Buddhism. University Park, PA: Pennsylvania State University Press, 1998.

"Metaphor, Translation, and the Construction of Kingship in *The Scripture for Humane Kings* and the *Mahāmāyūrī Vidyārājñī Sūtra*," *Cahiers d'Extrême-Asie*, *13* (2002): 55–83.

Overmyer, Daniel. "Values in Chinese Sectarian Literature," in David Johnson, Andrew Nathan and Evelyn Rawski, Eds., *Popular Culture in Late Imperial China*. Berkeley, CA: University of California Press, 1985, pp. 219–54.

Overy, Richard. "World Trade and World Economy," in Ian C. B. Dear and M. R. D. Foot, Eds., *The Oxford Companion to World War II.* Oxford University Press, 2001.

Ownby, David. "Chinese Millenarian Traditions: The Formative Age," *American Historical Review*, *104*(5) (1999): 1513–30.

Palmer, David A. *Qigong Fever: Body, Science, and Utopia in China.* New York: Columbia University Press, 2007.

Palmquist, Stephen. "'The Kingdom of God is at Hand!' (Did Kant Really Say That?)," *History of Philosophy Quarterly*, 11(4) (1994): 421–37.
Pankenier, David W. "The Cosmo-Political Background of Heaven's Mandate," *Early China*, 20 (1995): 121–76.
Park, Hyunhee. *Mapping the Chinese and Islamic Worlds: Cross-Cultural Exchange in Pre-modern Asia*. Cambridge University Press, 2012.
Pearse-Smith, Scott W. D. "Lower Mekong Basin Hydropower Development and the Trade-off Between the 'Traditional' and 'Modern' Sectors: 'Out with the Old, in with the New'," *Asia-Pacific Journal: Japan Focus*, 10(23) (2012).
Pecora, Vincent. *Secularization and Cultural Criticism: Religion, Nation, and Modernity*. University of Chicago Press, 2006.
Petri, Peter A. "Is East Asia Becoming More Interdependent?," *Journal of Asian Economics*, 17(3) (2006): 381–94.
Pietersee, Jan Nederveen. "Global Rebalancing: Crisis and the East–South Turn," *Development and Change*, 42(1) (2011): 22–48.
Pingree, David. "Hellenophilia Versus the History of Science," *Isis*, 83 (1992): 554–63.
Pocock, John G. A. *The Machiavellian Moment: Florentine Thought and the Atlantic Republican Tradition*. Princeton University Press, 1975.
Polanyi, Karl. *The Great Transformation: The Political and Economic Origins of Our Time*, introduction by R. M. MacIver. Boston: Beacon Press, 1957.
Pollock, Sheldon. "Axialism and Empire," in Johann P. Arnason, S. N. Eisenstadt and Björn Wittrock, Eds., *Axial Civilizations and World History*. Leiden: Brill, 2005, pp. 397–450.
The Language of the Gods in the World of Men: Sanskrit, Culture and Power in Premodern India. Berkeley, CA: University of California Press, 2006.
Posey, Darrell A. and Graham Dutfield. *Beyond Intellectual Property: Toward Traditional Resource Rights for Indigenous Peoples and Local Communities*. Toronto: IDRC Books, 1996 (http://web.idrc.ca/en/ev-9327-201-1-DO_TOPIC.html).
Puett, Michael. *The Ambivalence of Creation: Debates Concerning Innovation and Artifice in Early China*.Stanford University Press, 2001.
Qi, Jianmin. "The Debate over 'Universal Values' in China," *Journal of Contemporary China*, 20(72) (2011): 881–90 (http://dx.doi.org/10.1080/106 70564.2011.604506).
Queen, Christopher. "Dr. Ambedkar and the Hermeneutics of Buddhist Liberation," in Christopher S. Queen and Sallie B. King, Eds., *Engaged Buddhism: Buddhist Liberation Movements in Asia*. Albany, NY: State University of New York Press, 1996, pp. 45–73.
Radkau, Joachim. *Nature and Power: A Global History of the Environment*. Cambridge University Press, 2008.
Raegan, Laurie. "Healing Through the Emotions: The Confucian Therapy System of Wang Fengyi," 2012 (www.swarthmore.edu/healing-through-the-emotions-the-confucian-therapy-system-of-wang-fengyi.xml).
Raj, Kapil. "Beyond Postcolonialism . . . and Postpositivism: Circulation and the Global History of Science," *Isis*, 104(2) (2013): 337–47.

Rajan, S. Ravi. "Science, State and Violence: An Indian Critique Reconsidered," *Science as Culture, 14*(3) (2005): 1–17.

Rambelli, Fabio. "The Idea of India (Tenjiku) in Pre-Modern Japan: Issues of Signification and Representation in the Buddhist Translation of Cultures," in Tansen Sen, Ed., *Buddhism Across Asia: Networks of Material, Intellectual and Cultural Exchange.* Delhi: Manohar and Singapore: Institute of Southeast Asian Studies, 2014, vol. I, pp. 262–92.

Raulet, Gerard. "Critique of Religion and Religion as Critique: The Secularized Hope of Ernst Bloch," Trans. David J. Parent and Ed. Tim Luke. *New German Critique, 9* (1976): 71–85.

Rawski, Evelyn. "The Imperial Way of Death: Ming and Ch'ing Emperors and Death Ritual," in James Watson and Evelyn Rawski, Eds., *Death Ritual in Late Imperial and Modern China.* Berkeley, CA: University of California Press, 1988, pp. 228–53.

Ray, Rajat K. "Asian Capital in the Age of European Expansion: The Rise of the Bazaar, 1800–1914," *Modern Asian Studies, 29*(3) (1995): 449–554.

Reid, Anthony. *Imperial Alchemy: Nationalism and Political Identity in Southeast Asia.* Cambridge University Press, 2009.

Renan, Ernest. "What Is a Nation?," in Homi Bhabha, Ed., *Nation and Narration.* New York: Routledge, 1990, pp. 8–22.

Revkin, Andrew C. "Reefs in the Anthropocene – Zombie Ecology?," *New York Times,* July 14, 2012 (http://dotearth.blogs.nytimes.com/2012/07/14/reefs-in-the-anthropocene-zombie-ecology/?ref=opinion).

Richards, Marilyn, and Peter Hughes. "Rammohun Roy," Unitarian Universalist Historical Society (UUHS) 1999–2007, 2014 (http://uudb.org/articles/rajar ammohunroy.html).

Ricoeur, Paul. "Narrative Time," *Critical Inquiry, 7*(1) (1980): 169–90.

Time and Narrative, vol. III. University of Chicago Press, 1988.

Figuring the Sacred: Religion, Narrrative and the Imagination, Trans. David Pellauer, Ed. Mark I. Wallace. Minneapolis, MN: Fortress Press, 1995.

Riesebrodt, Martin. *The Promise of Salvation: A Theory of Religion,* Trans. Steven Rendall. University of Chicago Press, 2010.

Ringmar, Eric. "The Recognition Game: Soviet Russia Against the West," *Cooperation and Conflict, 37*(2) (2002): 115–36.

Saaler, Sven, and J. Victor Koschmann, Eds. *Pan-Asianism in Modern Japanese History: Colonialism, Regionalism and Borders.* London and New York: Routledge, 2007.

Salvatore, Armando. *The Public Sphere: Liberal Modernity, Catholicism and Islam.* New York: Palgrave Macmillan, 2007.

Sanderson, Alexis. "Saivism and the Tantric Traditions," in S. Sutherland, L. Houlden, P. Clarke and F. Hardy, Eds., *The World's Religions.* London: Routledge and Kegan Paul, 1988, pp. 660–704.

Sangvai, Sanjay. *The River and Life: People's Struggle in the Narmada Valley.* Mumbai: Earthcare Books, 2000.

Sartre, Jean-Paul. *Critique of Dialectical Reason: Theory of Practical Ensembles,* Trans. Alan Sheridan-Smith; Ed. Jonathan Rée. London: Verso, 1976.

Schiffman, Zachary S. *The Birth of the Past*. Baltimore, MD: Johns Hopkins University Press, 2011.

Schilling, Heinz. *Early Modern European Civilization and Its Political and Cultural Dynamism*. Menahem Stern Jerusalem Lectures. Lebanon, NH: Brandeis University Press and University Press of New England, 2008.

Schmid, Andre. *Korea Between Empires, 1895–1919*. New York: Columbia University Press, 2002.

Schmitt, Carl. *Political Theology: Four Chapters on the Concept of Sovereignty*, Trans. George Schwab, 2nd edn. University of Chicago Press, 2005/1985.

Schulze, Hagen. *States, Nations and Nationalism: From the Middle Ages to the Present*. Oxford: Blackwell, 1996.

Seibt, Johanna. "Process Philosophy," in Edward N. Zalta, Ed., *The Stanford Encyclopedia of Philosophy* (Winter 2012 Edition) (http://plato.stanford.edu/archives/win2012/entries/process-philosophy/).

Seiwert, Hubert, in collaboration with Ma Xisha. *Popular Religious Movements and Heterodox Sects in Chinese History*. Leiden and Boston: Brill, 2003.

Selden, Mark. "China's Way Forward? Historical and Contemporary Perspectives on Hegemony and the World Economy in Crisis," *Asia-Pacific Journal: Japan Focus* (www.japanfocus.org/-mark-selden/3105). posted on March 24, 2009.

Seligman, Adam B., Robert P. Weller, Michael J. Puett and Simon Bennett. *Ritual and Its Consequences: An Essay on the Limits of Sincerity*. Oxford University Press, 2008.

Sen, Nabaneeta Dev. "Crisis in Civilization, and a Poet's Alternatives: Education as One Alternative Weapon," paper presented at "Tagore's Philosophy of Education": A Conference Dedicated to the Memory of Amita Sen, Kolkata, March 29–30, 2006.

Sen, Tansen. "Ancestral Tomb-Paintings from Xuanhua: Mandalas?," *Ars Orientalis*, 29 (1999): 29–54.

Buddhism, Diplomacy and Trade: The Realignment of Sino-Indian Relations, 600–1400. Honolulu, HI: University of Hawaii Press, 2003, pp. 76–87.

"The Spread of Buddhism to China: A Re-Examination of the Buddhist Interactions Between Ancient India and China," *China Report*, 48 (2012): 11–27.

"The Spread of Buddhism," in Benjamin Z. Kedar and Merry E. Wiesner-Hanks, Eds., *The Cambridge History of the World*, vol. V: *Expanding Webs of Exchange and Conquest, 500 CE – 1500 CE*. Cambridge University Press, in press.

Sewell, William H., Jr. *The Logics of History: Social Theory and Social Transformation*. University of Chicago Press, 2005.

Shao Yong. *Zhongguo huidaomen (China's Religious Societies)*. Shanghai: Renmin Chubanshe, 1997.

Shanghaishi shehuiju yewu baogao (SSJYB) (Reports of the Shanghai Municipality Social Bureau on Enterprises and Activities), Jan.–Dec. 1930; Jan.–Dec. 1931, Jan.–June 1932, Jan. 1946. Shanghai: 1930–2, 1946.

Shapinsky, Peter. "Polyvocal Portolans: Nautical Charts and Hybrid Maritime Cultures in Early Modern East Asia," *Early Modern Japan*, 14 (2006): 4–26.

Sharma, H. D. *Raja Rammohan Roy: The Renaissance Man*. Delhi: Rupa & Co, 2002.

Sharma, Mukul. *Green and Saffron: Hindu Nationalism and Indian Environmental Politics*. Ranikhet, India: Permanent Black, 2012.

Shimazono Susumu. *From Salvation to Spirituality: Popular Religious Movements in Modern Japan*. Melbourne: Trans-Pacific Press, 2004.

Shiva, Vandana. "Conflicts of Global Ecology: Environmental Activism in a Period of Global Reach," *Alternatives*, *19* (1994): 195–207.

Shiva, Vandana, and J. Bandyopadhyay. "The Evolution, Structure, and Impact of the Chipko Movement," *Mountain Research and Development*, *6*(2) (1986): 133–42.

Shrivastava, Aseem, and Ashish Kothari. *Churning the Earth: The Making of Global India*. New Delhi: Penguin/Viking, 2012.

Shulman, David. "Axial Grammar," in Johann P. Arnason, S. N. Eisenstadt and Björn Wittrock, Eds., *Axial Civilizations and World History*. Leiden: Brill, 2005, pp. 369–94.

Sidaway, James D. "Spaces of Postdevelopment," *Progress in Human Geography*, *31* (2007): 345–61.

Simmel, Georg. *Essays on Religion*, Ed. Horst Jürgen Helle in collaboration with Ludwig Nieder. New Haven, CT: Yale University Press, 1997.

Sirkin, Harold, James Hemerling and Arindam Bhattacharya. *Globality: Competing with Everyone from Everywhere for Everything*. New York: Business Plus, 2008.

Skinner, G. W. "Creolized Chinese Societies in Southeast Asia," in Anthony Reid, Ed., *Sojourners and Settlers: Histories of Southeast Asia and the Chinese*. Sydney: Allen and Unwin, 1995, pp. 50–93.

Smart, Ninian. *The Yogi and the Devotee: The Interplay Between the Upanishads and Catholic Theology*. London: George Allen and Unwin, 1968.

Smith, Howard D. "The Significance of Confucius for Religion," *History of Religions*, *2*(2) (1963): 242–55.

Song, Shenqiao. "Wo yi wo xue jian Xuanyuan – Huangdi shenhua yu wan Qing de guozu Jiangou" ("The Myth of the Yellow Emperor and the Construction of National Lineage in the Late Qing"), *Taiwan shehui yanjiu jikan*, *28* (1997): 1–77.

Spears, Collin. "SINO + ASEAN = East Asian Unification? Not Quite: Part I," *Brooks Foreign Policy Review*, posted May 15, 2009 (http://brooksreview.word press.com/2009/05/20/sino-asean-east-asian-unification-not-quite-part-i/).

Statistics on World Population, GDP and Per Capita GDP, 1–2008 AD (vertical file, copyright Angus Maddison, University of Groningen) (www.ggdc.net/maddison/oriindex.htm).

Stein, William B. "The Hindu Matrix of *Walden*: The King's Son," *Comparative Literature*, *22*(4) (1970): 303–18.

Stengers, Isabelle. "Whitehead and Science: From Philosophy of Nature to Speculative Cosmology," n.d. (www.mcgill.ca/files/hpsc/Whitmontreal.pdf). *Thinking with Whitehead: A Free and Wild Creation of Concepts*, Trans. Michael Chase. Cambridge, MA: Harvard University Press, 2011.

Strenski, Ivan. *Contesting Sacrifice: Religion, Nationalism and Social Thought in France*. University of Chicago Press, 1997.

Stroumsa, Guy G. *The End of Sacrifice: Religious Transformations in Late Antiquity*, Trans. Susan Emanuel. University of Chicago Press, 2009.

Subrahmanyam, Sanjay. "Of Imarat and Tijarat: Asian Merchants and State Power in the Western Indian Ocean, 1400 to 1750," *Comparative Studies in Society and History*, *37*(4) (1995): 750–80.

"Connected Histories: Notes Towards a Reconfiguration of Early Modern Eurasia," *Modern Asian Studies*, *31*(3), Special Issue: The Eurasian Context of the Early Modern History of Mainland South East Asia, 1400–1800 (1997): 735–62.

Suemitsu, Takayoshi. *Shina no mimi kaisha to jishan kaisha* (*China's Secret Societies and Charitable Societies*). Dalian: Manshu hyoronsha, 1932.

Suk-san, Yook. *Chondogyo: The Religion of the Cosmos That Blossomed in Korea*, Trans. Young Hee Lee. Seoul: Central Headquarters of Chondogyo, 2002.

Sunchindah, Apichai. "The Lancang–Mekong River Basin: Reflections on Cooperation Mechanisms Pertaining to a Shared Watercourse," RSIS Centre for Non-Traditional Security Studies No. PO13–01, February 2013.

Suryadinata, Leo. "From Peranakan Chinese Literature to Indonesian Literature: A Preliminary Study," in Suryadinata, Ed., *Chinese Adaptation and Diversity*. Singapore University Press, 1993.

"Kwee Tek Hoay: A Peranakan Writer and Proponent of Tridharma," in *Peranakan's Search for National Identity: Biographical Studies of Seven Indonesian Chinese*. Singapore: Times Academic Press, 1993.

Swedberg, Richard, and Ola Agevall, Eds., *The Max Weber Dictionary: Key Words and Central Concepts*. Stanford University Press, 2005 (Google Books.htm).

Tagore, Rabindranath. "Nationalism in the West," in Ramachandra Guha, Ed., *Nationalism*. New Delhi: Penguin Books, 2009.

Tagore, Saranindranath. "Postmodernism and Education: A Tagorean Intervention," paper presented at "Tagore's Philosophy of Education": a conference dedicated to the memory of Amita Sen, Kolkata, March 29–30, 2006.

"Tagore's Conception of Cosmopolitanism: A Reconstruction," *University of Toronto Quarterly*, *77*(4) (2008): 1071–84.

Takashi, Shiraishi. "Evolving a New Order for the Asia-Pacific," *Topics of the Times*, December 9, 2011 (www.nippon.com/en/editor/f00003/).

Takeshi, Hamashita. "The Tribute Trade System and Modern Asia," in A. Latham and H. Kawasatsu, Eds., *Japanese Industrialization and the Asian Economy*. London: Routledge, 1994.

"Kōsa suru Indokei nettowaku to Kajinkei nettowaku: Honkoku sōkin shisutemu no hikaku kentō" ("Intersecting Networks of Indians and Chinese: A Comparative Investigation of the Remittance System"), in Akita Shigeru and Mizushima Tsukasa, Eds., *Gendai Minami Ajia 6: Sekai Sisutemu To Nettowâku* (*Contemporary South Asia 6: World System and Network*). Tokyo University Press, 2003, pp. 239–74.

Takizawa, Toshihiro. *Shyukyo chōsa shiryō* (*Materials from the Survey of Religions*), vol. III: *Minkan shinyō chōsa hōkokushō* (*Report on the Survey of Popular Beliefs*). Shinkyō (Xinjing): Minseibu (Minshengbu), 1937.

Taylor, Bron R. "Popular Ecological Resistance and Radical Environmentalism," in Bron Taylor, Ed., *Ecological Resistance Movements: The Global Emergence of*

Radical and Popular Environmentalism. Albany, NY: State University of New York Press, 1995, pp. 334–53.

"Environmental Ethics," in Bron Taylor, Ed., *Encyclopedia of Religion and Nature.* London and New York: Continuum, 2005, pp. 597–608.

Taylor, Charles. *A Secular Age.* Cambridge, MA: Belknap Press of Harvard University Press, 2007.

Taylor, Mark C. *After God.* University of Chicago Press, 2007.

Tay Wei Leong. "Saving the Chinese Nation and the World: Religion and Confucian Reformation, 1880s–1937," MA dissertation submitted to the National University of Singapore, 2012.

Tegbaru, Amare. "Local Environmentalism in Northeast Thailand," in Arne Kalland and Gerard Persoon, Eds., *Environmental Movements in Asia.* Richmond, Surrey: Curzon Press, 1998, pp. 151–78.

Thapar, Romila. "Was There Historical Writing in Early India?," in Cynthia Talbot, Ed., *Knowing India: Colonial and Modern Constructions of the Past: Essays in Honor of Thomas R. Trautmann.* New Delhi: Yoda Press, 2011, pp. 281–308.

Thompson, Kiril. "The Religious in Neo-Confucianism," *Asian Culture Quarterly,* 15(4) (1990): 44–57.

Tilly, Charles. *Coercion, Capital and European States, AD 990–1992.* Malden, MA: Blackwell, 1992.

Tilt, Bryan. *The Struggle for Sustainability in Rural Society: Environmental Values and Civil Society.* New York: Columbia University Press, 2009.

Tsing, Anna. *Friction: An Ethnography of Global Connections.* Princeton University Press, 2005.

Tuttle, Gray. *Tibetan Buddhists in the Making of Modern China.* New York: Columbia University Press, , 2005.

Tu Wei-ming. "The Structure and Function of the Confucian Intellectual in Ancient China," in S. N. Eisenstadt, Ed., *The Origins and Diversity of Axial Age Civilizations.* Albany, NY: State University of New York Press, 1986, pp. 360–74.

Valdes, Mario J. *Reflection and Imagination: A Paul Ricœur Reader.* University of Toronto Press, 1991.

van der Veer, Peter. *Gods on Earth.* London: Athlone Press, 1988.

Imperial Encounters: Religion and Modernity in India and Britain. Delhi: Permanent Black, 2006.

"Spirituality in Modern Society," *Social Research,* 76(4) (2009): 1097–1120.

van der Veer, Peter, and Hartmut Lehmann, Eds., *Nation and Religion: Perspectives on Europe and Asia.* Princeton University Press, 1999.

Vaudeville, Charlotte. "Kabir and Interior Religion," *History of Religions,* 3(1–2) (1963): 191–201.

A Weaver Named Kabir: Selected Verses with a Detailed Biographical and Historical Introduction. New Delhi: Oxford University Press, 1993.

Verellen, Franciscus. "Taoism," *Journal of Asian Studies,* 54(2) (1995): 322–46.

Vishwanathan, Gauri. *Outside the Fold: Conversion, Modernity and Belief.* Princeton University Press, 1998.

Walby, Sylvia. "Complexity Theory, Globalization and Diversity," paper presented to conference of British Sociological Association, University of York, April 2003

(www.leeds.ac.uk/sociology/people/swdocs/Modernities%20Globalisation%
20Complexities.pdf).

Wallerstein, Immanuel. "The Construction of Peoplehood: Racism, Nationalism,
Ethnicity," in Etienne Balibar and Immanuel Wallerstein, Eds., *Race, Nation,
Class: Ambiguous Identities*. London: Verso, 1991.

Wang, Aihe. *Cosmology and Political Culture in Early China*. Cambridge University
Press, 2000.

Wang, Edward Q. "Between Marxism and Nationalism: Chinese Historiography
and the Soviet Influence, 1949–1963," *Journal of Contemporary China*, 9(23)
(2000): 95–111.

Wang, Mingming. "'All Under Heaven' (Tianxia): Cosmological Perspectives and
Political Ontologies in Pre-Modern China," *Hau: Journal of Ethnographic
Theory*, 2(1) (2012): 337–83.

Wanguo Daodehui Manzhouguo zonghui bianjike, Ed., *Manzhouguo Daodehui
nianjian* (*Yearbook of the Manzhouguo Morality Society*). Xinjing: Wanguo
Daodehui Manzhouguo zonghui bianjike, 1934.

Wansbrough, John. *The Sectarian Milieu: Contest and Composition of Islamic
Salvation History*. New York: Prometheus Books, 1978.

Wasmer, Caterina. "Towards Sustainability: Environmental Education in China –
Can a German Strategy Adapt to Chinese Schools?," Ed. Werner Pascha and
Markus Taube. Duisburg Working Papers on East Asian Economic Studies,
Duisburg, Germany, 2005 (www.econstor.eu/obitstream/10419/23138/1/
AP73.pdf).

Weber, Max. *The Sociology of Religion*. Trans. Ephraim Fischoff. Boston: Beacon
Press, 1964.

Economy and Society: An Outline of Interpretive Sociology, Ed. Guenther Roth and
Claus Wittich. Berkeley and Los Angeles, CA: University of California Press,
1978.

The Protestant Ethic and the Spirit of Capitalism, Trans. Talcott Parsons, introduction by Anthony Giddens. London: Routledge, 1992.

"Sociology of Rulership and Religion," in *The Max Weber Dictionary: Keywords
and Central Concepts*, Ed. Richard Swedberg and Ola Agevall. Stanford
University Press, 2005. (www.cjsonline.ca/pdf/weberdict.pdf).

Wee, C. J. Wan-Ling. "'We Asians'? Modernity, Visual Art Exhibitions, and East
Asia," *Boundary 2*, 37(1) (2010): 91–126.

Weller, Robert. *Discovering Nature: Globalization and Environmental Culture in
China and Taiwan*. Cambridge University Press, 2006.

White, Hayden. *The Content of the Form*. Baltimore, MD: Johns Hopkins
University Press, 1987.

Whitehead, Alfred N. *Process and Reality: An Essay in Cosmology*, Ed.
David Ray Griffin and Donald W. Sherburne. New York: Free Press,
1978.

Whooley, Owen. "Locating Masterframes in History: An Analysis of the Religious
Masterframe of the Abolition Movement and Its Influence on Movement
Trajectory," *Journal of Historical Sociology*, 17 (2004): 490–516.

Willmott, Donald E. *The Chinese of Semarang: A Changing Minority Community in
Indonesia*. Ithaca, NY: Cornell University Press, 1960.

Wittrock, Björn. "The Meaning of the Axial Age," in Johann P. Arnason, S. N. Eisenstadt and Björn Wittrock, Eds., *Axial Civilizations and World History*. Leiden: Brill, 2005, pp. 51–86.

Wolf, Arthur. "Gods, Ghosts and Ancestors," in Arthur Wolf, Ed., *Studies in Chinese Society*. Stanford University Press, 1978, pp. 131–82.

Wongsurawat, Wasana. "Thailand and the Xinhai Revolution: Expectation, Reality and Inspiration," in *Sun Yat-sen, Nanyang and the 1911 Revolution*, Ed. Lee Lai To and Lee Hock Guan. Singapore: Institute of Southeast Asian Studies, 2011.

World Heritage Sites (http://whc.unesco.org/en/list/).

Wright, Mary C. *The Last Stand of Chinese Conservatism: The T'ung-chih Restoration, 1862–1874*. Stanford University Press, 1967.

Xiang, Shiling. "A Study on the Theory of 'Returning to the Original' and 'Recovering Nature' in Chinese Philosophy," *Frontiers of Philosophy in China*, 3(4) (2008): 502–19.

Xingya zongjiao xiehui (Revive Asian Religions Association), Ed. *Huabei zongjiao nianjian* (*Yearbook of the Religions of North China*). Beiping: Xingyayuan Huabei lianlobu, 1941.

Yang, C. K. *Religion in Chinese Society*. Berkeley, CA: University of California Press, 1967.

Yang, Erzeng. *The Story of Han Xiangzi: The Alchemical Adventures of a Daoist Immortal*, Trans. and Introduced by Philip Clart. Seattle, WA and London: University of Washington Press, 2007.

Yang, Guobin, and Craig Calhoun. "Media, Civil Society and the Rise of a Green Public Sphere in China," *China Information*, 21 (2007): 211–34.

Yeophantong, Pichamon. "China, Corporate Responsibility and the Contentious Politics of Hydropower Development: Transnational Activism in the Mekong Region?," Global Economic Governance Programme, GEG WP 2013/82, University of Oxford, 2013.

Yu, Anthony. *State and Religion in China: Historical and Textual Perspectives*. Chicago and Lasalle, IL: Open Court, 2005.

Yulin, Zhang. "'Tiandi yibian' yu Zhongguo nongcun yanjiu" ("'Upheaval on Heaven and Earth' and Research on Chinese Villages"), *Zhongguo yanjiu*, Spring (2009): 1–17.

Zhang, Taiyan. "Yazhou heqinhui yuezhang" ("The Charter of the Asia Solidarity Society"), in Zhu Weizheng and Jiang Yihua, Eds., *Zhang Taiyan xuanji: zhushiben*. Shanghai: Shanghai Renmin Chubanshe, 1982.

Zhao, Tingyang. "Rethinking Empire from a Chinese Concept 'All-Under-Heaven' (Tian-xia)," *Social Identities: Journal for the Study of Race, Nation and Culture*, 12(1), (2006): 29–41.

"A Political World Philosophy in Terms of All-Under-Heaven (Tian-xia)," *Diogenes*, 56(5) (2009): 5–18.

Zhong Yijiang. "Gods Without Names: The Genesis of Modern Shinto in Nineteenth-Century Japan," Ph.D. dissertation, University of Chicago, 2011.

Bibliography

Zhu, Renqiu. "The Formation, Development and Evolution of Neo-Confucianism with a focus on the Doctrine of 'Stilling the Nature' in the Song Period," *Frontiers of Philosophy in China*, 4(3) (2009): 322–42.

Zito, Angela. *Of Body and Brush: Grand Sacrifice as Text/Performance in Eighteenth-Century China*. University of Chicago Press, 1997.

Zürcher, Erik. "Buddhist Influence on Early Taoism: A Survey of Scriptural Evidence," *T'oung Pao*, 66(1–3) (1980): 84–147.

REPORTS, INTERVIEWS AND WEB MATERIAL

"A New Multilateralism for the 21st Century: The Richard Dimbleby Lecture," London, February 3, 2014 (www.imf.org/external/np/speeches/2014/020314.htm).

"Assessing Five Years of CEPF Investment in the Mountains of Southwest China Biodiversity Hotspot: A Special Report," Critical Ecosystem Partnership Fund, August 2008 (www.cepf.net/Documents/final_mswchina_assessment_aug08.pdf).

"Cabinet Nod for Asean FTA," *Times of India*, July 25, 2009 (http://economictimes.indiatimes.com/News/Economy/Foreign-Trade/Cabinet-nod-for-Asean-FTA/articleshow/4818081.cms).

"China's ENGOs Increase by Almost 8000," *People's Daily* (English Edition), March 5, 2013.

Emerging Asian Regionalism: A Partnership for Shared Prosperity. Asian Development Bank, Manila, 2008.

"Goldman Environmental Prize Winner Yu Xiaogang on Hydropower and Community in China," Alex Pasternak's interview with Yu Xiaogang, posted April 12, 2008 (www.treehugger.com/about-treehugger/goldman-environmental-prize-winner-yu-xiaogang-on-hydropower-and-community-in-china.html).

"Inter-Referencing Asia: Urban Experiments & the Art of Being Global," Aihwa Ong and Ananya Roy, Workshop Directors, International Conference on "Inter-Asian Connections," Dubai, UAE: February 21–3, 2008.

"Maid to Order: Ending Abuses Against Migrant Domestic Workers in Singapore," Human Rights Watch, December 7, 2005 (www.hrw.org/en/reports/2005/12/06/maid-order).

"Non-Governmental Organization," *Wikipedia* (http://en.wikipedia.org/wiki/Non-governmental_organization).

"Overview of ASEAN Cooperation on Environment" (comprehensive view of agreements and treaties as well as the institutional structure of ASEAN environmental governance) (http://environment.asean.org/about-us-2/).

Power and Responsibility: The Mekong River Commission and Lower Mekong Mainstream Dams. A joint report of the Australian Mekong Resource Centre. University of Sydney and Oxfam Australia, 2009.

The Straits Times, Review and Forum, May 5, 2009.

Index

CPSIA information can be obtained
at www.ICGtesting.com
Printed in the USA
BVHW041411250319
543613BV00024B/1733/P